Passionate Crusader

RUTH HALL

Passionate Crusader

The Life of Marie Stopes

Harcourt Brace Jovanovich
New York and
London

Published in Great Britain as *Marie Stopes*

/ 7 / (

Hall, Ruth, 1933–
    Passionate crusader.

    1.   Stopes, Marie Charlotte Carmichael, 1880–1958.
2.   Feminists––Great Britain––Biography. 3. Birth
control. 4. Marriage. I. Title.
HQ764.S7H35   1977   613.9'4'0924 [B] 77–73054
ISBN 0-15-171288-3

First American edition

BCDE

MARIE STOPES

"I will be canonised in 200 years' time." *Marie Stopes, marginal scribble in a Catholic Truth Society pamphlet, 1919.*

> "Jeanie, Jeanie, full of hopes,
> Read a book by Marie Stopes.
> Now, to judge by her condition,
> She must have read the wrong edition."
> *Children's playground chant, London, 1924.*

"The Empire today has three enemies – all from Munich. One is Hitler, the other Goebbels, and the third that doctor of German philosophy and science – Dr Marie Stopes. The greatest of these is Marie Stopes." *J. F. Coates, M.P., New South Wales, Australia, Parliamentary Debates No. 153, 3 April 1940.*

"In a final estimate, Marie Stopes may well prove to have been one of the most important and outstanding influences of the twentieth century – a judgment with which, one feels sure, she would be in complete agreement." *Margaret Pyke, Chairman, Family Planning Association, 1962.*

CONTENTS

Illustrations	*page* 9
Author's Note	11
1	Birth of a Superior Brain	15
2	False Starts	35
3	A Northern Experiment	51
4	East and West	65
5	A Fate Worse than Death	78
6	Gates v. Gates	89
7	Alone in the Wilderness	109
8	"Married Love"	128
9	Married Love?	137
10	Bell, Book and Candle	155
11	Improving God's Handiwork	175
12	God Fights Back	197
13	The Great Trial	213
14	A Son is Born	242
15	Unenduring Passion	256
16	"Remember My Sweet Youth"	280
17	Intimations of Mortality	298
18	Surprised by Death	311
References	328
Select Bibliography	341
Index	345

ILLUSTRATIONS

Between pages 80 and 81

Marie Stopes's parents *and* Marie and her sister
"An attractive figure, despite her forbidding capacity for hard work"
In the laboratory of Professor K. Goebel at Munich

Between pages 96 and 97

The youngest Doctor of Science in Britain
Kenjiro Fujii

Between pages 176 and 177

Charles Gordon Hewitt *and* Reginald Ruggles Gates
Aylmer Maude *and* Marie in 1915

Between pages 192 and 193

Humphrey Verdon Roe with an Avro 'plane *and* Humphrey and
Marie in court dress
Letters from readers

Between pages 272 and 273

With her son Harry
Harry with a candidate for adoption *and* Harry with his wife Mary

Between pages 288 and 289

Marie leaving the Law Courts during the Stopes-Sutherland case; On
the National Birth Rate Commission, *and* At the Mothers' Clinic in
Holloway
Keith Briant *and* With Avro Manhattan

AUTHOR'S NOTE

It is not surprising that the truth about Marie Stopes has never been told. The first biography of this remarkable woman appeared in 1924 when she was still only forty-four. Ostensibly written by her close friend, Aylmer Maude, the biographer and translator of Tolstoy, some of the book was dictated by Marie Stopes herself, and the rest she scrupulously supervised – even down to refusing to supply the date of her birth. Anxious to counter-attack after her recent battering in the law courts – only a few years earlier had she emerged from the remote world of academic palaeobotany into public fame (or, perhaps, notoriety) as Britain's foremost proponent of sexual technique and birth control – she and Aylmer Maude were somewhat uncritical of their subject, to the point, almost, of adulation.

At the time, when even to talk of sexual matters in public was tantamount to an admission of private depravity, this jealous guarding of her reputation was understandable. Later it became obvious to all except her closest disciples that the aura of saintly altruism through which she would have the world see her was suffused with a large and equally genuine self-esteem. She would tolerate no criticism; and it says much for the strength of her personality that she was able to exercise her veto even beyond death.

Marie Stopes's only other biographer was the late Keith Briant, whose book appeared in 1962, four years after she died. Like Aylmer Maude, Briant was an intimate friend of Marie Stopes, and himself realised the limitations which such close acquaintanceship imposes on a biographer. In an introductory note he remarked, "I have tried to assess the truth about the seemingly paradoxical character of Marie Stopes but, for a number of obvious reasons, it is impossible in this generation to set down certain details." Though Briant's book clearly made more attempt at objectivity, his discretion resulted in an interpretation still conforming closely to Marie Stopes's own image of herself.

Briant may also have been hampered by the daunting mass of

material she left behind. She bequeathed her papers – a collection, it has been estimated, even larger than Gladstone's – to the British Museum which, after her death in 1958, had to hire a three-ton lorry to transport them from her country home in Surrey. When Briant worked on the papers they were still uncatalogued, and he appears merely to have skimmed the collection, looking for those famous names which Marie Stopes herself so cherished but which in fact constituted the least important element in her extraordinary life. The British Library (as the printed books and manuscript section of the Museum is now called) tried to winnow down the collection; but the bulk of her correspondence, private and public, about law suits and about sex, mysticism, literature, religion and science, still takes up more than three hundred boxes in the Department of Manuscripts – not to mention a further collection in the Museum's State Papers Room from her own vast library of pamphlets, books and press cuttings, and the large miscellany of manuscripts and family papers belonging to her son, Dr Harry Stopes-Roe, to which I have also had access. It took the library's staff some eighteen years to complete a preliminary sorting of this vast accumulation, after which I began work on this biography.

I hope to have told as much of the truth about one of the twentieth century's most remarkable women as the limitations of length permit. (The British Library, following Marie Stopes's wishes, still imposes one or two restrictions on the use of material, but these are insignificant, relating only to a section of clinical case-sheets, which might eventually be of interest to academic historians of the early days of birth control.) Inevitably, with a woman whose life was devoted to the achievement of so many different ambitions – in science, literature and the improvement of the human race – there will appear to be faults of emphasis. Those primarily interested in coal research, for example, or in the minutiae of birth control administration, might well feel that I have spent too much time on Marie Stopes's own sexual and personal problems, particularly in the earlier part of the book. Yet it was precisely her experience of sexual and emotional misfortune that led directly to the career which assured her, as she put it, of "a place with the Immortals".

Her claim is not so grandiose as it appears. She was the central figure in that social revolution by which men, but more particularly women, were freed from the miseries of sexual ignorance and haphazard reproduction. Indeed, compared with her initial struggles, the activities of the women's liberation movement over the last decade appear in retrospect as mere mopping-up operations after a major battle.

Among the many millions who have benefited from her crusade, few know much of her history. Even fewer are aware of the complexity of the motives underlying her apparently straightforward philanthropy. Her personal life was an anguished paradox, the ideals of love she believed in and advocated for others perpetually eluding her own grasp. If, in the light of previous biographies, this book appears overly critical, it has at least been written in that spirit of objectivity to which Marie Stopes herself always laid claim.

Among the many who helped me with their personal reminiscences of Marie Stopes I thank particularly, and alphabetically: Professor W. G. Chaloner, Professor of Botany, Birkbeck College, London University, who also instructed me in the mysteries of palaeobotany; George Edinger who, as an undergraduate, first met Marie Stopes at the height of her fame in the 1920s; Dr Evelyne Fisher, doctor at the Mothers' Clinic in the 1930s; Baron Avro Manhattan, who knew her intimately in the last decade of her life, and who allowed me access to his personal correspondence; Warren Tute, who knew her in the 1940s; Sir John Waller, who encouraged her poetic ambitions; and Dr Helena Wright, one of the earliest pioneers of birth control in Britain.

I owe a special debt to Dr Harry Stopes-Roe, the only surviving child of Marie Stopes, who gave me unlimited access to the family papers. He, and his wife Mary, put up with my presence in their home, talked to me honestly (though sometimes contradictorily) and gave me many valuable insights, in addition to generous hospitality.

Among those who did not know Marie Stopes personally, but whose help was also essential, I thank Muriel Box, for permission to quote from her published transcript, *The Trial of Marie Stopes*. Peter and Margaret Eaton, the antiquarian bookdealers, gave me the run of their collection of early birth control literature. Richard Hall first suggested that I write a book and Ron Hall, my husband, by a judicious mixture of support, encouragement and stringent criticism, ensured its completion.

J. P. Hudson, of the British Library's Department of Manuscripts, was unfailingly helpful. Audrey Leathard allowed me to read her encyclopaedic doctoral thesis (to be presented to the London School of Economics) on the provision of family planning services in Britain; Diana Athill, my editor, was unstinting with encouragement and sensitive emendations. In Tokyo, Jenny Phillips undertook original research on Marie Stopes's stay in Japan 1906–9, and interviewed the few survivors from the Japanese botanical world of that period. David Samuelson, of Samuelson Film Service, lent me a rare copy of Marie Stopes's only film, *Maisie's Marriage*, and the British Film Institute gave me facilities to screen it. Elizabeth Smart never completed her own biography of Marie Stopes, but was generous enough to pass on all her material to me, and with Bernard O'Sullivan I enjoyed many fascinating discussions on the complexities of Marie Stopes's litigation. Elizabeth Donnelly, Christine Walker and Clive Unger-Hamilton were most helpful with additional research; Joan Kennedy typed the book and made many valuable suggestions.

I am especially grateful to Anne and the late James MacTaggart who, with the indefinitely prolonged loan of their house here in the Thames valley, gave me the peace and seclusion in which to write this book.

Kelmscott, 1976

Chapter 1

Birth of a Superior Brain

"Dear Madam ... I consider I owe my brain power to two factors: the inheritance through many centuries of a long line of cultivated ancestors on both sides, and the exceptional antenatal period which my parents arranged for me."

Marie Stopes to an admirer, 28 October 1921

THOUGH brought up to believe that she had suddenly appeared out of nowhere, Marie Stopes was born in the normal manner, on 15 October 1880, in Edinburgh. Years later, when her daughter was thirty-eight and considered old enough to know the facts of life, Mrs Stopes gave her an account of the event: "I can be fairly exact," she wrote. "I had chloroform at the last and when I waked you were *there*. I said to the doctor, 'Is it a boy or a girl?' 'A girl.' 'Thank the Lord. Is it all there right and normal?' 'Yes, all right.' 'Has it red hair?' 'No, I think it has none.' 'That's all right, then. What o'clock is it?' 'Half past three.' I thought the baby was dead, but he slapped it and took it by the heels and gave it artificial respiration and it came round all right."[1]

Marie Charlotte Carmichael Stopes, as she was christened, was the first child of what appeared on the surface to be a well-matched couple. Charlotte Carmichael, born and brought up in Edinburgh, was enormously proud of her Scottish forebears, a family traceable back – so her equally proud daughter claimed – to 1100. Of more importance, however, than her illustrious lineage – one great-grandfather had helped to design Edinburgh's elegant New Town, and her own father was the landscape painter, J. F. Carmichael – were Charlotte's own achievements. She was the first woman in Scotland to take a university certificate – the only qualification open to women who, although taking the same examination papers as men, were not allowed to attend lectures, or to be awarded degrees. The experience contributed to her passionate advocacy of Women's Suffrage long before the movement became fashionable. Her meticulous, rather staid, literary work – after marriage she established a first-class reputation as a Shakespearean scholar – was balanced by a real polemical gift, to which Marie was subjected from her earliest days.

"How can men become truly free that ignore, for others, the liberties founded on the same reasonings by which they enfranchised themselves?" raged Mrs Stopes in 1894. Firmly rejecting the romantic notion of "fair women and brave men", what the world needed, she argued, were brave women and fair men, "who can understand that none lose through another's gain and that theirs is not Liberty but License, that use a self-asserted power to the restriction of the rights and privileges of others."[2]

Henry Stopes should have been the ideal husband for the intellectual Miss Carmichael. They met, appropriately enough, at a meeting of the British Association for the Advancement of Science, and were married in 1879. Intellectually, it was a heady time. The certainties of Victorian Britain were crumbling under the impact of Darwin, Marx and George Eliot – not to mention the trial two years earlier of Charles Bradlaugh and Annie Besant for publishing a work on birth control, an event that scandalised most of the nation. The atmosphere in which Henry and Charlotte started their married life has been well described by George Bernard Shaw, who was just beginning to make his mark in London. In 1879, the year of their marriage, Shaw had joined a new debating society, the Zetetical:

... there was complete freedom of discussion, political, religious and sexual. Women took an important part in the debates ... The tone was strongly individualistic, atheistic, Malthusian, Ingersollian, Darwinian and Herbert Spencerian. Huxley, Tyndall, and George Eliot were on the shelves of all the members. Championship of the Married Women's Property Act had hardly been silenced even by the Act itself. Indignation at prosecutions for blasphemous libel was *de rigueur*; and no words were too strong for invective against such leading cases as those of Annie Besant ...[3]

Apart from the atheism – both Henry and Charlotte remained convinced Christians – Shaw's description of the radical freethinker's basic equipment could be taken almost as a blessing on their happy conjunction. The son of a prosperous Colchester brewer, Henry Stopes shared his wife's passion for minority causes. Though "bred a Brewer", as his wife rather tartly remarked in her obituary of him twenty years later, he qualified as an engineer and architect specialising in the building of breweries. He was founder and chairman of judges of the Malting Barley Competition, wrote numerous learned treatises on the art of brewing and, as the *East Anglian Daily Times* observed at his death, "cast himself heart and soul into the movement for Pure Beer, in which he greatly distinguished himself".

His major passion in life, however – in common with so many other late Victorians excited by the evolutionary theories of Darwin and T. H. Huxley – was archaeology. Despite being whipped at the age of eight for taking his fossils to bed with him, Henry went on to establish the largest private collection of prehistoric flint implements in the country. Marriage to Charlotte did nothing to quell his obsession. Though his wife was uninterested in archaeology, he spent much of their delayed honeymoon – by this time Charlotte was already pregnant with Marie – digging for fossils. For Henry, their four months' trip through Europe and the Near East was as rewarding as it was to the nascent Marie, who later referred to this "exceptional antenatal period" in terms suggesting that, by some curious osmosis, she had absorbed palaeontology directly through the amniotic fluid. In meticulous copperplate script, Henry recorded his unearthing of the first stone-axe to be found in Egypt. He enthused in his diary not over Charlotte, but over the specimen which later became known as the Red Crag Shell. If authentic, this find – a carving on shell of a human face – was not just the first human portrait to be discovered: it also indicated the existence of man in the Pliocene Age. So intense was the Church's opposition to such an idea – it differed profoundly from the biblical version of man's genesis – that Henry was obliged to withdraw his paper to the British Association in the following year and wait until public opinion was ready to accept his data.

Reticent about his new wife though his honeymoon diary remained, however, Henry took pride in the fact that Charlotte was no mere adjunct. In return for her forbearance with old stones, he firmly seconded her fight for New Women. Returning from their honeymoon, they set up home together in Cintra Grove, near the Crystal Palace in Upper Norwood. Two months after their arrival, Charlotte had already started a Shakespeare Reading Society, a Logic Class, and the Upper Norwood Discussion Society, to which Henry was allowed to deliver harangues on women's rights.

Some of Charlotte's enthusiasms must have been hard to live with. Her work for the Rational Dress Society was respectable enough. She contributed to the society's *Gazette*, and read a paper, *Some Errors in Women's Dress*, to the British Association in Newcastle.* But some of her other preoccupations may have seemed a little recherché to a husband less indulgent than Henry. Charlotte was constantly pestering editors with articles on such arcane matters as cotton grass, frozen meat and Newhaven fishwives. On frozen meat, she was gently rebuked by Oscar Wilde, then editor of *Woman's World*:

> With your contention that frozen meat ought to come into the scope of the Adulteration Act, I fully agree, and so I should think must everyone, but as to the prejudicial effects of the process of refrigeration on the flavour and nutritious properties of meat ... I cannot help feeling that your views are somewhat exaggerated and should be glad if you could see your way to modify your expressions ...[5]

Innocent of Wilde's predilections – his wife, Constance, after all, was a leading light in the Rational Dress Society – Charlotte invited him to her home for a meeting of the Upper Norwood Discussion Class. Wilde politely refused the invitation; he was, he explained, entertaining friends that evening.

Despite her apparent eccentricities, Henry Stopes was never less than loyal to his wife. Following a contentious correspondence sparked off by Charlotte's denunciation of smoking in the *Woman's Herald*, he took up his pen in support. His letter gives some indication of their life together, and of Henry's more conventional aspects in the role of protective, Victorian male:

> Madam, I have followed with some amusement and much interest the curious correspondence on this subject which you have permitted

---

* It was, commented the *Gazette*, "very well received, and an interesting discussion ensued, Miss Lydia Becker again ranging herself on the side of stays and corsets".[4]

to appear ... Mrs Stopes has refused to sit in the same room with any male relative or friend who smoked. Fortunately few of her relatives have followed the habit ... we have travelled together far and wide. When her polite requests proved insufficient to check the hardened smoker, I have often been compelled to give a very clear intimation that it was my intention to see her rights regarded and her wishes respected, and on some occasions I have had to resort to very strong measures. I can recall, for instance, an encounter with a young American, a very popular and witty priest from Dublin, in Upper Egypt, and with an Italian Senator from Rome, in an Austrian Lloyd's steamer, in the Levant. Due entry was made at the time in the ship's books, and proper protest lodged with the right authorities, but I have reason to believe that my height and width of chest, and perhaps the vigorous Saxon I can employ when required, had more to do with her freedom from persistent annoyance than any attempt to respect law or etiquette by these men ...[6]

Unfortunately, this loyalty and apparent harmony hid a problem as common in nineteenth-century middle-class society as detestation of tobacco. Charlotte, in common with most women of her class, knew nothing about sex when she married. The subject was never discussed. It was the white woman's burden, an indignity to be stoically endured in order to achieve the righteous goals of producing children and satisfying a husband whose sexual needs were different from her own. The virtuous wife, as the few marriage manuals pointed out, "submitted" unwillingly to her husband but – far from demanding satisfaction – was expected to feel ashamed should she experience any sexual gratification. In the marriage of Henry and Charlotte, this all too common disability was compounded by an unusual factor. When they married, in 1879, Henry was twenty-eight. But Charlotte – in an age when women were contemptuously dismissed as "on the shelf" at the age of twenty-five – was thirty-nine.* Even today – though it would no longer be considered a bar to sexual compatibility – such an age gap would be unusual. At the time, it spelt marital

---

* Keith Briant, the last biographer of Marie Stopes (*Marie Stopes, a Biography* Hogarth Press, 1962) says that Henry and Charlotte, on their marriage, were twenty-eight and twenty-six, respectively. Briant knew Marie Stopes, who often, for the sake of convention, falsified the facts. Charlotte's date of birth, and Henry's, are clearly stated on their marriage and death certificates.

disaster. At the age of thirty-nine, Charlotte had lost the malleability with which, in a much younger woman, Henry might have succeeded in overcoming the sexual inhibitions created in women by social conventions. Contemporary photographs of Charlotte show an un-smiling, thin-lipped, rather hard-eyed woman, secure in her own rectitude. The impression is not mere fantasy. When Charlotte died in 1929, at the age of eighty-eight, an old family friend wrote to Marie: "Ah! my dear, it is a long, sad story – your mother's married life and yours and Winnie's girlhood. Do you know how long I had known her and what a very old friend she was? I went to meet her ... in '74 or '75 ... and if ever there was a born old maid your mother was that woman – she should never have married and I was aghast when she wrote and told me she had accepted Mr Stopes."[7]

The sexual imbalance in their marriage revealed itself very quickly. Henry made no mention of Charlotte in his diaries, a fact which has led some to believe that he was more interested in palaeontology than in his wife, and that Charlotte, through no fault of her own, was unfairly deprived of the marital affection that should have been her due. The evidence suggests, however, that exactly the opposite was the case. In his personal correspondence with Charlotte, Henry revealed a passion totally at variance with Charlotte's dutifully affectionate protestations to him. In August 1880 he wrote to her from the British Association meeting in Swansea to 3 Abercromby Place, Edinburgh, where Charlotte was awaiting the birth of their first child: "My darling ... Tell me what is the other danger that may make you care less for me than you even now do? ... God bless you, my darling, Ever with fond love, Your Harry."

Physically and temperamentally, Henry Stopes was an attractive man. His rather regular features were enlivened by the dark chestnut hair and strikingly luminous eyes which his daughter Marie inherited. His passions were accompanied by deep affection and a whimsical sense of humour that made him spend hours, merely to amuse his children, training the domestic cats to sit at the dinner table, in front of a fully laid place-setting, and behave like human beings. Signi-ficantly, none of these qualities was attractive to Charlotte. She was interested only in Henry's other-worldly attributes. Years later, when Henry was dead, she wrote to Marie – as a matter for self-congratula-tion rather than expiation: "When I first met my husband his strongest attraction for me was his solid religion. I felt it would support my weaker faith. His first gift to me was a large Octavo Textbook, with a Text, hymn and address for every day of the year."[8] Charlotte was a member of the Free Church of Scotland, a group which in 1843 had declared itself "free and protesting" against the already protestant established Church of Scotland. Though the Free Church became increasingly broadminded – Mrs Stopes bitterly resented Marie's description of her mother as a "Calvinist" – she could scarcely tolerate Henry's more extreme Nonconformism. Officially a Congregationalist, Henry was also a Quaker – too individual a form of religion for even Charlotte to stomach.

The matter was rather more important to her than to Henry. Though another daughter, Winifred, was born in 1884, four years after Marie's birth, Charlotte would never accommodate herself to her wifely "duties". Henry was deeply upset by his wife's lack of physical ardour. Even in 1886, seven years after their marriage, he was still trying to break through the barrier of frigidity. On July 30 that year he wrote to Charlotte, then on a seaside holiday with the two children, hoping that when next they met she would be in better health and "with the scales taken from your eyes as to the effects and need of greater love existing between us ... Dearest, will you put from you the teachings of your splendid brain and look only into the depths of your heart and see if you can but find there the love that every woman should hold for the father of her babes? ... We would put from us the seven blank years that are ended and commence the truer honeymoon."[9]

Charlotte did not respond, and Henry gave up. After this, his letters dwindled into mere travelogues, usually ending up "Yours dutifully". There can be few sadder epitaphs to a sexually failed marriage than Charlotte's final letter to Henry after she had visited him on his deathbed in 1902: "... The sensual look has passed away from your face that so pained me, and you seem to have regained the chastened expression of your youth, which made me trust you. I have given you a heart-whole devotion even when I blessed your actions; and I have never even kissed another man all my life."[10]

It is highly unlikely that, as a child, Marie knew anything of her parents' difficulties. The subject of sex was discussed – but only in relation to the lower organisms. "I drew minutely the sex organs of earthworms and frogs," Marie later recorded, "and discussed them frankly and simply with my father – but they did not come into marriage. In our home, human sex was never spoken of at all."[11]

Charlotte was enormously proud of her first child, keeping a diary in which she recorded, after only two months of Marie's life: "Baby has shown great intellectual development." At the time, there were no financial worries – a cook, and a nanny for the children were then matter-of-course amenities and Henry had indulged himself by taking an Elizabethan manor house in the village of Swanscombe, near Dartford in Kent. He was convinced – rightly, as it turned out, since Swanscombe Man, the earliest skull of *Homo sapiens*, was later discovered there – that the nearby gravel pits would be rich in prehistoric relics. From her earliest years, Marie was trained to follow him, digging, washing and cataloguing the specimens Henry uncovered, explaining their significance to visiting academics, and learning the significance of an elephant's tooth and a flint-axe.

But, after several years of marriage, Charlotte's initial enthusiasm for her children appeared to be dampened. Her sexual deadness, and inability to feel, or express, affection, were exacerbated by Henry's shortcomings. Initially well-off, if not wealthy, he spent far too much time and money on his private archaeological passions. His architectural practice in London, originally his major source of income, began to lose money. Henry was also a visionary. Charlotte, with the dour caution instilled by her Scottish ancestry and upbringing, was horrified by Henry's speculative ventures – the most spectacularly unsuccessful of which was his plan to set up luminous advertising in Underground tunnels, to be activated by approaching trains. After a decade of marriage, Henry was in severe financial difficulties and Charlotte began to take more and more refuge in her own preoccupations with Shakespeare and the Suffragist movement. Though always a punctilious mother, she never achieved a loving relationship with either of her daughters. The consequences were mixed and – at least for Marie – crucial. At the age of seventy, Marie Stopes wrote: "To most adults childhood appears the happiest time. I am far happier today than when I was a child."

Religion still possessed enormous force in the late nineteenth century. Children were brought up in the shadow of a vengeful God, ever ready to punish misdemeanours, even unto the failure to eat lumpy porridge – a sin which evoked the classic parental response: "God sends us lumps to make us strong." For Victorian children – unless death intervened to waft them to eternally angelic playgrounds – it was Hell, not Heaven, that lay about them in their infancy. The Stopes household was unusually liberal. Charlotte had no time for "Popish" cant. Overhearing the young Marie confessing to her nursemaid one day, "Emma, I have been praying for more of the Holy Spirit", Charlotte promptly sacked Emma and took on the more Nonconformist Annie. Though Charlotte always stoutly denied that she had ever spoken of the "terrors of Hell" to her children they were, however, brought up in an atmosphere of plain living and high thinking. On Sundays, they attended church three times a day, and were allowed to read only "improving" books. After lunch, Mrs Stopes might permit herself a little needlework in preparation for Monday's laundry – but only, she explained, to save the consciences of her maidservants. During the week, she sang hymns to Marie and Winnie and listened to their daily prayers.

Despite Charlotte's protestations of liberalism, Marie developed an acute sense of sin. Until the age of twelve, she was educated at home by her mother. At the age of six, Marie later recalled in an auto-biographical chapter she contributed to her first official biography in 1924: ". . . my manifold sins had been made very evident to me, and I felt that if only I were a better girl I would *feel* the actual floods of the Blood of Jesus which would purify me . . . I remember placing myself at the foot of a long flight of stairs at the bottom of which was a sheepskin mat, dyed crimson, and I rubbed myself in the crimson wool of the mat and tried to picture the stream of the Blood of the Lamb cascading down the stairs and over me, purifying me and taking away my manifold sins."[12]

Allied to her sense of sin was a feeling of responsibility towards "those less fortunate", as the current cliché had it. The Victorian middle classes had a well-developed feeling of duty towards the lower classes – partly as an insurance policy against divine disapproval, but perhaps largely in expiation of guilt about the exploitation on which their own wealth rested. Always, as she remained, a child of her class, Marie took her responsibilities so seriously that, even as a child, they assumed a neurotic fervour far removed from the dispensing of chicken broth by which pallid young ladies were wont to assuage their charitable instincts. Everything, Marie felt, was all her fault: ". . . my guilty presence in the world was responsible for disasters to others. I remember clearly one day the lady with whom we stayed reading some paragraph from a paper about a great calamity abroad – I think an earthquake – when I burst out crying, and said: 'Oh, but I can't help it. It is really not my fault.' I have never entirely lost this sense of *burden*."[13]

Charlotte Stopes did nothing to allay her elder daughter's anxieties. She was as sparing in her praise as she was lavish in her exhortations to righteousness. Many years later, in a revealing gloss on Aylmer Maude's biography of Marie, she wrote: "It may be noted that her Mother had an early method with her and her sister. She impressed on their father and all others, never to repeat the children's 'clever things' before them, or to praise them unduly. So they developed and were able to speak without self-consciousness."[14]

It was a harsh discipline, and Marie never recovered from the feelings of inferiority instilled, no doubt with the best of intentions, by her mother. Charlotte's "advanced" ideas only contributed to Marie's childhood unhappiness. Over two small incidents – ridiculously trivial in themselves, but extremely painful to a sensitive child – Marie brooded bitterly and, even as an adult, never ceased to refer to them. There were, first of all, the rock cakes. Mrs Stopes distrusted dried fruit as fervently as she did frozen meat. For Marie's tea parties, she provided plain cakes – iced, but unfruited – where all the other mothers came up with standard rock buns. This, Marie was convinced, meant that her family was too poor to afford rock buns: she was a social outcast. The clothes Charlotte prescribed for her were an even worse affliction. As an adherent of Rational Dress, Mrs Stopes could hardly dress her daughters in the current mode, which was then a miniature version of the adult's, with fitted bodice, heavy skirts and numerous flounced petticoats. Instead, Marie was garbed in shameful – though sensible – knitted dresses. She became convinced – probably rightly – that all the other girls were laughing at her.

Comfort had to be sought elsewhere. Personally responsible as she was for earthquakes and other Acts of God, drowned in the Blood of the Lamb, deprived of maternal praise and rock cakes, and shrinking in her knitted dresses, Marie turned to the only other possible source of warmth. "MY DERRA PAPA," ran her first letter at the age of five "I LOVE YOU AND I WANT TO WRITE A LETTER TO YOU." It was the beginning of a lifelong passion, dangerous only to Marie. Until the end of her life, she remained convinced that her father was one of the greatest men who ever lived. Who could possibly bear comparison with him?

Henry Stopes was a passionate man. His strong affections, maritally denied, naturally devolved upon his elder daughter. Frequently away from home, either at his London office in Southwark, at scientific meetings, or abroad looking for fossils, he showered her with letters of a rare, sometimes lyrical tenderness. He wrote to Marie, then aged five, and on holiday at the seaside: "My Little Love . . . Play with the sand and the tiny little waves – the mightiest force on earth loves to play in the sunlight with little girls. Listen to the murmur of the ripples and hear what they say to you so that you may tell me . . . When you grow big Papa will tell you many things they said to him when he was little before his ears were hurt by the hard harsh words of cruel men and women."[15]

Marie, always anxious to please her adored father, immediately developed an intense love for the sea. At the age of five, unable to swim, she literally threw herself headfirst into the icy waves of the English Channel in mid-March – a childish folly that brought from Henry the admiring comment, "*That's* the sort of daughter I like." Charlotte always believed that it was her own firmness in dipping Marie in the sea at the age of nine months that created her daughter's passion for the sea. Henry's rather more sensual approach, however, offers a likelier explanation. In a curious way, Marie identified him with "the mightiest force on earth" who loved to "play in the sunlight with little girls". The sea became for her not just a universal panacea – she drank large daily glasses of sea water whenever possible – but also a mystical force with highly sexual overtones. One of her later poems, *The Bathe, an Ecstacy*, is in fact just that – a naked celebration of bodily union with the sea, whose breezes, "quiver up the flanks of sheltered bays".

Henry did not see his strong affection for his elder daughter as running counter to Charlotte's sterner approach; indeed, he was at pains to impress upon Marie the "greatness" of her mother's achievements and the necessity of living up to them. It is revealing to compare the two letters Marie received from her parents on her sixteenth birthday:

Charlotte, 14 October 1896:
"... Only as I sewed, I thought and dreamed and prayed that my girls may grow up servants of God and keep themselves unspotted from the world. I remain, Your loving mother, Charlotte Stopes."

Henry, 15 October 1896:
"My dear Marie ... I wish my little girl to feel that she is never forgotten if seemingly overlooked. The sense of responsibility has already come to you. With so great a mother life is (and must be) different in some of its aspects to other children's. It is now time to tell you that with such advantages as you possess you have to do (or at least to try) for yourself and others what your mother did with so few advantages. My own birthdays were always marked by sermons so I have preached to you. Now I want you to feel that you have the warm loving arms of a father round you. With fondest love, Your affectionate father, H. Stopes."[16]

It was fortunate that Henry had faith in his daughter's powers. No one else did. It was not until 1892, shortly before her twelfth birthday, that Marie first went to school. Apart from daily prayers, Sunday bible readings, and her father's intensive instruction in archaeology, her education had been limited to just one hour's lesson a day from her mother. Charlotte, with the usual Scottish distrust of English education, refused to sully her daughter's mind by sending her to one of the local schools in Upper Norwood. When Marie was five years old, Charlotte had started giving her lessons in Greek and Latin. Somewhat surprised and exasperated by her daughter's failure to become immediately proficient in those two languages, she was obliged to lower her sights to a less demanding course of home studies, comprising, she proudly claimed, "Grammar, Composition, Arithmetic, History of England and Scotland, Tales of Greece and Rome (all followed on the map)".

Eventually, even Charlotte had to admit that her educational experiments were not achieving the expected results. The school she chose for Marie and the seven-year-old Winnie was St George's High School, Edinburgh, founded only four years earlier by a group of Suffragists, "to provide sound instruction according to the best educational methods, to avoid overwork, and to evoke an interest in study". Not surprisingly, Marie was considered rather backward, and was put in a class of girls much younger than herself, thus further increasing her feeling of inferiority. Most eleven-year-old girls, in a strange city, separated for the first time from home and parents, and publicly branded as academically inferior, would have retreated into tears and solitary brooding. Significantly, Marie was already beginning to show her unusual capacity to react with positive aggression to any challenge or adversity. The first entry in her school diary, dated 4 October 1892, ran: "On Tuesday I went to school at 10 o'clock and did not like it at all. I went to bed very cross."

It was a narrow life in Edinburgh, enlivened only by hymn-singing, duty calls on her mother's old friends, letter-writing and the endless darning and sewing to which Victorian girls were subjected. "Marie, clean vest to go on at once. They took *four hours* to mend," wrote Charlotte, hysterically dashing between the British Museum and the Aristotelian Society. "Do not let them run down again and get into Jacob's ladders. Whenever you see a *stitch*, put on a clean one and mend the other." Marie spent the little spare time she had from her studies cataloguing her stamps and sea shells and collecting signatures for her Suffragists' Book demanding women's rights. Sundays, of course, were sacrosanct, tersely described by Marie in her entry for November 6: "Went to Church, it was a very nice sermon, came home and read the Bible till tea. Made a Bible Clock, Sang Hymns and went to bed."[17]

After two years at St George's, Marie was still no more than a very average pupil. Only once did she make any impact on either her teachers or her fellow-pupils. Henry Stopes had donated part of his collection of flint implements to the museum of the Society of Antiquaries in Edinburgh, and he asked Marie to present the collection. This she did, subjecting the museum's director to such a learned lecture on the exhibits – with precise instructions as to how they should be labelled – that, highly amused, he persuaded the headmistress of St George's to let her give a lecture to the whole school, and to university students. Marie was not too happy about her performance. "My first lecture, oh! dear it was *dreadfull*. Then I had to do it over again for the stu-dants, they are the ones that are going to be teachers," she wrote to her parents. But everyone else was impressed by her self-confidence and the nonchalant expertise she brought to a complicated subject.

Of more significance than this isolated success, however, was Marie's dogged refusal to accept her continuing lack of academic success. Her apparent mediocrity, coupled with her mother's withholding of any form of praise, could well have resulted, in a less strong-willed child, in a meek acceptance of inferior status. Marie's reaction was quite the reverse. "I love to do my lessons well to please my teachers," she innocently confided to her diary in her first term at St George's. Her longing to excel, to be admired by others, was by now well-established, already giving some hint of that ferocious ambition that was later to unleash such energy in pursuit of her ends. Unconsciously, Marie boosted her confidence by ignoring her own deficiencies and stressing her minor successes. "Went to school very early, as I was monitress," ran her diary. "At reading only nine of the girls knew it all the others have to stay in at play tomorrow. I have not as I knew my reading." This could be seen as an early form of that compulsive self-congratulation that later, when she became famous, created so much dislike among both enemies and friends; but, at the time, it was a necessary defence against her feelings of inferiority.

At fourteen, Marie, with her sister Winnie, came back from Edinburgh to London to attend one of the best girls' schools, the North London Collegiate. Once more, she was at a disadvantage. Academic standards at her new school were much higher than at St George's, and she was well behind her age group in most subjects. In addition, the two girls were allowed to attend school only in the mornings. Charlotte, admittedly, distrusted formal education; but a more likely explanation of this decision lay in Henry's financial insolvency. Though he had designed several noteworthy breweries in both London and Colchester, he was neither interested nor acquisitive enough to make a success of his architectural practice. Charlotte earned a little from her Shakespearean commentaries and pamphlets on women's rights but – as she never ceased to point out to her daughters – not nearly enough, given the high fees at the North London Collegiate, to make up for Henry's alleged deficiencies.

Socially, too, Marie felt deprived. Henry and Charlotte kept on the Mansion House at Swanscombe for weekends and holidays, but, to be near their daughters' school, took a house in Denning Road, Hampstead. The old village, whose salubrious heights had for centuries provided a refuge from London's plagues, was rapidly becoming a shelter – as it still is – for the middle-class avant-garde. Intellectual snobbery was already rife, and when Henry Stopes moved in to the quiet, yellow-brick suburban street, with his boxes of fossils stacked in the garden, a neighbouring professor of geology commented, "Good God, we've got a grocer moving in next door." The Stopes family never recovered from this initial condemnaton. Neither, after the rural seclusion of Upper Norwood and Swanscombe, were they prepared for urban sophistication. At Charlotte's insistence, Henry eventually allowed the two girls to attend the dances and parties given by their friends, but would not allow them to hold their own dances – a prohibition Marie found humiliating. Significantly, she blamed her mother for the failure to return hospitality, whereas in fact it was her father's disapproval of dancing, coupled with his lack of money, that dictated the ban.

At least in Hampstead, however, Marie had access for the first time to a large lending library. She read voraciously and secretly – comparative theology, Swedenborg, Kant, Confucius and the whole of Darwin. Her reading of Darwin brought about Marie's first conflict with religious bigotry. One of her Scottish aunts, a highly religious woman, expressed horror at Henry's even mentioning the name of Darwin in front of his daughters. Naturally, Marie championed her father, and confessed that she herself read Darwin, whereupon her aunt whisked her off to the study, demanding immediate repentance and recantation. Marie refused and was formally committed to hell. The experience contributed to her growing independence of judgement. She rejected the idea of a vengeful God and replaced her mother's rather narrow, formalised religion with the more direct approach to the Deity implicit in Henry's Quaker leanings. Even in the Society of Friends, however, Marie discovered a lack of charity which she could not tolerate. At the age of sixteen, she attended her last Friends' Meeting with her father. In one of her earlier poems, "The Brother", Marie hymned the secret joy she and her father shared, while undergoing a dreary Anglican service, in thinking of the Meeting:

> ... but seldom said where flew
> Our Sabbath-thoughts; but, he and I, we knew
> The joy of waiting in the plain wood pew
> Till winged inspiration should descend,
> And make one stand to pray, another bend.[18]

On this occasion, however, which Marie claimed was a "true, unvarnished account", an old carpenter attended the Meeting and asked everyone to pray for him as he had just killed someone. No one reacted except Marie, who offered to share her hymn book with him. He left, gave himself up to the police, and was later hanged. Disgusted by the Friends' lack of sympathy, Marie – though she occasionally called herself a Friend when convenient – never attended another Meeting. Nor did she ever again attach herself to any one religion, preferring to rely on direct communication with the Almighty.

The only reason for doubting Marie's claims about the nature and extent of her reading is that no trace of such an expansion of general culture appears in her letters from this period. They are remarkably childish, the script unformed, the content that of a child of ten. As late as her seventeenth birthday, she was writing to her father: "My dearest Father . . . I have had such a nice day and such a lot of presents too . . . Mother gave me a dear little mouse, with an india rubber tail, we fastened it on the curtain and so deceived Mrs Garnett [the house-keeper at Swanscombe] that she called us in from the garden to see it." Nor was her school career – initially, at any rate – much more promising. Academically, Marie was regarded by most of her teachers at the North London Collegiate as hard-working but rather dull. It was not until her very late teens that the combined effects of Charlotte's constant exhortations and Marie's own yearning to win her father's approval – "I want to kiss you," he wrote, when Marie came second in both her scripture and natural science classes – began to show results. Scathing though the classics mistress might be – she was almost affronted when Marie, against all predictions, matriculated in Latin – one or two teachers recognised her unusual gifts. Impressed by Marie's energy, intelligence, and enormous powers of concentration, the chemistry mistress, Miss Aitken, gave her special tuition. So effective was her coaching that Marie, when Miss Aitken was suddenly taken ill, took on the chemistry teaching for the whole school. Her zeal, and her obvious competence, were rewarded with five pounds from Dr Sophie Bryant, the headmistress, a leaving scholarship in science – and a vastly increased confidence in her own intellectual powers.

The apparently sudden transformation in late adolescence from mediocrity to brilliance is a fairly common, though not an easily explicable, phenomenon – Winston Churchill is the most obvious example. In Marie's case, the sudden flowering of her innate intellectual gifts was stimulated by several factors in addition to the parental pressures to excel. In common with one or two of her friends at school, she had developed an attachment to Miss Clotilde van Wyss, one of the younger science teachers at the school, and wished to impress her. Of more immediate importance, perhaps, was sheer financial necessity. By now, Marie was aware of her father's financial difficulties and realised that – unlike most girls of her social class – she would not be able to rely on either parental support, or the provision of a dowry resulting in that usual desideratum (except for Marie) a husband. Disillusioned both in business and in the lack of recognition of his archaeological work, Henry Stopes wrote touchingly to his daughters on the last day of the nineteenth century:

> Dec 31, 1899. My dearest Kiddies, I turn from very wearisome and trying letters to write the last letter of the Century to my sweet little girls to wish a Very Happy New Year ... Sorrow, pain and trouble are almost sure to come. I only hope there may be a fair share of joy, happiness and achieved success for each and both of you. But you cannot command success. Be content to make sure that you deserve it.[19]

Lack of courage was never one of Marie Stopes's defects. Merely deserving success was not enough; she was going to command it as well. Both her parents wanted her to attend one of the women's colleges attached to London University. Marie, however, at the age of nineteen, had her own ideas. She now had much more confidence in her intellectual abilities and, ignoring both parents and her headmistress, Dr Bryant, she enrolled as a student in the science faculty of University College. At the time, women were very much in the minority at U.C., but they were allowed to take degrees, and Marie was determined both to study under the best teachers – who would not normally be found in one of the women's colleges – and also to pit her brains against men students. Her will to succeed was immediately evident. Chemistry, Marie knew, was her strongest subject and she asked to do honours degree work straight away without taking the usual intermediate examination. Her request was turned down. Instead, however, of meekly acquiescing – which would have meant repeating work she had already done at school – Marie switched without hesitation to another subject. F. W. Oliver, professor of botany at London University, was more sympathetic to her ambitions than his colleagues in the chemistry department. He gladly took her on as an honours student, even though she had few qualifications and had so far shown little interest in the subject other than the fossil botany she had picked up privately during her father's excavations at Swanscombe. Her decision was crucial in establishing her development as a scientist and in determining the whole course of her life.

Professor Oliver was not disappointed in his new, unusually enthusiastic student. At the end of her first year, she won a gold medal and – by dint of secretly attending evening classes in addition to her normal studies – came second in her zoology class. In her second year, Marie's extraordinary energy and capacity for hard work yielded even more startling results. She had discovered that, though an internal student, she could take an honours degree in one year instead of three if she sat as an external student – provided she obtained honours in one subject and a first-class pass in the second. The Registrar of the University tried to discourage her from such a foolhardy venture, saying the whole project was "ridiculous and impossible", but Marie persisted, vowing that she would get not just one honours and a first, but two honours, in botany and geology. Privately, Marie was not so confident as she appeared. Her entering for the final B.Sc. examination after only two years at university was initially undertaken more as a practice run than a genuine attempt to take her degree. But in the summer of 1902, events forced her to take more urgently her light-hearted tilting at academic windmills. Henry Stopes had become seriously ill with cancer of the intestines. At first, Marie was not aware of the danger. Henry, though never officially separated from his wife, spent little time in London, where Charlotte, though complainingly, still maintained their Hampstead home for Marie and Winnie. He was more often to be found in Swanscombe, where the rest of the family occasionally joined him at weekends, or at Greenhithe in Kent, where a rich philanthropist had offered him a promising acreage of land to pursue his archaeology. It was from Greenhithe, where Charlotte punctiliously visited him from London once or twice a week, that Henry wrote his last birthday letter to his adored, and adoring, elder daughter. He was only fifty; but, though he did not menion to Marie the nature of his illness, she sensed, as she prepared in October to sit her finals, the valedictory nature of his letter:

My dear Mariekins, Thank you so much for your interesting letter. It cheers me so much in the lonely life I now lead to feel your own fresh young heart sometimes beats with love for one who loves you so very very dearly ... It is a pleasant world to those who have a superfluity of its goods. It is possible to be happy if endowed with only a sufficiency but to the needy it can be intensely hard. I know all this and have known it for long yet I can only offer you good wishes. These dear I send you and may you be able to build upon the wide foundations I have done my best to spread for you. It is poor and broken I know but dearest it is my best. In my daily work I *know* that no foundation I have laid will fail under its load and in one of the sweet joys of my life I have equal trust that my sweet girl will live up to her possibilities ... Ever your affectionate father, H. Stopes.

To Henry, dying in considerable pain, the thought of his daughter's success was some consolation for a life devoid of either worldly recognition or marital affection. His agony, he wrote on 3 November 1902, to Charlotte, who had returned to London, was "too exquisitely cruel and yet my brute strength is such that all the combinations of disease leagued against me have to war for weeks and months to come to break me up Oh it is too hideous."

Terrified that her father might die without even the comfort of her possible success, Marie asked Professor F. W. Oliver to get her exam results before they were officially published. On November 28, just a week before Henry died, came a hastily scribbled postcard: "1264 gets Bot. 1st Cl. Hons. Geol. 3rd Cl. Hons. F.W.O." Marie had achieved exactly what she had promised; and yet there is something just a little too neatly sentimental about the notion, accepted by her previous biographers (perhaps, since they both knew her, under the sway of personal persuasion) of Marie's altruism in achieving success in order to comfort her dying father. On December 5, the day of Henry's death, Marie wrote from London to her mother, who was with Henry at Greenhithe:

My dear Mother ... I have now something to tell you that will take some very careful understanding – you know that I am to take my degree next year and that I have worked for one year and the courses are arranged for two. Well, I thought this year I had better keep my work up and that it would be good for me to practise by taking the papers – The most unlooked for result is that *this* year *I have got my degree*, I am now B.Sc. Not only have I got it, I have got it very well, I have got 1st Class Honours in Botany ... also Honours in Geology 3rd Class and *am the only* candidate with honours, the others (men only) all failed, so my name stands alone in the list. As it is supposed to be impossible to take one honours in a year, to get two is very nice ...

Two questions immediately pose themselves. If Henry had been informed of his daughter's success, why did not Charlotte, who was with him, also know? Neither is Marie's own attitude easily explicable. She had, it is true, every reason to be proud of her achievements. In addition to taking double honours within two years, she had also been awarded the university's Gilchrist Scholarship, which would enable her to do a year's postgraduate work abroad. To indulge, however, in such a paean of self-congratulation on the day her father died would indicate an apparent insouciance bordering on the heartless. And yet there can be no doubt of Marie's love for her father; for the rest of her life she never ceased to defend publicly his reputation as an archaeologist and, privately, his supreme virtues as a man. Perhaps a juster explanation of her seeming egotism lay in her upbringing. Charlotte and Henry Stopes had done their work only too well. Their constant exhortations to succeed had produced in their elder daughter an ambition quite out of the ordinary. Charlotte's unwillingness to give praise and affection had created an equally unusual self-reliance. At twenty-two, however deeply she might feel, Marie was tough enough to subordinate her emotions to the fulfilment of ultimate aims. Charlotte was already beginning to cavil at the effects of an independence she had herself helped to create. Instead of meekly staying at home to comfort her widowed mother, as most girls would have been expected to do at that period, Marie was determined to advance her career elsewhere. Only Henry had ever shown faith in her potentialities; henceforth, resisting her mother's emotional demands, she would prove herself worthy of his trust, and of her own boundless will to succeed.

CHAPTER 2

False Starts

"I have no aim but to be as great, good, strong and true
as it is natural for me to be ... Other people don't come
into my scheme except to love me, or for me to love. I
will not attempt to influence them. I would rather merely
be as nearly my perfect self as I can be. My instinct,
desires and capacities all point to a scientific career."
Marie Stopes to Alvara Humphrey, 11 January 1905

ON 13 October 1903, just before her twenty-third birthday, Marie
took the boat train from Victoria, en route for Munich. Together with
copies of her articles on "The Leaf-Structure of Cordaites" and "The
Epidermoidal Layer of Calamite Roots", papers already published in
the *New Phytologist* and *Annals of Botany*, she also packed long
combinations against the Munich winter, and her favourite doll.

At one level, Marie's long-standing feeling of inferiority had changed
to a supreme self-confidence. Her unexpected success in taking her
degree so quickly meant that she had several months to spare before
taking up her postgraduate scholarship. Palaeobotany, the study of
fossil plants, which had originally been for Marie a second-best alternative to chemistry, had now become a major passion – "a chapter in
the Book of Life," she phrased it with characteristic romanticism,
"which is as well worth reading as any in that mystical volume."[1]
During her last few months at University College, she acted as research
assistant to her professor, F. W. Oliver, and D. H. Scott, both pioneers
in the study of the reproductive aspects of early plant life. Her experience gave Marie an unusually thorough grounding in original research
techniques, and reinforced her conviction that her life would be dedicated to science. Academically, she had achieved a status superior to

most of her fellow male students – and, in the unspoken competition for favour in her father's eyes, she had overtaken her mother. Socially, too, she had made some mark at university. Conventional though they were in other respects, neither Henry nor Charlotte Stopes ever countenanced the current belief that women were inherently inferior to men. The extent of prejudice against women startled Marie when she first attended University College. As president of the Women's Union debating society, she retaliated by starting – for the first time – joint debates with the men's union, taking the chair at the first debate and shocking the university authorities.

At another level, however, she was insecure, and untutored to a degree that would today be inconceivable. Her parents' only contribution to a sexual education – Charlotte understandably, but Henry from rather more complex motives – had been entirely to deprive her of one. So ignorant was Marie, even of mere social usage, that she could not understand why other students kept asking about her engagement; totally unaware of its significance, she had been wearing a ring, given to her by her mother, on her engagement finger.[2] The suggestion that she was engaged was doubly shocking to Marie, since her father had brought her up to believe that no nice girl would ever think of marriage before the age of twenty-five. Mutual adoration between father and daughter led to a willing complicity in the preservation of innocence; but what girl could fail to notice that married or engaged women proclaimed their status with rings on the fourth finger of the left hand?

In 1903, Marie Stopes was an attractive figure, despite her forbidding capacity for hard work. Of just under medium height, she was slim, full-breasted, her rather short legs disguised by the long skirts of the period. Under a mass of dark reddish-brown hair, inherited from her father, her eyes were her most striking feature – large, hazel and, according to those who knew her, varying in expression between the extremes of harsh intellectual contempt and a softly beguiling sexuality. Sartorially, she eschewed the stereotyped dress – mannish suit, hard collar and tie – affected by many women who shared her suffragist convictions. She had little money, and spent hours making up by hand floating pre-Raphaelite gowns in strange silks, usually of orange and green, and had already developed her devotion to large hats, jangly jewellery, a minimum of corsetry, and clothes that stressed her femininity rather than proclaimed her fiercely competitive entry into a world dominated by men. She was clever, bursting with ideas and, despite her earnestness, capable of high spirits. More important, perhaps, she exuded a yearning for passionate attachment – a quality which, since the world is largely composed of those who either do not possess it or are too frightened to pursue it, had a rare appeal. It was a yearning that she never lost, that led to her greatest disasters and to her greatest achievements.

Miss Clotilde van Wyss had been the first person to respond to these qualities. A teacher at the North London Collegiate when Marie was a pupil, she was young, blonde and intense. She was also addicted to theosophical speculation and nature walks – attractive preoccupations in a school atmosphere where, it seemed more worthy of record, one Winnie Ryder "received a blotter for sterling work in the Egg and Spoon Race".[3]

In 1899, when Marie was nineteen, Miss van Wyss wrote to her: "Dear child of mine . . . Need I say that I send my special love to you, you have won it already long ago. Whenever I think of you a strange gladness creeps over me and I feel rich in the thought of your love and less lonely."

It is not the usual mode of address between teacher and pupil. Marie's replies to Miss van Wyss were no less passionately expressed:

Psyche, my beloved . . . The picture that I send I chose a long time ago – when it seemed to me to put into form thoughts that were hovering in your mind – I would not choose it now. Accept it more as a memory of the past than as an expression of the present time . . . And my love that I send always. Is it the same each time? I think not, grown a little wider, deeper, wiser, it loves you more and feels still more the impossibility of true expression. Marie.[4]

In suitable vein, Clotilde van Wyss replied:

Mia Cara, I wonder if my thoughts reached you – even if I did not express them in a letter. I intended to reply to you straight off on my birthday but my heart was too full for words and so I went for a walk through a ripe cornfield ablaze with dream-flowers and gave myself up to passionate thoughts . . .

Miss van Wyss's attentions continued after Marie had left school. In April 1901 she invited Marie to spend a few days with her in Cambridge, where she was attending a course in further education. "Dear Winnie," Marie wrote to her sister from Cambridge, "Imagine my horror on unpacking to find no nightdress! (*don't* tell Father, it's too disgraceful!)" On Marie's return to London, her former teacher pursued her with expressions of extravagant affection. "My Marie," she wrote, "My soul aches with the pain of having been torn away from all I love with a great deep still love." It is unlikely, however, that their friendship had complete physical consummation. At the time, sexual deprivation and ignorance drove many women to channel their feelings away from the opposite sex and to express themselves in fiery and romantic language without realising its possible interpretations. Marie was totally ignorant both of homosexuality and of masturbation which, she wrote many years later, she had never even heard of until she was twenty-nine.[5] Yet the "affair" with Clotilde van Wyss was significant for Marie in reinforcing the ideas of sexual "purity" already instilled by her father. Some measure of its effect can be gauged from the fact that, at the age of forty-six, after she had achieved fame as sexual reformer and birth control propagandist, Marie was still brooding about the malign influence of Miss van Wyss. Though she cited no names, the account in *Sex and the Young* is obviously based on her own experience:

> A teacher in a large girls' school was most popular with both mistresses and pupils – so popular that before she had been long at the school there was always a long trail of girls wanting to walk home with her, eager to hold her hand on excursions or in the playground and to bring her flowers picked in their own gardens or purchased on their way to school.

> The teacher, Marie continued, established relations with about a dozen girls, managing to convince each that she was an especial favourite, and extracting vows of eternal chastity and dedication to herself.

> Each separately deluded girl felt herself pledged to remain all her life in a highfaluting kind of secret Order based on a muddled mixture of mysticism, pseudo-theosophical fantasies of "purity",

and crude physical expressions of personal love and sex feeling. The teacher accepted presents from the girls far beyond their means, which involved deprivations and saving up of pocket money and allowances for fares, books and so on, which they ought not to have spent thus.[6]

Marie's adolescent passion for Miss van Wyss was also important at another level. Her attraction towards other women remained for at least part of her adult life, making still more difficult the establishment of normal relationships with men, and resulting in a total rejection of homosexuality, either male or female, all the more violent for her own unacknowledged penchant.

Heterosexually, Marie had her chances. By the end of her first term at University College, Guy Pilgrim, a fellow-student, had added his epistolary blandishments to those of Miss van Wyss. Marie rejected him summarily, bringing the reproachful reply: "Dear Miss Stopes, I do not think you realise the intensity of my love for you, if you fancy that a week or a month or a year can crush it into nothing. You probably speak from the experience of a schoolgirl attachment, which made you feel unhappy for a bit." (Over this, Marie scribbled in pencil: "How dare you! Not I!") Time, concluded the unfortunate Mr Pilgrim, might heal the wound, but the scar would remain. "I am afraid you don't realise what a hopeless blank the future looks to me without you ... Little did I think when discussing life's disagreeables with you that day at Ely that it would be *you* who would cause me the greatest sorrow of my life ... I am very miserable ... Write me an answer to this if you are kind – and then for me – a life to be "lived" somehow: have you the heart to condemn me to that? Sincerely yours, Guy E. Pilgrim."[7]

Not trusting the postal services, Mr Pilgrim walked all the way from the lowlands of West Hampstead to the heights of Hampstead village, where he delivered his plea personally through the letter-box of the Stopes home at 25 Denning Road. His zeal brought little reward. Dated the same day, 3 December 1901, Marie's reply is worth quoting at some length. Here are all the puritanical certitudes that she was later to reject intellectually, but found almost impossible to dispense with; an idealism masking inexperience; and a temperament that saw people not as they were, but only in relation to her own demands:

Dear Mr Pilgrim ... If at present you feel sad and sorry (and I should only despise you if I thought you did not) I am sure that if you face it manfully there is no need to be "cynical" – there are lots of sweet women in the world, but if your feeling is strong enough to last thro' all your life you can make it a lifelong blessing for you can carve your life so that it is like some strong beautiful solitary mountain ... For there is nothing in the world I so reverence as beauty, whether of the world, of character or in a soul. And knowing this, if you are a true knight, you *will strive to the uttermost to build what I could admire, whether I see it or not* ... forget me, please, but remember that *it is of infinitely more value to be a grand, than a sensually happy man* ...[8]

Marie's failure to respond to his overtures was not entirely her own decision. Only a few weeks previously, she had made the mistake of confiding about Guy Pilgrim to Miss van Wyss, who was not slow to respond. She wrote to Marie from Cambridge:

Dear little one, I am sometimes filled with a vague dread that you are drifting beyond my reach ... As regards the subject of your last letter – a sickening dread came over me as I read. This thing ought not to have happened, Marie, I do not blame you for it, but it ought not to have happened. It is like a stain on your garment of purity. I am strict, perhaps pedantic in some ways, as you well know, and so took the matter to heart perhaps more than I need have done. I have my dreams of beauty too – and such things shatter one of them. I too trust you absolutely – I know that you in no way led the man to honour you with the offer, but I cannot help thinking that, if you retired into an inner coil of your shell – you would be safer from the touch ... Dear love, I wish you were here. I believe you would be happy though at first you would kick against the pricks ...[9]

Their relationship – particularly since Marie now knew from correspondence with her former classmates that she was not the only recipient of Miss van Wyss's favours – was unlikely to survive such deviousness. It was with some relief that she left behind the perils of assorted sexual feelings, and set off for Munich, there to pursue a purer reality in the shape of the fructifications of cycads. Ironically, her year in Munich was to provide much more serious problems. She fell deeply in love – and with someone even more unsuitable than either Miss van Wyss or Guy Pilgrim.

Munich was a revelation. Marie took lodgings in a dingy but respectable boarding house in Hessstrasse, close to the university and the *Englische Garten* and just on the edge of Schwabing, a district which, in its intellectual and artistic pretensions, closely resembled the Hampstead she had just left. For Marie, the similarities went unnoticed in her new-found freedom. Short of money as she was, she was fortunately within walking distance of Munich's old centre, and could spend hours exploring on foot the fascinating architectural jumble of Gothic and rococo, overlaid by the massive neo-classic monuments imposed on their capital by the nineteenth-century Bavarian kings. For the first time she could do exactly as she pleased, going to parties and dances, spending long evenings arguing about philosophy and poetry in one of Munich's innumerable cafés without having to account for every move to her strict and slightly envious mother. The escape from her mother's recriminations, indeed, was not the least of Marie's blessings. After Henry's death in 1902, and the payment of his debts, Charlotte was left with only eighty pounds a year for herself and Winnie to live on. Henry's houses in Swanscombe and Hampstead, it turned out, had both been rented, and no one was prepared to pay a good price for the only valuable asset Henry had left, his collection of fossils. Charlotte refused to economise by giving up any of her domestic help. Nor would she agree to Marie's suggestion that she supplement her income by taking in a lodger – what, argued Charlotte, would the neighbours think? The burden of her complaints – about money, the ineptitude of servants and the thanklessness of daughters – now fell on the inadequate, nineteen-year-old Winnie, to whom Marie wrote consolingly:

Dear Kid ... Oh dear, I wish our family could live happily the way I do here – cooking cakes in saucepans and making jam while composing German and going out and coming in just as the spirit moved it ... I understand your tied-up, helpless feeling and can't give any advice except be as happy as you can on bread and water when you can't get bread and milk.[10]

For Marie, it was a bread and milk period and she was not going to allow her family to spoil her enjoyment of the freedom for which she had worked so hard. She was determined to take full advantage of Munich's varied cultural riches. Munich was then, as it still is, Germany's foremost city in terms of the number and quality of its art collections. Musically, too, it was unusually rich – at least for lovers of Wagner, who owed much of his success to the initial patronage of Ludwig II of Bavaria. Not previously much inclined to music, Marie developed a passion for Wagner, visiting the opera twice, sometimes three times a week while *The Ring* was in production. She invariably attended fancy-dress balls as a Valkyrie in armour she made herself out of cardboard and silver paint. Even the intense cold of the Munich winter failed to dampen her enthusiasm and the high spirits generated by the sudden expansion of interests. The temperature in her tiny room in the Hessstrasse seldom rose above twelve degrees centigrade, she had not enough money for more than the occasional fire, and any water in the room iced up within five minutes even by day. If working at home, she habitually wore two thick dressing gowns over her outdoor clothes and, unable to afford a hot water bottle, used her iron to take the chill off the bed. One night, however, she dispensed with even this small luxury. Isadora Duncan, the dancer, was then at the height of her career – so much so that when she left Munich after a performance there in March 1904 there was a riot at the railway station and the train left festooned with admirers still clinging to the carriage doors. Marie was so intoxicated by Isadora's dancing that, casting aside her long combinations in favour of flimsy chiffon draperies, she stayed up all night dancing in front of her mirror while humming Beethoven's Seventh Symphony.

Some aspects of Munich life, as a well-brought-up English girl, she could not approve. To Winnie, she wrote that the Muenchener's capacity for beer was "truly appalling" (the estimated intake is, indeed, forty-seven gallons per person per year); and, after her first visit to the Hofbräuhaus, most celebrated of Munich's vast beer vaults, refused to join any more student expeditions to the *Bierkellern*. She was also a little shocked by the pre-Lenten excesses of *Fasching*, the annual carnival – though not sufficiently so to stay away. The Schwabing district might well resemble Hampstead, but there was nothing in London to compare with the processions of fantastically decorated floats along streets crammed with semi-drunken merry-makers intent on the temporary abandoning of all social conventions. Marie's letters from Munich at this time have a naturalness and gaiety that she rarely exhibited later:

Dear Mother . . . I must go on with an account of the *Fasching Zeit* . . . It is really the *whole* of Munich that goes mad – the very best people – as I said those in the richest carriages like the others. I saw two dear old clergymen, each at least 60 years of age – solemnly buy a packet of confetti and then begin pelting each other! There wasn't an officer in the street in his uniform – all were dressed as pierrots, clowns, Red Indians etc., and you know officers here are the tippest top of society . . . It is the boast of Munich that every woman who goes to Cafe Luitpold or *any* cafe fasching Tuesday night, gets kissed. I can boast that I went and did *not* get kissed – I was with two men and looked all the time like a block of ice and had my quietest clothes and a big cloak on – but usually that is not enough. Still, it would be a strange man that wanted to kiss a block of ice.[11]

It would indeed. Aylmer Maude was later to describe Marie at this period as "remarkably sexless". The description is only partly justified. Her demeanour was certainly prim – but understandably so. Germany was even slower than Britain in allowing educational opportunities to women. At University College London, Marie had been in a small minority; at the Botanical Institute attached to Munich University, she was – at least during her first term – the only woman among 5000 men. Naturally, she felt herself an object of some curiosity, and retreated into a protective shell of apparent coldness. Socially, too, she was exceptionally insecure and gauche (except with older men) a failing she resentfully ascribed to her upbringing. She wrote to Winnie, suffering from the same problem:

As to your being a baby – I expect it is due to your (and our, for I am not free from the same charge) babyish ignorance of many of the branches of feminine learning, some good, some bad, and some frivolous. E.g., we neither of us know anything about the doings of society ladies, and who married who last etc – also a considerable ignorance of the good usages of good society and the way to carry on and lead an intelligent and interesting conversation with either sex – there is a way of doing that that stamps people who have mixed with their equals. We have had next to no social intercourse with anyone – and none with well-educated young gentlemen – the people of all others to polish and refine women . . .[12]

Marie was never to lose the snobbery implied here – the envy of one who feels unfairly deprived of equality with those higher up the social scale. But there is no evidence that she was lacking in sexual attraction, or unaware of her own impact. While remaining impeccably circumspect, she enjoyed her literally unique position among so many men. "I was made much of, petted, danced with, made love to in various and sudden circumstances, and asked in marriage," she later recalled.* Among the frowsily dressed German women she felt almost elegant, and boasted of her little conquests to Winnie: "I have bought a lovely little round fur cap – it is *quite* round and flat on top – like a Russian a little but not quite. Of jolly black fur – and cost 2/6! It *ought* to be most unbecoming being small and round – but it isn't. When I wore it and a long cloak and a very short skirt and nailed boots – a strange *Herr* held open the letter box for me and took off his hat with a sweep."[13]

Some were tantalised by Marie's apparent lack of interest in the opposite sex. Alvara Humphrey was one of the two English students who fell in love with her in Munich – partly captivated, as Marie herself was, by her fur cap. "I remember," he wrote, "going and seeing what your name was on the paper before your place in the *Palaeontologische Hoersaal* and admiring your profile in your little fur cap and feeling sure you were English. I also admired the resolution with which you refused to show the slightest interest in me after once meeting my eyes in a lecture."[14] Marie's indifference to her various suitors was genuine – to the point of absentmindedness. At one point, she even found herself engaged to be married. Bored to tears by an importunate German youth on a botanical expedition in the Bavarian Alps, and with a still inadequate command of the language, she was

---

* The account (in *Black Breeding*, Hutchinson, 1942) may be a little exaggerated, the pamphlet being written in reply to Lord Vansittart's *Black Record*, a blanket condemnation of German education which was based, he argued, on hatred of England and the English.

reduced to murmuring a weary "Ja, ja, ja" to everything – including a proposal of marriage. Even after the mistake was sorted out, he continued to pursue her, and Marie's professor was obliged to intervene to soothe German family honour, affronted by her breach of promise. Marie was not interested. Why waste time on callow scientific youth, so far removed from her ideal of mature masculinity? There were, besides, ambitions to be fulfilled.

After her father's death, it had become obvious that, in addition to earning her own living, Marie might well become responsible for an impractical mother and a sister who was not just untalented but frequently ill. Winnie was already suffering from the heart disease that killed her in early middle age. She had shown no promise at school and now, at the age of nineteen, had begun a course in bookbinding. Knowing the stresses imposed by living with Charlotte, Marie was at this time highly sympathetic to her younger sister – even to the extent, during the middle of writing her doctoral thesis, of designing highly complex book-covers for Winnie to execute. Marie's very kindness, however – a quality she did not overly lavish on her peers – betrayed an all too justified lack of faith in Winnie's talents.

A far more potent driving force than her family's economic incompetence was Marie's personal ambition. She did not yet boast of her academic successes. "The best of it is," she wrote to Winnie from Munich, "no one, not even the Prof. knows I have done anything at my university at all." Yet, to Thekla Resvoll, a Norwegian botanist working at the Institute, she confided her firm intention of becoming a professor – not just that, but *"Dann werde Ich beruehmt"* ("I will be famous").[15] Marie allowed nothing to interfere with her work. She had chosen Munich for postgraduate studies largely because of the presence there of Professor K. Goebel, Europe's most eminent morphologist.

The study of plant fossils has never achieved the glamour associated with animal remains. A pleasurable terror attaches to the imaginative reconstruction of dinosaur and pterodactyl, and there is an intellectual appeal in the attempt to trace our own precursors. But, to most of us, a tree remains a tree, however problematical its pedigree. Marie felt differently. To her, the evolutionary process in the plant world was just as exciting as her father had found it in the sphere of *Homo sapiens*. Through her work with F. W. Oliver, Marie had become passionately interested in the reproductive habits of the cycads, the most primitive of the seed-bearing, as opposed to the spore-bearing plants (ferns, for example) still in existence – though tenuously, compared with their predominance millions of years ago. Professor Goebel had the most comprehensive collection of cycad specimens, both fossilised and living, and Marie was determined to work on the cellular structure of their ovules (the unfertilised seed) and ova (unfertilised egg cells).

At first, Professor Goebel was a little shaken by the intensity of his new student. No woman from the Botanical Institute, he warned her, had ever been allowed to take a university doctorate. Marie persisted. "I can lead that dear old professor round and round in an argument," she wrote to Winnie and bludgeoned her way into his laboratories, the first woman, she claimed, to gain entrance there. Once admitted, she worked a twelve-hour day, starting at eight a.m. At weekends, she sometimes worked for thirty hours at a stretch, sustained only by beef tea heated on a spirit stove. The German language received equally ferocious assaults. Eschewing the English community in Munich Marie insisted on speaking only German, preferably with Germans. Impressed by such zeal, Goebel relented. At his insistence, the university regulations were changed, and Marie was allowed to present her thesis on the cycads, reading and defending it in public, in German. There were a few titters at her unorthodox pronunciation – she had no gift for languages – but no doubt about the result: she was now Dr Marie Stopes.

"There was quite a sensation when I got back to the Lab," she wrote to Winnie, "a gorgeous armful of roses, a presentation card – handshakes and *grüesing* by the dozen – it's very rare indeed for a woman to be Doktor in Germany and I am the first in Botany here, also I got *magna cum laude* and all this year no one has got more than *cum laude* ... This week hasn't been exactly dull – a visit to Zurich, excursion with Prof. Schroeter, a German man's infatuated letters (he wants to marry me, or did) a Doktor examining results, flowers etc – a lovesick Englishman insisting on escorting me – ditto ditto a young German."[16]

If only, she yearned, someone would give her three hundred pounds a year for life, "I would be the best English botanist in fifteen years – and the best known in six – England is so insular and her men not half well enough known here, simply because they do not travel: and when they do speak only English!" Nor did the German students seem to offer any more serious competition to Marie, lacking as they were in idealism and high seriousness. The only sort of public-spirited things they went in for, she complained to her mother, were the Korps, "where the members drink beer together and are bound to fight a certain number of duels with the other Korps students. Naturally all this does not appeal to me, even if they would have me as a member."

Marie had little time for German men, in particular the large group of Prussian students at Munich. She detested their rampant male egoism – a lust, as she put it, "surpassing the love of women. How sure too they were that I, being essentially feminine, must be captivated by this male dominant idea!" A true child of Charlotte Stopes, Marie scorned such ideas and did not hesitate to express her dislike of the German attitude to women. She described it later: "I laughed when I first saw it, but was reproved for my laughter and told that I had no sense of values. No one but I laughed openly in the street on seeing a lady in a heavy rainstorm holding *her* umbrella over the head of a tall Prussian officer so as to protect him and his uniform while her thin silk dress was drenched. But I was severely reproved that my frivolous mind did not perceive that all the flourishes of a uniform should be preserved immaculate . . ."[17]

Properly handled, Marie's father had instructed her, every man was either a gentleman or a servant, and a lady should have no difficulty in distinguishing between them. Primed with this advice, Marie ignored the local custom of stepping into the gutter when the military walked down the sidewalk. She stared them straight in the face, waiting for their will to crumble. It never failed.

Scornful as she was not just of Munich's officer class, the accepted acme of desirability, but of her fellow-countrymen as well, Marie was obviously limited in her quest for the emotional involvement that had so far eluded her with Clotilde van Wyss and Guy Pilgrim. Among the 5000 unworthy men at the Botanical Institute, however, there was just one who might be allowed to encroach on Marie's preoccupation with cycads. Kenjiro Fujii was thirty-seven, and Marie Stopes twenty-three when they first met in Professor Goebel's laboratory. Midway in age and experience between the safe paternal charms of the professors with whom Marie liked to establish a daughterly relationship, and the crass

energy of her own age group, he had the attractions of both. Academically, he had qualifications sufficient to satisfy even Marie's taxing
demands and arouse her admiration. An assistant professor at Tokyo's
Imperial University, he was on leave in Europe to study with Goebel
and Strasburger. He had published widely, particularly on the structure
of gingko (the maidenhair tree), the only surviving species of a once
prominent and widespread genus. The botanical world was then
excited over the recent discovery of the manner of reproduction of this
extraordinary plant, held sacred in China and Japan, and Marie was
understandably impressed by Fujii's researches (the least esoteric of
his papers was entitled "Has the Spermatozoid of Gingko a Tail or
None?"). Academic achievement, however, was not Fujii's only
attraction. He was gentle, sensitive, well-read and, like Marie, given
to those long and passionate discussions about literature and philosophy
which she found impossible to obtain from her beer-drinking, duelling
fellow-students. Fujii was also, unfortunately, Japanese, an atheist,
and married.

At first, Marie was unwilling to admit her attraction. The two met
frequently in the laboratories but, on weekend botanical expeditions
in the Bavarian Alps, Marie was always careful to talk to other students
rather than to Fujii. Extremely sensitive as she then was to the opinions
of others, Marie was also embarrassed by the political implications of
being seen too often in Fujii's company. England was an ally of Japan's
in the current Russo-Japanese war and, for some inexplicable reason,
Marie disliked intensely the comment when she and Fujii were seen
together, "Look, there goes England and Japan." Neither was Mrs
Stopes likely to be sympathetic to her daughter's involvement with a
godless, married Asiatic. To allay suspicion – and also in an attempt
to exorcise her own feelings – Marie in her letters home stressed
Fujii's diminutive stature (rather unwisely emphasised by the Tyrolean
costume he sometimes affected), his botanical ambitions and his married
status. In March 1904 after she had been in Munich six months, she
wrote to Charlotte:

Dear Mother ... He and I went out together on Sunday – the
Chicks were to have met us and all gone together but at the station
they never turned up so we had to go without them. He is very nice
and very interesting and wonderfully western and observant in his

way. He is so tiny – smaller than I am, hands included – I sort of look after him. I am sorry for him with his wife in Japan while the war is on. He is a splendid botanist too – I have learnt heaps from him.[18]

A month later, Marie wrote again to her mother about "little Fujii", whose main role in her life, she gave the impression, was in encouraging her ambition to "get high in the botanical world". What she did not mention was an overnight excursion alone with Fujii, looking for ovules – an adventure she confided to her sister, though without betraying the extent of her feelings. They spent the night at a lakeside inn high up in the mountains:

I had the loveliest room looking down into the water and across to the snow mountains. We had breakfast at 6.30 on the veranda overlooking the lake, which reflected the tips of the snow mountains just glittering in the rising sun – and we started to go 24 miles before dinner! The sun got hotter and hotter, till little Fujii nearly collapsed, all that saved him was a great patch of snow on top of his little bald head ... Still we did it and got to the opera one minute before the appointed time ... I do like being a perfect wanderer and to go *"selbst weiss nicht wohin"* – I shall never look on little Fujii as a solemn and learned Professor again – after that snow on his head ... I will go walking tours all the rest of my life.[19]

Her rather tasteless attempts to make fun of Fujii hid a mutually increasing interest. There was, of course, no question of physical consummation. She was not yet twenty-five – the age her father had laid down as the lower limit for a respectable girl to think about marriage – and she would have been horrified at the mere suggestion of sex before, or without, marriage. Neither did she know at the time that Fujii's marriage was unhappy. Like most marriages in Japan, it had been arranged by his parents and he had met his wife only once before they were married in 1900. A daughter, Yuki, was born in 1900, but his wife was already in love with another man and wanted a divorce. Proud and diffident, both Fujii and Marie Stopes were unwilling to admit an attraction that seemed beset with so many problems. But by the end of June 1904 when Marie left Munich to return to England, sufficient contact had been established beneath the intellectual fencing that passed for courtship to make it probable that Fujii would try to follow her. Their relationship had not gone unnoticed. Among the friends who saw her off at Munich railway station was Alvara Humphrey, the young English student whose suit she had so firmly rejected. "Dear Miss Stopes," wrote the lovesick and jealous Mr Humphrey, "Was the sad looking little man who saw you off at München Professor Fujii? He looked utterly cast-down and hopeless; if he considers it his duty, however, you know he will be able to forget you in true Shinto fashion and bend his mind to work."[18]

Laughably tiny and Japanese he might appear to arrogant Europeans, but Professor Fujii had no intention of bowing out in Shinto fashion. The card he enclosed with Marie's flowers at the station was ominously idealistic. "We will meet as though we met not, and part as though we parted not. Out of dreams into dreams." Their frustrating relationship was to last five years – a long time for what turned out to be yet another false start.

CHAPTER 3

A Northern Experiment

"A good many people will be watching with interest
what is a new experiment up here and the future chances
of women for similar posts will depend a good deal on the
success or non-success of the present appointment."
F. E. Weiss, Professor of Botany, Manchester University
to Marie Stopes, July 1904

MARIE's natural reluctance to embark on a serious relationship with
Fujii was increased by doubts about her own scientific future. She had
been offered a post as research assistant in the botany department at
Munich University. The idea of staying on in the city she had found
so exciting was initially tempting, but the pay turned out to be too
little to live on – still less to help support Winnie and Charlotte.
Neither would such a post serve to advance her academic ambitions.

It was with little hope of success that, shortly before leaving Munich,
she applied for a vacancy at Manchester University, as a junior lecturer
and demonstrator in botany. F. E. Weiss knew of her work and
supported her application; but the university had never previously
appointed a woman to its scientific staff, and even he was not very
hopeful about the result. "Owing to the innovation of our recommending the appointment of a woman for the post of Demonstrator," he
wrote to Marie in July 1904, "the report has had to be sent to the
Council ... The Council has unfortunately some old-fashioned and
some timid members, which renders its decision a little uncertain."[1] A
week later, after a long and serious debate about the wisdom of such
a step, the University Council agreed to the experiment.

Marie's first reaction to her unexpected success was to write to

Fujii about it. Like most Japanese, Fujii had been brought up to think of women as inferiors, unworthy even of the gloss of gallantry by which the Western world sugared the pill of subjection. His three years in Europe, however, had modified his ideas and from Munich, he wrote to Marie in a spirit of genuine congratulation: "You are to show to the people how and what a woman can be. I am glad that you will be the first example in North England and I envy the college that got you ... If only the women's university in Tokyo, which was founded only four years ago, could get a lady, Japanese or foreign, who is so able to stand in such a position for science and English language!"

Apart from serving to advance her career, Marie's initial three years in Manchester were difficult and rather gloomy. After the delights of Munich, she found the endless vistas of mean red-brick streets and grimy municipal Gothic infinitely depressing, the inhabitants pale, stunted and ill-fed, the students dull and the damp climate intolerable. Almost immediately she began to suffer from catarrh and painful neuralgia, afflictions that disappeared whenever she left the city. Still only twenty-three when she took up her appointment, she felt herself on trial and approached her first lectures in "fear and trembling". Socially, too, she was monitored for defects. Her students were delighted with the science department's new and personable addition – the more conservative academic wives somewhat less so. Marie's attempts to recreate Munich's student gaiety caused some disapproval, particularly when she insisted on inviting lowly undergraduates to the Biological Fancy Dress Balls she inaugurated, herself appearing as a tropical pink moth in a dress held together only by safety pins. "Dear Miss Stopes," wrote the professor's wife, "... my husband says, and indeed I feel so strongly too, that it would be very inadvisable to invite individual *students* either to your rooms or to go with them to concerts, theatres, etc. Lecturers and external friends are different."[2]

Her personal life was equally beset by problems. Mrs Stopes showed no signs of mellowing with age, and it was not so easy to ignore her in Lancashire as it had been in Bavaria. Income and spirits varying with the publication of one slim monograph or another, Charlotte was resentful of her elder daughter's success, while at the same time paying lip-service to its necessity. Marie was for a time willing to sympathise with her mother's difficulties. A true child of her class, she shared her parents' assumption that someone else should undertake the boring quotidian tasks, in order to give full scope to the truly creative; but a short selection of the letters flying angrily between Hampstead and Victoria Park, Manchester, reveals the growing tension between them:

May 5, 1904 Marie to Charlotte: "I am glad some money has turned up – and hope a servant will follow. It is really scandalous and a reflection on the education of the country that you could have been so long without."

June 17, 1904 Charlotte to Marie: "I have been on the parish for a month already."

Feb 17, 1905 Charlotte to Marie: "My dear Marie ... I am sorry you do not spend the same amount of intelligence in understanding my letters, my position and my difficulties that you spend on your own work."

Feb 19, 1905 Marie to Charlotte: "As things are changing so rapidly, what is the use of my attempting to give advice, for by the time my letter reaches you it is stale and useless. I think ... the best thing is to leave it entirely to your discretion at the time of decision and I will try not to grumble at the result ... Remember, if it is of any assistance to you, I am quite willing to take over the responsibility of Winnie and do what I can for her."

Feb 24, 1905 Charlotte to Marie: "I was in financial despair. I had tried to borrow money from every friend I had, in vain, and the gas and water threatening and all my bills standing. Winnie had not train-money for another day and I had not a penny for another stamp."

March 19, 1905 Charlotte to Marie: "I am sorry that you are so indifferent to your mother's difficulties, as not even to read and answer my letters."

Marie was not indifferent, but Charlotte was an impossible woman to help. While deploring her younger daughter's inability to earn any money, she still refused Marie's offer to give Winnie a home in Manchester, which would have alleviated some of her difficulties. The two women were still battling for supremacy. Any boast from Marie about her growing standing in the world of palaeobotany was immediately countered by Charlotte's scholarly eminence. "They put me on the high table again," she wrote of a Shakespearean dinner, "the only woman *on my own account* – the others were wives and daughters of *men.*" The growing movement for women's rights provided further opportunities for quarrelling. Much to her daughter's distress, Charlotte supported the increasingly militant Pankhursts rather than the more modest and lady-like suffragists favoured by Marie. Was it unladylike, Charlotte retorted, if you found a burglar in the house, to hit him over the head with a broom – and had not women been burgled of their political rights ?[3] Carrying the battle into her daughter's camp, she asked for Marie to arrange for her to give a lecture at Manchester University. Marie's reply is not without a trace of malicious glee:

> Dear Mother ... I would rather, on the whole, not apply for any such thing ... I was speaking about the subject today and one of our most active members on women's subjects had never even *heard* of you ... I got an awfully good review in the *New Phytologist* ... it really was most flattering, "written with a breadth and knowledge not before met with in an English elementary book".[4]

Impatience with her mother was heightened by Marie's growing preoccupation with an even more emotionally wearing problem, her relationship with Fujii. He had arrived in London, ostensibly to study under F. W. Oliver, just before Marie left for Manchester in October 1904. They saw each other only briefly and, judging by letters, their attraction for each other was still undeclared. There were hints of it, however, among Fujii's attempts to explain Buddhism and Marie's grandiloquent expressions of contempt for mediocrity and for those whose life was not, as her own was, "pulsating with meaning". A week after she left London, Fujii wrote to her: "I am quite well, though I cannot say I am happy (except momentary happy thought and feeling which from time to time comes over me poetically)." In her reply, Marie approved his high opinion of Professor Oliver and made plans for Fujii to come and work in Manchester, plans to which he had already agreed and which therefore make her ambiguous references to "the future" slightly tantalising and not a little disingenuous:

> I am so grieved you are not happy – why is it ? Are they not kind to you in London? ... Yes, though in common talk one cannot use the word "lovely" as you did, yet I think it fits Prof. Oliver very

well indeed. True, also, that he attracts by his very calmness and noble aloofness – but it seems that Goebel attracts equally by his fiery living power, his very grand discontent with all the little thorns of life and all its stupid mediocrity. Is it not the whiteness of the lily that attracts us and the deep red of the rose? I could not say which is better of two such beautiful things ... Yes, there is much to say, we leave it always "to the future" which may never come. Perhaps it may. Yours, MCS.[5]

Fujii visited her briefly in Manchester. But by the end of her first term there, the relationship was still at an impasse, their frustrations finding release only in intellectual backbiting. In his letters, Fujii constantly rebuked Marie for her belief in immortality; why, he asked, could she not love where she loved, hate where she hated, and live life so fully that she could accept the finality of death? Marie riposted with jibes about Japanese materialism and lack of spirituality. His philosophy, she told him, was too small. "Can you conceive of a worm seeing in the sky at sunset all we see in it?" she wrote to him in December. "Can you not conceive of us as beings whose powers are as limited in relation to other forms as a worm is to us? But, as I think a worm would waste his time trying to understand sunsets, so I think we are absolutely incapable of understanding those above us, and the fate of us all." What a pity, she concluded rather frostily, that he had missed her lectures on cycadofilices – "They are the best I have ever given. Auf wiedersehen, MCS."[6]

While continuing to be half-excited by this postal flirtation, Marie would not allow herself to be convinced of its seriousness. Apart from anything else, she still felt, as she put it, "the strong British dislike of any thought of love between an Englishwoman and a foreigner". Certainly, the attraction was not permitted to interfere with her scientific work. Fujii's delicate musings were in strange contrast to her new life in Manchester. At the same time as his frequent letters on life's deeper import, a fellow-scientist was writing to her: "My dear Miss Stopes ... I must insist that in your paper you misunderstand my account of *Cephalotaxus*. When you say I found in its outer integ. '*zwei entgegesetzt ovientirte Bundel*' and then directly compare them with '*zwei entgegengesetzt ovientirte Bundel of Enceph. horridus*', what I say above is proved absolutely."

By the end of her first term she had established her dedication to science. In the laboratories she demonstrated methods of cutting fossil sections and preparing slides, gave lectures to medical and engineering students, and even tried to infect the Manchester slums with her enthusiasm for palaeobotany. Like her father, whose advertisements for public lectures always contained the rider, "Working Men Welcome", Marie felt a moral obligation to pass on her knowledge to the lower classes. What the factory workers of Ancoats and other slums made of cycads and inferior oolite has not been recorded, but at least Miss Stopes enjoyed her extra-mural lectures. "Dear Kidlet," she wrote to Winnie, "Life is a terrible rush – last night I gave a really good lecture to my working men – they were pleased I think. I feel like a small kitten impudently lecturing an old dog with these men, except when I roll out the long words they can't understand and then graciously explain them."[7]

Teaching commitments still left time for her own research. She was working for her London D.Sc. – which she took in 1905, becoming the youngest doctor of science in Britain – and collaborating with Fujii on the nutritive relations of surrounding tissues to the organs producing the female cells in gymnosperms (non-flowering, seed-bearing plants).[8] But most of her botanical passion was by now channelled into the study of coal, an enthusiasm she was never to lose. Manchester's main attraction for the fossil botanist was its proximity to the Lancashire and Yorkshire coalfields. The local mines provided the world's richest source – at least until their discovery in America – of "coal-balls". These, the most perfectly preserved of plant fossils, consist of a whole mass of vegetable matter petrified in irregular roundish masses and embedded in the coal seams. Unlike most plant fossils, consisting usually of a solitary leaf, or a fragment of stem, they provide a concentrated bundle of leaves, twigs, fruits, stems and sometimes seeds – in the nature, almost, of a botanical time capsule hundreds of millions of years old. During her first three years in Manchester, Marie published on several coal-ball plants, and also, with D. M. S. Watson, a Manchester contemporary, on coal-balls themselves, a study which remained for some years a standard reference work on the subject.[9] Unusually, Marie always insisted on going down the mines herself, instead of waiting for samples to be brought to her. This so impressed the pit-owners that they showered her with their own fossil collections, one of which yielded a species unique in Britain. She called it *Tubicaulis sutcliffii*, in honour of Mr Sutcliffe, a local mine-owner.

With confidence in her scientific future much increased after three months in Manchester, Marie had more time to think about Fujii. She returned to London to spend the Christmas vacation with her mother and Winnie in Hampstead. Fujii, depressed by his hotel, had moved to rooms in Southampton Row, and during the next few weeks the two saw a lot of each other. As a Christmas gift, he sent her an antique Japanese sword-ring (punctiliously enclosing gifts of equivalent value for Charlotte and Winnie). Their relationship, under conditions imposed by propriety – they met mostly in laboratories, at concerts of Wagner, in Kew Gardens, and spent December 27 picnicking on the muddy, windswept heights of Hampstead Heath – gradually deepened, accelerated by Fujii's commitment to return to Tokyo in February. He had already written to Imperial University asking for an extension of his leave in Europe and, while waiting for an answer, followed Marie to Manchester for the start of her second term. It is at this point that the story becomes a little confused.

In 1911, two years after the bitter end of their love affair, Marie Stopes took the extraordinary step of publishing her correspondence with Kenjiro Fujii. For *Love Letters of a Japanese*,[10] she took the pseudonym "G. N. Mortlake", editor of the letters between "Mertyl Meredith" and "Kenrio Watanabe", artists who had met in Germany and continued their love in England. Even with this disguise, the incidents and emotions described were accurate enough to convince those few friends privy to the affair that Fujii must be dead, otherwise such an account could not be published. This was not the case. It was merely the first example of Marie's lifelong habit of dispelling her personal traumas in print. Her claim in the introduction that the letters are unfictionalised appears to be justified. The two correspondents are ostensibly artists but there are no references in the book to visual preoccupations. More significantly, the letters that still survive in manuscript appear in *Love Letters* in exact transcriptions, even down to the date. Marie did, however, change some of the locations from which the letters were written, and this has created some confusion. Briant, for example, not having checked the published version with the manuscript originals, puts Marie in Zurich when she was actually in Munich, and in London when she was in Manchester. Even so, the parallels are sufficiently strong to justify the use of *Love Letters*, provided full source references are given; they are used here only when no autograph letter survives.

According to her editorial comments in *Love Letters*, it was not until April 1905 that she and Fujii admitted their attraction. Such was Marie's respect for convention that she could not tolerate the idea of being in love with a married man. Yet, a month earlier, on hearing that Fujii's stay had been extended for a month or two, she wrote to him in terms that were encouraging, to say the least: "You say we must finish all in May – finish our friendship and leave it embalmed as mere memory? Are we not rather planting the seed which will grow to be a tree, 'living and never finished'?"[11]

Marie was twenty-four when she received her first kiss. The experience did not live up to the high expectations engendered by such novels as *Mademoiselle de Maupin*, which, at the time, (though she found it slightly shocking) provided her only basis of sexual knowledge. Fujii shared the Japanese disgust with the Western habit of kissing, and had to be instructed by the equally ignorant Marie. The result, she told him later, with that chilling candour that helped to destroy so many of her relationships, was "quite horrid". At the same time, Fujii's innocence was deeply gratifying. Marie had always sworn that she would never marry a man who had kissed another woman, nor would she kiss anyone unless she intended to marry him. Her first kiss, then, disappointing though it was, was important both as a declaration and as a way of assuaging her guilt about being in love with a married man. Her scruples are apparent in the commentary to *Love Letters*:

As things stood it was impossible for them to be lovers in the normal way. He proposed to her, however, that they should consider their relations as if he were a free man. Knowing that morally he was free, and that legally it only required a simple formality on his return to his country to rid himself of the wife who had already broken her allegiance to him, and who was even more anxious for her freedom than he was, Watanabe asked only that Mertyl should be secretly betrothed to him, so that they should not waste the little time they had together, but should strengthen their love by exchanging vows. He won from her lips the first kiss she had ever given to a man, a kiss that she considered as binding as a marriage service. Their relations were still very much in the realms of spirit, however, for she felt the restraint of the knowledge that he was not legally free, however little he was bound morally.[12]

Fujii, remembering her earlier letter, sealed their "betrothal" with a box of red and white flowers. "Dear, – a bunch of flowers followed you, they could not help starting after you. *Bitte dich, gedenke an*: White of the lily as pure as my love and red of the rose as deep as my love. It will be as it is. Good night, dear, good night."[13] On the same day, 25 April 1905, Marie was elected a member of the Manchester Literary and Philosophical Society, in company with Mr Ernest Fearon, chemist to the Salford Corporation Gas Works. The occasion was celebrated by the reading of a paper, "On the Constituents of Manchester Soot".

Marie was occasionally conscious of the incongruities in her life, but the juxtaposition of lecturing to the Ancoats Working Men's Brotherhood on "Alpine Spring Glories" and pursuing her love for an unsuitable Japanese professor failed to weaken her faith in all-consuming passion. She spent part of the summer of 1905 on a working holiday in Munich, where Fujii was to join her before leaving for Tokyo. By now, their love was allowed free verbal expression, and from Munich she wrote with touching directness:

Dearest of all … sometimes when you are not there I begin to look at our love from an outsider's point of view, and cannot understand how the thing can be. When you are away, too, it all seems too strange, too sweet, too absurd, too like a strange novel, too impossible that I could have found so early in my life the man who can be perfectly my own, whom I can love. You know I never expected any one could be such as I wished; I never expected to marry … Beloved.[14]

Marie's sincerity was less obvious when she wrote of the physical side of love. She had absolutely no experience but, unlike Fujii, who saw love ideally as beyond bodily expression, she was already convinced, if only theoretically, of its importance. Fujii was slightly embarrassed by some of her comments – understandably enough, based as they necessarily were on the commonplaces of romantic literature. "Beloved," she wrote to him from Munich, "I never loved you so much as I loved you today. I do not know why, I cannot understand it at all, but the whole day has been one of love so great as to be almost pain. I woke with the feeling that you were near me, every nerve in my body tingling with longing for you, every pulse in my body throbbing with desire."[15]

While not admitting to throbbing desires, Fujii, too, was startled by the depth of his feeling. His command of English tottered under the strain of describing the sometimes bizarre effects of their now acknowledged passion. Before leaving London to join her in Munich, he wrote to her at the end of June: "Beloved, dear, dear, my dear ... You changed me so much, you overturned my thought, and even my person. Before I knew you my nails were not clean, my hair was nicely long not a bit, I have not shaved enough, and now if I don't do them every day, I feel that day I lost a dignity for myself."[16]

They managed to spend ten days together in Munich before Fujii sailed for Japan. To allay the suspicions of Mrs Stopes, Winnie was also in Munich, acting as chaperone; but they were alone together, wrote Marie, always anxious to preserve her respectability, as much "as the claims of society and of their work allowed ... They managed to go several times to the woods and to spend two days in the mountains." Before leaving on July 10, Fujii bought her a brooch, with Cupid's bow and arrows; she gave him a ring.

There is no reason to doubt Marie's protestations as to the "purity" of their relationship. Equally certain is her longing for physical expression, a need that was to be frustrated for so many years. On August 1, she wrote to Fujii about her desires in a much more convincing manner than her earlier self-conscious flights:

> Sweet, I long so for the physical touch of your hands on mine, and to look into your eyes. To be kissed, I sometimes long so much that I take a girdle and bind it tightly, so tightly that I can hardly breathe, round my waist and then close my eyes and dream that it is your arms around me. It gives me almost the feeling. You know I have never worn corsets. I have always been scornful of women who did. But do you know, dear, this teaches me that this is why so many women like to have them very tight.

Both were certain that they would eventually marry. Fujii addressed Marie as "sweet wife" and, back in Tokyo, exulted in her effect upon him. He had only to think of her, he wrote in September, for his whole person to become "mysteriously electrified till the minutest points. Oh, there is nothing so sweet and happy as the state of electrification due to you, Beloved." In reply, Marie addressed him as "husband" and considered herself morally, if not actually, married. Marie's intentions were clear and unswerving. In November of that year, after giving a lecture to 300 members of the Openshaw Working Men's Brotherhood, she went to tea with the secretary and his wife, both spiritualists. Marie was delighted by their forecast of her future, and promptly wrote to Fujii:

Sweet Heart ... He and his wife are quite simple people, but so *real* ... She told me that everything I do in my life will succeed (so far that has been true) and it is a pleasant thought. She also said that the man who is everything my heart desires is not yet born, as I set my aims *so* high – but that I shall marry wisely and well and that my marriage will be one out of the common in its perfection – She said I had not yet thought of a definite man to marry which was silly of her! But I told her that for fun. It amuses me so much to hear people's views about my possible marriage! and I dare not hint at the truth, that thou and I are one – dear heart it is known only to us, how sweet! But that she said she saw in me acting a strong old wise spirit that would make all I touch a success – pleased me even while I do not actually believe it. It helps towards success where people around expect success – *nicht wahr?*

She also told me people had seen me and told her I was beautiful! I was awfully glad for no-one here has told me and I feared I must be ugly in their eyes – and for your sake I wish that people find me a little beautiful. Dearest, I wish so much that your wife is beautiful, good, distinguished – all that is splendid so that men and women may think ..." [here, the letter, a rough draft in the British Library collection, breaks off][17]

Fujii was equally determined to marry Marie. Two months later, in January 1906, his divorce came through. He spent much energy in his letters reassuring her about their future together. Though she professed belief in a grand passion transcending convention, Marie was genuinely horrified by the stigma of divorce, the fact of Fujii's already having a child, and the thought of English prejudice against marriage with a Japanese. Fujii pointed out, quite accurately, that in Japan marriage had no connection with either religion or love – indeed, love matches were considered immoral – that his child, if considered in the European way as product of marital love, was what he called a mere "misprint", and that English prejudice was as nothing compared with Japanese distrust of the English (to Marie, a novel, and scarcely credible concept). It says much for the strength of his feelings that Fujii was prepared to discount his culture and upbringing to accommodate himself to Western ideas of a more holy matrimony.

After his divorce, it was agreed that they would marry in eighteen months' time. There were many problems. Fujii's academic career lay in Tokyo University. He was unlikely to visit Europe again for any considerable length of time. He also had his small daughter to bring up. There was only one solution: Marie would have to go to Japan. With no money of her own – anything left over from her salary went to help Charlotte and Winnie – some other way would have to be found of re-uniting her with the man she was determined to marry. Such a love, she felt, was so far above that of ordinary people, for whom marriage meant only "a vulgar affection for a short time, and then dislike and quarrelling", that no difficulty would be allowed to stand in its way. For the next academic year in Manchester, she maintained her respectable, humdrum life among her unstimulating students and the pursuit of fossils embedded in the inferior oolite of Brora, up on the east coast of Scotland. She was, noted the university students' magazine, "fond of hockey, rowing and walking"; but no one knew of her frequent letters to the absent Fujii: "Kiss me gently when we meet, or I will die."[18] The problem of financing such a consummation would have defeated a lesser person. Marie solved it with a typical combination of imagination and determination.

In common with the rest of the botanical world, she was fascinated by the question of the origin of the angiosperms. These – flowering plants, as opposed to the non-flowering gymnosperms – now dominate the earth's surface and are, indeed, what most people today think of as a "plant". Fossil historians, however, were puzzled by the angiosperm's decisive takeover from the gymnosperm. How had they arisen so suddenly and spread so fast? Such rapid evolution (over a period of a mere seventy million years) was difficult to accept, and in 1879 Dawin complained that the angiosperms were "an abominable mystery. I would like to see the problem solved." Today it has still not been solved; but in 1906 scientific bodies were already willing to finance research into the mystery. In common with other palaeobotanists, Marie was well aware of the angiosperm impressions discovered much earlier in Japan and elsewhere. What she was more interested in was the much rarer find – a petrified specimen, revealing the structure of the plant rather than merely its impression. With the thought of a trip to Japan no doubt reinforcing her scientific curiosity, Marie sent off to Fujii for samples from Hokkaido, Japan's most northerly island, and the area she thought would be most likely to produce such petrifactions. The nodules arrived shortly after her twenty-sixth birthday, and the first section she made revealed an angiosperm. Convinced by her case – and justifiably, in view of her subsequent discoveries there – the Royal Society had little hesitation in awarding her a grant to go to Japan, the first time such help had been given to a woman.

She planned to join Fujii in Tokyo in the summer of 1907. As the months passed, there was no diminution in the force of her commitment. Her letters were accompanied by gifts – including once a box of red roses and white heather which Marie, unable to resist an experiment, embalmed in mercuric chloride. They arrived in Tokyo six weeks later, rotted and smelling.

At first, Marie did not notice the lessening of Fujii's feeling for her. He had always suffered from attacks of vague, undefined illness, and she was not too worried by their increasing frequency. Her own career was going well. In the first half of 1907, her work was published in *New Phytologist*, *Annals of Botany*, and *Geological Magazine* and, a fortnight before she left for Japan, her paper on a new plant-bearing deposit, "The Flora of the Inferior Oolite of Brora", was read to much acclaim at the Geological Society. Marie had even reconciled herself to the thought of living with a ready-made daughter in Tokyo ("tho' I wish she was a boy," she wrote to Fujii) and instructed Winnie to have her favourite doll refurbished at a good doll's shop: "You know Frenchie, don't you, the jolly big one with a porcelain face, who used to have big white kid shoes. I shall let Prof. Fujii's little girl play with her, but I shan't *give* it to her unless she is an awfully nice child."*

* According to Fujii's second wife, Keiko Tanaka, who is still at the time of writing alive, the doll was kept for many years on a corner table in the Fujii home. (Information from Jenny Phillips who interviewed Keiko Tanaka in Tokyo in September 1975.)

It was not until shortly before she left for Japan in July 1907 that Marie became upset by Fujii's apparent coldness. His letters had become much less frequent, he addressed her as "Dear" rather than "Ideal Dream", and even asked her to postpone her visit for a year. At that stage, of course, with all the arrangements made, and the Royal Society eager for botanical discoveries, it was impossible for Marie to change her plans. She was hurt, and wrote to Fujii: "My luggage is nearly packed, such a lot of it. I have had to find out and do everything for myself; all the help and advice you promised has to come ... Perhaps you may remember that you love me by the time I get to Yokohama, and may help me with the Customs. Your behaviour is rather curious."[19]

A month later, on July 3, Marie sailed from Genoa on the *Prinz Regent Luitpold*, bound for Yokohama. Guy Pilgrim, her former admirer, had heard of her latest adventure and wrote to her from Calcutta: "Farewell! I hope you will have a good time in Japan. But don't go and marry a Japanese whatever you do." Marie had every intention of marrying a Japanese. Fujii, it is true, had not fulfilled his promise to meet her halfway and share the delights of Japan's Inland Sea. Once together, however, it would surely be simple to re-establish a passion which had subsisted for eighteen months only on the written word. It was unthinkable that Fujii, her first and only love, could have changed his mind.

CHAPTER 4

East and West

"Why couldn't I love someone whom it would be simple
and easy to marry – or why couldn't I stay as cold-
hearted to wooers as I have hitherto been? But of course
I always knew I should love some day and do it passionately, made as I am it was inevitable."

Marie Stopes, Tokyo, to Professor F. E. Weiss,
Manchester, 21 May 1908

AFTER five weeks at sea, Marie arrived in Japan on 9 August 1907.
Fujii met her at Yokohama, but – after two years' impassioned correspondence – neither of them recorded the meeting. Certainly,
Fujii's letters had not prepared her for the vast cultural differences
between Japan and Europe.

Despite Commodore Perry's enforced opening-up of trade in 1853,
Japan still remained in many ways an enclosed, highly conventional
society. The revolution of 1868, inaugurating the Meiji régime, had
installed the Emperor in place of the Shogun. Previous feudal attitudes
were succeeded by an intense chauvinism, bolstered in the first decade
of the twentieth century by Japan's unexpected success in the recent
war against Russia. Japan still felt herself superior to the West (particularly to Christianity, which for most Japanese typified the most
ludicrous superstition) but at the same time was dependent on Western
expertise in engineering, commerce, medicine, education – all the
skills that could increase her prosperity. Equally, the fashionable
revival of "Old Japan" was accompanied by a snobbish and contradictory admiration for the Western way of life. At court and diplomatic functions, at performances of the classical Nō plays, it was not

uncommon to come across descendants of the *daimyos* (the old nobility) incongruously dressed in kimono, surmounted by black frock-coat and top hat, their wives in the latest Paris fashions, but with their unaccustomed corsets worn outside the gown.[1]

Marie was determined to refrain from transferring to Tokyo the lifestyle of suburban London. Japan by now had railways, factory chimneys, and brick buildings that soared above the grey, wooden, one-storied houses that still made up most of Tokyo. She chose to lodge in an old house in Koishikawa-Ku, near to the Botanical Institute. She happily slept on the floor, under silk quilts that were put away during the day, delighting in the lack of furniture, the starkness and simplicity of a room that could be quadrupled in size merely by sliding back a few paper screens. Initially, almost everything was aesthetically pleasing after the heavy decor of the Victorian interior, the elaborately varied meals, and the baroque curlicues of the women's dress against which her mother had so vehemently inveighed. She even liked Japanese food. Breakfast, lunch, and dinner were so similar – a conglomerate of rice, raw fish and eggs – that there was no point in thinking out new menus. Marie delighted in the indigenous. In the journal she kept throughout her eighteen months' stay in Japan, she deplored the sewage system (the commonest manure was unashamedly human) but did not allow this to influence her appreciation of Japan's visual genius: "The tawdry fluffiness of most of our women's dress and hair seemed like flannelette beside rich satin as compared with her ... I wonder till I verge on lunacy how it is that the West has not yet discovered the glory that lies in smooth curves and gleaming surfaces, and in lines of cloth, unbroken by frilling and tucking and ruching and pleating ..."[2]

Such aesthetic considerations bore little relation to the actual status of women in Japan. As a sop to Western culture, a Women's University had been founded seven years earlier, but Japan was much more inimical than the West to women whose ambitions extended beyond the domestic role allotted them.

Women were innately inferior. Permitted to serve tea, they took no part in the conversation. If invited out, they took a separate rickshaw behind their husbands.* Marie was much impressed by the fact that

---

* "Above all, be constantly polite and conciliatory in your demeanour towards the people. Whereas the lower classes at home are apt to resent suave manners, and to

the new university concentrated on teaching women how to bring up children: "... by far the largest number of the women graduates go back to their homes and get married," Marie commented admiringly, "so that nearly all the students are studying for the *culture*, not working for exams, so as to be able to become teachers ..."[3] Obviously, she did not consider herself part of that female sex whose devotion to the "culture" she objectively approved. As a Westerner, her own application to exams was different. With an estabished scientific reputation in Europe, she could afford such *de-haut-en-bas* attitudes. There were no women scientists in Japan, and women were not allowed to study at Imperial University, except as research assistants. It says much for Japanese politeness that Marie was accorded the status of an honorary man.

Only ten days after arriving in Tokyo, Marie set off on her fossil-hunting expedition to Hokkaido, then one of the least explored of the islands, covered in ice and snow for half the year and inhabited partly by the aboriginal Ainos, much despised by the rest of Japan. Despite her protestations, the authorities insisted on providing an interpreter, two guides, thirty coolies and a policeman (there were no major crimes in the jungle, but he turned out to be very good at catching fish for breakfast and carving chopsticks out of bamboo). Marie wrote to her sister:

Dear Kid ... They take the dangers earnestly, or not so much the dangers as the difficulties and when I sit in a white muslin dress and pink silk sash and tell them I don't mind walking several miles up a river bed and that I don't mind sleeping on stones they think I am not treating the hardness of their country with proper respect.[4]

She very quickly discarded white muslin and pink sashes in favour of short, blue Japanese trousers and jacket, leggings and sandals. Her search for coal-balls in the Yubari coalfields of Hokkaido was not too arduous. Once outside the mining settlements, however, there was nothing but trackless forest, carpeted with six-foot bamboo. The river beds provided the only path. Too strong and rapid to allow

imagine that he who addresses them politely wishes to deceive them, every Japanese, however humble, expects courtesy, being himself courteous. His courtesy, however, differs from that of the West in not being specially directed towards ladies." *Murray's Handbook to Japan*, John Murray, 1913.

navigation, they were shallow enough to provide a route for anyone determined to pick a way between one bank and the other. In her journal Marie gave a vivid account of the quest for post-Carboniferous coal-balls:

August 24: – Really, it is hard work to carry tents and everything along these rivers. Often I alone find it difficult to go, and I have nothing to carry – except my fan and hammer, both of which are in constant use. Sometimes it would be impossible to go where we have been with boots, the straw sandals give such a clinging grasp that we are able to get a foothold on a steep rock which in boots it would be mad to attempt.

Fortunately the river into which one would be precipitated is seldom deep enough to be dangerous. The day's scientific results are solid, but not thrilling. Tents are a luxury, but I would rather sleep out under the stars. With all these coolies and people I am not allowed to do my own cooking, but I most fervently wish I might. The food is rendered needlessly trying by their attempts at European cooking – but they mean so well! They even carried a chicken for my consumption, but will only cook it for ten minutes, so it is as hard as the stones we are hunting for![5]

As a white woman, she was an object of great curiosity. Wondering crowds gathered whenever she went swimming, demanding to know why she was so white – and so foolish as to wear clothes in the sea. Marie proved to be much more adaptable than most of her compatriots. She was amused rather than horrified when, on rail journeys, Japanese businessmen in sober European suits would suddenly strip down to the skin and slip into a comfortable kimono. She approved Japan's total lack of prudery about the human body, and even got used to the constant procession of observers when she took a bath. "The Japanese argue (really far more purely and logically than we do)," she wrote to Winnie, "that all necessary things are pure and that if it happens that while one is necessarily naked during bathing and another by accident opens the bathroom door, there is no thought of harm – *no one* peeped or pryed the whole time I have been here, though they openly stared in through open doors."[6]

Marie's powers of adaptation did not extend, however, to the assumption of woman's inferior role. Infuriated by Tokyo's muddy, largely unsurfaced roads, and by the impossibility of finding her way around (houses were haphazardly numbered according to the date when they were built) she bought a bicycle – eccentric for a European, inconceivable for a Japanese woman. *"Très moderne,"* commented the French Ambassador sarcastically when she turned up on her bicycle for a reception, in full evening dress splattered with mud. Marie sometimes liked to see herself as the Intrepid White Woman, maintaining civilised values in unmapped territory where no white foot had ever trod. In fact, both in Tokyo and on her scientific expeditions, she was heavily insulated from the discomforts endured, for example, by Isabella Bird, the Scottish missionary who twenty years earlier had travelled on horseback through Hokkaido, living with the Ainos, their vermin, contagious diseases and inedible food.[7] In Tokyo, through no fault of her own (it is still difficult for Westerners to build up strong social contacts with the Japanese) her life outside the Botanical Institute was limited to diplomatic circles and to the wives and families of British businessmen. It was a world of ladies' hockey matches, tea parties and stiff receptions. Marie soon found it unwise to enthuse too much about such social occasions even when she was genuinely excited. One evening, shortly after her return from Hokkaido, she received an invitation to the Imperial chrysanthemum party at Akasaka Palace. "It was amusing to see the awe with which my landlady viewed it – the Imperial Crest being almost sacred in this country," Marie wrote in her journal. "She took it in her hands as a good Catholic might a piece of the true cross, and raised it three times to her forehead, and asked leave to take it to show her husband. I shine from the reflected glory."[8] Such naked delight in her little social triumphs was obviously not going to appeal to Mrs Stopes. Why should Marie be having such a good time? Replying to this latest instalment of Marie's journal (circulated among family and friends in lieu of letters) Charlotte demanded that Marie return home immediately, get married to someone rich and respectable, and support her aging mother. Marie lost her temper. "Dear Mother," she replied in January from Tokyo:

You bemoan the fact that you have not a married daughter – but what steps have you ever taken to assist either of us to get married? What dances have you ever chaperoned us to? What young men have you introduced us to? When I mix as I do here, among ordinary people and see the kindly helpfulness (not to be confused with husband-hunting) of mothers for their girls in the way of social things I sigh indeed for my abnormal youth and for Winnie far more. Of course I could have been married often, it is my own high standard as regards certain things, which debars me – but what chances has Winnie had? ... Well, you ask me to foreshadow my plans ... All I know is that I shall have to remain a long time yet in Japan over these fossils ...[9]

Marie tried to placate her mother by admiring references to the growing support in London for the Suffragettes – but spoiled the effect by congratulating herself on being out of the country – "for tho' I don't have so much sympathy with the rowdy ones, I should have probably got drawn into it and it would have seriously damaged my career as a scientist".[10] Whatever Marie did, in fact, was wrong from Charlotte's point of view. If she enjoyed herself, she was heartlessly self-indulgent; but if she failed to capture the sparkle of Tokyo society, Charlotte complained about the lack of social repartee in her letters. To one such complaint, Marie replied in a fury:

My dear mother, who on earth do you suppose utters *bons mots* or *jeux d'esprit* for me to gather up and transcribe? With the exception of Miss Ballard, the amusing missionary, it is not mere conceit that makes me say I am usually the most brilliant conversationalist at a gathering here ... No, I don't think I shall ever be present at Court – why should I? I shouldn't be in the set at all at home and it would waste a lot of time and money to attempt it.*[11]

Marie's impatience with her mother's demands was exacerbated by the stagnation of her love affair with Fujii. She had been right in suspecting, even before she reached Japan, that his affection had cooled. Like many another traveller before and since, Fujii had begun to see the difference between a romance which had been exciting while he was abroad, and a marriage which would seem embarrassingly unsuitable at home. Marie's official reason for being in Tokyo was her joint work with Fujii on angiosperms. There was no reason why, as Marie's

* More a way of contradicting Charlotte than a statement of her own feelings. Marie had already approached an old family friend for advice about how to be presented at Court, but decided it was too expensive. Some years later, she spent considerable time and money engineering her presentation, and finally managed it in 1924.

sponsor, he should not have accompanied her on the Hokkaido trip. He preferred instead to send another Japanese botanist who spoke English but knew little of their work together. On her return to Tokyo, Fujii refused to undertake laboratory work with her in the evenings, claiming that this might damage her reputation – even though he was by now divorced, and though no stigma was attached in Japan to non-marital relationships. Marie was unwilling to admit that something might have gone wrong. In April 1908, six months after arriving in Japan, she wrote to her revered mentor, Professor Oliver, about her difficulties:

> This job seems much bigger than I anticipated. Perhaps I should not say much bigger but much *slower*. Japan is not yet fully western-ised even though she has electric tram cars in the city and her men sport "foroko-coatos" – (you must realise Japanese has no consonants without vowels attached) and time seems to be no object with them – also Prof. Fujii my nominal colleague is busy – and now is ill, really very seriously ill, in danger of losing his sight.[12]

It is difficult now to assess just how far Fujii's alleged illnesses were real or feigned. In *Love Letters of a Japanese*, Marie ascribed the break-up of their relationship to his ill health. At first she accepted his explanation as genuine, and was prepared to devote the rest of her life to supporting an invalid. Only a month after writing to Professor Oliver, Marie decided to force the issue by consulting one of her academic colleagues about the possibility of a life for herself and Fujii in England. At the time, and for many years afterwards, there was considerable prejudice against married women in the academic and teaching professions, and they were frequently dismissed on marriage. Marie did not readily confide in friends, and her letter to Professor Weiss, head of her department at Manchester, was long, confused, and unusually hysterical. She was, she told him, "desperately lonely and unadvised". She swore him to secrecy and begged him to read the letter twice before forming an opinion:

> My dear Prof. W ... Now there is no good beating about the bush ... I am in love! and of course thinking about marrying. But it is all so extraordinarily tangled and furiously complicated that I fear it will never come off at all ... Now please don't be vexed and

throw the letter down and say "of course – another woman lost
to science" – or something of that kind. Science comes largely into
my calculations and I will be no worse a scientist because I am
married. Are you?

I had better tell you who it is. It is Prof. Fujii – you know how
nice he is and how everyone likes him – I alone know how exquisitely sweet he can be, for I alone have [experienced?] his
love – that I know well.

What did it matter, Marie argued, that Fujii was so ill all the time,
and in danger of going blind? She could read to him, and they could
still work together: "He is ballast and I am the sails in our work
generally" – (a description that would scarcely have appealed to
Fujii). But, of course, the main reason for their projected marriage was
love: "*the* argument in favour of the marriage, to bring forward any
others is to insult that greatest thing in the world". Perhaps she should
marry before returning to England? But then she would more or less
have to support Fujii, his salary being so small. Would Manchester
University still employ her if she were married? Surely the only
objection could be the possibility of children . . .

Now in my case there are very many reasons why I will never have
children. So many, so vital are they that you can feel perfectly
safe . . . The best answer I ever saw to that cynical question, "Why
marry?" was "Because Love commands." Everything looks very
easy to me, in spite of the many difficulties, if you in Mnch. feel as
I feel that marriage makes no difficulties to one's capacities as a
scientist and I can take on my work in England just as I would if I
returned without the little gold ring on my finger. I ought to mention, perhaps, that I will still retain my first name, as I have always
said I would, whoever I married, even if he were a Lord . . . Please
guard my secret well, so many things may happen to prevent the
marriage, and if so, I couldn't bear that people knew. You know, I
rather prided myself on being a Diana . . .[13]

There is no record of Professor Weiss's reply, or of Fujii's attitude
(if, indeed, he had been consulted). Fujii's health, allegedly, deterior-
ated further. It is only too likely that, in an attempt to extricate himself
without damaging Marie's pride too much, he exaggerated his bodily

ailments. He knew that Marie, in common with most Europeans, was terrified of leprosy. In her journal for February of that year, Marie wrote that she was haunted by the sight of lepers: "They are not allowed to *live* in the city, when in an advanced state of disease, but they are allowed to come in and beg. One may easily touch one by accident! Today I was within a foot of one before I noticed it. They hold out their hands, with the fingers eaten away, gruesome sights, and mumble prayers for alms . . . On the whole, the Japanese do not fear leprosy nearly so much as we do, they say we over-rate its contagion; but how can they pretend to civilisation with such sights in their streets?"[14]

She deplored the fact that lepers were allowed to marry and beget children – why couldn't they be transported to some remote island and allowed to die out? – and in April 1908 she determined never to use public transport again: "The horror of my last ride! A leper came and sat down beside me, almost on top of me, and the cars are so crowded I could not get away. He was not in the worst stages, of course, but some of his finger tips were eaten away and one eye was blinded – there is none of the 'white as snow' business about lepers, it is an eating away of the digits, and finally the limbs."[15]

In August of that year, Marie recorded in unusually emotional vein:

Are the gods never going to have mercy and stop their cruel play of battering Professor F—, and through him, me and our fossil work? Instead of coming early in the morning, as we arranged, he came very late, with the horrible news that he had just heard that the people who lived in his house before him (he moved last year) had a *leper* in the family! Consequently he and his household have stood grave danger of getting this ghastly disease, and may actually have it now, the latent period is so uncertain . . . On my way back I saw several beggars, ghastly creatures, kneeling by the wayside, with fingerless hands, all purple blotched . . . I am not really afraid for Professor F— (and through him, for myself) but I fear the removal will still further hinder the progress on our fossil work.[16]

Fujii lived until the age of eighty-six – eight years longer than Marie. After the dissolution of his first marriage, and Marie's departure from Japan, he had, consecutively, two common-law wives, one of whom he finally married at the age of eighty-two. According to those who remember him, he remained in excellent health until his death in

1952. His son, Shin'nichi Fujii, born in 1925, recalls no talk of leprosy; nor does Shin'nichi's mother, Keiko Tanaka, whom Fujii married in 1949. Those of Fujii's former students who still survive – Professor Yudzuro Ogura, Professor Yoshinari Kuwada and Dr Yosito Sinoto – were amused at the idea. Fujii's "leprosy", they agree, must have been an expedient to rescue him from the embarrassment of a liaison he no longer wished to pursue.*

It was, indeed, a measure of Fujii's desperation that he was driven to such fabrications to avoid the pain of overtly rejecting Marie. Though she did not admit it openly, she recognised that the affair was over. In August 1908 she wrote to her mother in reply to yet another of Charlotte's complaints about Winnie's gaucheness in society. Marie still maintained to her mother the fiction of Fujii's happy marriage – two years after his divorce – and her response to Charlotte's boasting about her admirers was, if only to herself, an admission of failure:

> Dear Mother . . . I am sorry the Kid is so stupid as to be disinclined for Society and the chance of a husband – little fool, now is the time, she will never be either younger or prettier than she is now. As you have two charming men in hand, keep one for me, I should like a Sir Galahad husband and you say one of them is that. When I return I shall be willing to marry a man suitable in tastes who lives in a University town (preferably London) and who adores me – I can't take to any of those with whom I am already acquainted. I fear I shall have to give up the idea of a botanist, it limits my choice too much . . . Your affectionate daughter, M. C. Stopes.[17]

Even Marie's robust constitution was unable to cope with her gradual realisation of Fujii's rejection. Most unusually, she became subject to fits of weeping, and in September, a month after the leprosy scare, she herself became ill. She took to her bed with a high fever, and even submitted to the humiliation of calling a doctor. A true hypochondriac, Marie distrusted doctors (a feeling vindictively reciprocated by the medical profession much later, in her campaign for birth control) and put her faith in self-medication. In Tokyo, she had already got rid of sixty-six warts on her hands, she told Winnie, by "the simple

---

* I am indebted here to Jenny Phillips, who interviewed in Tokyo in 1975 members of Fujii's family, and as many of his former students – now very old – as could be traced.

application of nitric acid". Despite the doctors, she survived her four-day attack of psychosomatic leprosy and went back to the wearisome round of dull, diplomatic parties and solitary sessions in the laboratory. She had no one in whom to confide her miseries, and only hinted at them in her journal. One of her ambitions had always been to be an ambassadress, but even the diplomatic life, on which she had embarked with such enthusiasm, had lost its savour. "Who would believe it?" she wrote, "I am only too thankful that I know what a life it is, and will never need to fear that I drop into it dazzled and unawares. It is an endless round of calling and dining; they profess to complain of it themselves, but take little interest in anything else."[18]

Neither were Marie's attempts to enliven the social scene very successful. Following Charlotte's example in Upper Norwood, Marie started a ladies' debating society. One of the first debates was on the motion: "That the unmarried life is the happier." Marie did not record the outcome, but her comments make it clear that she did not range herself on the side of the militantly anti-male spinster. She found the whole debate "fortunately rather superficial":

> The people here are not in touch with all our modern types, and I did not need to speak against the ranting type, who rave against men and marriage and prove themselves deformed. No, there were no such problem people here, only young spinsters who didn't dare or wish to speak against marriage, and elderly spinsters who were clever enough to be amusing without touching a fundamental note. The ranting type seems mercifully to be confined to big communities; I suppose it is an inevitable result of city life, where some must sterilise . . .[19]

While reserving the right to criticise Tokyo's circle of expatriates, however, Marie was deeply offended if left out of any of its functions. From about this time, her letters take on an acerbic, high-handed tone which later became habitual when she felt herself ignored or in any way criticised. In November of that year, she wrote to Sir Claude McDonald, British Ambassador in Tokyo. The letter was dated the day before his big reception for the eminent biologist, Sven Hedin, to which she had not yet received an invitation:

> Dear Sir Claude . . . I take the perhaps rather unwise step of writing to you directly because it seems to me much hangs on this – were

it merely for the pleasure of a social function, I would not dream of questioning whether or not your invitation went stray ... but tomorrow representatives of the university are coming to you to meet S.H. – and if they find that I – the only British scientist in Japan, and one moreover for whom they have put themselves so much about – am not invited to meet Dr H at my own embassy – what will they conclude?[20]

Sir Claude was not to be intimidated. He had sent an invitation, he replied, and found her writing to him "hasty and inconsiderate, and the concluding paragraph in which you say that 'were it merely for the trifling pleasure of a social function' is also – I venture to think – discourteous. You are perhaps unaware that there is no obligation whatsoever on my part to entertain anybody at this Embassy outside the strictly official and diplomatic circles."[21] The invitation finally arrived, but Marie, piqued, did not attend the reception. She did, however, write again to Sir Claude, pointing out her absence. He was not sufficiently perturbed to reply.

Two months later, on 24 January 1909, Marie sailed for home from Yokohama, via Vancouver, on the *Empress of Japan*. Kenjiro Fujii, along with one or two other friends, came to see her off; but this time there were no enigmatic avowals, as there had been at Munich, among the chocolates and flowers.

"Why I didn't break down and howl on the platform I don't know," Marie recorded in her journal. During her eighteen months in Japan she had achieved everything, except the one thing she had gone for. Scientifically, because of Fujii's illnesses, she had been stretched to her limits. The results of their collaboration – though Marie always gave him joint credit – were in fact mostly her own achievement. She had found in Japan no coal-balls, but she had discovered what was at the time the earliest example of a petrified flower and her publications about Japan over the next few years confirmed her reputation as a palaeobotanist of some originality.[22] But the affair with Fujii was over. Summing up her feelings about Japan, Marie concluded that the Japanese were neither so artistic nor so clever as Westerners accused them of being. Nor were they so insensitive to the possibility of "deep friendship between the East and the West".

Despite their apparent coldness, some Japanese had "a beauty of feeling which only the exceptional Westerner could match ... The apparently immobile face is immobile only because we ourselves are not alive to its subtle changes. When you know a Japanese face it is as eloquent as that of a sensitive English girl. And the moods and feelings it mirrors are not alien to ours ... In the 'changeless eyes' of the Japanese I have seen fire and mist, radiance and storm. I have seen men's tears welling up from the sweetness beneath to veil the eyes that looked on sorrowful things, or things so beautiful as to be a pain – as is Mount Fujii in an opal morning."[23]

This tribute to Fujii, whose eyes had proved to be insufficiently changeless, was doubly generous, written as it was at the time of her leaving Japan. The end of their love was a severe blow – not just to her faith in the consuming and eternal nature of passion but, more importantly, to her pride. She never recovered from it, and all her subsequent endeavours can be seen as furious compensation claims for emotional injury. Over fourteen years later, when they were once more in touch, they addressed each other as "Dr Stopes" and "Professor Fujii". Marie never saw the sacred Mount Fujii without its covering of clouds; and possibly only Fujii would have realised the significance of the telegram she sent to him in Tokyo on his seventieth birthday, in 1936, over thirty years after they first met: "May the glow of immortal life burn beneath the snow capped peak of Fujii's seventy epochs."[24]

CHAPTER 5

A Fate Worse than Death

"To a woman who deeply loves a man, broken betrothal
is as death itself – indeed, it is worse."
Marie Stopes to C. G. Hewitt, Tokyo, 19 April 1908

ONE of the ways of coping with the pain of rejection is to plunge into
emotional promiscuity, rather than to retire altogether from the problems of human involvement. A month after leaving Japan, Marie had
decided that the best way to repair her damaged self-esteem was to
prove her own attractiveness.

"Why do I always fall in love with women?" she complained in her
journal, extolling the beauty of an American woman she had met at a
diplomatic party in Tokyo. "On her soft white neck were the loveliest
little blue veins, I never saw anything so suggestive of living marble.
She was like white marble, with an underflush of rose and violet . . .
She is the only woman in Tokyo who has bewitched me."[1] Marie's
question was easily answered. A man, Fujii, had let her down. She
turned for reassurance to those who could give her warmth and
admiration without the problems of bringing heterosexual affection
to a socially acceptable fruition.

Marie was twenty-eight when she arrived in Vancouver from Japan,
en route to England. She was worried about being unmarried – most
women were considered "on the shelf" at the age of twenty-five, or
even earlier – and she decided to stay on a week or two in Canada,
giving lectures to women's societies about her experiences in Japan,
and exploring the local fossils. Dr Helen McMurchy was nearly twice
her age, and took Marie under her wing. Few of Marie's letters to her
survive, even in the rough drafts which she so rarely discarded; but

Dr McMurchy's letters to Marie were preserved. Reading them, in the British Library collection – they have hitherto been ignored – it is possible to build up a picture of a violently frustrated woman responding to a younger woman's need to be loved, a need so intense that Marie was driven to encourage the older woman's admiration to a point beyond the bounds of convention. "My Darling," wrote Helen McMurchy from Toronto, as Marie left for Montreal:

> That is what I have been wanting to call you ever since the express took you away from me to Montreal. In that moment I knew I loved you – when I found it in my heart to take you into my arms and kiss you ... You have "got me" – dear – and what a sweet thing that you *knew* that you had got me and were a little glad about it.
>
> There will be true lovers for you, Darling – instead of that false and cruel one – You are sure to be admired and liked – and loved – by many men ... I claim you for mine, dear – forever – as you said. I shall always have a share in you and in what you do – You dear genius ... Midnight and mail time. It must be goodbye – and was I the only person who kissed you in Canada! You darling – what am I to call *you*? Ever yours affectionately, Helen McMurchy.[2]

Marie had obviously confided in her new friend about the hard-hearted Fujii, and Dr McMurchy's somewhat extravagant sympathy was by no means rejected. Marie's reply – she was by now on board the *Lusitania* on the way back to England – evoked another effusion:

> February 24, 1909: "My Darling, It has been a little hard to make up my mind to write to you, Dear, tonight. I think I wanted to ask *you* if you meant it all! ... You see I know so little about you, Dear – and yet so much. I know you mean it all – I know *you* knew what you were giving me – and yet I want you to tell me once more."

It was a typical lovers' correspondence, with neither party willing to commit herself. Dr McMurchy's letters continued throughout February and March, and Marie was, apparently, upset by a slight diminution of the total devotion she expected. On March 29, Helen McMurchy wrote to her:

... And the letter of March 4th wasn't half so warm as the previous ones! Then this shall make up for it, dear – I remember that letter and remember just how I felt. You know it was a bit hard for me after you went away – Before I knew it, I had given you your place in my heart and it hurt to let you go ... Then when your letters came and I found you really *did* care – perhaps – I thought very much about you ... It seemed too good to be true that you really cared for me.

With Marie back in England, the passion lapsed.* Dr McMurchy had served her purpose, but was a little cloying. In Manchester, where Marie had now been promoted from demonstrator to lecturer in botany, with in addition, a commission from the British Museum to undertake a full-scale compilation of the Cretaceous Flora, she felt it was time once more to test the tepid waters of heterosexual attachment.

Henry Bassett was tepid enough. A fellow-student at both London and Munich, he had been in love with Marie for six years. Like most chemists he felt himself despised by the civilised world; but at least Marie consented to go on nature trips with him, walking or cycling. After one such trip he wrote to her in June of 1909:

Dear little Sunbeam, I will christen you thus for to me you are indeed like a ray of light in the darkness. I am rather a lonely person as I do not easily form big friendships and, with the exception of my dear old Father and Mother, I think you are the only person who really understands me at all ...

Incompetence and insecurity were never attractive qualities to Marie, but she filed Henry for later reference. His devotion was beyond question; but what swooning delights could be expected of a man who diluted his avowals of love with a disquisition on the nature of coal grit? Marie was after rather more taxing quarry. She found it – and was defeated by it – in Charles Gordon Hewitt.

· · · · ·

* Their correspondence was not resumed until 1927, when Marie Stopes, by then famous as the apostle of birth control, wrote to "Minky", asking for statistical data. Helen McMurchy, not amused by such familiarity after such a long lapse, wrote back very stiffly: "My dear Doctor Stopes ..."

Bottom:
Marie (*right*) with
her sister Winnie

Top: 'An attractive figure, despite her forbidding capacity for hard work'

Bottom: In the laboratory of Professor K. Goebel at Munich, Marie on the Professor's left

Like herself, Charlie Hewitt was a promising academic. They had known each other briefly before Marie went to Japan and, while she was there, he confided in her about the break-up of one of his frequent betrothals. He was morally obliged to call off the marriage, he explained, because only one of his lungs was working. In April 1908 when Fujii's coldness was already becoming apparent, Marie wrote to him, begging him not to break off his engagement:

> Don't do it, don't don't. To a woman who deeply loves a man broken betrothal is as death itself – indeed it is worse, for death we believe means either dreamless sleep or an all enhancing comprehension, but a broken betrothal is an endless agony of pain, of constant little reminding pains that turn very simple daily duty and pleasure into torture ...
>
> Do you remember Isolde? flying to the man she loves to die in his dead arms. A great love is so much greater than any mere sickness or death ... I do not know of course how strong your love was, but I fancied I saw in your face the promise of a great and beautiful love and it has hurt me to think of it lying with broken wings – I love lovers so ... the real deep love of a man and a woman is so vital, so glorious, so holy, that *nothing* should make them break their betrothal ...

Intrigued by such idealism, Charlie Hewitt pursued the friendship when Marie returned to Manchester. Though he was engaged yet again, to a Miss Edith Garner, there could be nothing wrong in scientific discussions; their paper, "On the Tent-Building Habits of the Ant, Lasius Niger Ninn, in Japan" was published in 1909 by the Manchester Literary and Philosophical Society. In July that year, he wrote to her from Filey in Yorkshire:

> Beloved friend ... It's horrible to think that it will be such a long time before I see you again ... I think my going away is a good thing – it will help me to see things in their proper perspective when the personal element is eliminated – and I shall never take a step which cannot be retraced until I am absolutely certain ...

It seems fairly obvious that Marie – though she knew of his engagement – was forcing him into some form of action. A month later he wrote to her:

... You say one should pluck the flower of life in youth – is there not such a thing as plucking a flower and regretting it afterwards? Is not youth synonymous with inexperience? It is because I feel that because I gain experience, see things from different aspects day by day that I feel the awful risk of snatching a few moments' happiness – of a very transient nature – that I hesitate ...[3]

Four days after this, Marie replied from 14 Well Walk, Hampstead. Finally escaping Charlotte, who still lived a few streets away, she had set up home, when not in Manchester, with Winnie. Her letter was highly provocative:

Best beloved of friends – all last night I slept little but there was a feeling in my hands, so strong as to amount to an actual physical feeling, that I held in them something rare and beautiful and sacred. Even if we were never to meet again I would thank you for that vow on bended knees. Difficult – you said – sweet knight I know – but not too difficult for your beautiful strength.

Hewitt had decided to take up a new academic appointment in Canada, but Marie, bitterly disappointed at the outcome of her affair with Fujii, was determined not to let him escape. Between Hewitt, Edith and herself, an extraordinary correspondence developed with Marie manipulating at the centre. Swearing eternal secrecy to both, she demanded to see their correspondence. Curiously, both Hewitt and Edith Garner meekly acquiesced – and Marie promptly betrayed one side to the other. Rather late in the day, Edith recognised that Marie was trying to "steal" her fiancé – particularly when, soon after arriving in Canada, Charlie broke off their engagement. She finally plucked up courage to confront Marie with her suspicions:

Dear Dr Stopes ... Do you love Charlie Hewitt and wish to marry him and does he return your love? I must know, so trust to your honour to be honest and straightforward with me ... I will not mention my own feelings in this matter or how I have suffered through a great love ... I have always known of your friendship towards him and have always trusted you, for I know you have many things in common with science, etc – but if it is something more than friendship, that is love, between you, be merciful and tell me all.

For Marie, the quality of mercy was not a problem. In March 1910 she invited Edith to spend the night at her home in Manchester and to bring Charlie's letters. She then briskly informed Edith that Charlie no longer loved her, and that he was in love with Marie. She confirmed it by letter on March 15:

Dear Miss Garner ... He was essentially loyal to you even after he had broken off his relations with you. It was only in the last few letters that anything further than friendship was spoken between us. I need not tell you he has never kissed me (Ah! how I envy you). Yes, he has told me that he loves me but at present I do not know whether he *really* loves me or not but I think that I do know the truth about his relation to you and that he does not love you as you wish, I think is absolute fact.

On March 21, a few days later, Marie wrote to Charlie Hewitt. "My conscience," she said, "has been giving me no peace so long as I keep you in ignorance of this." Marie hated to see Edith, she claimed, clinging to the false idea that Charlie still loved her:

It seems to me that probably she would write to you and you to her and that it is essential you should know of this correspondence; tho' I think it would be kinder to her not to tell her you know – only answer according to your knowledge. I think from what I have observed that if she was once definitely convinced that you would never see her again she could find happiness later on with someone else ...

Having established her good faith with Charlie, all Marie now needed to do was to extract an admission from Edith that she, in turn, no longer loved Charlie. Two days later, on March 23, she wrote to Edith:

Dear Miss G ... I have been thinking that it would be *so* good for him if you would write to him and let him know that you do not love him any more (you know what false ideas he has about his value in women's eyes) ... At present I suppose his male vanity is flattered to think of you and others languishing for him ... It may seem a queer way to do good, but truth and bitter medicines are good for naughty children. I was so glad you came to see me and talked with me ... You are worth more stable love than he gave ... In writing to him it would perhaps be as well not to say much about me and of what I told you for then he would think you only wrote out of pique and the salutary truth would not be brought home to him.

Marie was not prepared for the counter-attack. Edith had been corresponding with Charlie and, in accordance with Marie's instructions, sent on to her Charlie's confidential letter about his feelings for Marie Stopes. So great was Marie's need for self-justification that she copied the whole letter – twelve pages – by hand. These extracts are from her autograph copy of Charlie's letter:

Edith ... It's a long history and for your sake I must be brief. You have seen Miss Stopes; for that I'm glad but she will have told you only her side and she understands things as little as you did.

He had really loved Edith, he argued, until Marie Stopes came along:

I had no more intention of saying anything to Miss Stopes than I had of committing suicide. It was on account of my feelings towards her that I recognised the unenduring character of my love for you – but it was the *ideal* that she set me and not herself that I really loved ...

Charlie had told Marie, he said, that in view of her idealism he would never dare to ask her to marry him:

She replied – a long letter – she told me she loved me, that I held her happiness in my hand and as I would never ask, then she must ask me to marry her – You can never put yourself in my place. I was simply overwhelmed. I asked for three months to think it over and see whether my feelings were real and lasting ... then I felt here is another woman – the one for whom I have most affection and whose ideal has inspired me and if I refuse, I make her unhappy – Edith, what *could* a man do?

By saying no to Marie, Charlie argued, he was atoning to Edith for his betrayal. Miss Stopes, he wrote, "is as unhappy as you were, but I feel in a way I cannot help it and I feel that she is more in love with Love than with me. I can see that to her the man is only the personification of her great ideal love – that I cannot be."[4]

That was probably one of C. G. Hewitt's more perceptive remarks. Enclosing the letter, Edith wrote to Marie in May 1910. Her comments on Marie's part in the affair are touchingly naïve, but she did manage to get in a parting shot:

Dear Miss Stopes ... The irony of it all is, that it has been through you, and your influence, I have lost what to me at one time was everything most precious in life, but I feel sure you had no idea what you were doing ...

I can see that had we married with any feeling of doubt on his side, we should have been miserable – I never doubted his sincerity. How could I help it after all he had said and written to me? He has done the same to you, and I see that towards you, too, his love has not lasted ...

To the last, Marie refused to accept Charlie's version of the affair; she could not afford to put herself in the position of a woman who had offered marriage to a man, and been refused. On 23 May 1910, the day after receiving Hewitt's letter to Edith, she wrote back:

My dear Miss Garner, It is good of you to send the letter ... "In truth, I fear he is a plausible villain" and much loves to keep our good opinions of himself. I agree with you that you cannot accept his statement ... I am returning the letter at once – and will, of course, not tell him that you let me see it ... I am glad you are going to have a good time abroad. Send me some of your wedding cake. Happiness be with you.

To Edith Garner, it seemed that Marie Stopes had destroyed her relationship with Charlie Hewitt. No such worries troubled Marie. All she wanted were her letters, so that she could "understand" his motivations, and thus justify her own actions. In July 1910 she castigated Charlie:

On May 18, I asked you to let me see all my own letters, which request repeated by cable, you have had the discourtesy to disregard. Since my childhood I have never prayed for my daily bread and forgiveness of trespasses, but only – and often – to *understand*.

The one way for me to understand this unimaginable situation is to go through all our letters carefully, now I can judge both you and myself.*

Foiled by the charming but fickle Hewitt, Marie fell back on Henry Bassett. In the middle of her involvement with Charlie and Edith, she gave Henry reason to believe that he might not have waited all these years in vain. His response was ecstatic. From 9 Prospect Vale, Liverpool, he wrote to her:

Dear little Marie ... If you only knew how for the last five years I have hoped against hope that in time you might come to love me a little, unworthy object though I felt myself ... Then last Saturday I learned there was some hope for me but it is terrible to think that I may still be found wanting. Luckless wretch that I am, that I cannot urge my cause more fitly but can only lay my simple honest love, quite unadorned, at your feet ... do come and comfort your unhappy slave, Henry Bassett.[5]

Until recently, Marie wrote two days later, he had never had a chance. But now there was some hope – "and if you like to take the risk and try really to win me you may go in and try – the lists are open and I can only repeat there is a ghost of a chance".[6] Unfortunately, she told him, he was not really artistic enough. True, he liked camping, but he had no appreciation of music, poetry, books and painting, and did not seem to notice whether things were beautiful or not. Bassett replied to her on 18 May 1910:

Dear little Marie ... However you may eventually judge me I could hardly be more unhappy than if disposed of summarily now ... I wonder if I am quite as bad as you think. I do care for music and books and painting in my own way but I am not so clever as you and have always had to work so hard at my own subject that other things have gradually had to go ... You must remember that you are a very exceptional little person. I have never come across a man who cares for all the things you care for.

* If Charlie Hewitt sent back his letters, they have not survived in the British Library collection. It may be that Marie destroyed them, anxious as she was to appear as the pursued, rather than the pursuer. Their correspondence was apparently not resumed until March 1911, on Marie Stopes's marriage to another man.

It was obvious that Henry Bassett had little chance of winning the lady's favours, however open the lists. He was, for a start, available – always an unattractive quality from the idealist's point of view. And he failed to conform to her current *beau idéal*. Marie had for some time been infatuated with the works of Maurice Hewlett, a now-forgotten novelist, author of the popular "Senhouse" trilogy. "Oh, Senhouse," Marie wrote ecstatically to Hewlett in 1910, "You have such a quality, such a power of beauty in your writing and suggestion, that I think it must be a cleansing sunshine to thousands."

The hero of Hewlett's latest novel, published in 1909, was Jack Senhouse, son of a rich mine-owner, who gives up his inheritance for a life of freedom, camping in tents, painting, communing with Nature and washing his own trousers – while still, of course, remaining a perfect gentleman.[7] He falls in love with a beautiful girl, Sanchia, whom he treats both as an unattainable Greek goddess and as an apt pupil for instruction in poetry, painting and his philosophy: ". . . salvation in this world is the power of using every faculty we have to the full – every available muscle to the highest tension, every ounce of brain to the last drop, every emotion to the piercing and swooning point."[8]

It was the perfect expression of Marie's own romantic longing for intensity. Wanting masculine freedom and at the same time needing to be adored by someone she could admire, she saw herself as a combination of Senhouse and Sanchia. Henry Bassett, though admirably faithful and fond of camping, was never likely to push every emotion to the piercing and swooning point. Something drastic would have to be done. She was thirty, an age which at that time consigned her to the status of a desiccated old maid. In July that year, she resigned her lectureship at Manchester, giving as the reason her ill-health caused by the appalling climate there, and returned to live in London.

The Hewitt-Garner imbroglio was not allowed to affect her work as a scientist. That year, as well as lecturing in Manchester, she published seven major papers, among them her long study with Fujii on the Cretaceous plants.[9] Her reputation had been further increased by the publication of her work on coal-balls with D. M. S. Watson, and of *Ancient Plants*, the first popular account of fossil plant study. Indeed, Marie now felt secure enough to undertake what she had always threatened to do – produce her own magazine satirising the botanical world. The first issue of *The Sportophyte* (from *sport*, the current term for what is now known as a mutant, and *phytos*, a plant) came out on 1 April 1910. Marie wrote most of it herself, under pseudonyms like S. O. Crates, T. H. E. Orist and S. Ilias. The humour now appears stunningly peurile,* but at the time it was considered rather daring.

Back in London, and with the cataloguing of the cretaceous flora in hand, Marie could not assuage her restlessness. Fortunately, there was no longer any difficulty in getting financial support for travel and research. Within her relatively restricted field Marie was, at the age of thirty, established as one of the leading palaeobotanists of her time.[10] She set off to attend a series of scientific conferences in America and Canada, where the government had invited her to undertake a study of the carboniferous flora of New Brunswick. It would be tempting to think that, in accepting the offer, Marie was committing the same folly by following Hewitt to Canada as she had in pursuing Fujii to Japan. But this time her aim was different. Charlie Hewitt had been proved sadly deficient. What she now needed was the final solution of all her frustrations as a single woman wanting to be married, a consummation Hewitt was much too capricious to provide.

Within six months she was married. The second issue of *The Sportophyte* carried the item: "Dr Reginald Gates arrived in England by the 'Empress of Britain' on April 1, 1911. Curiously enough, another British botanist, Dr Marie Stopes, was travelling on the same ship. As the steamer was a day later than the travellers had anticipated, they can hardly claim to have premeditated the date of their arrival, appropriate though it was."

The irony is obvious only in retrospect. Marie, married just a fortnight, had been fooled again. In marrying Dr Reginald Ruggles Gates, she could not have made a worse choice. The marriage was to be a disaster. It was also to change life fundamentally, not just for Marie Stopes but for millions of others.

---

* A typical example from *The Sportophyte*, 1 April 1910: "From a demonstrator's notebook: Q: How is the balance of the atmosphere maintained? A: Plants breathe in carbon dioxide and breathe out oxygen, and animals breathe in oxygen and breathe out carbon dioxide. As a consequence, if you take a rabbit and a cabbage and seal them together in a hermetically sealed tube, they will both live for ever."

CHAPTER 6

Gates v. Gates

Q: Did you live together, occupying the same bed, after
your marriage?

A: On a very large number of occasions we occupied the
same bed. We sometimes had two rooms because I am
a light sleeper; but he always had access to my room.

Q: Did he use to occupy your bed?

A: Constantly, yes.

Q: And at the beginning, I suppose, he occupied your
bed?

A: Constantly.

Q: With regard to your husband's parts, did they ever get
rigid at all?

A: On hundreds of occasions on which we had what I
thought were relations, I only remember three occasions on which it was partially rigid, and then it was
never effectively rigid.

MR JUSTICE SHEARMAN: He had made many attempts?

A: Yes.

Q: And he never succeeded in penetrating into your
private parts?

A: No.

8 May 1916, hearing in the Probate, Divorce and
Admiralty Division of the Royal Courts of Justice,
London, before Mr Justice Shearman

AT the age of thirty-one, Marie Stopes knew very little about sex.
She had, it is true, spent most of her adult life researching the male –
female reproductive aspects of plant life, but had made no attempt to
apply the pollination principle to the field of humanity. She can
scarcely be blamed for this. She had been brought up – like her
mother – to believe that ignorance of sexual matters was synonymous

with the "innocence", the purity from physical feeling demanded by the Victorian male, who saw his wife as inviolable property and therefore immune to the sensual transports (usually feigned) that he guiltily bought from prostitutes. In spite of her ignorance, Marie's reading suggests that her inclinations were more sensuous than her mother would have approved. She read Browning and Swinburne and, ignoring Charlotte's advice, found "the real Shakespeare" not in the plays but in the Sonnets and *Venus and Adonis*. Her great expectations of sexual experience appear to have been derived from these, from novels, and from the only book on sex that she had read before her marriage.

Edward Carpenter was a Marxist. His book, *Love's Coming of Age* was published in 1896, and was enormously influential. From the number of references in her letters, Marie had obviously read his book, and many of her ideas were taken from it. She had little enthusiasm for his politics – Carpenter argued that women in general should ally themselves with the working classes to overthrow capitalism, which for so long had exploited both groups – but to most of his ideas she gave unqualified approval. In common with many writers of the period, Carpenter was trying to reconcile the flesh with the spirit, and Marie's romantic nature responded ecstatically to his vision of true lovers, whose glances "penetrate far beyond the surface, ages down into each other, waking a myriad antenatal dreams".[1] He inveighed against nineteenth-century prudery and the "enforced celibacy" of women. The archetypal middle-class Englishman, "a picture of beefy self-satisfaction", should learn to understand a woman's sexual needs, rather than treating her merely as an outlet for gratification. The prime object of sex, he argued, differing from all religious thinking at the time, was not the procreation of children, but "*union*, the physical union as the allegory and expression of the real union". Rather like D. H. Lawrence a few years later, Carpenter could assuage his own guilt about physical passion only by elevating it to a mystical level. The "unclean" element must be removed from the idea of sex, and the young should be taught: "How intoxicating, indeed, how penetrating – like a most precious wine – is that love which is the sexual transformed by the magic of the will into the emotional and spiritual!"[2] Too often, Carpenter argued in his chapter on marriage, the "civilised" girl was led to the altar "in uttermost ignorance and misunderstanding as to the nature of the sacrificial rites about to be consummated. The youth too is ignorant in his way ... Impatient, he injures and horrifies his partner and unconsciously perhaps aggravates the very hysterical tendency which marriage might and should have allayed."³ To the present-day reader, however, the most remarkable aspect of *Love's Coming of Age* is that it contains scarcely any physiological information, of even the most elementary kind. This may perhaps be because Edward Carpenter was himself homosexual. At any rate, it provided little practical help to neophytes like Marie Stopes, other than to provide her with a framework of mysticism to accommodate the uncomfortable facts of physical passion.

Marie Stopes met Reginald Ruggles Gates in January 1911 at a scientific congress in St Louis. They were immediately attracted to each other. Two years younger than Marie, Gates was rapidly establishing a reputation in the comparatively new field of genetics. Reserved and sensitive, he yet had a decisive quality that could hardly fail to appeal to Marie, weary as she was of vacillating Fujii, devious Hewitt and the colourless Henry Bassett. Dr Gates was also pallid, his blondish hair merging into pale, regular features; but at least he knew what he wanted. Within a week of their first meeting, he proposed and was accepted. Marie had some misgivings – but about herself, not Ruggles Gates. On February 11, she wrote to her sister Winnie, with instructions for redecorating the house in Well Walk, one of the rooms to be painted a bright sunshine yellow:

Dear Kid – For, my dear kid – tho' I can't be sure till I am actually married, I want that room for a *man*! A man who will be my husband before I sail, I expect, if he stays as nice as he seems to be ... Except that he has a stupid little nose he seems *absolutely* perfect! I couldn't have made him better myself. He is a Canadian and a darling ... He is quite simple-minded and a dear and is not rich but has just a little private income. I didn't know this at first and was prepared to marry him and keep him myself ... *Don't* tell a soul. It is a dead secret. You see, I am a "sudden" person and in the middle of the ceremony I may say *no*! I don't want it to be known until I am actually married. I am pretty delighted with him – he really does seem the perfectest thing!

In her next letter to Winnie, a week later, Marie had to correct part of her previous letter. Dr Gates, it turned out, did not have a permanent private income after all – "so we'll continue to be poor – but blissfully, beautifully, happy, I hope. He is *such* a dear." Winnie was told to break the news gently to the difficult Mrs Stopes, still enjoying the contradictory responses of bewailing her daughters' single state, while deeply resentful of any threat that they might actually marry. "He is so *gentle* in every sense – I hate him to have to see *her*," Marie wrote. With the vigorous practicality that contrasted so oddly with her high-flown romanticism she told Winnie to continue decorating, to arrange a reception in Hampstead for the beginning of April, and to send out invitations: "As you may imagine, it is so important that particularly my bedroom should be a pretty, restful, sweet-memoried place ... If people ask you what I would like for wedding presents, say table silver, cutlery, glass, a dinner or tea service – latter blue and white china, preferably Copenhagen!"

It was an odd courtship. The couple had met only in January, spent barely a week together and did not meet again until shortly before their marriage in mid-March. In early March, Marie wrote to Winnie from Montreal with final instructions:

Dear Kidlet ... I am going to see him the day after tomorrow – I am really wondering what he'll be like, it is *so* long since I saw him – more than two months.

I shall wire you one word – "married", then you can break it to Mother and anyone you like.

There should be an evening party I think, of just our local friends, to meet him. Get two rooms at Prince Arthur's library – have a few palms hired in to make it pretty and get invitations out directly you get the wire ... Have light refreshments only.

Best love from Bun

P.S. Of course, if you get a wire to say I am *not* married, don't send out the invitations!

They were married at the Windsor Hotel in Montreal on 18 March 1911 by a Methodist minister. Among the guests were two former admirers – Dr Helen McMurchy and Charlie Hewitt. On her divorce five years later, Marie Stopes was still a virgin.

. . . . .

For the first year, Marie had no inkling that her marriage was unusual in any way. She had achieved married status – still considered by most to be woman's ultimate goal – while at the same time maintaining her independence. Back in England, she lost no time in going to lawyers to establish her legal right to her own name, rather than her husband's. She then sent to those friends who did not already know of her marriage a printed statement of her position:

Dear ... As there is a considerable diversity of opinion among my friends as to what they should call me, and as I find there is a very widespread misconception as to the law regarding married women's names, I think it may be useful to make a definite statement regarding both these subjects.

In the first place, notwithstanding my marriage, my legal name is Marie C. Stopes. As I have been for some time, and still am entitled to the courtesy of the title of "Doctor", the situation is relieved of any difficulty regarding the application of either "Mrs" or "Miss" to that name. Privately, for the few friends who cannot escape the bonds of custom, I add the name of my husband by hyphen – Stopes-Gates.

As the replies came in, Marie took pleasure in listing, on the back of an old envelope, twenty-five variants of her name. One of the replies should have given her cause to think. What, asked Henry Woodward, editor of *Geological Magazine*, about children? "I allude to the very remote possibility, which sometimes arises after marriage, I mean the birth of children. I always think these little persons should be considered in the question of nomenclature." Marie wanted children, but, incredible though it now seems, did not link their appearance with anything beyond botanical chit-chat in Liberty-printed drawing rooms and passionate, if inconclusive loveplay in her sweet-memoried bedroom. She was determined to be ecstatically happy, and the world believed her. In August, six months after her marriage, Charlie Hewitt sent congratulations on her obvious happiness. He had, he confessed, been worried – particularly in view of her idealism and fear of being stifled by marriage – but she had proved him wrong.[4]

It is difficult now to assess the extent to which Marie's own temperament contributed to her husband's impotence. Gates was both sensitive and extremely conventional. Marie's high-handed pomposities about her name, her support for the Suffragettes and her fight for tax reform – she objected strongly to being taxed jointly with her husband – were more than merely embarrassing: they were an insult to his status as head of the household. Professionally, too, he felt overshadowed. Marie's academic standing had originally been one of her attractions; but, as is so often the case with men who marry clever women, his pride could not tolerate the reality. On the recommendation of Professor Oliver, Marie had been appointed lecturer in palaeobotany at University College – the first such post to be created in Britain. While she was increasingly noticed and admired – the *Daily Chronicle* even sent a reporter to her inaugural lecture, who described her as "extremely youthful and unprofessional in a dainty pink costume" – Gates was reduced to lecturing on biology to medical students at St Thomas's Hospital, a post far below his academic potential.

Under these pressures – not to mention his awareness of his own impotence – the gentle Dr Gates became increasingly ill-tempered, veering between extremes of violent, jealous rage and childish expressions of nursery affection. In June 1912 just over a year after their marriage, Marie was still sufficiently fond of him to try to boost his confidence. Posing as an anonymous, eccentric donor, she wrote, through solicitors, to Imperial College with an offer of twenty pounds for a series of six lectures on plant genetics, the emphasis to be on mutations. Delighted, the college suggested a promising Cambridge scientist. Oh no, came the reply, he must be a London scientist, and had they thought of approaching the Royal Botanic Society? Not very much to the anonymous donor's surprise – her husband, after all, was an active member, and specialised in plant mutations – the society recommended one Dr R. R. Gates.

He gave the lectures; but Marie's machinations – and her twenty pounds – were not enough to repair the marriage. The situation was further complicated by the arrival at 14 Well Walk of a lodger, Aylmer Maude. A distinguished man of letters and the official translator and biographer of Tolstoy, he had met Marie at a dinner party at the end of 1912. He was twenty-two years older, but still a handsome man, in the prophetic, flashing-eyed mould of Havelock Ellis. Estranged from his Russian-born wife, he was immediately attracted by Marie, and within two months he was installed with the Gateses in Hampstead. For the next year, until thrown out by Gates, he took part in an extraordinary triangular turmoil that eventually descended to base wrangling, violence, separation and the divorce courts. First as confidant, later as her platonic lover, Maude was the first to make Marie realise the incompleteness of her marriage. Of Ruggles Gates's side of all this, little is known. A prolific writer, he left few non-scientific records, never talked about his first marriage (he married again, much later in life) and did not contest the divorce suit. Marie was not so reticent. With the same scant regard for other people's sensitivities that she had shown in publishing her correspondence with Fujii shortly after marrying Gates, she enshrined the three of them in a play.

In 1926, thirteen years after the events it described, *Vectia* was ready for performance. The Lord Chancellor, Lord Cromer, refused it a performing licence, on the grounds that the theme was unsuitable. Vectia (Marie Stopes), is "a delightful English girl" married for three years to William (Ruggles Gates) "an ordinary Englishman, rather thin and ascetic looking with pale, dun-coloured hair and face". She longs for a child and cannot understand why, after three years of marriage, she is still childless. She is rescued from ignorance of her husband's impotence by Heron, their next-door neighbour (Aylmer Maude) – "keen, well-cut face and humorous lips; a well-groomed, virile, attractive man". With his encouragement, she defies her husband's threats to drag her scandalously through a divorce on the grounds of her adultery, and brings her own – successful – nullity suit.

The Lord Chancellor's refusal of a licence sparked off Marie's only directly personal account of her marriage, a description that has not, until now, been published. Denied a stage production, Marie sent copies of *Vectia*[5] to Thomas Hardy and the playwright, Alfred Sutro. Hardy found the plot – even if true – incredible; but it was in reply to Sutro's more detailed strictures that Marie wrote one of her longest, most confessional letters. Like Hardy, Sutro found Vectia's ignorance of sexual matters inconceivable: surely she had women friends, if not a mother, who could have helped? And how could she have been happy, when her natural healthy desires were unsatisfied? Nor was it fair, Sutro went on, to turn the wretched husband, suffering from such an appalling and ghastly affliction, into a brute. Marie wrote back in a rage, trusting him, she said, "with facts never put on paper before".

Impressed by her revelations, Sutro read the letter twice, then destroyed it as too personal for his archives. Marie, ever mindful of posterity, preserved her own rough draft, from which the following extracts are taken:

Really, truly, dear Mr Sutro ... Now I'm going to be as tho' in the witness box and answer your categoric questions.

You: Is it conceivable that Vectia shouldn't have known? – Yes, and moreover *she didn't* and *I* am Vectia.

The play is almost unadulterated autobiography. Is this not rather specially of value in view of the fact that I was already then a doctor of science and had passed through the dissecting rooms of a University. It is the *truth* about one who has since become known as an expert on sex and hence proves that ordinary girls wd. be even more in the dark.

You: She has women friends, if she hasn't a mother. – Yes – I had both, my mother living all the time in her own house in the next road. More, I had a *family doctor*, and when, after three years, I went to him and said, "Look here, I really don't believe I'm properly married, I wish you'd examine me or my husband or something, as it is beginning to worry me and I do want to know." He *refused* even to look into the facts. So I wasted a whole year. After it, *I had a family solicitor*; I went to him and he said I had no legal redress! So I had to read up law – Lord Halsbury's Laws of England in 33 or so volumes – do you know it? That wasted another year but in the end *I instructed my solicitor* how to conduct my case and won it as a virgin wife after *six* years of marriage.

You: Could she have been really happy at first even? – Yes, I was quite happy for a long time and thought we were completely married.

You: Why go out of your way to make him such a brute? – Contrariwise, in real life such impotent paranoics are much *worse* brutes, and I softened and toned down and reduced his brutishness and unreasonableness so much as to leave him far nicer than is natural!

You: Suddenly he becomes horrible. – Quite. – that's one of the points. In real life quite as horrible and even more sudden. Actually instead of pretending to kill himself, he really tried to kill me with the bread knife. Too "unnatural" for the stage, so I softened that too ...

1905 – the youngest Doctor of Science in Britain

Kenjiro Fujii

Your letter makes me sad, for I so crave tender understanding and love and *hate* so to startle or revolt or disgust or frighten people. I'm *not* really clever, and only try to be good (I'd so *like* to be understood and loved while I'm alive, as I think posterity could love me only it will have forgotten all about me! ...)*[6]

Marie was not exaggerating when she claimed that *Vectia* was "almost unadulterated autobiography". All her life, she cherished enormous literary amibitions, but she did not command the alchemy by which personal experience is transmuted into artistic truth, and an exclusively scientific training had done nothing to remedy this weakness. To her, the literal, laboratory-dissected truth was by its nature more artistically valid than mere invention. For this reason, *Vectia* is a bad play, but an accurate guide. Many incidents, even whole chunks of dialogue, tally exactly with her life with Gates and Maude at 14 Well Walk as recorded in her correspondence thirteen years earlier. Reading the play, then, it becomes obvious that Will/Gates was as ignorant of sex as Vectia/Stopes. In an exchange with Heron, her lover, Vectia explains how she had come to be married to Will:

HERON: You are still just a pretty little maiden.
VECTIA: Don't – anyway, the year I married Will, two other men asked me to marry them.† But they'd ... both ... kissed other women, and I ... didn't like the idea of a secondhand husband. And so when Will proposed I asked him if he had! (Laughs. HERON laughs too – a short, good-tempered laugh.)

Just think what a thing to ask a man! But I did. And when he solemnly assured me he'd never kissed a girl, never wanted to, I not only believed him, I thought it was fine and noble of him. That's how I had been brought up, you see.[7]

There are constant hints throughout the play, though the word is never used, of homosexuality. In her long and passionately argued preface, Marie railed against the current dramatic stereotype of the strong, over-sexed male dominating the frail, yielding, under-sexed woman. Her own play, in distinction, had the temerity to portray "a

---

* The sentence in parentheses has been scored out in the rough draft by Marie Stopes. All italics are hers.

† Presumably, Charlie Hewitt and Henry Bassett.

woman who is simple, pure and normally sexed, and a man who is futile and weak as a result of the poisoning of his youth ... thousands of women ... are suffering today not from man's simple lust and over-developed and excessive virility, but from his weakness, due to youthful ignorance and corruption, and his consequent marital impotence. Who in the world should know this better than I? ... Lest the deluded or prudish among you think this arises only with a few perverts and effeminate men, let me assure you that many of those in the throes of this intensely difficult problem for themselves and their wives are virile in external appearance and potential character, and have been contaminated and weakened in their early youth."*

Towards the end of the play, when Will/Gates has been unmasked as an impotent monster, Heron/Maude expresses some sympathy for his plight:

HERON: Yes. It's damned hard on you *now* when it's too late to alter. Poor devil! I suppose you're another product of –
WILLIAM (quickly): I've done no wrong. Till I married Vectia I had never touched another woman.
HERON (with scorn): *Women!* Bah! – they're not the only –
WILLIAM (shamed): I –[8]

The play is resolved, as it was in real life, by the lover eliciting the truth about Vectia's sexual ignorance (he shows her a diagram of basic human physiology and the truth finally dawns) and assuring her she will have no difficulty in bringing a nullity suit against her husband. So accurate a representation is Vectia, that there is even a reference to Marie's favourite character – the Virgin Una who, in Spenser's *Faerie Queene*, represents true religion and whose safety is guarded by a lion. Marie liked to be called Una – at least by Aylmer Maude:

VECTIA: Heron, I'm dazed. You have been so good, what should I have done without you?
HERON: Una generally finds a lion.

* When Reginald Ruggles Gates died in 1862, *The Times* obituary remarked: "He was almost effeminate in his gentleness but he had a core of resilience." The play's hints might equally well be taken as attacks on masturbation – of equal anathema to Marie Stopes. My interpretation is based on comments she made to friends – in particular Sir John Waller (interview with the author, 21 August 1975).

On only one major point does fiction diverge from reality. In *Vectia*, Marie was at pains to stress the purity of her relationship with Maude. A note to the producer demands that Vectia and Heron "must make it quite clear that their relation is a pure and straightforward one and that there is not the smallest hint of flirtation or love-making on either side, but there is an old-standing friendship". In fact, her relationship with Maude was neither straightforward nor very pure – except at the most immediately physical level.

Aylmer Maude moved into the Gates's home in Hampstead in February 1913. Only a fortnight later Marie, on a walking holiday with her husband, was already confiding to Maude her marital difficulties. She wrote to him from Haslemere: "Oh Maudie dear, I am so very sorry you are being so miserably neglected in my house . . . my husband is beside himself with rage against 'the women' and the wife too for not condemning them." Marie's support for the Suffragettes – she had, in the previous year, joined the Women's Social and Political Union – was not Dr Gates's only complaint. He sought to compensate for his impotence by violent criticisms of Marie – of her friends, her books, the daily newspaper she read, even of the fact that she tried to win at chess, a deliberate manoeuvre, he argued, to ruin his self-esteem. His jealous rages were becoming insupportable, and in August of that year, Marie finally gave herself up to the luxury of confession. "Dearest Friend," she wrote to Aylmer Maude:

> There was another pathetic scene – and a grand Reconciliation last night and this morning – and my head aches and I am as numb and unfeeling as a dead, hunted-to-death doe. I felt a brute not to be able to feel, but I simply can't. I don't feel a spark even for *you*, except admiration for your many, many dear and noble qualities and the feeling that I ought to feel ever so warm a gratitude and affection; but I don't . . . Yours ever sincerely, Marie C. Stopes.[9]

The mood did not last very long. As she had done after her rejection by Fujii five years earlier, Marie salved her pride by inviting the admiration of others. Only four days later, she again wrote to Aylmer Maude, cleverly appealing to his chivalry and to his amorous hopes:

> Dear and lovely and precious person – In answer to my letter that was intended to give you peace you say it did not, that your heart

bleeds ... I suppose the things that hurt you were my speaking of a grand reconciliation and also laying so much stress on the deadness of my own heart ... I thought you did understand how worn out, dead, all personal feeling is in me. Why should the thought of it hurt you so, dear one? You know, the bigger, impersonal love, admiration, tenderness, you arouse in me, *you* beyond any one ...

Do you want further reasons why my personal heart should be so dead? How permanent do you think the Reconciliation was? Do you know that the other day, the day you left, he threatened to strike me and was within an inch of doing it ... and only $2\frac{1}{2}$ years ago marriage seemed to me something holy and perfect, a relation in which anger was unthinkable ... It has taken just $2\frac{1}{2}$ years to make me a thing abhorrent to myself – could I feel enough to care.

Ruggles, she went on, had threatened to shoot Aylmer – but his aim was not very good. Also, she had reminded Ruggles that five minutes previously he had said he had been in hell since the week after they were married – therefore he could hardly blame Aylmer Maude for his marital unhappiness.

If I give him a few kisses and play a little, as my buoyant-physical nature finds it easy enough to do – all is well. At present we have had 24 hrs of light and happy calm and kisses. *Real* kisses would still matter to me *immensely* – his I put in a different category. *They* don't really matter. But *you* don't want kisses like that! If ever I kiss you, it must be with a piece of my soul – if my soul ever comes back to me again ... Dear one, dear one, Oh don't you know that I *ache* to understand you? I had wrenched myself open to show you all I could of myself ... Do you want me always to be taking out and talking over and fingering the deep and difficult things we have to face? ... Ever sincerely, M.C.S.[10]

This seems like sexual flirtation, however rarefied, and Maude apparently took it as such. He replied with a love letter and Marie, on August 23 wrote back:

Very dear one – It is well nigh *incredible* to see how we have got tangled up in two weeks' correspondence ... the reason I am writing to you is the letter I got yesterday, yours of Thurs 21 – Dear, it was a love letter! and, dear, I didn't *quite* understand it, but I'm

awfully afraid what I said in my last letter may have been misunderstood by you.

It was, she said, sheer thoughtlessness on her part that made her
yearn for days *and* nights in which to talk to him – "when I might
have foreseen you would interpret it in a personal way".

By October 1913 Marie was already in correspondence with a firm
of Canadian solicitors. She asked if divorce were possible on the
grounds of 1) abusive language of the husband 2) a single, open act of
adultery by the wife, undertaken purely in order to get free 3) remaining with another man for a period of time – again, in order to obtain
her freedom and 4) collusion between the two married partners to
provide evidence of adultery. The solicitors replied that, under
Canadian law, none of these grounds would qualify her for a divorce.
They had no suggestions to make as to how she might extricate herself. Marie's own doctor and solicitor in London were equally un-
helpful. It was at this point that Marie decided to take matters into her
own hands. "Her life became quite intolerable," Aylmer Maude wrote
later, "and I heard her say one day: 'I should go mad if it were not
that I say to myself, "Why have I a scientific brain and all my scientific
knowledge, if it is not to find out things that seem to puzzle every-
body?"' and, in a very impersonal manner, she took up her own case
as a piece of scientific research. She went to the British Museum and
read pretty nearly every book on sex in English, French or German."[11]

For the next six months, Marie read her way solidly through English
law and through Marshall and Starling's treatises on the physiology of
reproduction (Starling's pioneering work on hormones was just beginning to affect thinking on sexual matters). At a less technical level, she
found ample support for deploring her own sexual deprivation – and
that of the majority of women – in the complete works of Professor
August Forel, whose *Sexual Ethics* and *The Sexual Question* had
recently been translated from the French. Alice B. Stockham's *Karezza*,
not published in Britain and only available in the restricted access
section of the British Museum (coyly known as "Cupboard") openly
advocated the advantages of coitus reservatus, thus substituting
physical pleasure for procreation as the prime sexual motive. In
Edward Carpenter, Marie found a precise statement of her own feelings,
in particular what Carpenter called "Nature-sex-mysticism", an

instinctual combination which had, he argued, been destroyed by modern civilisation and to which we should attempt to return. She was also much impressed by his theory that both male and female benefited physiologically through the mutual absorption of secretions during the sexual act.

Possibly the most formative influence on her thinking at this time, however, was Havelock Ellis. In *Man and Woman*, published in 1894, and *Studies in the Psychology of Sex*, the last of whose volumes came out in 1910, Ellis, a medical doctor, stressed the ills that befell sexually deprived women. Men must stop regarding women as a cross between "an angel and an idiot", overcome their ignorance, and exercise some imagination and sensitivity. "We have to imagine a lock," he wrote, "that not only requires a key to fit it, but should only be entered at the right moment and, under the best conditions, can only become adjusted to the key by considerable use ... The grossest brutality may be and not infrequently is, exercised in all innocence by an ignorant husband who simply believes that he is performing his 'marital duties'."[12] Perhaps of greater importance to Marie were Ellis's major preoccupations. Impotent for most of his life, Ellis was married to a Lesbian and suffered, in addition, from urolagnia.*[13] His own problems gave him enormous sympathy with sexual abnormalities and, not unnaturally, he concentrated on them in his writings. This aspect of Ellis disgusted Marie – reading the *Studies*, she later recalled, was "like breathing a bag of soot; it made me feel choked and dirty for three months".[14] The experience reinforced her feeling that what the world needed was sexual guidance for the relatively normal, like herself.

As her knowledge increased, and with it her awareness of the intractable nature of her marital problems, Marie relied more and more on the support of Aylmer Maude. While not committing herself to Maude in any way, she could not afford to dispense with his friendship. Her husband's constant taunts and abuse were wearing her down. His torrent of horrible words, she wrote to Maude in December 1913 had "sent her soul to hell" and left her body "in an incompetent and devastated condition". Defeated, she fled to Switzerland, and wrote to Maude on December 22 from Villars:

---

* Sexual excitation through other people's urinating.

My most precious ... Beloved, *how* I wish you were here! All yesterday I thought of you practically all the time – Do you know those 3 unexpected kisses in the Tube as I was leaving you, echoed so yesterday and time and again sent my heart pulsating and my whole body throbbing towards you ...

On New Year's Eve – following her father's habit of summing up the year – she wrote once more to Maude:

Dear Heart ... I have only one more day here, alas! It has done me so much good, but the time is really too short; one cannot restore in 10 days what 1000 days have ravished ...

It seems *such* a little while since I left – oh! I don't want to get caught again in the iron bands of all that gloom and misery! But I must of course – just set my teeth and plunge again. But at first when I get back, before the holiday is undermined, I shall be strong and seize the opportunity to give *you* a tiny little holiday. Do you know what I'm going to do? Send you to bed and keep you there all day ...

For Aylmer Maude, there was little hope of the sensual rewards here so provocatively offered. Marie was still living with Ruggles Gates and – if she was to obtain a divorce on the grounds of nullity, rather than to consent to being divorced by Gates – she would have to remain a virgin. The strains on Aylmer Maude and Marie were considerable, their frustration reaching to an almost marital tension. Like Gates, Maude did not approve of the Suffragettes, and in February 1914 just after Maude had been thrown out of 14 Well Walk, Marie loosed her anger on him. Had he ever had to wash street garbage from his hair, she demanded? Had he had the soft flesh of his neck stung with horse dung from the road? With a good deal of sense, she argued that Maude was operating a double standard:

Where do you think the crowds of "good" pharasaical suffragettes would be today, who belong to "law abiding" societies and condemn those who take any real burden on themselves? Nowhere. They would still be non-existent – asleep. Nor are you consistent. You urge me to resist Ruggles' private impositions and wrongs to me, object even that I forgive so much and bear with as much as I do – you see clearly enough in a personal case that touches you nearly, that to forbear with conscienceless wrongdoers only breeds further wrong. Why can you not see it in the case of bigger and impersonal issues? ... I am glad we shall not be seeing each other for a week ...[15]

Maude was worried about Gates's threats – not just to kill him, but to cite him for divorce. Marie was worried about safeguarding her reputation as a virgin – and also about preserving Maude's adoration. He tried to get out of the situation, but Marie, on 1 April 1914, gave him just that little encouragement to go on. She wrote to him from University College:

What unexpected blows you strike. Today as I said goodbye first at the Tube, I had no thought at all but that we were parting – under rather strained and saddening conditions – for perhaps a fortnight.

I said goodbye in that sense – and you insisted on coming down the Hill with me, and in the High St., in the face of all the people, amid the noise of traffic, you made it goodbye for ever.

Did you expect me to cry out before all the people and plead with you? Perhaps it disappointed you that I did not.

We have had a number of things in common – "you know it is always a bit of a wrench parting with anyone", you said. It is nice to feel that it is no worse for you than that – and also that when you come to reckon it up you will find yourself free to select someone more amenable and less costly than I – someone you can get without having to face a divorce.

Only – if you have any pity in you, don't go for another woman of my make, unless you enjoy torturing as well as slaying your fellows. M.C.S.

Her job at University College was taxing, and she came home to violent scenes with Ruggles. His taunts and abuse were so vicious, she said, that she felt as if she were drowning in sewer filth. Her health began to suffer, she had a permanent headache, and frequently contemplated suicide.

Instead, she wrote to *The Times*. Her excuse for a public expression of disillusionment with marriage was London County Council's recent ban on the employment of married women doctors. Her own experience of marriage, she informed *The Times* – "the innumerable coercions, restrictions and encroachments on liberty ... has brought me to the point of being ready to condone ... a life lived in serious and binding union with a man to whom she is not legally married. Three years ago such a course would have filled me with horror."[16]

Her letter was not mere bravado. She was seriously thinking of living with Aylmer Maude. He, unfortunately, was not so keen. "The idea of the house," she wrote to Maude on April 14, "had seemed to me so beautiful a solution of so many problems and to you it only appeared as a sudden and irritating decision involving money." Nor had marriage destroyed her ardent pursuit of elusive sexual perfection. If only, she added wistfully, she and Maude could spend more time together, "we might touch some pinnacles of delight and comradeship – but it needs *weeks* of intercourse to grow ... We never seem to reach the jumping-off point into infinity."

Something more positive would have to be done. On May 6 Marie finally visited a doctor – more sympathetic than the previous one – and came out with a certificate attesting her virginity. Three days later, on May 9, she wrote a poem, burning with frustrated sexual energy. Masquerading as a description of the fusion of atomic particles, the poem apostrophised the "flame of life".

> Flame of life! that steals between
> Atoms of all vital dust
> In their motions only seen;
> Flame that lights the woodland lust
> Sets the sexes nerves afire
> So that merge with each they must
> When they tingle with desire:
> Burn, oh flame that weak men flee,
> Fusing molten dust with lust
> Burn till true Love's trinity,
> Leaps toward Heaven, from earth outthrust.[17]

Two days later, on May 11, Marie Stopes left her husband and her home. The next few months were to prove the justness of her complaints to *The Times*. She was well aware of the damage to her husband's pride that would be caused by a nullity suit, but she had no alternative. Gates was prepared to carry on the marriage, but the blustering and bullying that were the natural compensation for sexual inadequacy made life intolerable. In revenge, he refused to leave the house himself; by forcing her to do so, he manoeuvred her into forfeiting her rights. Marie felt this particularly unfair: not only was the lease on 14 Well Walk in her name, but she had paid more than half the rent, and had bought most of the furniture.

Possibly the saddest element in any marital break-up is the wrangling over possessions. The only correspondence that survives between Marie Stopes and Reginald Ruggles Gates is of this nature. There is in it no hint of their former love, of affection or even of the regret that might accompany the sundering of two people who had lived together for three years. In July 1914 Gates wrote to Marie from 14 Well Walk. He was trying to let the house – to anyone except Marie – and demanded her share of the rent.

Dear M, Your share of the rates, £8.16.4d. for the past year, will be about £4, and of the rent for last quarter £7.3.9d, making a total of £11.3.9d. I shall be glad to receive this as I need the money. The reason the house is not let quickly is because the rent was raised. Yours, R.R.G.

*

Dear Ruggles, In reply to your request for me to send you money, I can only return a refusal. You prevented me living peaceably in it: you prevented me letting it to friends: you assumed of your own free will absolute responsibility and told me I had "abdicated all my rights": you have been living in undisturbed possession of it having moreover the use of my property in it and after locking me out. Your request, therefore, is, to say the least, unbecoming; and you had better understand that I shall not pay one penny. Yours sincerely, M. C. Stopes.[18]

As the wrangles developed over who owned the blue glass lamp in the hall, the gas brackets and fluted curtain poles, a dispute affecting rather more people – at least initially – had begun. On 4 August 1914, when Britain declared war on Germany, Marie had temporarily retired from her personal struggle to live alone in a tent on a beach in Northumberland, on the Longhaughton estate of Lord Howick, nephew of the Foreign Secretary, Sir Edward Grey. With her usual ability to live life on several different levels at once, Marie saw nothing odd about the simultaneity of passionate letters to Aylmer Maude, demands to her estranged husband for the restoration of furniture, and worry about how to deal with the unspeakable Huns. She wrote to Aylmer Maude, on 4 August: "Dear Love – This isolation and anxiety is *intolerable*! Come to me! Are you coming on Thursday? *Please telegraph a message in any case* ... if you come for only a few days here, at least we can talk, advise each other, consult. Should I enlist in the Red Cross? Will it be possible to live in London at all?"

The day after, Marie wrote again. She had decided to enlist in Lady Howick's branch of the Red Cross, but was still suspected, by the local militia patrolling the beach, of being a spy:

My precious beloved one ... I am still on my solitary shore in the little tent: daily, I fear, becoming the wonder of the neighbourhood as 3 warships sailed slowly up the bay – aeroplanes are overhead and 3 soldiers are now stationed on my shore to patrol it. I am beginning to wonder myself whether it is bravery or foolhardiness or a joyous callousness which keeps me here solitary o' nights ...

Dear Love, you are not *yet* ruined; your American shares may become very valuable. I may 1) die or 2) get rich: I *may* still get Well Walk and a boarder and so be able to give you daily comfort: the war may only last a few weeks – and *you* may get rich ...

In October, Marie filed her nullity petition in the Probate, Divorce and Admiralty Division of the High Court of Justice. Clause 3 of her petition – issued in the name of Marie Carmichael Gates (but with the qualification insisted upon by Marie, "otherwise Marie Carmichael Stopes") pleaded: "That the said Reginald Ruggles Gates was, at the time of the said marriage and has ever since been incapable of consummating the said marriage and that such incapacity is incurable."[19] Though the case did not come to court until 1916, almost two years later, Marie was sufficiently sure of the outcome to write to Ruggles Gates's father in Canada. She did not go into details, but pointed out that "Reginald has failed in almost every way possible for a husband to fail."[20] In her first volume of poems, published that year, in 1914, she allowed herself a more personal statement:

To have loved, to have kissed,
And – oh, God! – to have missed
The completion of Love! ...
A more pitiful thing
Than the broken wing
Of a bird that has soared,
Is one driven by fate
To return with hate
Where she once adored.[21]

CHAPTER 7

Alone in the Wilderness

"... I was alone in the wilderness and have led them to the promised land."

Marie Stopes, 1930

ALL reformers like to refer, in retrospect, to that particular episode in their lives when it suddenly became obvious what must be done to save humanity. Much weightier than mere argument, Saul's blinding by the truth probably brought more converts than all his Epistles. The lifelong justification for Marie Stopes in her campaign for sexual reform, her burning light on the way to Damascus, was the experience of her first marriage. The campaign later focused on birth control, but began with a general concern for sexual education. In her preface to *Married Love*, first published in 1918, she wrote: "In my own marriage I paid such a terrible price for sex-ignorance that I feel knowledge gained at such a cost should be placed at the service of humanity."[1] In fact, the genesis of the book was rather more complicated than such a statement of simple concern for humanity suggests.

In the summer and autumn of 1914, when her marriage was breaking up, anyone reading her correspondence could have been forgiven for thinking Marie, if not mad, at least suffering from delusions of grandeur. Already, in print, she had mapped out a life for herself: twenty years in scientific research, twenty in philosophy and poetry, and a further twenty "in the direct service of humanity".[2] But, after only ten years of the scientific period, the three ambitions were becoming hopelessly mixed. By 1914, Marie had completed her catalogue of the Cretaceous flora for the British Museum, but a concern for the fossils of the Lower Greensand contributed little to the more grandiose destiny she confidently expected. Writing to Aylmer Maude in 1913, she had already referred to "a haunting idea that has hung over me for a very long time":

> One of the things I specially want to talk to you about is something you mentioned in your letter. You said ... you wd. not grudge me if I felt I wanted or had to, die for something big – bi-sexual, not, like the women's movement, unisexual – What is there at present bigger than the women's movement that I *could* die for? And supposing I was anxious to die – what is there my death could really, materially benefit? *Do* tell me seriously, very, *very* earnestly I want to know ...

Four days later, she wrote to Maude again, informing him that she had decided not to die after all – it was too easy. She would continue with the task that she felt "called" to undertake. In May 1914, shortly after she had finally left her husband, Marie was still unforthcoming about the nature of her call, but was at pains to reassure Maude that God had not entirely usurped his position. From Hindhead, where she was staying with friends, she wrote on May 16:

> Joy – My work is cut out for me here – there is a soul and body I must re-make ... I came to rest but find I have stores of strength which a sweet worn soul is fading for want of – God seems to be making me a healer, out of the wrecks of my joy he is strangely building a *more* translucent joy but a less personal one ...
>
> Dear one, when I think of all you have done for me, your tender consideration and help when I was so nearly submerged with the throttling vampire at my throat – I feel that I owe you all myself, but at other times I *know* I was put in such a position in order that you might have the joy of saving me and that I should afterwards be the medium of a divine message to several people who would never have opened their hearts to me otherwise.
>
> But dear, *dear*, though in hours of inspiration and when the strength flows through me for my work, I feel so livingly conscious of the divine in me, using me – most of the time, naturally, I am human, and then you, dear, *dear*, matter so much ...

The divine message was transmitted on several levels. At the least worldly, it consisted of plans for "The People's Bible – brought to them by Marie Carmichael Stopes".* The new bible would contain prayers, a creed, and "Epistles to wives, husbands, prospective mothers, The Unhappy, The Abnormal, The Radiant etc." The first chapter opened with the invocation: "Come, oh Churches, I would win you to hear the words of your God, who has spoken amidst terror and slaughter the things of peace and joy."

Marie decided, however, that the world was not yet ready for such direct evangelism: she would appeal to humanity at a more beguiling level. Her play, *The Race*, or *Ernest's Immortality*, was written in late 1914, and embodied all Marie's sexual frustrations and her intense desire, as a virgin married woman, for children. The heroine is Rosemary Pexton, daughter of a country solicitor. Asked for in marriage by the local squire (titled, of course) she has meanwhile fallen in love with a young soldier, off to the Front in three days' time. Her father disapproves of the engagement and, at a ball shortly before Ernest leaves to defend King and Country, Rosemary/Marie sums up her readings on sex at the British Museum:

ROSEMARY: To think that it is *my* father who makes it impossible for us to bring *your* child to gladden the world! Why should we allow him to commit murder? The murder of the children which might be ours? Why should my father rob you of fatherhood?
ERNEST: Rosemary! What do you mean?
ROSEMARY (with a look of mystical devotion): My beloved, may God grant that you live for ever, in thy children's children. (She leans forward ... He goes towards her eagerly, but incredulously.)

In Act II, Ernest is killed and pressure put on Rosemary, for business reasons, to marry a solicitor. Refusing, Rosemary holds up a baby garment that she is knitting:

PEXTON (her father): Good God! Could any honourable man foresee that his daughter would be an abandoned woman?
ROSEMARY: It seemed to me then, and I shall always think, that the world would be a better place if there were more men like Ernest in it. Heredity *does* matter ... for the sake of our race, all fine young

* This work exists only in manuscript, in the Stopes–Roe collection. There is no date, but by the handwriting and by internal references to "the clouds of war", it appears to have been written in late 1914.

men such as Ernest should have children – and the others should
not ... Is it not *more* wrong that not only Ernest, but all the
fine, clean strong young men like him who go out to be killed,
should leave no sons to carry on the race; but that the cowardly
and unhealthy ones who remain behind can all have wives and
children?[3]

The Race is interesting not so much dramatically (Ellen Terry sent
it back with the comment that it was all very well but what the public
wanted was "a little bit of fluff") but for the light it throws on the
development of Marie's ideas. At the time, she knew little about
contraception and so easily fell into the logical trap for which, so
often later, she was to castigate the Catholic church – the equation of
contraception (in this case, by abstinence) with deliberate murder.
She was much more interested in achieving sexual satisfaction and in
having a child herself – obsessions which, particularly since her
marriage had broken up, shocked the older generation. "You seemed
the last 3 or 4 times I saw you to be bent on vindicating your right to
have the 'full life'," rebuked one of her mother's friends. "I want you
to have a lovely child; but I don't want suffering for you. Once let
that sex feeling run only in the sensual channel and we, as a Nation,
are done for."[4] On the play's central theme, however – the need to
improve the Race by breeding from fine young men like Ernest, even
if this offended conventional morality – Marie felt better qualified to
argue.

Today, her eugenic ideas appear extreme. The heredity/environment
argument still continues, but few would nowadays support the proposition that qualities like cowardice are inherited. In 1914 such ideas
were part of the unthinking "commonsense" of the period – so much
so that, discussing their suitors, girls would coyly describe their
prospective husbands as "VGTBW" ("very good to breed with").
Intellectually, eugenic ideals had a respectable basis. Marie was steeped
in Darwin, whose theory of natural selection was widely interpreted
to mean that if the fittest survived, they deserved to do so. As a cor-
ollary, it was surely better to breed from such strains rather than from
genetically determined inferior stock. Marie had also read the works
of Darwin's cousin, Francis Galton, who coined the word "eugenics".
In *Hereditary Genius*, Galton argued the existence of a natural élite:

"It is in the most unqualified manner that I object to pretensions of natural equality," he wrote. Comparing differences in intelligence between the various races, he was horrified by the performance of the blacks: "The mistakes the Negroes made in their own matters were so childish, stupid and simpleton-like as frequently to make me ashamed of my own species."[5] Most people believed in the infinite perfectibility of the human race, a vision defined by another of Marie's heroes, H. G. Wells. He foresaw, in 1900, a world state which would favour the procreation of: "what is fine and efficient and beautiful in humanity – beautiful and strong bodies, clear and powerful minds, and a growing body of knowledge and to check the procreation of base and servile types, of fear-driven and cowardly souls, of all that is mean and ugly and bestial in the souls, bodies and habits of men".[6]

Like most great propagandists, Marie was a product of other people's ideas, a link between their originality and her own awareness that others might need such knowledge. As early as 1912, only a year after she married Ruggles Gates, Marie firmly told the *Daily Chronicle* that all children ought to be instructed about the functioning of their own bodies – only thus could eugenic ideals be pursued. "Personally, I am a great believer in heredity. We inherit two-thirds of our nature and make up the rest for ourselves."[7] Before she had any inkling of the problems that marriage would bring, Marie had already started work on a book about sexual relationships. She sent her manuscript to Maurice Hewlett, who fictionally most nearly summed up Carpenter's ideal combination of "Nature-sex-mysticism". He wrote back:

Dear Miss Stopes ... I read it last night and recognised immediately its enthusiasm and amiable intention. At present, it seems to me there is no more in it. It is a kind of first sketch for a thing, which, when complete, might be romantic, poetical, philosophical ... but which must be completed to make it so. It is much too short, and has no conclusion; the verses are not really part of the book ... The question you must decide is whether there is enough of it left in you to urge you to begin again and make a book of it. If your Ms, as it exists now, were my own, I should keep it by me until I felt a recurrence of the mood, and when that happy moment arrived I should begin slowly to recopy it ... I have a dozen things – prose and verse – in exactly the same state as yours. If the Gods are benign, they will all be born anon. I think that you express yourself more naturally and clearly in prose than in verse. Forgive this forthrightness, and believe me, Sincerely yours, M. Hewlett.[8]

Marie took his advice to begin again, and – a rare feat for one who kept even bus tickets and dinner menus – burnt most of the manuscript and rewrote it.

Marie's separation from her husband had removed one of the immediate causes of her unhappiness; but it did little to alleviate the misery she felt throughout the years of the First World War. Though she recognised that he was much too old for her, she preserved Aylmer Maude's adoration. In April 1915, as the first Zeppelin raids began over London, they spent a holiday together in Cornwall. Maude's return to London was closely followed by a stream of affectionate letters, hinting at greater delights to come. "Precious dear one," she wrote from "The Ledge, Lizard", "I am *so* glad that we have had just a little peep of peace together – peace that perhaps might have heralded joy had it not been chased off the field by business . . . Sleep well, and work well, and love-me-well, Your M."[9] The sinking of the *Lusitania* by German submarines in May 1915 resulted in a national wave of anti-German fury. Marie's response was more personal. "My dearest heart," she wrote to Maude on May 9:

It was a real joy to get your letter this morning, my own dear, and to feel that the world with all its horror and anguish is not the supreme thing of power its very solid outside would lead one to believe. When the news of the Lusitania came, my first thought was of you and how I wished that if any closer danger which might touch us should arise that we might be *together*.

More and more intensely do I feel that the one thing worth bringing into and trying to increase in the world is love, love and its joy and beauty in every form and every possible expression. That is why I am beginning to revolt against so much of the so-called "intellectual" work, the gloomy realistic novels, the problem plays – light, trust, joy, the palpitating burning beauty of simple things and greatly lived, simply lived lives is what I should like to portray if only God will give me the power . . . Dearest, I know I could give you so much more if we were simple and true in all things . . .

In August that year, she stayed on at the Penwith Temperance Hotel, Land's End, after Maude had spent another holiday with her. Her letters were even more promising. "My darling dear," she wrote on August 27, "It has been far the nicest day since you left . . . The day-dreams were all lovely ones, with us married and you and Henry James and I all went slowly touring to all the lovely places in Europe. You and I went off alone honeymooning by ourselves all day . . ." The honeymoon remained a day-dream: Marie was once more immersed in the more theoretical aspects of love and had already completed the second draft of her book hymning the joy of love and the palpitating burning beauty of simple things (at this stage, *Married Love* went under the title *They Twain*). Her determination to publish it was strengthened that summer by her meeting with Margaret Sanger, the American birth control pioneer.

Mrs Sanger, a former nurse who had, she felt, delivered far too many babies in the New York slums, was three years younger than Marie. Bored with her marriage – which had at least been consummated to the extent of three children – she started a monthly magazine, *Woman Rebel*. Militant in tone, it called for social and political revolution, and promised information on contraception. This was tantamount to inviting prosecution. In the United States, under the Comstock Law – so called from the zeal of Anthony Comstock and his Society for the Suppression of Vice – it had since 1873 been an offence to mail "obscene, lewd or lascivious articles" – including information on contraception. Mrs Sanger was duly indicted on nine counts. The day before her trial was due to open, she left America and – without a passport, under the assumed name, "Bertha Watson" – sailed for Britain. Arriving in Glasgow in October 1914 the first thing she noticed, she later claimed, was that the streets were full of "fighting shiftless beggars. Hundreds of women were abroad, the big shawls over their heads serving two purposes: one, to keep their shoulders warm; the other, to wrap around the baby which each one carried . . . Older children were begging 'A ha'penny for bread, Missus, a ha'penny for bread'."[10]

She and Marie Stopes first met at Mrs Sanger's meeting at the Fabian Hall in London in mid-July 1915. The two women were later to become firm enemies, but at the time there was no jealous rivalry to mar their friendship. Such reputation as Marie had was limited to palaeobotany and coal research, and she was delighted when Mrs Sanger accepted her tea and dinner invitations to 14 Well Walk. With the outbreak of war, Dr Gates had returned to Canada, and Marie was once more in possession of her Hampstead home. In *My Fight for Birth Control*, Margaret Sanger later gave her impression of their meeting:*

> She was then writing a book, *Married Love*, which was to deal with the plain facts of marriage. She expected it to "electrify" England. She then explained to me that, owing to her previous unfortunate marriage she had had no experience in matters of contraception nor any occasion to inform herself in their use. Her husband, she said, had been unable to make her happy and her marriage had not been consummated ... She realised, however, she said, from the address I had given in Fabian Hall, that such knowledge of contraception was important in the lives of women. Could I tell her exactly what methods were used and how they were used? I replied that it would give me the greatest pleasure to bring to her home such devices as I had in my possession. Accordingly, we met again the following week for dinner in her home, and inspected and discussed the French pessary which she stated she then saw for the first time. I gave her my own pamphlets, all of which contained contraceptive information.[11]

The vignette of two earnest ladies, one a virgin and the other struggling to escape matrimonial shackles, discussing rubber pessaries over the roast lamb, is intriguing. It was also useful to Marie. Mrs Sanger's championing of sexual satisfaction for women reinforced her own ideal† and her pamphlets provided a background for the very short chapter on contraception that she had now decided to incorporate in *Married Love*. In return, when Margaret Sanger once more faced prosecution on going back to the States that autumn, Marie organised a petition to President Woodrow Wilson. She enclosed with the signatures – among others, of H. G. Wells, Arnold Bennett and

---

* Marie Stopes's own copy of this book, now in the Stopes-Roe collection, has been heavily scored by H. V. Roe, her second husband, with a marginal comment: "False. Damned liar." In later years, Marie never liked to admit that she had learned anything from anyone, particularly not from Margaret Sanger.

† In her pamphlet, *Family Limitation* (1914) Mrs Sanger argued that "a mutual and satisfied sexual act is of great benefit to the average woman, the magnetism of it is health giving, and acts as a beautifier and tonic". – Quoted in *Birth Control in America*, David Kennedy, Yale University Press, 1970, p. 25.

Professor Gilbert Murray – a remarkable covering letter. It received
a lot of publicity in America, and was probably the first appearance of
that distinctive, highly emotional rhetoric that later proved so seduc-
tive to the millions who bought her books. The letter was doubly
remarkable coming from a woman who desperately wanted a child.
"Have you, Sir," she harangued the President, "visualised what it
means to be a woman whose every fibre, whose every muscle and
blood-capillary is subtly poisoned by the secret, ever-growing horror,
more penetrating, more long-drawn than any nightmare, of an unwanted embryo developing beneath her heart? While men stand
proudly and face the sun, boasting that they have quenched the wicked-
ness of slavery. What chains of slavery are, have been, or ever could
be so intimate a horror as the shackles on every limb, on every thought,
on the very soul of an unwillingly pregnant woman?"[12]

Whether or not President Wilson was swayed by her passionate
prose, the prosecution was dropped. At the time, Margaret Sanger
expressed undying gratitude to Marie, though her reactions were a
little mixed. She would now, after all, have to find another occasion
for the martyrdom so necessary in publicising her cause.*

Throughout the war years, Marie was suffering from financial as
well as sexual problems. In her divorce case, the costs had gone against
her husband, but Gates had left the country. Marie got into fairly
heavy debt by paying them herself. Her lectureship at University
College was barely sufficient to keep her, let alone Winnie, who was by
now a semi-invalid. Still only thirty, she wrote to Marie in May 1914:
"If only you could make my heart stronger! Think of it, Bun, 13
years! Nearly all in pain and weariness – all the best years of my life."
There is a limit to the amount of support relatives can muster for the
permanently ill and inadequate. It is difficult not to feel sympathy for
Winnie, with her heart trouble, her rheumatism and the constant feeling
of inferiority towards her elder sister. But she insisted on spending
Marie's hard-earned money on faith-healers, and she refused to live
with Marie, which might have cut down costs. "Dear Bun," she
wrote, "You say I am not just to you ... That I am a beast I can't
help. I have done all I can to try and do and be what you wished and
it has been an absolute failure, because our whole natures are so

---

* She achieved her ambition on 29 January 1917, when she was sentenced to thirty
days in prison for opening a birth control clinic in New York.

different ... I never was a real companion to you because I hadn't the brains and now more than ever when I am perfectly aware my mental capacity is failing very rapidly there would be no real pleasure for you."[13]

Marie's attempts to make money were as novel as they were unsuccessful. Her constant requests to be given some important war work commensurate with her talents had led to a part-time appointment in coal research at the Home Office experimental station at Eskmeals in Cumberland. Incidental to her researches there, she had discovered a new dye from coal; why not market it? In great excitement, she wrote to Professor Knecht, a chemist at Manchester School of Technology. She was, she explained with unusual modesty, not a chemist, but she would be willing to hand over the secret of production for the professor to finish off – provided they went half shares in the sales of the dye. Nothing came of the idea, and Marie reverted to her former plan to make money by conquering the world of entertainment.

Her energy was considerable. Throughout the war years, she bombarded theatrical producers with plays. There were at least eight of them, plus a musical comedy and a film scenario, *Germany Miscalculates*. Unfortunately, her judgement of what audiences wanted was not very sound. Where soldiers on leave wanted *Chu-Chin-Chow* or the slightly risqué jollity summed up by "Mademoiselle from Armentières", she offered long disquisitions on the joys of Nature (one play called for a live sheep on stage throughout Act I, "if convenient"); where their wives and sweethearts called for jingoistic militarism, or the sentiment of "Keep the Home Fires Burning" Marie came up with a plea to end war by forming a world parliament. Ironically, the only production she achieved was Clarence Raybould's opera, *The Sumida River*, based on one of the Japanese No plays she had translated, with Professor Joji Sakurai. Though assured that it was normal practice for an opera to be known by the composer's name, she was furious at her name appearing in a smaller type than Raybould's and scribbled across the poster advertising the Birmingham production of the opera in 1916, "Note his cheek!"[14]

Undeterred by constant rejections, she sent her play, *The Race*, to George Bernard Shaw. She had met him in August 1917 on a cycling holiday to the Fabian summer school at Godalming. Though her sympathies were always Conservative, Marie attended Fabian Society meetings as assiduously as she supported the British Association for the Advancement of Science – partly for stimulus, but also for the contact with celebrities who might prove useful. She found Shaw, she wrote to her mother, "very amiable and friendly" and far more like-able than she expected. At the age of sixty-one, Shaw's twin eminence as playwright and pet *enfant terrible* ready to pronounce pungently on any topic, was undamaged by the wartime levity that had reduced demand for his plays. He found Marie's earnest enthusiasm rather appealing, if slightly "dotty", and adopted towards her the paternal, teasing attitude to which she always responded in older men. His unequivocal response to *The Race* was thus more hurtful than all the polite excuses of theatrical producers. In September that year, he wrote to her from Ireland:

Dottissima, Short of rewriting this play, I can do no more with it than cut 20 pages just to shew you how you should cut the rest. You haven't used your brains on it one bit. Would you find *me* very interesting if I had nothing more to say than "dowdy frocks, prudish ideas, blue stocking and spectacles" and such-like reach-me-downs . . . You must cut out everything that does not get your play along; and if you wish to convey that your hero's hair is turning grey, you must leave that to his wig-maker and make-up box and not spend pages of irrelevant twaddle on it. Until you take the stage more seriously than you take a coal mine you will never do anything with it. Or shall I say that until the stage interests you as seriously as fossils do you had better leave it alone. At present you are doing nothing half the time but enjoying the amateurish delight of making-believe; it's so interesting to invent a room with doors and windows and furniture and a man named Smith, aged about 45, in it, that you imagine they will interest people who haven't invented them. They WONT. So there![15]

Marie's reply was signed, "Yours meekly appreciative", but she had difficulty in stifling her rage. Though she claimed that she was grateful for his "slings and arrows of outrageous insult", did not Shaw rather over-rate the value of intellect? "I know I have much to learn about plays and at present I lie a meek valley at your feet, grateful for stones hurtling down from your steeps at me. But the day will come when I arise as a peak also . . ."[16]

Marie was also in difficulties with the book that would "electrify England", as she had put it to Margaret Sanger. In their biographies, both Maude and Briant followed their subject's myth that she had deliberately delayed publication of *Married Love* until the times were more suitable. In fact, she could not find a publisher. As early as 1915 she had sent her manuscript to Blackie & Son who had published her *Ancient Plants* and *A Journal From Japan*. From Glasgow, Walter Blackie replied:

> Dear Dr Stopes, Thanks. But the theme doesn't please me. I think there is far too much talking and writing about these things already. The world is suffering from too many physiologists and psychologists and it's not me that will lend a hand.
>
> Pray excuse the suggestion, but don't you think you should wait publication until after the war, at least? There will be few enough men for the girls to marry; and a book would frighten off the few.[17]

Marie replied that she would send him a copy of the book when it was out. "*What* an idea of marriage you must have," she rebuked him, "if you think the truth about it will frighten people off."

Reactions to "the truth" were varied. Turned down by Blackie, Marie, in her first attempt at the art of marshalling support – an exercise at which she later became so adept – sent her manuscript to everyone she admired. Edward Carpenter thought it "excellent, and most enlightening" and invited her to his cottage near Holmesfield, on the edge of the Derbyshire Peak District. They went through it page by page. "You certainly get in a *lot* of important points," he wrote in May 1916: "menstruation, positions, ejaculation without penetration, birth control, insemination etc – which will terrify Mrs Grundy; but she, poor thing, is in a very moribund condition already, so the book may only hasten her end!"[18] Carpenter, himself a highly secretive author, suggested that she publish first in French to avoid possible complaints from Mrs Grundy. The idea did not appeal to Marie – she was after as wide an audience as possible. Maurice Hewlett, too, was enthusiastic about the new draft of the book he had first criticised in 1911. It was, he said, very well written and "exceedingly good doctrine. The intelligent, I should say, or at any rate those who have 'intelletto d'amore' have made your discoveries for themselves –

but it is proper that all men should be plainly told what are women's dues in such a matter."

Others were not so happy. In July 1916 Marie asked P. Chalmers Mitchell, FRS, secretary of the Zoological Society, to write a preface for her book. He refused, on the grounds that it was not scientific enough, and contained "statements that seem to conflict with normal experience". Even more distressing was the attitude of Dr R. V. Wheeler, her colleague in coal research at the Home Office experimental station in Cumberland. She respected him enormously, he was one of the few friends with whom she never quarrelled, and together they published the results of their research in a work to which reference is still made.* Dr Wheeler's reaction to *Married Love* was ambiguous. Some of the writing, he said, was wonderful:

> You can understand then, how it is so appalling to be suddenly knocked down by a grisly word or a brutish sentence ... On looking through them again I see that in nearly every instance it is the insistence on the animalism of the act of sex-relation which has aroused my anger ... it is a tribute to the power of your writing to say that you have almost convinced me that man should model himself on "other mammalia" – and so have disgusted me with the whole idea of marriage relations.
>
> My fear is that, as it stands at present, your book would, if widely read, establish among Englishmen that abominable calculating condition of mind where women are concerned that is so characteristic of Frenchmen ... I mentioned before the ugliness of many of the words you have chosen (perforce?) – "orgasm", "intumescent", "ejaculation" & so forth. I know you can change them if you put your thinking-cap on.[19]

At that time a great many people would have felt the same distaste as Dr Wheeler. Marie's own ignorance was far from unique, and innumerable young women shared the experience reported by Frances Stevenson, Lloyd-George's† private secretary and mistress, when she described a visit to an old college friend in her diary for May 1915: "She was telling me of the way in which they have been brought up,

---

* *The Constitution of Coal*, monograph published by HMSO for the Department of Scientific and Industrial Research, 1918.

† At the time, Chancellor of the Exchequer.

in such ignorance of the world, that she on her marriage day knew absolutely nothing of what was expected from a wife to her husband on marriage. The consequence was that she was frightened and unhappy."

Sexual relations were discussed in only two languages – the scientific terminology of abstruse medical journals, and the literary euphemisms that translated an orgasm into "the moment of supreme bliss". Mostly, of course, sex was not talked about at all. It was against such a background of ignorance and prejudice that Marie Stopes tried to fuse the two languages.

As a scientist specialising in reproduction – though, admittedly, only of plants – she was not shy about using accepted scientific terminology. She had a frank, candid manner – already noticed by Margaret Sanger – and was able to put at their ease people unused to talking about their sexual problems. They confided in her, further increasing the more solid aspects of her book, which she constantly revised throughout the war years. In the closed society of the experimental station up at Eskmeals, she found ample scope for more human experiments. By August 1916 she had become much involved in the small community there, and felt, she told Aylmer Maude, as if she were manipulating characters in a play. She told him about a marital situation in which she was confidante to both sides: "I have great hopes. But he is very puritanical so I fear when my true character and mission is revealed, it may shock him horribly. I have to go wisely and carefully, as he is only *ignorant*; all his wife wants is in him, part dormant and part consciously repressed." Next month, the wife left her husband, and Marie dosed them both with manuscript copies of *Married Love*. On October 1, the husband – a colleague of Marie's at Eskmeals – wrote again, marking his letter "Private – to be destroyed on day of receipt". I quote from the undestroyed letter:

Assuming that she returns ... there comes the question of conception. As a Catholic I cannot make use of women's bodies for personal amusement, nor can I enforce suffering ... I may say that I am unaware of any methods save rubber appliances the use of which seems to me to savour of the Greek comic stage rather than of real life ... Could you inform her of any form of protection that she could wear which, while preventing penetration of sperm to the vagina would not produce the grotesque features of affixing a cover to the penis.

I feel sure you will forgive my frankness as much depends on her realising not only what you have written in the book, but also the possibility of her experiencing the physical as well as the comrade-like expression of love in her own case . . . I have been starved for over a year considerably . . .[20]

This was the first of what became, as soon as *Married Love* was published, an avalanche of problems. At the time, Marie appears to have been much more open-minded than after publication, when the pressures of fame thrust her into a necessary respectability. Her professed abhorrence of abortion, for example, lasted until her death in 1958. But sandwiched among her personal correspondence for 1916 is a note in her handwriting. The date, address and signature have been carefully removed. It reads: "*re* the girl who wishes to escape the consequences: I have not my notes here, but I remember that at the normal monthly period is the most likely time and for 2 or 3 days then very hot baths and a purgative should be taken. I believe pennyroyal is used with no danger and satisfactory results, but no lead containing drugs should be touched . . . Don't let her fiddle about with hair pins and things as some women do, they are horribly dangerous."[21]

The year 1917 was a nadir for Marie. The general background was bad enough. Until recently, the civilian population had been little affected by the war, except as an excuse for heroics. But now, as the grisly battle of attrition pursued its inconclusive course, casualties mounted and the streets were filled with the blue-garbed figures of the wounded and mutilated. Food and fuel were running short, public transport was slow, crowded, and often non-existent. As she struggled by unheated trains between Cumberland, London, and her new home in Leatherhead – another attempt to save money – Marie had no cause to be any more satisfied with her personal life. Her work, as usual, was successful enough; but, in her thirty-seventh year, she was without husband, child or lover. For much of the time Aylmer Maude lived with her in Leatherhead. He was still in love with her, but her feelings for him – marked earlier at least in her letters by a longing for passionate physical expression – had dwindled to affection. True love cannot subsist for ever on paper and ink, and from being "Dearest

Love" and "Most Precious Person", Maude was now relegated to "ducky" and "goosie". In August, on the cycling holiday during which she met Shaw, she wrote to Maude: "Ducky dear . . . I got a nice lovish letter from you this morning – and it pleased me – a little – *but*, but, but – I will try to concentrate on your nicer points . . . I'm really quite fond of you – but fondness isn't love as *I* could love. Yours, with a kiss."[22]

There is some evidence that at the time Marie's despair was strong enough – and she was still open-minded enough – for her seriously to consider satisfying her sexual and maternal longings outside matrimony. Her letters to T. H. Holland, a colleague from her Manchester days, have not survived; but, hidden among her scientific papers, one or two of his letters were kept.* In February 1917 Holland wrote a highly ambiguous letter from his office at the Munitions Board, Simla, in the Punjab. Marie's decree nisi had been granted four months previously, and he apologised for not having been able to give more help during her troubles with Ruggles Gates: ". . . One feels mean to sympathise without being able to help, and I am sure you understand why active assistance would have been worse than help when you had to prove that you had a good physical reason for demanding relief from your intolerable bond . . ."[23]

The implications are extraordinary. Had Marie discussed the possibility of an affair with him? It is difficult to know what other interpretation to place on "active assistance", though such a suggestion would have been contrary to all her upbringing and her later protestations of disapproval of the whole idea of free love. Rather more certainly, she confessed to Holland her determination to have a child, with or without matrimony. In October 1917 Holland replied:

I can understand your natural desire, but the world is so badly constructed that if you had your way, except in only one way, you would handicap for life your gift to the benefit of the world that would condemn you . . . The world is the richer for your scientific products, and would be still richer if the better types, among whom you can be counted, were allowed to add to its wealth; but you

---

* It is known that shortly before her death in 1958, Marie Stopes destroyed a number of papers. Among them were probably all Aylmer Maude's letters to her during the First World War, before her second marriage (after this, his correspondence is entirely preserved); and perhaps her letters to T. H. Holland.

have to think of the handicap you would leave for your own. I know you wouldn't care what narrow-minded people thought of yourself.[24]

Marie's threat to have a child was more an expression of her unhappiness than a statement of intent. She was far too conventional to flout accepted codes of behaviour. She also genuinely believed that children should be the embodiment of that true, undying love she had pursued so long and so unsuccessfully. Unfortunately, she was not in love; and her latest admirer was even less suitable as a possible solution to her problems than Aylmer Maude.

Marie had long been a member of the Society of Authors, Playwrights and Composers and in January 1917 the society nominated her to represent them on the Cinema Commission of Inquiry, set up by the National Council of Public Morals. Marie's contribution was slight, chiefly remarkable for the first of her many battles with T. P. O'Connor, MP, the Chief Film Censor, and a Catholic. She did, however, catch the attention of the commission's president, Russell Wakefield, the Bishop of Birmingham. A widower, with four sons, and a pillar of the Established Church, he had to be circumspect. But he was much attracted to Marie. In later years, she liked to represent herself as the cool, indifferent object of his passion: "The Bishop was so devoted to me," she wrote to Lord Alfred Douglas, "he implored me to marry him and said he would give up being a Bishop if I would only promise. But of course he was far too old for me ... I always think of him with deep affection, tho' I always failed to return his love."[25] The correspondence that survives, however, reveals a degree of flirtatiousness on Marie's part only too typical of her responses when deprived of the adoration she felt her due. In May 1917 she had apparently turned down his proposals. "Dear Friend," wrote Birmingham, "I now know what you think of men – However though the opened chapter is now closed, still we will be friends." The next day, May 9, Marie replied provocatively: "So you think the crackling outside of an onion is its heart: and that from one who has just been hurt by half-jesting and is half-jesting to hide the hurt, you hear the truth of what she thinks about men or anything else? O, profound observer of character."

In June, Birmingham was still sufficiently encouraged about their possible liaison to write: "I become more and more conscious that I have no longer the power to be more than friend i.e. I cannot give you the vigour I once possessed. Whether even my counsel as to life is as virile as it once was I question ... You are young, you have to be one of our *great* women ..."[26] By August, he assured Marie that she really needed a man to look after her, and by the end of November, Marie apparently felt it necessary to restore his flagging zest. She sent him the proofs of *Married Love*, and wrote, from Leatherhead: "Dear, precious friend ... enclosed are Proofs of my existence ... And you? Have you no Proof for me of your existence for me? ... At present all my writing and work is scientific – that work goes very well – but the deeper thing, the thing that matters *most* is breaking my heart since I saw you last. Men seem to be disappointing creatures. May Heaven guard you."

So ambiguous was their correspondence, however, that the letter may equally well refer to Marie's continuing difficulties in finding a publisher for *Married Love*. Along with the Bishop of Birmingham, she had met on the cinema commission the secretary of the National Council of Public Morals, the Rev. James Marchant. He disapproved of some aspects of the book – at the cheap price she wished it to be published, what effect would it have on the young? – but sent the manuscript, with a recommendation, to Stanley Unwin, the publisher. Publishing history is full of "the ones that got away". Unwin was in favour of publishing *Married Love*. His colleague, C. A. Reynolds, disagreed, preferring, if a risk were to be taken, to put his faith in a novel about homosexuality. Since both their signatures were required on any agreement, they published neither book. The firm that eventually published the novel was prosecuted and heavily fined. "Of *Married Love*," Sir Stanley Unwin, as he later became, recorded with anguish, "more than a million copies were soon sold".[27]

Even though Marie was by now prepared to finance the costs of publication herself, no publisher or printer cared to risk his reputation – not, at least, without the sanction of a Church of England dignitary. The Bishop of Birmingham refused to write a preface, as did W. R. Inge, the Dean of St Paul's, the most "advanced" of the church's thinkers. The weight of moral and religious authority was against the use of mechanical preventives: "I have a good deal of respect for authority in ethics, and for this reason I neither practise nor recommend these methods."* Her mention of artificial impregnation was "most repulsive", and he also protested against her statement that very few men lived in perfect continence: "I have had a long experience of public schools and universities, and my opinion is that in that class and at that age, the proportion of those who entirely abstain from illicit relations with any other person is between 80 and 90 per cent."[28]

Apart from Aylmer Maude who told her she would be lucky if she sold two thousand copies in twenty years, there were few to encourage her. One of them was Dr Binnie Dunlop, secretary of the Malthusian League. A virgin himself, Dr Dunlop mildly disapproved the recommendation in *Married Love* of separate bedrooms, and also the disparagement of coitus interruptus, but offered to back the book. If there was not a sufficient number of backers, he said, almost as an afterthought, "I have a rich young man (who wishes to start a birth control clinic for poor women in Manchester) in my mind who might well be glad to be the means of launching such a progressive work. When he was in Town the other day I told him a little about it and the difficulty of publication, and he said he would like to see it."[29]

Within six months, Marie Stopes had married the rich young man, published *Married Love* (the small publishing house of A. C. Fifield was eventually persuaded to take it on and it was published in March 1918) and finally tested her sexual theories against reality. Few marriage ceremonies can have afforded such a neat literary irony: it was solemnised by the Bishop of Birmingham, the bride was given away by Aylmer Maude, and the best man was Dr Binnie Dunlop. Marie Stopes, it seemed, had indeed come out of the wilderness and was ready to lead her people to the promised land.

---

* It is interesting to compare this with Dean Inge's complacent statement only sixteen years later. "Now, birth-control clinics are supported by a long list of titled ladies, and by some of the leaders in the great professions. I believe I was the first clergyman to face obloquy by urging that the question ought to be discussed as freely as any other social or economic problem." *Vale* by W. R. Inge, Longmans Green, 1934, p. 34.

CHAPTER 8

"Married Love"

"... a light in great darkness to many of us, though a
light shining through a lantern which was possibly not
in the best taste."

Naomi Mitchison on *Married Love*, 1930

"... responsible for providing instruction to girls of
initially dubious virtue as to how to adopt the profession
of more or less open prostitution."

Dr C. P. Blacker on *Married Love*, 1924[1]

IN 1935 a number of American academics were asked to list the twenty-
five most influential books of the previous fifty years. Their findings
were collated and in the final list *Married Love* was accorded sixteenth
place out of the twenty-five – just behind *Das Kapital*, *The Golden
Bough* and Havelock Ellis's *Psychology of Sex*, but ahead of Einstein's
Relativity, Freud's *Interpretation of Dreams*, Hitler's *Mein Kampf*
and Keynes's *Economic Consequences of the Peace*.[2] What was the nature
of a book that could arouse such extremes of gratitude and anger,
and yet be mentioned in the same company as Einstein, Hitler and
Keynes?

Today, when sexual satisfaction does not necessarily imply the
participation of the opposite – or, indeed, of any – sex, the impact
of *Married Love*, with its stress on the sublimity of sex within marriage,
is difficult for anyone less than middleaged to understand. It was a
book that held old men from the chimney corners of their London
clubs, that middle-class wives read avidly before hiding it within the
covers of the Anglican prayerbook, and that their sons read with
prurient giggles in public-school dormitories. I lost count, while

researching this book, of the number of people who told me of such reactions. To us it is such an innocent, even puritanical, book, but sixty years ago, when the majority still thought of the sexual side of marriage in terms of man's "rights" and woman's "duties", it had explosive force. Its main argument is best summed up by the author herself towards the end of the book's mere 116 short pages:

Man, through prudery, through the custom of ignoring the woman's side of marriage and considering his own whim as marriage law, has largely lost the art of stirring a chaste partner to physical love. He therefore deprives her of a glamour, the loss of which he deplores, for he feels a lack not only of romance and beauty, but of something higher which is mystically given as the result of the complete union. He blames his wife's "coldness" instead of his own want of art. Then he seeks elsewhere for the things she could have given him had he known how to win them. And she, knowing that the shrine has been desecrated, is filled with righteous indignation, though generally as blind as he is to the true cause of what has occurred.[3]

From the first sentence of the first chapter – "Every heart desires a mate" – Marie Stopes was at pains to stress mystical "oneness", a sum greater than its parts, that would result from a satisfactory physical relationship.* The frequent troubles that arose, she argued, were not the fault of "our educated girls, composed of virgin sweetness shut in ignorance". Nothing, after all, could alter "the pristine purity of a girl of our northern race". Nor were such problems entirely the result of modern city life, with its haste, greed and artificial surroundings. Opportunities for peaceful, romantic dalliance were to be found less "in a city with its tubes and cinema shows than in woods and gardens where the pulling of rosemary or lavender may be the sweet excuse for the slow and profound mutual rousing of passion". No. Even given the lack of rosemary and lavender in Central London, the problem was much deeper than that. It arose from nothing less than the ignorance and insensitivity of men.

Men, experiencing a fairly continuous level of sexual desire, were

---

* Her bookplate consisted of a well-pruned rose tree, with the motto: "Ex libris M. C. Stopes, omnia ex uno, omnia in uno, omnia ad unum, omnia per medium, et omnia in omnibus."

not aware of their partner's much more fluctuating needs – sexual desire usually being felt in a monthly curve at its height around menstruation, with a smaller peak in the middle of the month. Because women had become dependent on men not just for luxuries but for necessities, they had concealed and distorted their natural sex impulses and given in to men's constant demands, even when they felt least desire to satisfy their "racial instincts":

> ... the husband's regular habits of intercourse, claiming her both when she would naturally enjoy union and when it is to some degree repugnant to her, have tended to flatten out the billowing curves of the line of her natural desire. One result, apparently little suspected, of using the woman as a passive instrument for man's need has been, in effect, to make her that and nothing more.[4]

The results, Dr Stopes argued, were bad for both. Confronted by a wife whose apparent frigidity (biologically determined) appeared as mere capriciousness, the husband's sexual life degenerated into a mere surface need, "quickly satisfied, colourless and lacking in beauty". The wife, disgusted by his selfish indulgence when her "sex-tide is at the ebb", became disillusioned.

The situation was further complicated by a society that, at one level, extolled sensual pleasure for both men and women and, at another, deprecated it. Thus a husband could hate his wife for both her frigidity and her (variable) sensuality; while the wife could be hurt by his brutish demands and also made to feel ashamed of her genuine sexual desires:

> Welling up in her are the wonderful tides, scented and enriched by the myriad experiences of the human race from its ancient days of leisure and flower-wreathed love-making, urging her to transports and self-expressions, were the man but ready to take the first step in the initiative or to recognise and welcome it in her. Seldom dare any woman, still more seldom dare a wife, risk the blow at her heart which would be given were she to offer charming love-play to which the man did not respond. To the initiate she will be able to reveal that the tide is up by a hundred subtle signs, upon which he will seize with delight. But if her husband is blind to them there is for her nothing but silence, self-suppression, and their inevitable sequence of self-scorn, followed by resentment towards the man

who places her in such a position of humiliation while talking of his "love".[5]

It is astonishing that a virgin of thirty-eight could talk so much good sense, deplorably flowery though its expression now appears. Ideologically, there was little originality in *Married Love*, though it succeeded in pulling together scattered ideas from her reading of Edward Carpenter, Ellis and Olive Schreiner. She felt that society could be changed and rebuilt on a foundation of satisfactory orgasms and a renewal of the once instinctive sexual tenderness, but – rather like D. H. Lawrence in *The Rainbow* – she was unable to suggest how this would come about. Her basic dilemma lay in the conflict between her idealised view of marriage, involving the fusion of two equal individuals into a higher but exclusive unity, and her awareness of the individual's duty to the community, which she saw as a "super-entity". The conflict is implicit in *Married Love*, though not formulated until 1935 when in *Marriage in My Time*, she categorised "true marriage" as: "essentially an escape from the herd into the seclusion of the lair ... In the lair, its entrance secured by legal process, the two may retire from the herd and afford each other warm comfort on a mutual basis wherein is an element of mystical contact with cosmic serenity."[6]

In *Married Love*, she could only resolve the conflict with the rather lame conclusion that happiness makes people work better:

The happiness of a perfect marriage, which enhances the vitality of the private life, renders one not only capable of adding to the stream of the life-blood of the community in children, but by marriage one is also rendered a fitter and more perfect instrument for one's own particular work, the results of which should be shared by society as a whole ...[7]

Lacking any political or societal framework for her arguments, she sought justification in science. She made great play with the physiological benefits to be derived from the mutual absorption of each partner's seminal and vaginal secretions during sex, a contention for which there is absolutely no evidence (if such absorption did take place, it would be infinitesimal, and of equivalent benefit to the oral ingestion of, say, half a vitamin tablet per year).

Similarly with her Law of the Periodicity of Recurrence of Natural

Desire in Healthy Women. She agreed with others that the peak of sexual desire in women occurred at or about menstruation, but promulgated as scientific fact her "discovery" of a smaller, mid-month peak. As a professor of physiology pointed out to her at the time, her carefully drawn graphs merely represented her own prejudices, unsupported as they were by any evidence or statistics.*

Marie's intellectual confusion extended to the more usual areas of sexual conflict. While recognising the social basis of women's sexual problems in their economic dependence on men, she was at the same time unwilling to renounce current sexual mythology. Though Woman should be more than what would today be called a "sex-object", she nevertheless had a duty to preserve her femininity. It might attract a man, once or twice, to see his goddess "screw her hair up into a tight and unbecoming knot and soap her ears"; but the proceeding was too unlovely to retain lasting enchantment:

> The man, with the radiant picture of his bride blurred by the daily less lovely aspects, may cease to remind her by acts of courtship that her body is precious ... In this respect I am inclined to think that man suffers more than woman. For man is still essentially the hunter, the one who experiences the desire and thrills of the chase, and dreams ever of coming unawares upon Diana in the woodlands ...[8]

It was this very confusion that contributed to the success of *Married Love*. Women felt that they should be liberated from being a passive sexual receptacle, but they still wanted to retain the traditional role of the eminently desirable goddess pursued by the lustful hunter. Men could feel that increased sensitivity to their wife's physiological difficulties would increase both their own sensual pleasure, and that of their wives, and thereby the gratitude and devotion that were the male's due.

The true originality of *Married Love* lay in its expression. From

---

* It is only fair to add that Havelock Ellis (himself a doctor of medicine, as Marie Stopes was not) was impressed by her theory, finding it "the most notable advance made in recent years in the knowledge of women's psycho-physiological life". He published an article, "The Menstrual Curve of Sexual Impulse in Women", supporting her thesis. Havelock Ellis to Marie Stopes, 9 November 1918. BL-S., enclosing typescript copy of his article.

Havelock Ellis, Marie Stopes took her nonchalant use of physiological terms – penis, clitoris, vagina and mucous* were used freely for the first time in a popular work. Edward Carpenter provided the "mystical" justification for a sensual pleasure that was still frowned on; and Marie glued the whole uniquely together in a style at once sickly, inflammatory, imaginative, simple and direct. On one page she would refer from her own experience to the confessions of an ignorant young wife who felt something lacking in her husband's love:

> Her husband has never kissed her except on the lips and cheek, but once at the crest of the wave of her sex-tide . . . she felt a yearning to feel his head, his lips pressed against her bosom . . . Because she shyly asked him, Mrs G's husband gave her one swift unrepeated kiss upon her bosom. He was so ignorant that he did not know that her husband's lips upon her breast melt a wife to tenderness and are one of a husband's first and surest ways to make her physically ready for complete union . . .[9]

On another page, she would indulge mystical fantasies undreamt of by Carpenter. The fusion of joy and rapture between two mates, she argued, was not purely physical:

> The half swooning sense of flux which overtakes the spirit in that eternal moment at the apex of rapture sweeps into its flaming tides the whole essence of the man and woman, and as it were, the heat of the contact vapourises their consciousness so that it fills the whole of cosmic space. For the moment they are identified with the divine thoughts, the waves of eternal force, which to the Mystic often appear in the terms of golden light.[10]

Only six pages later – such was her sense of reality – she is advocating what amounts to mutual masturbation during pregnancy. The wife cannot allow her husband to enter the sacred portals of her body when it is developing a new life; but she also has to consider the strains which nature imposes on her husband: "The tender and loving wife will readily find some means of giving him that physical relief which his nature needs . . . With an ardent man, wholly devoted to his

---

* Many medical men still subscribed to the nineteenth-century error that vaginal mucous fluid "happens only in lascivious women or such as live luxuriously." (*Rees's Cyclopaedia*, 1826.)

wife and long deprived of her, the time will come when it will
be sufficient for him to be near her and caress her for relief to take
place without any physical connection." So much for the apex of
rapture.

The intellectual confusion in *Married Love* is also evident in her
attitude to the liberation of women. She extolled marriage as every
woman's ultimate goal in life, a state in which the giving of her jealously
guarded "all" to a man would be rewarded with a lifetime of physical
and spiritual bliss. Equally, however, women had a right to their own
intellectual development – an idea somewhat at odds with the concept
of a woman's main treasure being the bestowal of her body:

> Still, far too often, marriage puts an end to woman's intellectual
> life. Marriage can never reach its full stature until women possess as
> much intellectual freedom and freedom of opportunity within it as
> do their partners.
>
> That at present the majority of women neither desire freedom for
> creative work, nor would know how to use it, is only a sign that we
> are still living in the shadow of the coercive and dwarfing influences
> of the past.[11]

Marie's ideas had not yet ossified into dogma, and, a week before
Married Love was published, in March 1918, she poured out all her
doubts and confusions in a long letter (there is no appellation, but it
was probably addressed to the Bishop of Birmingham, whom she often
called "Friend"):

> Dear Friend, Fancy wanting to write to you since Wednesday ... I
> wanted to write because my brain has been following out a train of
> thought I think so important ... It is to me strange, desolating
> almost, but I am beginning to wonder whether that attitude, so
> noble in some of its aspects, which you and I and people of ideals
> like us think so right, that attitude that in giving her body in love
> a woman gives her "all" (while a man scarcely does as much) has
> not been responsible ultimately for a great evil, the horrible tri-
> partite division of womankind? Today what have we among us,
> 3 groups of women.
>
> a) The unmarried – never allowed any sex joy or relief, however
> much they fundamentally suffer for lack of it, with *no* sex life.

b) The married (possibly burdened without limit with childbearing) with perhaps a normal (but often excessive) sex life.

c) The outcast – in order to balance the unhealthy percentage of unmarried, they are overworked to the point of sex machines ...

Now the question haunting me at present, would we have Class C of women to anything like the extent we have it if we had not Class A? – and would we have Class A, *de facto* if we had not the – I fear to my horror I was going to call it the fetish, of the idea that a woman once having given herself in love has nothing left?

Dear, you are so *wise*, I want to think this out with you, I believe it is a cornerstone of immense importance to the whole community. That a woman should *never* give herself save for love, is an axiom; but it is outrageously violated in our social system (as a result of the fact that we tend to think a woman has lost everything when she has once given herself. Isn't it in reality a laying far greater stress on the physical side of things than should be?) I, if anyone, has a right to ask this, for few women married for years, have still "all" to give! Most women don't dare to think this aloud lest people think they are excusing themselves ...[12]

That was an example of genuine free-thinking that she was to achieve with increasing rarity after 1918.

Married Love was an immediate success. It "crashed into English society like a bombshell," Marie wrote later. "Its explosively contagious main theme – that woman like man has the same physiological reaction, a reciprocal need for enjoyment and benefit from union in marriage distinct from the exercise of maternal functions – made Victorian husbands gasp. A week or two after that book was published in 1918 all London was talking of it, and when I lunched with the very distinguished Secretary of the Royal Society of Medicine, Sir John MacAlister, he said to me: 'If it is true it is the most incredible, but the most wonderful thing for mankind; a new gospel of hope.'"[13] The book sold over 2000 copies within a fortnight and by the end of 1918 was already into its sixth edition. Marie took great pleasure in passing on the details of its success to Walter Blackie, one of the publishers who had turned it down. "I see you said in 1915," she wrote, "that this book might frighten off the few men left of marriageable condition, but that is not my experience, and among my most ardent correspondents are young lieutenants recently married."[14]

The very success of *Married Love*, however – and the birth control crusade to which it contributed – created a necessary circumspection. Marie might have a "new gospel of hope", but gospellers have to be above reproach if their pronouncements are to carry any weight. From now on, Marie Stopes was a public figure. She was also married, a useful adjunct to her new career as sexual reformer, and could afford to forget her agonisings over the vast army of sexually deprived women, of which she had so recently been a member.

CHAPTER 9

Married Love?

> "There are other types of women who . . . are not capable
> of the full experience of marriage until the early thirties.
> On the whole, the late maturing is the lasting type of
> woman, as the slower growing oak outlives the rapidly
> shooting sunflower."
>
> Marie Stopes, *Marriage In My Time*, 1935

MARIE STOPES was thirty-seven when she married for the second
time. She was a virgin, and felt the ignominy of her position. It was,
surely, not her fault? Evolution, and the artificiality of modern life,
had created a type of woman – particularly among the more intelligent – who did not develop physiologically until well into their
thirties. The argument became a tenet of her creed, and a justification
of the inexperience from which she had written so persuasively about
the joys of married love. It was too late to be a sunflower but anyway
oaks were better.

Humphrey Verdon Roe was thirty-nine when he met Marie. The
fourth of seven children of a prosperous Manchester doctor, he joined
the army immediately after leaving school and his army crammers,
fought through the Boer War, and endured the Siege of Ladysmith.
The experience cured him of military ambitions, and he resigned his
commission in 1902, returning to Manchester to take over the family
firm of Everard & Co., webbing manufacturers specialising in the
manufacture of braces.

Disillusioned with the army and already a little bored with the
business world, he soon found scope for his enterprise in the exploits
of his brother, Alliott. Known as "A.V.", Alliott Verdon Roe was a

year older than "H.V." A departure from the family type, hitherto limited to the church, the army and the professions, Alliott was an inventor of considerable originality and tenacity. Aviation was scoffed at in 1906, and a passionate letter from him to *The Times* defending the Wright brothers' experiments was published with the editorial rebuke: "... all attempts at artificial aviation are not only dangerous to human life but foredoomed to failure from an engineering standpoint".[1]

Despite the usual disasters – his planes were always coming down in the sewage farms at Brooklands race track – Alliott persisted in his mad ventures, and in April 1909, Humphrey, by now making a healthy profit from Everard & Co., decided to invest in his brother's inventive genius. The partnership caused some ribaldry. At the time, Alliott recalled in his memoirs, "the most successful single product of Everard & Co was an article of men's wear sold under the proprietary name of 'Bullseye Braces'. Naturally, when people came to know that the 'Avro' machines were financed by H. V. Roe there came a stock joke that 'Avro' biplanes were kept up by Bullseye Braces, which was financially true."[2] Under their agreement – clinched with £1 – Humphrey undertook to cover all his brother's debts, in return for a half-share of profits. His faith was justified. In July that year – the same month that Blériot flew the Channel – Alliott made the first 100-foot flight in a British plane powered by a British engine. By the time war broke out in 1914, Humphrey had invested £10,000 in the company.

In August 1914 Britain had a mere 100 aircraft – only forty-three of them serviceable – but Humphrey's business skills ensured that Avro was equipped to supply machines for the new aerial warfare. He piloted the planes as often as his brother and, in November 1912, claimed the odd distinction of being the first man to type while flying – in an Avro 501, an enclosed biplane built for the International Aeroplane Competition at Salisbury.[3] In the same year, Humphrey later recalled, he had "the pleasure of flying over Portugal in a machine of our own make, an Avro, labelled 'Republica', which helped to distract the attention of the populace from a revolution they were contemplating".* It was an Avro that brought down the first Zeppelin

* Humphrey was no political revolutionary – his brother, Alliott, still less so. In 1939, Sir A. V. Roe, as he had then become, published his opinion that Hitler and

over Britain, and the first air attack – on the Zeppelin sheds at Fried-richshaven – was made by Avros. By the end of the war, the firm had produced 10,000 planes, and both brothers were rich. They had, however, quarrelled, and in 1917 Humphrey gave up his interest. He joined the Royal Flying Corps and became an aerial observer and night-bomber with the 100th Squadron. It was at this stage, in early 1918, that he met Marie Stopes.

They were introduced by Dr Binnie Dunlop, MD, Secretary of the Malthusian League, who was anxious to help Marie with financial backing for the publication of *Married Love*. At first, over lunch at a Lyons café, neither realised who the other was. "Dear Dr Stopes," Humphrey wrote two days later, "Dr Dunlop told me you had dis-tinguished yourself at Munich, so I pictured you as some stout German frau, a weighty and ponderous piece of goods. I was therefore very surprised when I met you at the Lyons Popular to see a young girl instead ..."4 Marie was equally surprised. She expected "an elderly gentleman with a broad watch chain on an expansive front, and thinking that my host had provided a handsome and fascinating khaki-clad* officer in his stead, I forgot the Manchester manufacturer and found a very thrilling companion in Mr H. V. Roe, the Aviator ... It was right at the end of the party before we realised that we each were the person we had been invited to meet! but by that time Cupid had already driven his shafts. Indeed, Heaven had made us for each other and essentially what we both said was "Hello! *You* at last? Why on earth didn't we meet sooner?"5

Humphrey's interests, for an aviator, were as surprising as his

---

* While paying lip-service to the horrors of war, Marie was herself not above indulging in Kiplingesque chauvinism. On a scrap of paper, she preserved one of her poems written at the time:
Won't you kindly leave 'old of me Tommy
When you kiss me as 'ard as all that
You do nothin' but ruin me temper and cockle the brim of me 'at.
You're so tall and fine in yer khaki
You're a match for a 'undred wild Huns,
You're as cool and as straight as the guns that they 'ate
And you'll silence their blastin' big guns. (MS in SR-Coll.)

Mussolini were both working for the betterment of civilisation: "This brings me to the Jewish question ... one should not overlook that they are the race who form the backbone of the underworld and they have been able to obtain great power by getting control of the creation of currency." (A. V. Roe, *The World of Wings and Things*, Hurst & Blackett, 1939, p. 187.)

personable appearance. Walking through the slums of Manchester, he had developed an interest in birth control long before he met Marie. He had drawn up a list of requirements for a birth control clinic – even down to the number of washbowls and towels – and in October 1917 summarised his arguments for the benefit of St Mary's Hospital, Manchester: "... far too many children are brought into the world without their parents appearing to care about their future prospects ... Everything goes to prove that John Stuart Mill was right when he wrote 'Little improvement can be expected in morality until the producing of large families is regarded with the same feeling as drunkenness among other physical excess'."[6] He offered St Mary's £12,000 in his will, and £1000 a year for five years to set up a birth control clinic. The offer was refused, on the grounds that it might deter other patrons.

Humphrey was just as prepared to take a risk with Marie as he had been with Alliott. Immediately after meeting her, he sent a cheque for £200 to finance *Married Love*. Their mutual attraction had not been declared – unusually for Marie, who rarely indulged in the playing-hard-to-get game – but they corresponded when Humphrey returned to France only three weeks after their first meeting. A gentle, rather simple man, with the kind of schoolboyish charm that was still, at forty, endearing rather than irritatingly naïve, he was enormously flattered by Marie's interest. On February 20, he wrote to her from the R.F.C. Officers' Rest House in France:

> Dear Dr Stopes ... Have you got a spare photo to spare, PLEASE? I would very much like to have one autographed by you. It would make a very interesting addition to my all-too-small collection of celebrated people. I have Phil May, Tom Brown, Joynson Hicks and I believe that is all. So I do hope you will favour me with a photo of yourself. Be a brick! Yours very sincerely, H. V. Roe.* [7]

The two were to meet again sooner than either expected. Returning from a night-bombing raid over the German lines, Humphrey's plane – not an Avro – came down with engine failure, and he was sent back to England at the end of March with a broken ankle and jarred

* Presumably HVR's heroes – Phil May was a cartoonist, William Joynson-Hicks an extreme right-wing Conservative, much-hated Home Secretary and fervent anti-Bolshevik.

spine. Forgetting all her other commitments – "Why, oh why run away at this critical period?" lamented her publisher, A. C. Fifield – Marie rushed to visit him at the R.F.C. Hampstead hospital on March 26 – the day *Married Love* was published. She managed to engineer a day's leave for him and on April 1 he came down to Leatherhead. "Dear Duckie," Marie wrote to Aylmer Maude, who was still living at her home there, "please be home in time for dinner and not late (velvet jacket required) as I have an unexpected and important visitor. A 'wounded' from France whom I am rather fond of. Please call me Una. Don't tell him I have never spoken of him!"

It might be April 1, but Marie was not going to be fooled again. She had already decided that she was in love with Humphrey. On April 4, not revealing her sex, or the nature of her doctorate, she wrote to the Commanding Officer of Humphrey's hospital, on London University paper: "Now that Lieut. H. V. Roe is making good progress, Dr Stopes begs to suggest that a few days in the sunny open air of Leatherhead might assist in his recovery. Dr Stopes undertakes that Lieut. Roe will lead a strictly disciplined life, be out of doors all day, go to bed early and touch no alcohol if the short leave is granted him to visit Dr Stopes' private house in Leatherhead."[8] The plot did not work: if Lieut. Roe was well enough to go to Leatherhead, he was fit to go back to the Front, where the German offensive on the Somme had been raging for over a fortnight.

There was also another slight problem. They had now agreed that they loved each other and wanted to marry; but Humphrey was already engaged. He let the truth be known only gradually, probably a wise decision. It could scarcely contribute to his recovery to have two women wrangling over his hospital bed. Possibly remembering her similar predicament ten years earlier with Charlie Hewitt and Edith Garner, Marie was in no doubt as to what he should do – throw up his fiancée, Ethel Burgess, and marry Marie immediately. "It may be only a matter of weeks," she harangued him on April 14, "before you are back at the Front. Anything may happen. If we marry at once I might already be carrying your child while you are away." Miss Burgess was equally adamant. If she was to be discarded propriety demanded a period of at least six months before her fiancé married someone else. An honourable man, Humphrey did not wish to hurt Ethel; nor could he say, like Charlie Hewitt, "a plague on both your parties" and scuttle off to Canada. He was genuinely in love with Marie.

Storming down from Manchester, Ethel demanded to see the enchantress, and on April 21, she and Humphrey turned up unexpectedly at Marie's Leatherhead home. It was not a happy interview. Ethel accused Marie of fortune-hunting, and of not feeling a genuine love for Humphrey – how could it all have happened so quickly? Furious, Marie wrote to Humphrey after they had left:

> ... I might have been less hurt and surprised and therefore more patient had I not had the shock of seeing her on the doorstep in such an aggressive aura. (By the way, do you realise that I generally feel and sometimes see other people's aura? That may partly explain what seems to her so impossible, my loving you so *quickly*. Sometimes I know people's inmost secrets in a few seconds.) ... Time, I am sure, will set her on her feet again. She is not your mate, and I sincerely hope her mate will turn up ... You may tell her that my power of love is not less than hers and that she need have no anxiety that you are being married for your money! How comic to think of it! By the way, even if you settled on me half of all you possess, it would be annually much less than I am securely earning for myself, and so I risk being the poorer for marrying you for I risk my own earnings if our child makes me very ill ...

This was disingenuous in the extreme. Marie knew that he was rich,* and he was upset by her attitude. "All your plans are being made on the assumption (a cold, calculated one at that) that I shall be killed or maimed," he wrote to her. On the other hand, there was the possibility that, without marriage and a child, she would have a nervous breakdown: "that I do not like to consider possible." In despair, Marie resorted to her usual practice of canvassing acquaintances to find out the truth. Councillor Margaret Ashton, the Manchester philanthropist, replied rather frostily. She trusted H. V. Roe herself, she said, "But of his private life I know nothing, nor do I know who are his friends ... I have thought him rather an isolated person – of strong individuality

---

* In an undated autobiographical fragment, Marie later recalled the time when, shortly after their first meeting, H. V. Roe "left £50,000 one day in his overcoat pocket at a meeting of the R. [Royal] Society where the coats are hung on an outside peg". (BL-S.)

– perhaps not very easy to get on with, or easily making friends."[9]
Councillor Ashton's assessment of Humphrey as a strong person was
obviously wide of the mark, and Marie did not take her advice. Humphrey had already given up. Guilty about both Ethel and Marie, he
gave way to the stronger. "You give your orders as to what is to
happen in future. Or if you don't give orders, you let me know your
wishes. It's all the same," he wote to Marie.[10]

Their engagement was announced in the *Morning Post* on May 7.
Marie may have felt some qualms about Ethel Burgess.* They were
not sufficiently strong to deter her. On May 16, they were secretly
married at the Register Office, St George's, Hanover Square, only
three weeks after Humphrey had signed a declaration to Ethel Burgess
not to marry for six months. By mutual agreement, he had settled
£20,000 on Marie, with a further £10,000 for the furtherance of birth
control.

Aylmer Maude was one of the two witnesses at the secret wedding
– even Marie's mother, though she was aware of the engagement, was
not told of it. Maude put on a brave front, but he was deeply upset
by the sudden shock to their relationship. "My very dear one," he
wrote shortly before her marriage, "Oh, my dear, you do not know
how many conflicting thoughts and feelings rise in my mind and
heart when I think of you and of our past, present and future friendship. I want you to be happy and to live a normal life with children
of your own and I am deeply grateful to you for having befriended
me in my loneliness from December 1912 onwards ... Au revoir,
my dear one – It is such a joy to think of your cleverness, your sanity,
your originality, your taste, your looks, your grace and – when you
please – your sweetness. Your loving Aylmer."[11]

Whether or not it was the kindest thing to do, Marie sent him a
progress report on the day after her marriage. "Dearest Duckie," she
wrote from Craigvara, Leatherhead, where she and Humphrey had
spent their first night, "Thank you for your nice little letter – I have
often thought of you and am very, very fond of you. Humphrey and
I were very happy last night and this morning – the marriage is
consummated, but naturally, I haven't had it at its best yet ..."[12]

---

* Perhaps in an attempt to justify Ethel's unworthiness as a mate for Humphrey, she
copied passages from his diary: "June 27, 1914, Ethel out by side door. June 27, 1914,
Ethel sleeps with another man." (Notes in Marie's handwriting, SR-Coll.)

The next day, May 18, Maude replied, generously stifling his grief: "My dearest Una, Your kind letter is a great comfort to me. It came when I was feeling myself a useless failure with no future before him. Your friendship cheers me and is the most precious thing I have. I am very glad things have gone well with you. From what I have seen of Humphrey he seems to be a really good sort, simple, straightforward, solid and capable . . ." Marie, now on honeymoon in Cornwall, where she had spent several holidays with Aylmer Maude, replied by return: "Dear Ducky . . . Humphrey is dearer and dearer, the more I know of him, and seems so utterly made for me I am unable to believe in the *reality* of anything happening now. It is *too* good . . . I often think of you and shall always love you . . . I need your kind of love as well as Humphrey's as one needs relatives and friends as well as a mate."[13] As if this were not congé enough, Marie added five days later that he could stay for three nights in Leatherhead after their return from honeymoon but after that would have to leave – "the days are too few and fateful to have *any* reduction of their content".

He had still another trial to endure. Humphrey's return to the Front had been indefinitely postponed, and Marie insisted on a proper church celebration of their marriage. As she no longer had a father, she also insisted on being given away by Maude. He found it hard to reconcile himself to the idea. "I have never had enough of you – nor indeed could ever have," he wrote. On June 19, the marriage was solemnised at St Margaret's, Westminster, by the Bishop of Birmingham. He had some trouble persuading her to use the word "obey", but Marie, to save him embarrassment, eventually agreed. The ceremony and reception, the invitations stipulated, would be of the simplest nature, owing to the war. Nevertheless, Marie wore cream satin, silver brocade, and a tulle veil, held by a wreath of orange blossoms. Mrs Stopes, as usual, was critical. Immediately after the ceremony she wrote to her daughter: "The *back* which was chiefly presented to the congregation was very neat and artistic, the veil fell in folds just right, and the *heels* were not seen *much* . . . The bridegroom's back was strong and sturdy, is he not *heavy* for an aeroplane? You should both be weighed; father and I were $9\frac{1}{2}$ and $7\frac{1}{2}$ stone."[14]

Maude soon found an opportunity to escape his humiliating position. Following the Russian Revolution in 1917, Allied forces had begun their intervention in Russia in July 1918. Maude had spent much of his youth in Russia, spoke the language fluently and had married a Russian wife. He had no hesitation in following the British troops to Archangel, as war correspondent, and lecturer for the YMCA. In November that year he wrote sadly to Marie: "It would be a much greater wrench for me to go to Russia if it were not that your marriage has cut us apart to an unexpected and painful extent." Marie wrote to him very rarely while he was away – a lapse which further hurt him – and they never reverted to their former intimacy.*

Marie had some excuse for neglecting her friends. Humphrey was "simply adorable", she wrote to her mother on August 5, "and now that I know what a true marriage should be I know enough to know how very exceptional he is." With customary vigour, she threw herself into the scientific proof of hitherto theoretical pleasures. A day later, she was writing to Humphrey: "My darling sweetheart . . . I want to *admire* you more and more as well as to love you darling – you can't think how strange it is to find a man I can really admire, so keep the proud distinction . . . I wish our first experiment on last night's lines had been in a big beautiful bed, in a pretty room and not so cramped and sordid."15

They were often apart, Marie up at Eskmeals or in London, Humphrey in Manchester or on unspecified, desk-bound war work. They wrote to each other once, sometimes twice a day, with the touching and (to others) embarrassing silliness that affects lovers. Humphrey was "Tiger Humphlekins", Marie was "Wood Nymph". "Don't get growner up than you are, please," Marie wrote on September 24, "I wish I were with you this minute, I'd pounce on you and *make* you roll on the ground and I'd pull your hair and tickle you and behave altogether like a wild pussy kitten. So I'll send little scattering scurrying kisses instead to the great, big growly silky curly Humple Tiger, from his Tiger Kitten Wife." Humphrey could not quite match such effusions, contenting himself with expressions – totally sincere – of disbelief at his own good fortune in capturing such a wife. "My dearest little lonely Wood Nymph," he wrote, "Fancy finding a glorious loving wife and all the other things thrown in, what a lucky man I am . . .

---

* They did however remain close, though critical, friends until Maude's death in 1938, at the age of eighty. To Harry Stopes-Roe, only surviving child of the marriage, Maude was always "Grandpa" – an indication of the status to which he was now relegated.

You could have captured anyone you wanted. Yet little me has won this great prize."[16]

Significantly, Marie's reciprocal infatuation did not impede her critical faculties. "Oh dearest lover, sweetheart Tiger," she wrote in October, "I have so very often thought of a moment when we were together in that 'new way' last week and a look came on your face and your eyes closed – a kind of look that was so beautiful I don't know how to describe it . . . otherwise this last weekend you were not at your best."[17]

Three weeks later, on October 24, Marie, worried about his feckless attitude to money, sent him an agreement to sign. Of course, she added, if he *really* wished to risk his money – "which represents our possibility to do patriotic birth-control and other racial work" – they would tear it up together. The agreement read: "I hereby register to my wife Marie my inviolable promise not to part with or to re-invest sums totalling more than five thousand pounds without previous complete and full discussion with her." The agreement was duly signed by Humphrey and witnessed by Alice Gertrude Heap (their housekeeper). It did little to curb Humphrey's speculations, but for the moment at least reassured Marie.

The problems of adjusting to marriage – complicated by attempts to reconcile Humphrey with his family after his quarrel with Alliott – were an additional pressure on Marie. There was no let-up in her scientific work. On November 11, when the armistice was signed, England went wild. In London, people held parties on the open upper decks of buses, there were bonfires in Trafalgar Square, and total strangers copulated openly in the streets.[18] Marie spent the evening – with Humphrey in the audience – lecturing on coal to the Birmingham & Midland Institute, Paradise Street. "Darling Husband," she wrote to Humphrey next day, on her way back to Cumberland, "'The greatest days in the history of our Race', as the papers call the present, don't seem to leave any particularly joyous or beautiful memories to *us*, do they? I shall never forget all the horrible ugliness and *futility* of 'rejoicings' at Birmingham."

That year, Marie's wartime work with Dr R. V. Wheeler on the constitution of coal – a Government-sponsored project – had been published. It led to Marie's independent researches that established her work internationally. Sewing by a coal fire one day, she romantically recalled – putting her discovery on the level of Newton's apple, Watt's kettle and Archimedes' bath – she noticed that some bands in the coal burned in a different way from others, creating tiny volcanoes. This gave her the idea of examining the different bands microscopically, using very thin sections. She then correlated the microscopic and macroscopic aspects of the four constituents of coal and defined their nature in the words vitrain, clarain, durain and fusain.* The terminology, with some modifications, is still used today.[19]

Marie's labours were complicated by the unexpected success of *Married Love*. Some rejected it. "Hardly suitable for *The Times*," commented A. C. Drew, a subsidiary editor, who returned the review copy. But most agreed with G. B. Shaw's verdict on the book, lent to him by Aylmer Maude, a fellow-lecturer at the annual Fabian summer school. It was the best thing of its kind he had ever read, Shaw wrote to Marie in August 1918; and while on the subject, could she give him any advice as to an impotent friend of his?[20]

At first, Marie was intrigued and flattered by the letters occasioned by her book. One of the earliest, in May 1918, was from a doctor who had a patient whose ignorance of the female curve of sexual desire had wrecked her nerves. He suggested that the husband should only approach his wife when she invited him by wearing a pink ribbon round her neck. Marie scribbled enthusiastically over the letter: "Mention in next edition, but say against the true ideals for a woman to advertise to her husband that she is wanting."[21] By October, the response had become almost out of hand. A. C. Fifield complained that he could no longer deal with orders, an odd complaint from a publisher with a bestseller on his hands. But Marie was at last able to repay one of her debts. On October 2 she wrote two letters to Humphrey. One was addressed to "dearest lover, sweetheart Tiger". The other read:

> My Dearest Lieut. Roe, I am very glad to be able to tell you that the business partnership which we formed over my book "Married Love" has so far been successful that I am able to return to you the whole of the £200 capital you invested together with the £100 profit which we agreed on closing the transaction . . . I thank you

* "The Four Visible Ingredients in Banded Bituminous Coal", *Proceedings Royal Society*, Vol. 90, 1919.

warmly for your ready co-operation, for the results might have
been so very different and you so promptly and generously took the
risk. Yours very sincerely, MCS.

Like Malthus, enthused Binnie Dunlop, delighted at his own part
in the book's success, she might well now "spend the remainder of a
long and happy life bringing out new editions of your Essay with
more and more data and evidence".[22] Marie, of course, had no intention
of limiting herself in any such way. *Wise Parenthood*, the second book
in her new field of research, had already been written, and was published on 18 November 1918. Marie always presented this work – a
concise guide to contraceptive methods – as a necessary sequel,
rather unwillingly undertaken in response to popular demand, to
Married Love, a myth which her biographers have accepted. In fact,
it was completed in 1917, before *Married Love* was published.[23]
Possibly she thought that such a stance would allay criticism. It did
nothing of the sort. Booksellers were "appalled" by it, poor Mr Fifield
complained. Even Bumpus had refused it, and how could she write
articles about birth control in popular newspapers, resulting in a flood
of orders that made his work as a publisher impossible?

Wise Parenthood, like *Married Love*, now seems totally innocuous.
But it took Marie several pages of tortuous argument to get to her
central point, delivered with all the bravado of a Luther nailing his
theses on the gates of Wittenberg: "On physiological, moral and
religious grounds, I advocate the restrained and sacramental rhyth-
mic performance of the marriage rite of physical union, throughout
the whole married life, as an act of supreme value in itself, separate
and distinct from its value as a basis for the procreation of children."[24]

The argument was unlikely to endear her to the Protestant Church,
still overwhelmingly Pauline in its attitude to marriage. Her advocacy
of contraception was equally contentious. Forestalling objections that
contraception would increase promiscuity, she stressed that her book
was addressed only to the married. If it fell into the hands of those "who
have not put any religious or civil seal on the bond of their love",
then it would reduce "the racial dangers which are so often coincident
with illicit love". While if it enabled a few wives entirely to avoid
having children: "It is surely well that such women should not be
mothers, for motherhood is too sacred an office to be held unwillingly"

– a piece of logic no Church would have been willing to accept at the time.

Medically, too, she was on dangerous ground. The dissemination of contraceptive knowledge has never been illegal in England, and Marie felt that her book would correct the "ill-informed and often debased instruction" that was freely circulating in pamphlet form. Unfortunately, contraceptive knowledge was in its infancy. Marie disapproved of the "safe period" – but such was the state of medical knowledge that no one disputed her definition of it as roughly the middle of the month (when, as we now know, conception is most likely to take place). What doctors could more easily quarrel with was her advocacy of the cervical cap – not so much in itself, but because she made the mistake of saying that it could be left in place for several days, or even weeks, without removal.

The third area for disapproval was sociological. Marie was herself a product of the Protestant ethic and viewed with horror, like many members of the richer middle classes, the growth in numbers of "the less thrifty and conscientious":

> The thriftless who breed so rapidly tend by that very fact to bring forth children who are weakened and handicapped by physical as well as mental warping and weakness, and at the same time to demand their support from the sound and thrifty ... this half is not free and untrammelled, but is burdened by the partial support and upkeep of the unfit portion of the population, and hence is less able to support children of its own good type than it would were the incapables non-existent.[25]

Such a class-oriented attitude would not appeal to radicals. At this time Marie's efforts were not directed at the working classes where, logically, they should have been focused. As a measure of her profound ignorance of working-class reality, she extolled the virtues of the cap, which "could be fitted at any convenient time, preferably when dressing in the evening".[26]

None of these points would have caused so much stir had Marie not brought them out of the world of theological disputes, academic footnotes and medical journalism in to the sphere of public debate. The war had created a profound change in the public's attitude towards sex. By 1918, so great had been the slaughter, there were now 1096 women to every 1000 men – an imbalance quickly noticed and talked about, especially by those women (still a limited number) who had at last received the vote. There was a general loosening of conventional attitudes towards sex – one in five of the returning heroes had contracted venereal disease – and people were now as ready to discuss such problems as the rapidly growing popular press was eager to cater for them. As the author of *Married Love*, and a member of the Birth Rate Commission, Marie was much in demand. She would write for practically anyone, and her outspoken articles for papers like the *Sunday Dispatch* made sneers from the scientific establishment almost inevitable. The *Eugenics Review*, which might be expected to be favourable, talked glumly only of the lacerations and probable cancer which the cap would cause – and as for leaving it in for several days – "We think it a pity that this book has been published."[27] Criticism also flourished at less exalted levels and in June 1919 the *News of the World* offered a willow-pattern tea tray to every "proud mother of ten children ... useful for taking up mother's cup of morning tea, or for serving father's evening refreshment".[28] The most vicious attack came from the *New Witness*, which was particularly incensed that Arnold Bennett had contributed an introduction to the fifth edition of *Wise Parenthood*:

> After much consideration [proclaimed the paper] we have decided that a thundering attack would please this most unpleasant woman almost as well as ardent support ... The peculiar horror of her book is that it is couched in pseudo-scientific terms, and is addressed to the married woman ... Mr Arnold Bennett bears an honourable name: he can hope to bear it no longer if he does not at once dissociate himself from Dr Marie Stopes and her rubber goods. The introduction he has written to her filthy book is a disgrace to him and to his (and our) profession.[29]

The attack, by a cruelty transcending mere irony, came just after Marie had lost her first child.

The first sentence of *Wise Parenthood* – "A family of healthy happy children should be the joy of every pair of married lovers" – was not just rhetoric. Both Marie and Humphrey wanted children. In the autumn of 1918 they spent a holiday together at the Land's End Hotel,

Cornwall, with conception in mind. Also on holiday there was another recently married couple. For the young Dr Helena Wright, her first meeting with Marie Stopes remains a vivid memory. "I saw this floating creature in a long-skirted white lace dress against the rocks – most striking figure. At the time, she was capable of being impersonal and could still accept criticism. We discussed the medical aspects of *Wise Parenthood* and she listened with proper scientific interest. She was a person of flexible intelligence – very interesting and to the point."[30] Marie's comparatively deferential attitude – to a much younger, medically qualified woman – was unusual. By this time, the constant praise from readers of *Married Love* appears to have turned her head a little, and when Humphrey left Cornwall in September, she wrote:

Darlingest Tiger-Humphles ... Thanks so much for seeing about the sugar. It is so strangely precious in these days.

I got an M.L. [Married Love] letter today saying "You have done more to promote the happiness and welfare of humanity than all the priests, prophets, philosophers and social reformers in history." That is not stinted praise, is it? I have for a long time had the feeling I am a kind of priest and prophet mixed – but it sounds too incongruous to say so when at the same time I would like to be always a girl and beautiful and beloved and in love with an adorable husband ...[31]

The prophecies, however, would have to wait. Marie's instinct about Cornwall had been right. "Fertilising coitus," as she charmingly put it, had taken place and she was pregnant. The child would, of course, be a girl, and was already referred to as "Margaret".* Humphrey pestered her with injunctions to eat lots of apples and oranges, never mind the cost, and Marie replied unromantically with requests for a bottle of his urine. Germs had appeared.

Suddenly in the middle of the night I realised *you have* the symptom – acute frequent passing of water ... and of course infected me ... I am *fundamentally* so sound and healthy! I almost hope you *have* got them for then that would be an adequate explanation of several

---

* Probably in honour of the daughter in *Dear Brutus*. In late 1917, Marie wrote to Sir James Barrie, saying how much the play had made her love him – "Margaret's father behaved *so* like my darling, long dead father ..." (28 December 1917. BL-S.)

things which have worried me and of your troublesome habits ...
I haven't time now to write a love letter, but all my thoughts are
love for you. Margaret was very active yesterday but didn't hurt
her mummy.[32]

Dr Amand Routh, Marie's gynaecologist, was also worried – not
about the infection, but about a thirty-eight-year-old woman, pregnant
for the first time, who refused to stop work. "Dear Dr Stopes," he
wrote on 27 February 1919, "Do let me hear how you are for I cannot
take the responsibility of such a piece of animated quicksilver unless
I am a bit in touch. What with your coal expert work, your botany,
yr Birth Control and yr Baby and yr B. coli, I am aghast."

Neither did Dr Routh approve of Marie's insistence on having
"Twilight Sleep" for the birth. A newly fashionable analgesic for childbirth, it involved injections of a fairly critical mixture of morphine and
scopolamine. Marie herself had doubts. In May, just before the baby
was due, she confessed her fears to a friend who, three years earlier,
on Marie's totally theoretical advice, had used Twilight Sleep. "Dearest
Marie," wrote Mollie Wrench, ". . . of course you are not going to die
... you must have something back in part-payment for all you have
already done, and I think that a month's quiet rest with your little
Margaret in your arms will give you such exquisite joy that you will
know it is the crown of all things in wedded life ... really, with
Twilight Sleep there is nothing to dread."[33]

With the baby more than a month overdue – though her calculations
may have been wrong – Marie went into a nursing home at Teddington on July 16. Humphrey was instructed to keep a diary of events:

5.42 p.m.	Dr comes out, says the 1st Injection given.
7.05	Brown says M asks for chloroform.
7.30	Brown gives the 2nd injection. I have dinner with Brown and his wife.
8.53	Very beautiful sunset from the seat outside M's room. During this time M is sometimes quiet and sometimes she is sighing and moaning.
9.21	Brown goes in to inject again.
9.23	M sighs, again at – 28, now almost continuous.
9.40	Dr Brown said no more morphia.
9.45	M is quiet. I stay outside the room on and off ...

10.35	In M's voice, "Give me Chloroform, for God's sake." M now sighing and moaning.
10.50	M. "I can't endure it."
10.53 ½	– cries "Oh Nurse do be quick."
11–00	Bell & Brown come out, they tell me they cannot hear the child's heart ...

17th July

12.30	Quietness broken by sighs from M.
–43	Oh. Oh, what is it? cries M.
–44	Fiendish. OOOh, cries M.
–48	The bell was rung. Nurse returns with hot water.
–57	M cries Oh and sighs. Oh.
1–10	Bell & Brown had gone into the Study & I leave.[34]

Two days later, Marie dictated to Humphrey her account of how she had delivered her stillborn child. She wanted to be delivered first kneeling, then on her back. The doctors would not listen to her. "Every time I endeavoured to get into such a position I was hauled round, my hands and wrists and finally my legs were held, till I felt like a trapped and frenzied creature wantonly tortured. In the position to which I was hauled, my unusually well-developed muscles were unable to work. Also, as they allowed me no support, not even the bars at the top and foot of the bed, there was nothing to lever against ... There was nothing in the way of the "harness" which even intelligent savages give a parturient woman ... I was now frenzied and becoming incoherent with their folly in not allowing me to deliver myself in the position which suited my child and my muscles ..."

Dr E. B. Brown's version was different. On 21 July he wrote to Dr Routh: "... the delivery was quite natural, no forceps being used, the child lying in the L.O.A. position, at 10 pm there were no foetal heart sounds. She delivered herself of a male still born child at about 12.15, the liquor was mixed with mecomium and the placenta, which took a long time to deliver itself was very large and almost typically white and greasy ..."

To doctors, of course, the implication was syphilis – a suggestion immediately communicated to both Humphrey and Marie. Humphrey rushed the dead baby up to the London Hospital for a pathological report. There was no trace of syphilis – and meanwhile Dr Brown had destroyed the placenta. Grief-stricken and enraged at the suggestion of VD, Marie threatened to sue the doctors, and was in turn threatened with a libel action by the London & Counties Medical Protection Society. Humphrey had a photograph taken of the dead child. On the back of one of the copies was the inscription: "Henry Verdon, 12.15 a.m. 17 July, 1919, died just before birth, photograph taken 12 noon same day ... would have been born alive but for the interference of the doctor." Marie always remained convinced that the doctors had "murdered" her child.

By September, both she and Humphrey were in separate nursing homes in Mandeville Place, London – Marie for an operation to correct an inadequately sewn-up birth injury, and Humphrey with some unspecified complaint, about which Marie wrote to him: "You and the doctor must settle it. I had nothing to do with the *nature* of your illness tho' I know the results of neglecting it. M." After all their hopes, it had been an embittering year. On 31 December Marie wrote to Humphrey from St Ann's Hotel, Buxton: "Tender love on this last day of this cruel year, from your still Unknown wife, Love, sweetheart, friend, playmate, partner and Woodnymph." They were both weary, and tragically disappointed. "Dear Dr Stopes," wrote the doctor she had consulted in Buxton, "You must really try to take matters more easily ... Can you tell me if there is any change in the disappointing nature of the orgasm as yet? I had hoped that was simply a passing phase due to all the nervous worry you had so recently passed through. Have you considered about the advisability of conception again?"[35]

It was not Marie's first concern. There was, she replied to the message of sympathy from members of the Birth Rate Commission, "more than a personal grief in the destruction of our splendidly strong and beautiful boy, and his mother's crucifixion by the presumptuous ignorance of a series of persons. Through these agonies came gradually the realisation that I was thus learning facts of general significance to my countrywomen ..."[36] A little harder, more suspicious, more vengeful, St Joan was ready to fight again.

CHAPTER 10

Bell, Book and Candle

"The childless old Bishop of Gloucester,
A family wishing to foucester,
Was very much vexed
To find himself undersexed
When his fancy girl said, 'You Impoucester'."
H. V. Roe, unpublished limerick, following
the *Times* correspondence on birth control, 1925[1]

"Most of the people belonged to various chapels, but
many had Roman Catholic friends who used to bring
them the small thin candles meant for lighting to the
Virgin and they would push these up through to the
cervix. The candles were blunt instruments and not all
that dangerous but the women would bleed so badly that
I used to have to clear out the uterus."
Dr Evelyne Fisher, on her work in a Welsh
colliery practice in the 1920s[2]

BY 1920 Marie Stopes was well on the way to becoming a national
figure. "Humphies, I could be a *Society Lion*, if I chose to chuck my
coal-work and roar," she wrote to her husband, with a tale of the
London club where *Married Love* was so much in demand that
members were allowed to read it for only an hour at a time.[3] In
fact, without giving up coal research, she managed to roar loudly
enough to evoke violent responses from every stratum of society. Her
achievments, today taken for granted, can only be understood
against the background of opposition from the various churches,
from all political parties, from women themselves and the public at
large. Her vast correspondence at the time reveals both the extent

of human sexual misery and the prejudice against any attempt to ameliorate it.

Protestants

The official Anglican attitude, followed by most of the non-established churches, had as its basis St Paul's doctrine that, failing celibacy – the highest ideal, as practised by himself – man was permitted to contain his fleshly desires within matrimony.* The doctrine had been reinforced by Puritanism which, with its rejection of pleasure, saw children as the only justification for sexual satisfaction (and also as the basis for economic advancement). In 1917 the Bishop of Southwark, Hubert Burge, was on record with the belief that "The only thing that justifies ultimately the intercourse between the man and the woman is the purpose and the desire to have children . . . I disapprove entirely of intercourse if there is any other motive." A few eminent divines were not quite so obscurantist. Dean W. R. Inge,† one of the earliest members of the Eugenics Society, took the trouble to look up *Who's Who*. He found that of the forty diocesan bishops, one had five children, two others four each, and the remaining thirty-seven had a mere twenty-eight children among them.[4] Like many "radicals" of the period, his support for the limitation of population was based on concern for the middle classes, groaning under the burden of the constantly breeding, genetically inferior lower classes. Artificial contraceptives were, he thought, "a *pis aller* which high-minded married persons should avoid if they can practise self-restraint . . . but this is emphatically a matter in which every man and woman must judge for themselves and must refrain from judging others."[5]

Such restraint in condemning others was rare; and in July 1920 the Lambeth Conference of Anglican bishops passed a resolution calling on all high-principled men and women to bring pressure to bear on national and local government to remove "such incentives to vice as indecent literature, suggestive plays and films, the open or secret sale of contraceptives, and the continued existence of brothels".[6]

At more humbly pastoral levels, however, the Anglican church

---

* "I would that all men were even as myself . . . But if they cannot contain, let them marry: for it is better to marry than to burn." (Paul, I Corinthians, 7:7–9.

† Dean of St Paul's 1911–1934.

was ready to welcome *Married Love*. In May 1919 an Essex vicar wrote to Marie Stopes about his frigid wife: "She is slow to rouse, once or twice a year, possibly four times, I find heaven in *her* unspeakably sweet joy. *Can it be oftener? Can it be fairly regular?* I am afraid too often I bore her and that ends by boring me inexpressibly. Single lust is a feeble squib. I want fireworks!" Despite her threat to charge two pounds for consultation by letter, pleas from the ignorant guilt-ridden and disaffected clergy and their wives continued to pour in:

27 May 1919   Mrs Doris Boden, Mirfield Vicarage, Yorks, horrified by sex:
"Dear Dr Stopes ... I have only a very few times looked at that part with the aid of a mirror – and then only for a minute. I cannot describe the horror and dread I have of putting a finger in anywhere there ... I shall *never* forget the terrible torture when the doctor examined me before Baby came ..."

14 June 1919   Rev. C. S. Carey, St John's Vicarage, Gosport; wanting to know whether orgasms were bad for his wife:
"... p.s. I have noticed that if in 'love making' I have touched my wife near the entrance she is much more 'lively' and satisfaction comes much more readily. I always feel it is wrong to do this but having done it once or twice I have noticed the difference. I feel dreadful having written so frankly."

20 August 1920   Rev. E. Lyttelton, D.D., Overstrand, Cromer:
"You emphasise ... the importance of conjugal intercourse being a joint act, i.e. the gratification of the discharge should not be confined to the male, but should be shared by the female ... But the difficulty must often be that the discharges do not coincide in time. If that of the woman is late, it is difficult to see what ought to be done, as to prolong coition would be for the man a serious strain ..."

(Undated) Mrs M. E. Hemingway, Liverpool:
"Dear Dr Stopes ... I am a married woman, the wife of a *very* poor curate and have had three children in less than three years which we can ill afford to keep. I now find myself 8 days overdue and am terrified that I am again in that way ... I have done all I can in the way of hot hip baths but so far without any effect ..."

Marie marked this last letter "No Answer", obviously suspecting a plot to trap her into giving abortion advice. She was more on home ground – her reputation still being based on *Married Love* rather than birth control – with the Newark vicar, who wrote in November 1920 about premature ejaculation – one of the saddest letters from her Anglican correspondents:

> Dear Madam ... the third point is how best to arouse. I have had no instruction in what you call the Art of Love ... This Art of Love is so often referred to, p. 42 "romantic advances", p. 50 "charming love play", p. 82 "ardently to woo her" ... these and other passages seem beyond me. They raise pictures I long for, but do not know how to attain to. After the poetry of your book what actually has happened? We got to rest, my Wife always lies with her back towards me, I make a "tender advance" and suggest that she turn round so that we may chat and cuddle – the end of the poetry is "I do not like your breath in my face!!!" ... I fear that my loved one has not known rapture. I know nothing of the transports (p. 54) which prostitutes simulate ...[7]

Worse was to come. Intrigued by the unsolicited problems of the Anglican clergy, Marie sent out a questionnaire asking for information not just about the number of children, but about any contraceptive methods they had used. The response would have surprised the (mostly) celibate bishops, extolling at the Lambeth Conference the joys of self-denial. There were, of course, complaints. Several questionnaires were returned with comments such as: "What an abominably impudent question! M.A." or "As a Christian woman I would scorn such things" (from the wife of a vicar). The Rev. E. C. Aspinall, of Norwich, married for nineteen years, with nine children, scrawled across his form, without filling it in: "Thou shalt do no murder. If God sends the babies, he sends their breeches." But on the whole, recipients were only too eager to talk about their sexual problems. Disgust with sex, largely caused by the church's attitude, was a major obstacle. One vicar's wife was unable to complete the section on children since, after eleven years, there had been no consummation of the marriage: "... My husband, affectionate and quickly moved, had so severe a training in chastity as to amount to inhibition – The doctor who knows me best is distressed at the state of affairs, but though I envy women to whom the night brings more than rest, I have much for which to be proud and thankful – But there are times when the false position of my husband's ignorance of the nature of my suffering is very trying . . ."

The extent of ignorance bore out all Marie's book-learning. Some men had never even heard of the sheath, still less the cap and quinine pessary, and the commonest form of contraception appears to have been abstinence, sometimes for a period of eleven, twelve or even fifteen years. One method perhaps not envisaged by Marie – though in her list of contraceptive measures, she gave space under "g) other means" – was painstakingly answered by a Yorkshire clergyman. "Yes – occasionally," he answered; "rubbing 'stuff' out of erect penis by hand – self – wife – and a middle-aged widowed cook in absence of wife."

The method would scarcely have been approved by the Anglican church, which equated the "sin of Onan" with both masturbation and coitus interruptus.* A diary sent to Marie Stopes, from a "married clergyman who has a travelling appointment" showed even more clearly what "perversions", in Marie's eyes, the church had accomplished, and how far practice was from the edicts of the bishops:

Nov.	21	away	abuse
	26	home	abuse
Dec.	2	away	abuse
	12	home	abuse
	24	home	abuse
	30	(M: member withdrawn just before ejection [*sic*] – gave wife "manual" climax)	
Jan.	5	M: sheath used – no "feeling" for wife, though tried with hand	
	9	away	abuse
	25	home	abuse . . .
	30	M: (wife "had it" I did not except as a nocturnal omission [*sic*] afterwards in sleep)	

* Onan, in the Old Testament, brought the wrath of God upon him by "spilling his seed upon the ground" during coition with his dead brother's wife, thus avoiding his duty to raise children to his brother.

The world of "omissions" and "ejections", of wives who, with seven children, had never experienced an orgasm, of men terrified to touch their wife's breast in case it caused cancer, was now part of Marie's life; but it was unlikely to impress the bishops. They would have to be talked to at their own level. Marie, with her Calvinistic upbringing, and her Quaker access to God through the direct line of inner conscience, was amply equipped to direct their deliberations. In June 1920, she recorded later, she became aware of the forthcoming Lambeth Conference of Anglican Bishops.* While she was sitting under a yew tree, she wrote, God had spoken to her and had given her a message to pass on to the bishops. She duly addressed them, if only in print: "My Lords, I speak to you in the name of God. You are his Priests. I am His Prophet. I speak to you of the mysteries of man and woman." Her message, *A New Gospel*, was circularised in early July to the 267 bishops attending the conference.

What did it matter that Paul had not spoken of birth control? "Paul spoke with Christ nineteen hundred years ago. God spoke with me today," she argued, going on to a discussion of the necessary interchange of vaginal and seminal fluids:

> No act of union fulfils the Law of God unless the two not only pulse together to the highest climax but also remain there in a long brooding embrace without severance from each other . . . Ignorance of this truth has led the multitudes into a befouling and debasing view of the union in which the man is encouraged, even by Ministers of the Church, to look upon his own part in this holiest of sacraments as a mere gratification of his own lust instead of a mutual enrichment for God's service.[8]

God through science, she argued, had revealed the archaic nature of the sexual act, in its wastage of millions of sperms (i.e. the vestigial remnants of the evolutionary process) while at the same time endowing mankind with a unique potentiality for good within the sexual act "so far above our fellows the other animals as to be but a little lower than the angels". This potentiality, enhanced by scientific contraception, Marie saw almost as the equivalent of the Holy Ghost in its relation

---

* She may have been influenced by the fact that Dr C. Killick Millard, M.O.H. of Leicester, and a prominent birth control worker, had already sent a memorandum to the bishops (3 May 1920, Millard to Stopes. BL-S.)

to the other two members of the Trinity – man and woman. In her enthusiasm to communicate the revelation, her language attained biblical fervour:

> Harden not your heart, O leaders of the Christian Churches. Desire no longer to maintain in bondage the rich new spirit of life springing upwards ever higher and higher in the service of God. Rise to meet the new revelation. Perceive and bow the knee to the mystery of the sanctity of marriage, the complex powers of good in the truly welded pair, the holiness and divine beauty of the union of loving and lifelong mates. Perceive that in our midst the highest expression of human life is the pair united in profound and complex union, who use the means which God now sends through Science to raise the race. Thee shall lead the peoples of all the world to a higher potentiality for His service than ever has been known.[9]

What the Anglican Bishops of Bethlehem, Calcutta, Tokyo and Zululand made of this extraordinary work, in relation to their own flocks, has not been recorded. But the Anglican Church as a whole was not slow to respond. Resolution 70 of the Lambeth Conference expressed firm opposition, though it did not mention Marie Stopes by name, to the "teaching, which, under the name of science and religion encourages married people in the deliberate cultivation of sexual union as an end in itself".

A New Gospel was damaging to Marie's reputation at many different levels. "You will hardly disagree," wrote Dr Killick Millard, "if I say that it is very didactic and no people – least of all those in exalted positions – like to be told that they *ought* to take such and such a view."[10] Her editor, C. Huntington of Putnam's, the publishers, found the whole concept of prophecy "out of date", while *The Star* regretted that Dr Stopes had fallen prey to one of the pitfalls of genius "which we may charitably describe as megalomania ... many (of her supporters) must strongly object to its manner and form. They cannot believe that the Deity makes special revelation to Dr Stopes, and it can only injure her propaganda that these methods should be employed in it."[11] It was from the Catholics, however, that the strongest objections came.

The Catholic Church

The church's thinking in 1920 was based on Augustine and Aquinas. Augustine held that original sin was transmitted through the sexual act. The sin was rendered venial only by marriage, the primary purpose of which was the procreation of children to replace the fallen angels. All forms of contraception – other than chastity by mutual consent, leading to the spiritual contemplation of God – were condemned. Aquinas was not quite so sweeping. Pleasure in the sexual act was not automatically sinful, provided its purpose was the procreation of children. Later, Aquinas's doctrine of "Natural Law" was used to justify the "safe period" and to condemn any "unnatural", i.e. mechanical, contraceptive methods.

By the early twentieth century, however, the gradual spread of education had resulted in a population much less amenable to priestly discipline. A declining birth rate – particularly in France, where "artificial" contraceptives had been in use for well over a century – in conjunction with the birth control movement generally, drove the church into reactionary and sometimes ridiculous positions. In 1917, the report of the National Birth Rate Commission under the chairmanship of Dean Inge, recorded the evidence of Monsignor Canon Brown, later Bishop of Pella. Driven into a corner about the prevention of conception when a parent was syphilitic – at the time, children of syphilitics would almost certainly have been born with permanent mental and physical damage – he argued that it would be *less* wrong for syphilitics to have children than to use contraceptives, since they did not *intend* to pass on syphilis.[12] The church's general attitude to contraception was best summed up by P. J. Hayes, Roman Catholic Archbishop of New York, who in his Christmas pastoral for 1921 saw it as worse than abortion:

> Even though some little angels in the flesh through the moral, mental or physical deformity of parents, may appear to human eyes hideous, misshapen, a blot on civilised society, we must not lose sight of this Christian thought that under and within such visible malformation there lives an immortal soul to be saved and glorified for all eternity ... To take life after its inception is a *horrible* crime; but to prevent human life that the Creator is about to bring into being is *Satanic*.[13]

Marie's first brush with Catholic dogma was relatively mild. In December, 1917, after both Dean Inge and the Bishop of Birmingham had declined to write a foreword to *Married Love*, she sent the manuscript to Father Stanislaus St John, SJ. He replied with a glowing appreciation of the book, though, naturally, taking exception to the chapter on birth control. His attitude to Marie's example of the worn-out mother of twelve sickly, half-starved children was that "the loss of health on her part for a few years of life and the diminished vitality on the part of her later children would be a very small price indeed to pay for an endless happiness on the part of all". Rather unwisely, Father St John gave permission for his letter to be used in *Married Love*. It appeared at the beginning of the first edition in 1918 – almost as an imprimatur – with Marie's reply (about which she did not inform him). Despite his protests – he was in immediate trouble with his superiors – she went on using it for several editions.

Other Jesuits were not so tolerant. On 7 October 1919, Father F. M. de Zulueta wrote to her:

> Madam . . . I consider it most useful to pray God that your writings may not do as much injury to morals – to the souls of the ignorant poor especially – which they are calculated to do . . . indeed I find no sure evidence in your books that you hold any *definite* Christian doctrines at all. It appears to me that a pagan might have written as you do – though he would probably not have quoted the Word of God in the sense which you – to any sincere Christian shockingly – quote "He giveth unto His beloved sleep" [Married Love] . . . I had hopes no woman would write such books.*

A week later, on October 15, he wrote again, enclosing a doctor's opinion about her recommendation of the cervical cap, which could lead, he said, to neurasthenia, neuralgia, menorrhagia, and dysmenorrhea, "and I have heard that women of this kind become prurient and foul-mouthed and foul-minded with advancing years". His most violent objections, however, were to Marie's *New Gospel*:

> Madam . . . I regard it as a most profane compound of imaginary mysticism and pornography. It may perhaps serve the purpose of

---

* Marie scribbled on this letter "replied . . . much desire to know how R.C. Church reconciles the castration of boys with Christ. principle?" and added that she was a Christian, a Quaker. (BL-S.)

that type of young medical student who needs a veneer of religiosity to dignify his sexual pruriency, but could only revolt anyone with a real sense of religion ... I know from some experience of life that when a woman gets to the point of saying "I spoke to Christ yesterday" but has no idea of submitting her imagined inspiration to the judgment of any recognised spiritual authority, it is waste of time to reason.

There was sufficient truth in this to sting Marie to an equally violent reply, bringing up the usual anti-Catholic arguments about castration and Inquisitorial tortures. Three days later, he withdrew from the correspondence, in a manner calculated to cause the deepest offence to a prophet of God:

> ... It only remains for me to offer my poor prayers to God that He may enlighten your ignorance of His Law, remedy your self-complacency and prevent your doing the amount of harm to others – in body and in soul – which your expedients are calculated to produce. I remain, Madam, Yours obediently, F. M. de Zulueta.[14]

Marie was by now far away from her earlier admiration of the Catholic church.* "I wonder if you have noticed," she wrote to Huntington at Putnam's, in June 1919, "that the Roman Catholics are now openly going for me? – Rather awkward for them to say, as they do, that my book incites to mortal sin, when for the first five editions I had that Preface by Father St. John! But still they rely so much on the ignorance of their flock. I shall be having a magnificent fight with them shortly." The fight did not materialise until three years later; and in 1919, Marie could be forgiven for her nonchalant under-estimation of the adversary she was determined to take on.

Medicine

Unlike priests and ministers, medical practitioners could not retire to the safety of accepted dogma. There was no dogma. Sexual physiology and birth control were not taught at medical schools except, of course, for practical obstetrics. Indeed, there was little to teach. The study of

* "The Roman Church knows how to attract the people," she wrote to her sister from Munich in 1904. "I have often been in churches, early in the morning even, where every inch of standing room is taken – and the congregation very largely of men. Where in a Protestant church would you see that?" – Marie to Winnie Stopes, 23 March 1904. BL-S.

hormones was in its infancy, and most of the medical profession believed, like Marie Stopes, that the "safe period" occurred in the middle of the menstrual month. There had been no full-scale studies of either the efficacy or the possible dangers of contraceptive appliances. The individual doctor was free to give information if he had it, or to withhold it, depending on his religious, political or social prejudices. Since there was no state medicine, a doctor's income was to some extent dependent on the repeated parturitions of his women patients, a factor Marie Stopes was quick to recognise.*

Understandably, medical opinion was spread over a much wider field than the churches'. Supporting Marie Stopes at one level was Dr C. Killick Millard, Medical Officer of Health for Leicester, and a member of the Birth Rate Commission. Eschewing divine inspiration, he had the temerity to assert in 1917, in the middle of war, that opposition to the declining birth rate was based on militaristic considerations.[15] "Is it not probable," he asked, quoting Julius Caesar on the causes of war,† "that if the decrease in the birth rate had set in in Germany 25 years earlier, the deadly doctrine of pan-Germanism would have been sapped at its roots?" Worse than this, Millard argued, was the discrepancy between the classes. In Hampstead, predominantly middle-class, the birth rate had declined from 30 per thousand in 1881 to 14·8 in 1914: in Shoreditch, a working-class area, it remained constant at 31 per thousand. "It does seem to me something approaching hypocrisy for the educated classes ... to be quietly and privately availing themselves of the knowledge and means which science has placed at the disposal of mankind, in order to escape from what they regard – and with good reason – as the evil of over-childbearing, and yet to join in a conspiracy of silence to keep this same knowledge from reaching the poor who need it so much more."

On a less sociological level, Dr George Jones, of the West End Hospital for Women, was much more liberal than Marie, putting into

---

* "... That there may be medical men who do not approve of birth control is natural, when one remembers that a doctor has to make a living, and can do so more easily when women are ailing with incessant pregnancies than when they maintain themselves in good health by only having children when fitted to do so. Opinions of medicals, therefore, must be sifted. The best doctors are with us; the self-seeking and the biassed may be against us." – Marie Stopes, letter to *Sussex Daily News*, 17 Nov. 1921.

† Julius Caesar: "propter hominum multitudinem agrique inopiam" ("because of hordes of men and need of land"). There is no need to point out the connection between Millard's argument and Hitler's actions twenty years later.

words what she dare not even think. Marie was always careful to stress that her message was addressed only to the married. She expressed horror at the idea that her books might be read by the unmarried, thus encouraging "immorality" – an attitude which, when *Wise Parenthood* was published in 1919, brought a well-justified rebuke from Dr Jones. Surely, he argued, since the illegitimate child had a much worse chance in life than the legitimate, "the prevention of conception is just as important for a lascivious housemaid or milliner of 18 as for a married woman of 35 with 9 sickly children". The publication of *A New Gospel* brought a further salvo from Dr Jones:

> Dear Dr Stopes . . . The proper way to regard the relation of the sexes seems to me to be non-religious or non-moral . . . Two people meet and like each other and their liking matures with mutual desire for sexual relations . . . To say they propose to administer the matter of a sacrament to each other is sheer nonsense . . . To say it is moral or immoral is no better. If they keep at arms length they injure no one except perhaps themselves. If they go the whole length again they injure no one. There is no more immorality in the enjoyment of sexual intercourse than in the enjoyment of mince pies . . .[16]

Such a free-thinking attitude was as foreign to most doctors, however, as it was to Marie Stopes. Much more typical were the opinions of Dr Amand Routh, MD, FRCP, consulting obstetric physician at the Charing Cross Hospital. Marie's own physician during her first pregnancy, he addressed the Church Congress in October 1919. While admitting that twenty per cent of uterine and neo-natal deaths were caused by syphilis, he deplored the use of prophylactics because they weakened "moral resistance". As for the books then available on contraception, "whilst they state there is not yet an ideal method, they do not state what I believe to be the truth, that all such artificial methods are harmful . . . nervous exhaustion, inability to mentally concentrate . . . Women may develop pelvic troubles when pregnancy is desired later on."[17]

As usual, Marie decided to do her own research. She sent out a questionnaire to doctors. From the 129 replies, it seemed that doctors had as many problems as the Anglican clergy though at least the medical profession had access to instrumental correction if all else failed. Again, abstinence was common, along with coitus interruptus and douching:*

> Wife used a douche but conceived shortly after marriage. After birth of child coitus interruptus for about two years. She however hated sexual intercourse from the beginning and after two or three years of struggling and utter misery all relations ceased. Later I became intimate with a professional woman. Was happy with her for about ten years. She used a douche for first 6 or 7 years – then douche and rubber cap. Twice in this period she went a week or fortnight over her periods and an instrument was used, but it is not clear that this was really necessary . . .

Another doctor confessed that his wife had had five abortions, and an MRCS tersely summed up his married life: "First wife was victim of puerperal insanity after birth of son: became permanently insane later and died in asylum. Second wife delicate, no relations of a sexual character ever took place as there existed no object as past childbearing age." Not all doctors were so forthcoming. A Dr Bradley replied:

> Madam, My first thought on receiving your circular letter re Married Love and the use of preventatives was to put it in the waste paper basket – I have decided to send it on to our MP and to ask him if he gets a chance to get to legislation to prevent the country being flooded with this rubbish . . .

and a Stockport consultant had no hesitation in revealing his religious allegiances:

> Mr Brennan, MRCS, is acquainted with the writings of Dr Marie Stopes and her methods which he regards as more in the interests of pornography than of science.
>
> He agrees with Mr Hilaire Belloc that "the Catholic Church is an expert in man's nature and man's needs", that She has the wisdom of 18 centuries with her and the direct guidance of the Holy Ghost.
>
> When Dr Marie Stopes has these two qualifications Mr Brennan will be pleased to communicate with her again and to reveal to her the intimacies of his sex life.[18]

---

* According to the 1911 Census, doctors produced the smallest families of any occupational group – while themselves often refusing to give contraceptive advice to their patients.

Marie, it appeared, would have to wait considerably more than two hundred years for canonisation.

The Public

> "It is a remarkable fact that, while one may say . . . whatever one likes about religion and politics, while one may publicly preach atheism and communism, one may not make public mention, except in a scientific work, of the most rudimentary physiological facts. In most modern countries the only state-supported orthodoxy is a sexual orthodoxy."   Aldous Huxley, *Proper Studies*, 1927.

Starting at the top, Marie sent a copy of *Married Love* to Queen Mary (mother of seven). Her covering letter asked for a word of regal encouragement for "one who hopes in her life time thro' knowledge to *stamp beauty* on the deepest facts of life, that the human race may be transformed and glorified".* Queen Mary did not reply. Undaunted, Marie tried Queen Alexandra (five children) who, after nearly fifty years of marriage to Edward VII and a further ten years of widowhood was perhaps not the most obvious recipient for birth control literature. "Madam," Marie wrote, "May I humbly beg you as the gracious Queen Mother to read the enclosed pages about help my husband and I are trying to bring to the desperately poor and ignorant mothers of your Majesty's realm . . . we are not asking for a penny from anyone. This, the *most* urgent and most fundamental of all help for our race we gladly give ourselves." On February 23, 1921, Colonel Henry Streatfeild, private secretary, replied from Marlborough House:

> Madam, I regret that it is not possible for Queen Alexandra to give you an expression of her opinion upon the subject alluded to in the pamphlet, or to grant her personal support to Dr Stopes' scheme, as it is Her Majesty's invariable rule never to allow her name to be associated with any movements which might prove of a controversial nature.†

---

* Marie signed the letter "Your humble and devoted subject", then crossed out "humble" and substituted "loyal". (Rough draft, 21 March 1920. BL-S.)

† The only member of the royal family to support birth control – though not until after his abdication – was the Duke of Windsor, formerly Edward VIII. He sent several cheques – for £10, £20 and £30 – to help finance the Marie Stopes clinics.

Nor were politicians – partcularly once in power – any more helpful. Support for a controversial issue like birth control could easily lose votes. In 1921 David Lloyd George, Prime Minister of the post-war coalition government, refused to lend his name to the movement, though he was personally sympathetic to it.* Before the general election in 1922, Marie sent out another questionnaire – this time to prospective candidates. She asked them to sign a declaration:

I agree that the present position of breeding chiefly from the C3 population and burdening and discouraging the A1 is nationally deplorable, and if I am elected to Parliament I will press the Ministry of Health to give such scientific information through the Antenatal Clinics, Welfare Centres and other institutions in its control as will curtail the C3 and increase the A1.

There were 23 replies from Conservatives, 91 from Labour, 37 from Liberals. Even those who signed the declaration, however, appeared to have only a hazy idea of what was involved. The Conservative candidate for Ealing added the puzzled footnote: "N.B. At the same time I am at a loss to understand how the Ministry of Health is going to regulate this matter – and would *certainly never* lend my name to the use of preventives." Labour candidates tended more to the feeling that birth control was irrelevant, or perhaps, even a threat, to the large-scale economic and social reconstruction that now, for the first time, seemed within their grasp.† Robert Williams, Labour candidate for Coventry, wrote back:

---

* In 1914, Frances Stevenson, secretary, mistress and later wife of Lloyd George, recorded that she and the then Chancellor of the Exchequer were "both of the opinion that these ill-conditioned women should not be able to get married and have children, whereas girls who would make splendid mothers don't get a chance of having children". She quoted the case of a school for mental defectives. "One woman used to bring up an idiot child regularly once a year, until the head mistress got tired of it, and said to her "You are a wicked woman to have so many children!" "Lor, Mum, don't be so 'ard on us! It's the only pleasure we gets in life!" – *Lloyd George: a Diary* by Frances Stevenson. Hutchinson, 1971, p. 18.

† Sidney Webb, in 1907, saw the answer to the declining birth rate (deplored by all political parties) and the growing disproportion between the middle-class and working-class birth rates, not in birth control but in family allowances, free meals, school milk and more educational scholarships. "Once the production of healthy, moral and intelligent citizens is revered as a social service and made the subject of deliberate praise and encouragement ... it will attract the best and most patriotic of the citizens." (Sidney Webb, *The Decline in the Birth Rate*, Fabian Tract, No. 131, 1907.) In so far as anything definite can be said about population, it appears that increased affluence, educational opportunities and social welfare lead to a *reduction* in the birth rate, not, as Webb hoped, an increase.

Dear Mrs Stopes ... I am not sure that I am entirely at one with you, as I think that the improvement of the conditions of the people through the economic changes proposed by the Labour Party will be more effective in securing a better race than the selective breeding which seems to be implied in your declaration.

The Liberals, their power very much on the wane, could afford to be less serious. Alexander Lyle-Samuel, candidate for the Eye division of Suffolk, responded:

Dear Dr Stopes, I think your question to Parliamentary Candidates is very funny and trust you do not take this matter too seriously ... We are all, I take it, opposed to "breeding chiefly from the C3 population". If we assume that we are A1 ourselves, and it is without prejudice to our own individual rights, I think that the idea you have that things will be better if they were better is one to which each one of us can subscribe, but how any Institution is going to tell millions of people that they must not breed, or how you are going to get physical and mental deficients, who sometimes are returned to Parliament, to vote for the extinction of their rights, and to reflect on their parents by passing an Act of Parliament, I do not know."[19]

Marie did not succeed in her attempt to make an election issue out of birth control; but the population as a whole was not so dismissive as the politicians. The war had profoundly shaken accepted attitudes. Britain had lost three-quarters of a million men. Of her armies, another $1\frac{1}{2}$ million were permanently damaged by wounds or gas, and one in five was affected by VD.[20] Socially, Britain scarcely lived up to Lloyd George's promise of "a fit country for heroes to live in". Those that remained came back to continued rationing, unemployment – over 2 million by June 1921 – an acute housing shortage (no houses had been built during the war) rising prices, and a pound that was worth a third of its value in 1914. At another level, the imminence of death over the last four years had to some extent broken down sexual prudery. "Leave ladies", as they were politely called, openly advertised their comforts in the personal columns of respectable daily newspapers. Soldiers were issued with condoms – as an anti-VD, not a birth control, measure ; and Miss Ettie Rout, secretary of the New Zealand Volunteer Sisters, issued her jolly directive to the army:

... If you have spent a whole night with a woman who may be infected, of course it will not be so easy and simple to apply disinfection successfully as it would be if you merely had contact with the woman behind a fence for a moment or two. If you leave a gun out in the mist for a few minutes, it is easy to clean, if you leave it out all night, it is difficult to clean ...

It is impossible to imagine Florence Nightingale issuing such advice at Sebastopol. People were now much readier to talk about their problems and also to see them not as inevitable, God-given disasters, but as the product of social conditions and religious and medical obscurantism. A. C. Fifield, Marie's publisher, complained in April 1919 about "the never-ending and unprofitable correspondence with the angry, stupid and dirty-minded people who have been attracted in shoals to *Wise Parenthood*". Fifield gave up, and the letters came to Marie. Typical of one strand of the middle classes – at the time making up most of Marie's audience, since few members of the working classes could afford, or would have heard of, her books – was the letter from a journalist whose wife had just died in childbirth, after being warned not to have any more children: "In my own case the doctor who told me my wife must not have another child fobbed me off with a jest when I asked him to tell me how to obey his mandate; and ironically enough she had been dead a fortnight when your little book *Wise Parenthood* was brought to my notice ..."[21]

Another came from an ex-nurse in Manchester, aged thirty-seven:

Dear Madam ... I wish to know the ethics of birth control and my reasons are good ones – two husbands, four children. My husband is middle-aged (by the way, out of work two months now). Who is going to bring those children up. I am in very bad health. Debility. Tubercular. Pulmonary and heart trouble ... It takes me all I know to do the ordinary housework of a small house and to keep the little ones clean. The boy and girl have had phthisis and it has taken me five years of great care and nursing to get them right ... Now baby is under suspicion. Now I ask you for advice and I am sure I don't know anyone who needs it as much as I do ... I am so afraid of conception that I cannot bear for my husband to even speak kindly to me or even put his hand on my shoulder for fear he wants his rights and it causes a lot of anger and misery. It is two months since I last allowed him intercourse.[22]

Much more typical, however, were the letters from the upper end of the middle classes. Their arguments against birth control were based on Empire, militarism and – perhaps unconsciously – resentment at the lower classes daring to aspire to the perquisites of their superiors. Such attitudes were neatly summed up in a 1920 newspaper letter, headed "The Decline and Fall of England":

Sir ... The late war has either destroyed, or removed from the effective list, a very large number of our best men. In natural course these would be replaced within two decades or little more. But an insidious propaganda now proceeds for limiting families, and thus interfering with nature's reparation for our terrible war losses ... What is remarkable about the new propaganda for destruction of primary life, is its advance on methods advocated 40 years ago by the Bradlaugh, Besant School ... leading booksellers offer, in ordinary course, books with diagrams, showing methods unheard of by even the most extreme of the old teachers of life limitation. The movement is insidious, though girls and young men may often be seen in public eagerly perusing the books which make for the decline and fall of the British Empire ... This has a force now it never had before in English history, with impaired lives everywhere, and Labour organised not for a higher standard of life, but means to obtain luxuries, formerly impossible to any but a very limited class ...[23]

Lower down the same stratum were the *arrivistes*, anxious to prove middle-class membership by stressing their respectability. "Madam," wrote Sidney John Clift, a Shelley enthusiast, from Fulham in 1919:

Is it a desire to put bank notes into your pocket that you wrote such stuff as *Married Love*? ... Do you really think that my wife and I and our poverty-stricken friends (though none of us can afford to have more than two or three children) are sadly in need of such dirty advice as you offer? ... You deliberately misrepresent Malthus, who advocated moral restraint ... Alas, is there not proof everywhere in this ghastly modern world that a large house, a large income and the superior education beloved of H. G. Wells have

little to do with the creation of a genuine artistic let alone moral
sense ... And really some of the things you propose in your book
might have emanated from the brain of a Kaffir woman. Sidney
John Clift (a lover of Shelley).[24]

Marie's own middle-class background was only too evident in her
de-haut-en-bas attitude to the working classes. In 1919, her article
"Mrs Jones Does Her Worst" was rejected by the *Daily Mirror*, as
too strong. It appeared in the *Daily Mail*. Marie invited the reader
to go down "the mean streets" of any city: "Are these puny-faced,
gaunt, blotchy, ill-balanced, feeble, ungainly, withered children the
young of an Imperial race?" Why, she asked, has Mrs Jones had nine
children, six of them dead, and one defective? "Nor is it for Mrs Jones
to take the initiative. Isn't it for the leisured, the wise, to go to her and
tell her what are the facts of life, the meaning of what she is doing and
what she ought to do? ... The serious truth is that not many of the
leisured and the learned have bothered to think out the meaning of
what she is doing. If they realised it, surely an outcry of dismay would
be raised; *for Mrs Jones is destroying the race!*"[25]

Marie's class bias did not go unnoticed. *Radiant Motherhood*, her
third book on marriage and sex published in 1920, was well-received.
Concentrating as it did on pre-natal influences, diet, and how to choose
a nursery maid, it was, said the Medical Press, "unblemished by those
defects of taste and good breeding which made its predecessor, *Married
Love*, such unpleasant reading".[26] It was left to Mary Stocks (later
Baroness Stocks) to point out that "according to the régime set forth
in her latest book, motherhood is going to require a family income of
at least a thousand a year in order to attain the necessary degree of
radiance."

Such accusations were doubly galling to Marie. True, she did not
have first-hand experience of life in the slums, but her knowledge and
understanding of working-class problems, she felt, had broadened
considerably. As a direct result of *Married Love*, she was asked in
1919 to join the National Birth Rate Commission. This gave her a
wide range of evidence to support her own beliefs – and further proof
of the strength of the feeling against birth control. While generally in
favour of controlling the birth rate, a majority of the commissioners –
among them her old friend, the Bishop of Birmingham, her own

gynaecologist, Dr Amand Routh, and Dr Mary Scharlieb, an un-married Catholic – signed a reservation condemning, on medical grounds, artificial contraception. Marie wrote to all eleven asking for medical evidence – which none of them supplied – and drew up a minority report dissociating herself from the reservation, along with three other commissioners, Lord and Lady Willoughby de Broke and Dr C. W. Saleeby.[27]

Marie had also, in 1919, produced a pamphlet addressed specifically to the working classes.[28] She herself published *A Letter to Working Mothers*; but how was she to persuade them to read it? Her first forays into the working-class hinterland were not encouraging. Mrs E. B. Mayne, one of Marie's admiring correspondents, was deputed to undertake the conversion of London's East End slums. "I find the women on the whole suspicious," she reported on 12 February 1920: "I judge they are a good deal bothered by Mothers' Welcome people, health visitors, Social Welfare Workers and I am regarded in most cases as yet another intruder come to tell them how to wash the 'bayby' . . . The words on the cover 'How to have healthy children' frequently raise trouble so I lay stress on 'How to avoid weakening pregnancies'." Mrs Mayne called at twenty slum dwellings that day, but only five women took the free booklet. Prejudice was reinforced by fear of husbands – one of whom, Mrs Mayne reported on February 26, became very angry and wanted to know "'ow they'd keep the nation goin' if the poor didn't 'ave children, as the rich wouldn't."

Mrs Mayne concluded – as Marie had long been thinking – that the poor just would not bother. Some form of direct action was needed. Confronted by apathy from those who ought to have access to birth control but didn't want it, by opposition from those who had it but disapproved of others having it, and by individuals who wanted it but could not get it, Marie was driven to the conclusion that she would have to set up her own birth control clinic – and to publicise it so efficiently that no one could ignore any longer the message as divinely revealed to Marie Stopes.

CHAPTER 11

Improving God's Handiwork

"Utopia could be reached in my lifetime had I the power
to issue inviolable edicts."

Marie Stopes, 1920[1]

THE heading on Marie's clinic writing paper consisted of a rather
ill-drawn lamp, emitting radiant beams against the motto: "Joyous
and Deliberate Motherhood. A Sure Light in Our Racial Darkness."
It was an apt choice. In its literal sense, birth control has always existed,
if only as abortion and infanticide. Society's justifications, too, have
remained the same – the need to manipulate its numbers, in whatever
direction ("deliberate motherhood", in Marie's terminology) and the
desire to eliminate undesirables ("racial darkness").

By the end of the nineteenth century, Utopia was further away than
ever. Civilisation had been no help. As early as 1621, Robert Burton
complained in his *Anatomy of Melancholy* of the deplorable modern
tendency to tolerate all sorts of men, and even allow them to marry,
thus creating "a vast confusion of hereditary diseases, no family
secure, no man almost free from some grievous infirmity or other . . .
our fathers bad, and we are like to be worse". Man's growing humanity
to man, far from reducing the number of defectives, had merely
preserved them to breed more. By forbidding the ruthless annihilation
practised by earlier societies, it also threatened to confirm Malthus'
gloomy prediction of a population increasingly greater than the
resources necessary to maintain it.

Birth control was the obvious answer. Malthus himself, an orthodox
clergyman writing at the end of the eighteenth century, could only
recommend abstinence as a solution, or marriage at a later age

than usual. Stimulated by his ideas, others were not so cautious. Though the dissemination of birth control knowledge, *per se*, has never been illegal in Britain, it was always possible to prosecute on indirect grounds, such as obscenity. Francis Place and Charles Bradlaugh were both prosecuted after publishing books advocating "artificial" as opposed to "natural" contraception. Bradlaugh's trial in 1877 led to the formation of the Malthusian League. "We think it more moral to prevent conception of children," ran his argument, "than, after they are born, to murder them by want of food, air and clothing."

The support for contraception was further boosted by Darwin's theories. Given "natural selection", it was surely right to help Nature by discouraging procreation of the "unfit". The Eugenics Society was formed in 1908 to give "the more suitable races or strains of blood a better chance of prevailing speedily over the less suitable", as its president, Francis Galton, put it.[2]

The aims of the two societies were different, the Malthusians concerning themselves with population and economics, the Eugenics Society more with academic work on heredity. Yet there was a considerable cross-membership between the two, their main idea in common naturally being birth control. It seems odd that no major advance was made by either society in providing practical help for the recklessly breeding defectives who were threatening their ideas, particularly since contraceptive methods had advanced so rapidly. The male sheath had been around for centuries, first in linen, then sheep's intestines. For women, there were soluble pessaries, the half-lemon, squeezed out and inserted over the cervix, as advocated by Casanova, and in 1826 Dr Waters, in *The Philosophy of the Sexes, or Every Woman's Book*, advised "as large a piece of sponge as can be pleasantly introduced. An English Duchess was lately instanced to the writer, who never goes out to dinner without being prepared with a sponge. The French and Italian women wear them fastened to their waists and always have them at hand." The discovery of rubber in the nineteenth century increased the reliability of the condom, and also facilitated the development of the Dutch cap, invented in 1881 by a German, Dr Mensinga, of Flensburg. The term "Dutch cap" is significant. Holland was for many years the only country in the world where birth control was officially approved. In 1882, the year after Mensinga's inven-

Charles
Gordon Hewitt

Reginald
Ruggles Gates

Top left: Aylmer Maude, 1922
Top right, and bottom: Marie in 1915, her romanticism undimmed
by her disastrous first marriage

tion, Dr Aletta Jacobs opened in Amsterdam the world's first birth control clinic. Within a few years Holland had thirty such clinics in operation.

Lacking governmental encouragement, the two major English societies were not very effective. Their members came largely from the medical, legal and academic professions, and were terrified of damaging their reputations. During the First World War, the Malthusian League distributed birth control leaflets at their open-air meetings, but so cautiously that anyone interested had first to post off a form swearing to being married before any information was sent. Whatever else may be said of Marie Stopes, at least she had the courage to cut through the fears and prejudices that beset everyone else in England at the time, and to do what needed to be done. Her motives were as mixed as her advantages were unique.

Marriage to Humphrey Roe in 1918 had made a considerable difference to her life. The death of their first child in 1919 had given their home at Elmer, Leatherhead, unhappy associations, so they moved to a much grander country house, Givons Grove, in the same area. The grounds, bordering on Lord Beaverbrook's estate at Cherkley, were enormous and the house itself very different from the cramped rooms in Hampstead to which she had been accustomed. There were house-warming parties (no smoking indoors) and the *Westminster Gazette* described indoor delights, should the weather fail: "... if wet, there is to be dancing indoors. The music room at Givons Grove is a spacious apartment, with a parquet floor and windows that look both South and West. Out of it opens the drawing room, where, in corner cupboards fronted with trellised gold wires, are some of the china and other treasures which Dr Stopes collected during her stay in Japan several years ago, before she married her airman husband. People with preconceived notions of scientific women always get a shock on first meeting Dr Marie Stopes, so charming is she, and always so prettily dressed."[3]

Marie was rather disturbed about the cost of Givons Grove. At the time she gave little hint of it, except to reassure her mother that despite the numerous stables, farmhouses and unused wings, it was not nearly so big as it appeared. With hindsight, ten years later, she thought differently:

When I married H.V.R., I had no male relatives at all to look after a settlement and I was very romantically in love and peculiarly sensitive about money as I knew so many marriages wrecked by it. A gossip had said I was marrying H. for money* and that made it impossible to ask for anything.

After our marriage when looking at Givons Grove I told H. I *feared* it, it was too big. I also said, "It would take a very rich man to keep it up." He said, "I am very rich" ... After he bought Givons he never gave me any money either to keep it up or run the servants or feed us or even to buy the extra furniture we needed ...

This may be retrospective bitterness. At the time Humphrey was well-off which Marie may well have resented, even though she was still employed at University College and beginning to make considerable sums of money from her books. At Givons Grove she had her own laboratory. When not teaching in London she undertook private research projects, mostly on the structure of coal, for the Department of Scientific and Industrial Research who also paid for her research assistant. Between her and Humphrey, all appeared to be well. In March 1920 Aylmer Maude, having survived his capture by the Bolsheviks, wrote to Marie after a visit to Givons: "My dearest Una ... I behaved very nicely in that I suppressed, as far as I could, all external signs of my very warm admiration for you and my appreciation of the fact that neither your tremendous success as a writer, nor your position as the wife of the owner of a stately mansion has spoilt you." Marie and Humphrey were happy together and it was generous of Maude to write in July of that year: "Dearest Una, Glad as I was to see you again ... Glad, too, as I am to know of Humphrey's devotion to you, there is something just a trifle embarrassing in the frequent osculatory interruptions of conversations or other occupations."[4]

Marie's prosperity, in relation to most of postwar Britain, was reflected in her writings. Her suggestion, in *Radiant Motherhood*, that a parturient woman should spend at least six weeks recuperating in bed after the birth would have been laughable to most women, had they read it. But, gradually, Marie was developing a more realistic approach. The extra work created by the success of her books was "so

---

* Ethel Burgess, presumably.

appealing", she wrote to her literary agent in 1920, "that I cannot resist helping ever so many more people than I have time to." The majority of the requests for help came from the middle classes, and were not even limited to sexual matters. Marie spent much of the early part of 1920 organising an unsuccessful campaign against the decision of the Rhondda Valley education authorities to sack all their married women teachers. Her activities were widely reported in the press and, as her fame spread, Marie began to receive more letters from working-class women who had often clubbed together to buy her books. Under the title *Mother England* she later brought out a selection of such letters. While not casting doubt on their provenance, however, their general tenor in print appears so uniform that I prefer to rely on the extant manuscripts not quoted in *Mother England*. One such letter came from the wife of a farm labourer in Shepperton. She was expecting a fourth child, at the age of twenty-seven, and the family were living on £1 7s a week:

> ... I have got into trouble with the school, becaus my boy did not go, as I had no boots for him to wear and could not get any. I wrote and told my Mother but she cannot help me becaus My Father has died and left her with 3 children going to school and she said she cannot own me if I keep on having children, I cannot go out to work becaus of the children, neither me nor my Husband have had bad carictors for work, the only thing is the children and the money and they do not have enough to eat and I cannot get boots for them to wear ... do you think it would be best if I leave my Husband and go into the workhouse until the children have grown up a bit so that we don't have any moor, I have gone without food to try and win money in football but everything I try fails me. If you can kindly advise me I would be very grateful.[5]

In her reply, Marie advised against football pools, sent all her pamphlets on birth control and enclosed ten shillings to buy a pair of boots for the boy. Such practical generosity, revealing a genuine sympathy with individual cases of hardship among the working classes, must be set against those of her beliefs that today show Marie in a much less favourable light. It is often assumed that because she fought so vigorously for birth control against established authority, all her ideas must be of a radical, libertarian nature. This was not the case. Indeed, anyone short of an extreme reactionary would today regard some of her ideas with horror. It is important, of course, to see her ideas in the context of current thinking; but even so, she went beyond the bounds of what was considered acceptable.

The first foundation of Utopia, Marie wrote in 1920, could be achieved in her lifetime, "Had I the power to issue inviolable edicts. Alas! that the age of a beneficent autocracy has never been and is not here today!" Instead of quickly achieving a perfected human race, it would be necessary to take the much slower course of creating in every individual "that intense consciousness of the race which will make it impossible for individuals ever to tolerate the coercion of enforced and miserable motherhood, with its consequent poison of the racial stream".[6] Fortunately, Marie had no power to issue inviolable edicts. If she had, posterity might justifiably have linked her with Hitler, the exercise of whose "beneficent autocracy" in the field of eugenics threw that science into considerable disrepute.*

The middle classes had some grounds for thinking that they would be taxed out of existence to support those defectives and incompetents officiously kept alive. Before the war, a rich man would have paid only eight per cent of his income in tax – afterwards, he was paying about one-third, much of which went to support the new social services, in particular unemployment benefits. His fears were increased by the differential in the declining birth rate. From about 1870 the birth rate had fallen steeply, but much more noticeably in the middle than in the working classes. Was the pure stock of the educated English gentleman to be destroyed by the fecklessly breeding inferior classes?

Marie was in no doubt about the answer. In a central passage of *Radiant Motherhood*, written in 1920, her beliefs are clearly stated:

> ... society allows the diseased, the racially negligent, the thriftless, the careless, the feeble-minded, the very lowest and worst members of the community, to produce innumerable tens of thousands of stunted, warped and inferior infants. If they live, a large proportion of these are doomed from their very physical inheritance to be at

* On 14 July 1933 a law was enacted in Berlin for the compulsory sterilisation of anyone suffering from mental deficiency, schizophrenia, manic-depression, epilepsy, Huntington's chorea, hereditary blindness, deafness, and alcoholism. It came into effect on 1 January 1934. Only doctors of "Aryan descent", of course, were allowed to decide who qualified for sterilisation.

the best but partly self-supporting, and thus to drain the resources of those classes above them which have a sense of responsibility. The better classes, freed from the cost of the institutions, hospitals, prisons and so on, principally filled by the inferior stock, would be able to afford to enlarge their own families, and at the same time not only to save misery but to multiply a hundredfold the contribution in human life-value to the riches of the State.[7]

Nor was Marie at all attracted by the socialism of her friends in the Fabian Society like Shaw and Sidney and Beatrice Webb (whom Marie consulted at one stage about the possibility of standing for parliament, an ambition she never achieved). Following the success of the Russian Revolution in 1917, the growing popularity of the Labour party, and the advent of the "Red Clydesiders", the upper classes in Britain were as terrified of revolution as their forbears had been after the French Revolution in 1789. Marie shared their fears. The "hydra-headed monster of the revolutionary spirit", she argued in *Radiant Motherhood*, was caused by the envy of the lower classes, who mistakenly felt that they would be better off with a fairer share of the wealth and possessions of others. What they really needed were "new bodies and new hearts. Most of the revolutionaries I have met are people who have been warped or stunted in their own personal growth ... The secret revolt and bitterness which permeates every fibre of the unwillingly pregnant and suffering mothers has been finding its expression in the lives and deeds of their children. We have been breeding revolutionaries through the ages and at an increasing rate since the crowding into cities began ..."

How was society to get rid of its defectives and to preserve its best stock from destruction by hydra-headed revolution? By a few simple acts of parliament, Marie suggested, Britain could achieve within two generations "a new and irradiated race":

It is, however, neither necessary to castrate nor is it suggested by those who, like myself, would like to see the sterilization of those totally unfit for parenthood made an immediate possibility, indeed made compulsory. When Bills are passed to ensure the sterility of the hopelessly rotten and racially diseased ... our race will rapidly quell the stream of depraved, hopeless and wretched lives which are at present ever increasing in proportion in our midst.[8]

Nor was her sterilising zeal limited to the defective. Like many of her generation, Marie, notwithstanding her earlier penchant for Professor Fujii, strongly disapproved of inter-racial marriage. Today opinion tends more to the beneficial effects of miscegenation which, it is argued, creates "hybrid vigour" – an idea that might have occurred to Marie from her botanical work (one explanation of the rapid take-over by the angiosperms, or flowering plants, from the earlier gymnosperms is the enhanced vigour created by outbreeding). But she always advised correspondents against mixed marriages, and in a newspaper interview which she herself passed for publication, went even further: ". . . Somehow we wandered on to the subject of sterilisation on which the Dr has most interesting and ardent opinions. She believes that all half-castes should be sterilised at birth. Thus painlessly and in no way interfering with the individual's life, the unhappy fate of he who is neither black nor white is prevented from being passed on to yet unborn babes . . ."[9]

Her ideas were too extreme even for a climate favourable to eugenic ideals. Her beliefs sometimes drove her into cruelty. To a deaf and dumb father of four deaf children, who had written asking help in getting his son admitted to the Royal School for Deaf and Dumb Children at Margate, she wrote back asking how it was possible, "if you and your wife were brought up at the above institution, that you did not realise your duty to the community and to refrain from bringing more misery of the sort into the world. Did no one tell you that if you married, children would be likely to come, and did no one make you think about your responsibility in this matter?" On the same day, Marie also wrote to the chaplain of the Royal Association for the Deaf and Dumb. "Do you think it advisable," she asked, "that two defectives, both brought up at public expense should be permitted to produce four defectives to be brought up at public expense, and where is this geometrical progression to stop?"[10] The chaplain wrote back, with some justification: "Dear Madam, The purport of your letter appears to be censure on me for strongly recommending the admission of a Deaf child to a residential school for the Deaf. Ought I, then, to have recommended the lethal chamber?"

Lacking support for her more drastic remedies, Marie was thrown back on birth control as a way of improving the human race. The failure of her Rhondda Valley campaign on behalf of married women teachers* brought from Marie a violent attack on men in general and, in particular, their cavalier manner of dealing with the problem of "surplus women". "How long would civilisation as we know it today last," she harangued readers of the *Sunday Chronicle*, "if every woman of marriageable age was married and bearing children with no domestic help? Civilisation as seen today would fall to pieces ... But every woman would like to be married. Granted – were men all fine and splendid creatures; but as things are with so many men in all classes drink-sodden, work-shy, permeated by disease, stunted, lanky and physically unsound ... the 'superfluous' woman is too often made by the 'superfluous' man and racially all diseased and inferior men are superfluous."[11] It was stirring stuff and newspapers were eager to report any of Marie's doings, whether it was her campaign against joint income tax, "a tax on marriage", as she put it, for the non-payment of which she was prepared to go to prison (though not actually doing so) or her attacks on the Birth Rate Commission.

It is a mistake to think, as some historians have,† that birth control was respectable in 1920. In *The Control of Parenthood*, a symposium published in that year and edited by Sir James Marchant, secretary of the National Birth Rate Commission, prejudice against birth control was all too evident. Professor Leonard Hill argued that "the woman who uses preventives tends to lose her beauty early, becomes thin and neurotic". Dean Inge, while deploring "the multiplication of the most undesirable section of the population" had nothing but contempt for "the woman who despises the honour and responsibilities of motherhood". Sir Rider Haggard, KBE, wondered where we should all have been "and where would the Allies have been, if during the late war Great Britain had only possessed half her present population". And Dr Mary Scharlieb, a practising gynaecologist for forty years, feared that the use of contraceptives would lead to too much sexual enjoyment. "It is as if the loathsome practices of Heliogabalus made

---

* Marie's class bias was as evident in her attitude to the liberation of women as in her racial theories. The right of married women to teach was self-evident; but in May this year, Marie replied to the Skilled Employment and Apprenticeship Association, who had asked for her support: "I strongly disapprove of your association, apprenticing girls to such work as the furnishing and leather trades and not training them as they should be trained in household occupations." (27 May 1920. BL-S.)

† "A satisfactory diaphragm for women was invented in 1919. Soon afterwards Dr Marie Stopes made contraceptive devices respectable in a somewhat gushing book, *Married Love*." – *English History, 1914–45*, A. J. P. Taylor, O.U.P., 1965.

perpetual eating and drinking possible." Indeed, she went on, contraception should not be discussed at all. "The mere discussion of contraceptive methods is lowering to the moral sense and to the innate reserve and purity of decently brought-up young people. That such a subject should be made the matter of public discussion is a deep injury to the conscience of the nation."

Dr Scharlieb was the only contributor to mention Marie Stopes by name, though not in a totally critical spirit. Others were not so shy. Marie was horrified by the publication in 1920 of *Wedded Love or Married Misery*, by W. N. Willis, a former Australian MP, and author of *Why Girls Go Wrong*, *White Slaves in a Piccadilly Flat* and *Should Girls Be Told?* Willis's ideas would have been laughable had they not been so widespread. About the cervical cap, for instance, he agonised about the danger "of an untrained lay person penetrating the delicate interior of her body with such a germ and dirt carrier as the finger. Just the least little atom of foreign matter under the nail, just a scratch from that nail, and a woman would bring about a septic condition that will inevitably lead to great pain, illness if not death itself."[12] No mention was made of that much more potentially infective source, the penis. Similarly, deploring Marie's attempts to increase the physical enjoyment of sex, Willis lamented her advocacy of imagination in the use of different positions:

> It is really impossible to find words strong enough to condemn any suggestion of employing the imagination in sexual matters. This is a terrible recommendation for any author to be guilty of making. The imagination should, it can never be sufficiently emphasised, be subdued on all sides.[13]

Most hurtful of all to Marie, however, was Willis's suggestion that she was encouraging immorality. In his introduction, he sneered:

> Mrs Stopes may lay this flattering unction to her soul – her books have given great joy to the various rubber-goods shops and contraceptive vendors who have for years been invidiously preaching the doctrines she now openly advocates, and who find a very ready and profitable market among their nefarious clientele for such works as support their traffic ... Mrs Stopes has stepped out of her legitimate sphere of flower and fungus into the province of a medical doctor ...

Willis's ignorance – he argued that a woman could only conceive if she actually enjoyed the sexual act – was fairly typical. Marie's conviction that she must open her own birth control clinic was further strengthened by the reappearance of Margaret Sanger, the American pioneer of contraception, who had originally coined the term "birth control". In October 1916, along with her sister, Ethel Byrne, also a professional nurse, Margaret Sanger had opened a clinic in Brownsville, a squalid part of Brooklyn. It was raided by the police after only nine days, both sisters were imprisoned for thirty days, and Mrs Byrne was forcibly fed when she went on hunger strike. After the war, Mrs Sanger decided to open a clinic in London instead. Marie, who was already beginning to think of herself as the onlie begetter of birth control, was not at all pleased. She was "naturally disappointed", she wrote back to her American counterpart in May 1920. "Mr Roe and I have long been planning to found our own Birth Control Clinic in England as a memorial to our own marriage. We were introduced and first met over this question."

It was the beginning of a long and bitter rivalry, a competition which extended even to the romanticisation by both women of their "moments of vision". Margaret Sanger's conversion, she claimed, came about through the death of Sadie Sachs, a New York slum-dweller, who had been warned not to have any more children, the only contraceptive advice offered by her doctor being that her husband should sleep on the roof. For Mrs Sanger, who nursed Sadie Sachs through her fatal self-abortion, it was "the dawn of a new day ... I was resolved to seek out the root of the evil, to do something to change the destiny of mothers whose miseries were as vast as the sky."[14] Not to be outdone, Marie riposted with her own experience in Manchester. In 1906, she always claimed (though no mention was made of it at the time), one of the women medical students in her botany class told her of a patient all of whose four children had died shortly after birth:

The doctor put her off with some soothing platitudes, but the woman driven to despair said: "I believe there's something wrong with my man. If there's something wrong with my man I won't have babies no more – it's just cruel to see them miserable like this and have them dying one after the other. Won't you, for God's sake, tell me whether there's anything wrong with my man or not?" This was met by the assurance that there was nothing wrong, and she should go on having babies and do her duty by her husband. My medical woman student said that it was glaringly obvious that the baby was syphilitic. I asked her why she did not immediately tell the mother the truth. She shrugged her shoulders and said: "I've got my exam to pass; if I did a thing like that Dr – would stop me going to the hospital. I can't afford to take risks like that".[15]

"I vowed to myself," Marie wrote, "that I would never forget that mother, and that some day I would batter at the brazen gates of knowledge on her behalf." As it happened, Margaret Sanger's plans to open a London clinic fell through, and Marie was free to open what she rapidly convinced herself was the world's first birth control clinic (though she could legitimately claim that it was the first such clinic in the British Empire). So determined was she that, at the end of 1920, though she continued her scientific work privately, she resigned her lectureship at University College, on the grounds that it afforded "neither full facilities for research nor a living wage". Three months later, on March 17, St Patrick's Day – one of the few public jokes Marie permitted herself – she opened the Mothers' Clinic for Constructive Birth Control, a description which, she hoped, would encourage those who might be deterred by the more negative aspects of the venture.

Not everyone was delighted. After taking her decision to open a clinic, Marie had approached every conceivable source of support. In February 1921 Mrs Florence Booth, wife of the founder of the Salvation Army, wrote back: "The General and I do not feel free to add our names to your Society as requested ... As a mother of seven children, I feel very strongly that if the members of the Medical profession would do more to encourage women to suckle their children,* this would greatly increase Mother-love and prevent too quick an increase in the family ... I should greatly deplore anything which induced the poorer people to use the means for the prevention of conception which are now so prevalent amongst the middle classes."[16] But, by the time the clinic opened, Marie had mustered an impressive array of patrons.

---

* It was a common belief at the time that a woman could not conceive while breast-feeding.

Among them were Arnold Bennett, Edward Carpenter, Sir James Barr (a former vice-president of the British Medical Association), Dame Clara Butt, the singer, and Lady Constance Lytton, suffragette. Marie felt it vital to stress her respectability. A few days before the clinic opened, she wrote to the Chief of Police at Scotland Yard, complaining about a police instruction book which included "birth control" under the same heading as "abortions". She also enclosed a form to be signed and declared before a Commissioner of Oaths by all nurses working at her clinic: "I solemnly declare that so long as I am in any way associated with *The Mothers' Clinic* I will not in any circumstances whatever . . . impart any information or lend any assistance to any person calculated to lead to the destruction *in utero* of the products of conception."[17]

Her puritanism was to some extent forced upon her. As she explained in 1920 to a desperate New Zealander who had searched *Wise Parenthood* in vain for contraceptive advice for his virgin wife: "It was on purpose that I did not put in instructions regarding the first few days of marriage. I have to meet many kinds of opposition and if I made it easy for virgin girls to use Birth Control methods I should have laid myself open to certain dangers which I have avoided." At the same time, she had a genuine horror of any sexual abnormality. Like Havelock Ellis and Edward Carpenter, Marie had gained the emotional impetus for her revolutionary activities from her own abnormal sex life; unlike Ellis and Carpenter, however, whose difficulties created in them a warm sympathy with the "perversions" of others, Marie's problems merely served to intensify her own prudery. In January 1921 she wrote to a worried lesbian that it was all right to live with her friend "on rational, hygienic lines, without any hysterical excess", but that they must never go in for "mutual self-abuse which often leads to very considerable nervous breakdown".*

Marie's respect for convention was naturally extended to her birth control work. She might lyrically praise the sexual habits of the lily which, she told the perhaps puzzled readers of the *Sunday Chronicle* in February, opened its white petals "to reveal to the light of day and

---

* When Radclyffe Hall's sensitive novel about lesbianism, *The Well of Loneliness*, was published in 1928, Marie was disgusted and offered to write an attack "giving accurate, clear scientific reasons why, how and where the book is corrupt . . . it would, of course, make enemies of the homosexuals". (19 October 1928, MCS to C. Huntington. BL-S.)

the delighted eyes of mankind not merely the outer vestibules of sex but their very organs";[18] but in March of that year no such nakedness accompanied the opening of her clinic. Her brochure almost succeeded in disguising among a mass of idealistic verbiage, the clinic's true function and quite a number of those who read it assumed its purpose to be ante- rather than anti-natal. The whole venture, Marie wrote, was imbued by reverence – not just for the "fruitful mother" and wife, but "reverence for the child that it shall not be allowed to come unwanted and unloved to play a miserable part among us; reverence for the Race, that it shall be represented on this earth by the most perfect and God-like individuals that it is in our power to call forth in His Image". Unable to escape at some point the mention of birth control, Marie added that such knowledge would be given "not in the crude repulsive form it is advocated in some quarters, but as the key-stone in the arch of progress towards racial health and happiness".

The new race was to spring forth from the rather unpromising surroundings of Marlborough Road, Holloway, a poor area of North London deliberately chosen so as not to intimidate working-class women. The house she and Humphrey bought for the clinic was small, but Marie was proud of her décor, which she described as "Botticelli Blue, with reproductions of beautiful babies on the walls".[19] A sympathetic woman journalist, writing in the *Star* two months after the clinic opened, shared Marie's enthusiasm: "Fresh willow-blue curtains in the windows; on the walls clean white distemper and cool blue paint; a pedestal holds a little plaster model of a meditative baby angel looking just as though he had accomplished his flight 'from the everywhere into here'. And on the old Jacobean table a huge jar of pink-and-white roses with upclimbing branches of tender green. A place to disarm fear, to invite confidence in its callers."

An even more disarming feature – at least for the poor – was the possibility, for the first time, of obtaining free contraceptive advice. The establishment over the previous twenty years of ante-natal and child welfare clinics had led to a remarkable decline in the maternal and infant death rates; but contraceptive advice at such clinics, which would have been the logical outlet had the Ministry of Health been so minded, was nowhere available. At the time, there were few donations coming in, and Humphrey and Marie supported the clinic themselves (though Lambert's, the manufacturers, donated the first gross of cervical caps, doubtless seeing it as a worthwhile investment). Consultations were free, and to avoid any charges of profiteering, all contraceptives were sold at cost price, and even this charge was waived if the woman was too poor to afford it. Running costs for the first year, leaving out the initial purchase of the house, were £1100 – roughly equivalent to Marie's income from her books that year. Certainly, no one could justifiably accuse her of financial self-interest in opening the country's first birth control clinic. Medically, however, she was more open to criticism. Herself a doctor of science, not of medicine, and with a long-standing distrust of the medical profession, Marie was convinced that women would respond more readily to trained nurses than to doctors, who were then, for the majority, associated only with expense, severe illness, death and the whole alien world summed up in the word "Them" – the other half, those in authority, the moneyed, educated and with the right accent. Examinations and recommendations at Marie's clinic were carried out by a qualified midwife. If she suspected anything abnormal, the case was referred to the clinic's woman doctor, who visited only once or twice a week. In employing this procedure, Marie was far in advance of her time, a precursor of the paramedical approach to contraception which is now widely canvassed. At the time, her approach merely antagonised the largely conservative medical profession, jealous of any poaching on their preserves.

Press coverage of the Mothers' Clinic was disappointing. There were one or two brief reports of its opening, but most newspapers took the same line as the *Daily Mirror*, which replied to the invitation: "I am afraid there is an absurd idea in this office that the subject is not appropriate for discussion or publicity in a 'family newspaper'."[20] With the propagandist's true instinct, Marie hid her disappointment and claimed immediate success – naturally enough, since one of her declared objects was to prove that working-class women were not, as many held, averse to birth control, if only they had the opportunity. Just how successful was she in bringing health and racial hygiene to the poor, cervix-torn, "slave-mothers", producing their annual crop of "puny infants" and, as the clinic's brochure put it, "callously left in coercive ignorance by the middle classes and the medical profession"? Her uncritical admirers were in no doubt. Helen Macdonald in 1921 reported in the *Star* that the clinic was always crowded. "In the long afternoon hours a string of perambulators adorns the pavement outside, while within the mothers of London are learning new truths." In 1924 Aylmer Maude wrote that the clinic "was very soon overtaxed to such an extent that it has hardly dared to advertise its existence."[21] And in 1962, Keith Briant affirmed that "women poured in, many of them so poor that they had to save for their fare across London to reach the clinic".[22] These enthusiastic reports – all of them stemming from Marie – are not borne out by her own clinical records. By the end of 1921 only 518 women had visited the clinic – 471 wanting contraceptive information, 47 looking for help in becoming pregnant, an aspect of her work that Marie liked to emphasise. This works out, at the most generous estimate, at an average daily attendance of three patients, scarcely an overtaxing of resources.[23]

This initially disappointing response – though never publicly admitted – did not discourage Marie. Her direct propaganda, in the form of pamphlets to various health departments advertising the clinic's unique facilities, brought the usual adrenalin-producing opposition.* On 12 April 1921, three weeks after the clinic opened, Dr John Buchan, Medical Officer of Health for Bradford, wrote to Marie: "Personally, I have doubts with respect to your new Clinic ... in Bradford and the West Riding gross forms of birth control have given rise to the most grave abuse and the population is slowly controlling itself out of existence ... The population is aged, jaded, and non-virile and materialistic to a degree. It is a population of married old maids and married old bachelors ... This is the sort of result that birth control brings about and I personally would be slow in associating myself with such a movement."[24]

Two days later, Dr Mary Kidd, medical officer at the Hampstead ante-natal clinic in London, told the Mothers' Clinic to stop inviting her nurses and health visitors to send their patients: "I entirely and utterly disapprove of Dr Marie Stopes' action in setting up this Clinic, both as a doctor and as a woman and as a Christian. My health visitors therefore will do no such thing as to send my patients along to you."[25]

---

* The Lancet's comment deplored the lack of education of medical students in sexual and reproductive matters, but on the grounds that "any qualified doctor should be placed in a position to inform first himself and then, at his discretion, his inquirer, firstly of the arguments for and against contraceptives, and secondly, *of the relative degree of nervous wreckage to be anticipated from the use of any one method*". – The Lancet 26 March 1921 (author's italics).

Obviously, something more drastic was needed than either polite notes to the medical profession, or the provision of facilities. Marie always claimed that the idea of a vast public meeting to "make birth control respectable" was suggested to her by Lloyd George, then Prime Minister. He had turned down her invitation to become a patron of the clinic, but they appear to have met once or twice, and had certainly exchanged letters − of such an extraordinary nature, at least on Marie's part, that they seem scarcely credible in the context of her newly opened clinic.

By 1921, the postwar boom was over, and Britain was in the grip of a severe economic depression. In the three months since December 1920 unemployment had more than doubled and by mid-1921 reached two million. The coal industry, in which, as a palaeobotanist, she was still deeply involved, was the focal point for what Marie's despised revolutionaries hoped would be a general strike, leading to the final overthrow of capitalism. The coal mines had been taken over by the government during the war but were to be handed back to the owners on 31 March 1921. The mine-owners offered only a cut in wages, and a return to the old system whereby miners on richer seams earned more than those in inferior pits. The miners refused these terms, and were locked out on April 1. After their threats to flood the mines, Marie took it upon herself to save Western capitalism. She wrote to Lloyd George in April:

> My Dear Prime Minister, May I implore you *on no account* to yield to the threats of the miners' leaders, but absolutely insist on the safety of the mines being secured . . . You know, I think, that I was the only person to see the miners' delegates last Thursday after their fateful meeting and before they went north: I did this by barring their door with my arm and telling them they could miss their train but they must have a word with me.

She had, she went on, had a long talk with Frank Hodges (the miners' secretary) but did not get very far. Why not, she suggested to Lloyd George, send Marie in as a private guerilla force to subdue these pestilent miners?

> . . . if you will find a few wiry strong men to come with me, pistols in their pockets, I'll go again, *lock* their door and *make* them send

out notices to all the safety men to go back to work ... I know *publicly* you would have to repudiate my behaviour or even know nothing about it, but I'm willing even to go to prison to save the mines of the country. The miners' federation is the easiest place in the world to walk into and capture if no hint at all is given. Their pistol being at our heads, the last things these bullies expect is to find our pistols at theirs. Bullies are cowards and I won't hurt the creatures at all, but if they are shut in and *made to listen to me* it would only be a question of hours before they yield.[26]

Marie may well have been right in her estimate of the miners' inability to withstand several hours' listening to her. But on April 14 Frances Stevenson wrote gently back from 10 Downing Street: "Dear Dr Marie Stopes, Mr Lloyd George is very much obliged for your suggestions in connection with the present crisis, but he fears that it is not a practicable one, and I am sure you will understand the objections to taking such a course." The next day, April 15, is still referred to as "Black Friday" – the day on which other trade unions withdrew support from what the miners hoped would be the final showdown with capitalism.

Deprived of complete autocracy over the State – an ambition so innocently grandiose as to be comic rather than sourly threatening – Marie concentrated on her meeting. She booked the Queen's Hall in London for the evening of May 31. It was to be an evening in the Aimee Semple MacPherson tradition, with half an hour of organ music beforehand, followed by stimulating speakers. In her notes to the chairman, G. H. Roberts, MP, a Privy Councillor and former Minister of Labour, Marie stipulated that "the speakers are all limited strictly to ten minutes, with the exception of myself". She also drew attention to the appearance on the platform of Admiral Sir Percy Scott, KCB: "Our greatest living admiral. Will speak for ten minutes on the need of the Navy for fine men strengthened by the knowledge that they have happy homes."

Marie's plans aroused the usual opposition. Lord Beaverbrook sent back his tickets, *The Times* refused to accept the advertisement for it, and the *Morning Post* said she could have it in the personal column, but not the Court Circular. On May 7, the magazine *Plain English*,

Top: Humphrey Verdon Roe with one of the 'Avro planes kept up by Bullseye Braces'
Bottom: Marie *and* Humphrey in Court dress, 1925

...months I can scarcely walk with...
...womb dropped, and varicose
...ins, and my last baby was
...8 hours of terrible agony in
labour, a baby that weighed 11
Pounds. I think before I would
face it again, I would rather
commit suicide, my hussband is
a very strong man, and as
he is only a labourer, we
can scarcely manage as things
are so terrible,...

...together as friends, close
After three years, I bought your
book and, without my wife knowing
I put your teaching into practice
wooed her as I had never done before
I married her, and gradually I...
her back. Previously she showed...
passion, taking life as a matter of co...
and resignedly yielding to me. Now
however, a new spirit has come in
our home. I must thank you for
teaching us how to find a paradise...
had never imagined to be there. A...

Married Love and *Wise Parenthood* gave rise to a correspondence
described by Marie's publisher as 'never-ending and unprofitable'

under the headline BIRTH CONTROL AT THE QUEEN'S HALL said:

> This woman Stopes is the writer of the book to which we referred last week as being declared obscene by the Court of Special Session, New York. The publisher was fine 250 dollars ... Evidence has reached us which goes to prove that Stopes has, by means of her disgusting books, done an inconceivable amount of injury ... When she mounts the platform of Queen's Hall we assume that she will be supported by Hygienic Inge, who will no doubt be prepared to add to what he has already said in favour of "Birth Control", which in other words means grave immorality.*

On the day before the meeting, Miss Bandulska, a friend of Marie's, wrote to warn her that there was an organised attempt on the part of Catholics to break up the meeting: "You would do well to admit no priests and to have strong police support."

In the event, all went off smoothly. After dinner at the Ritz, Marie, Humphrey, Killick Millard, Sir Percy Scott, Aylmer Maude and Dr Jane Hawthorne, visiting doctor at the clinic, turned up to find a packed, orderly and sympathetic audience. The only dissident note had occurred outside the hall, when two men approached a Catholic priest with the suggestion that nuns should be allowed out of their convents to breed more Catholics. "'We will breed you all out,' the priest snarled back."[27] Otherwise, as Mrs Edith Zangwill put it, the audience were neither morbid nor even particularly curious:

> There was one young couple with a fat, sleepy baby. Their interest was doubtless entirely practical ... Otherwise the audience looked very much the same as at a Shaw play, or a Chaucer lecture or, indeed, at the meeting of any progressive and little-known society. Men were in a minority: some were bearded, but none I saw wore the new fashionable "prick" moustache. The women were largely of the Hampstead type, sallow and soulful and badly gowned. It may have been partly by contrast that the two lady speakers appeared so dazzlingly arrayed ...[28]

* *Married Love* had been published in America but, despite toning down by its publisher, Dr W. J. Robinson of The Critic and Guide Co. – an action for which Marie Stopes never forgave him – had been declared obscene and unmailable under U.S. laws.

Marie was accused of wearing a dress both too short and too décolleté: but, after the dispassionate intelligence of Killick Millard, the sentimentalities of Jane Hawthorne, and the naval demands of Admiral Scott – "We only want A1 men for the Navy, not wastrels" – her speech was much admired. She had a musical voice, far removed from the shrillness normally associated with the prophetic zealot. "Why have I gathered round me this great multitude?" she appealed to the Queen's Hall, from the depths of her fragile femininity. "How glad I am that you have responded to my call ... We, tonight, consciously and publicly step into the first days of a great new era of human evolution ... we will bring forth an entirely new type of human creature, stepping into a future so beautiful, so full of the real joy of self-expression and understanding that we here today may look upon our grandchildren and think almost that the gods have descended to walk upon the earth. (Applause)."[29]

What, all this time, was happening to Humphrey Roe, Marie's necessary partner in the creation of a god-like race? Though one of the instigators of the birth control clinic, he appeared already to be dimmed by his wife's dynamism. He had become a local councillor in Leatherhead but, though Marie's dedication to him of the ninth edition of *Married Love* in April 1921 read: "To the Sweetest Sweetheart on His Birthday, from the Wood Nymph", she seemed now to find him more of a burden than a mate. In May, she wrote to a Harley Street specialist:

> Yesterday, my husband, Mr H. V. Roe, suddenly developed pustules on his neck and the edge of his scalp which caused me anxiety and made me think instantly of *Staphylococcus aureus*: he went to the local medical man who treated it trivially and gave only a mild ointment. Feeling that this was quite inadequate I myself first washed the areas in hydrogen peroxide, then cut the hair off and painted the skin round the outbreak of the scalp with Iodine ...

Marie obviously believed in the marital advice she contributed so copiously to women's magazines. "A woman's first baby should be her husband ... he needs just the simple, loving petting that is demanded by a child."[30] Whether shaving his head and painting him with iodine could be described as "petting" is a debatable point; but Marie was determined to "manage" Humphrey as she would a child; and her ministrations at least ensured a reasonably presentable appearance when Humphrey, as co-founder of the clinic, was allowed on the platform at the Queen's Hall meeting.

Press coverage of the meeting was again disappointing,* and Marie rushed out a transcript of the major speeches. This, again, was greeted with a deafening silence, but Marie's activities had not gone unnoticed. On July 7, while she was away in Cornwall, looking for a holiday home where she and Humphrey could enjoy a "second honeymoon", another meeting took place in London that was to prove of far greater importance in Marie's publicity campaign than any of her stirring calls to action. In the same month that the *Daily Express* ran a competition – with a prize of £25 – for Britain's largest family, Dr Anne Louise McIlroy, Professor of Obstetrics and Gynaecology at the Royal Free Hospital, read a paper attacking birth control to the Medico-Legal Society. The ensuing discussion provides a fascinating cross-section of current thinking on the subject. Earl Russell (John Francis Stanley, the second earl, from whom his brother Bertrand later inherited the title) provided the most cogent arguments against the enforced provision of further cannon-fodder and Empire-builders. Bernard Shaw, too, was in favour of birth control – but only because he did not like to see human beings as slaves to nature: he disapproved of the condom ("reciprocal masturbation") and deplored the fact that most people were too poor to have separate bedrooms. The double bed, he argued, involved "a large amount of quite unnatural and unnecessary stimulant". Dr Bernard O'Connor was unable to see any difference between those who killed "germs" (i.e. sperms) and those who murdered children: "And if the latter may bring a person into the dock at the Old Bailey, it seems to me that logically the germicide should stand beside him." Dr H. G. Sutherland argued that the poor women in his own practice with lots of children "are not so much to be pitied as the Society woman who is losing her looks and her excitement and who has not got the natural happiness that comes from the child". In her summing-up, Professor McIlroy stressed once more the happiness of Irish peasants with large families. Only incidentally did she refer to the medical aspects of contraceptives. She knew nothing of the harmful

* Though one letter, signed "Beethovenian", arrived. A music-lover, he had read of the meeting, and said he would never again attend concerts at the Queen's Hall. It had been "sullied for ever". (5 June 1921. BL-S.)

effects of quinine, she said but "the most harmful method of which I have had experience is the use of the pessary". (The rubber check pessary was the method most widely recommended at Marie's clinic.)[31]

Dr Halliday G. Sutherland, like Marie, was born in Scotland, though two years later, in 1882. Educated at the Edinburgh and Aberdeen medical schools, he had led an adventurous life, on a whaler in Shetland, as a doctor in Spain and, during the war, as a naval surgeon. He had done original work on tuberculosis and was now deputy commissioner for TB medical services in England and Wales. Brought up in the Church of Scotland, he was converted to the Roman Catholic faith in 1919. Converts being notoriously more enthusiastic than those brought up in it, it is not surprising that Dr Sutherland was the only person to note Professor McIlroy's comments on the check pessary. Only a few months later, he incorporated her criticisms in a hastily produced book on birth control.[32] Here, he argued that birth controllers were exposing the poor to experiments. Their ordinary, decent instincts, he went on, "are against these practices, and indeed they have used them less than any other class. But, owing to their poverty, lack of learning, and helplessness, the poor are the natural victims of those who seek to make experiments on their fellows. In the midst of a London slum a woman, who is a doctor of German philosophy (Munich), has opened a Birth Control Clinic, where working women are instructed in a method of contraception described by Professor McIlroy as 'the most harmful method of which I have had experience' ... It is truly amazing that this monstrous campaign of birth control should be tolerated by the Home Secretary. Charles Bradlaugh was condemned to jail for a less serious crime."[33]

These few words – no more violent in tone than many other attacks she had already attracted – gave Marie the opportunity to indulge in the battle for which she had long been spoiling. Sutherland's remarks led to one of the twentieth century's most remarkable legal trials. The rewards, in terms of publicity for her cause, were great, but the costs, financially and emotionally, perhaps even greater.

CHAPTER 12

God Fights Back

> "The art of leadership ... consists in consolidating the attention of the people against a single adversary and taking care that nothing will split up that attention."
>
> Adolf Hitler, *Mein Kampf*

SOME of her friends – though not her best friends – were Catholics, but Marie had no doubt where her single adversary lay. If Dr Sutherland, by referring to her Munich doctorate, could tap Britain's anti-German feelings, why should she not counter with an appeal to the hatred – of much longer standing – of the Scarlet Woman of Rome?

The Catholic Church was worried. The 1920 Lambeth conference of Anglican bishops, with its vague condemnation of both contraception and "sex as an end in itself", had been reassuring enough. But in 1921, at the Church Congress in Birmingham, Anglicans were subjected to a much more subversive influence. Lord Dawson, personal physician to King George V, president of the royal College of Physicians, and the first doctor to receive a peerage,* told the conference that their bishops were on the wrong track. The love envisaged by the Lambeth conference, he said, was "an invertebrate, joyless thing – not worth the having ... Has not sexual union over and over again been the physical expression of our love without thought or intention of procreation? Have we all been wrong? Or is it that the Church lacks that vital contact with the realities of life which accounts for the gulf between her and the people?"[1]

---

* Except for Lister, whose peerage had been awarded for scientific rather than medical achievements.

His speech was widely reported. The *Sunday Express* demanded that Lord Dawson should be dismissed from his court position and, if possible, divested of "the grimy mantle of Malthus, the greasy robes of Bradlaugh and the frowsy garments of Mrs Besant". Others welcomed his unequivocal statement – "Birth control is here to stay ... No denunciations will abolish it." Marie, of course, was delighted, seeing Dawson's speech almost as a triumph for herself. "I am glad to see," she wrote to *The Times* (the letter was not published) "that my views receive cordial support and commendations in your columns ... even if, in order to get this attention, they have to be echoed by Lord Dawson."*[2]

Catholic alarm was further increased by the spread of practical provision for birth control. In November 1921, a month after Dawson's speech and eight months after Marie's clinic opened, the Malthusian League opened their own clinic, at 153a, East Street, in Walworth, a slum area of South London. The league had hitherto been a quiet, rather intellectual organisation, limited mostly to the discussion of Malthus' economic arguments for population control. In the summer of 1921, however, perhaps stimulated by Marie's more emotional approach, the league organised a three-weeks' campaign of open-air meetings in South London and distributed thousands of leaflets. Their clinic opened to a torrent of abuse. Eggs, stones and apples were thrown, men shouted "whore" and "abortionist" at the clinic's staff, and the door was smashed in.[3]

Marie had long been a member of the league, but quickly joined in the attacks. She had several complaints. The clinic was run by Dr Norman Haire, an Australian Jew who, in view of Britain's continuing anti-semitism, had changed his name from Zions on coming to London. A gynaecologist of considerable experience, he favoured the Dutch cap (the diaphragm) on the grounds that, for most women, it was much easier to insert than the small check pessary fitting precisely around the cervix. Though there was little evidence to support her theories, Marie believed passionately that the diaphragm would stretch the vaginal walls irreparably, thus reducing the woman's capacity to exert internal

* In 1934 when Lord Dawson was persuaded to introduce a Bill in the House of Lords limiting the sale of contraceptives, Marie tried to bully him into withdrawing. "How glad I am," he wrote, "that I never allowed myself to be enrolled under her banner." – *Dawson of Penn* by Francis Watson, Chatto and Windus, 1950.

muscular grip. At her own clinic, she almost invariably recommended the small check pessary which she had designed herself, after French models, and christened the "Pro-Race" cap. Her disapproval of Dr Haire's methods was equalled by her dislike of the Malthusian League's reverential attitude towards Charles Bradlaugh. Marie had carried out her own research into the early history of birth control but, after only three years in the movement, she now felt personally responsible for its creation. It was with some justification that in November 1921, when the league's clinic opened, the *Literary Guide* described Marie as "a talented lady who has been advocating birth control so effectively that she is inclined to suppose that she is the inventor of it". Any laudatory reference to Bradlaugh and other pioneers infuriated her. She resigned from the league, and attacked both the Malthusians and Norman Haire in print and on the public platform. "Personalities do not matter to me," she mendaciously wrote, "but the truth does. The fact that I will not bow the knee to Bradlaugh and have researched to unearth the truths ... is anathema to the Atheistical School, for curiously enough, they insist on a kind of reverence to Bradlaugh which is the exact mental equivalent of the R.C. reverence to the Pope."[4]

Marie was not going to tolerate any god, atheistical or otherwise, except her own personal deity. Though she constantly invoked the Christian God, He bore little relation to either the God of the scriptures (except in her own, highly individual interpretation) or to the doctrine of any Christian church. He was, however, created in her own image, a useful ally.

Chagrined by competition from the Malthusians, Marie multiplied her own activities, further increasing Catholic opposition. In August 1921 she founded the Society for Constructive Birth Control and Racial Progress, a separate organisation to drum up support for her clinic.* G. B. Shaw refused her invitation to become a vice-president of the CBC, as the society became known. Birth control bothered him, he said, "because the method most commonly employed changes genuine intercourse into reciprocal something else"[5] – but many other luminaries were willing to lend their names. The society held monthly

---

* Sometimes, with ludicrous results. In October 1921 Mr W. Baldwin Raper, MP, resigned from the society. "Until a couple of days ago," he wrote, "I was under the firm impression that your Institution was nothing more nor less than a Babies Welfare League. I now find, however, that it goes much further than that." (11 October, BL-S.)

meetings and social events and in May 1922, at a nine-course dinner at
the Hotel Cecil, Marie triumphantly produced as a surprise tenth
course the first issue of her newspaper, *Birth Control News*. The
occasion was enlivened with a lecture by Aylmer Maude, entitled, "The
Proposal of the Doukhobors to Murder their own Children".* W. H.
Smith's refused to distribute *Birth Control News*, but some managed
to get hold of it, and its value was touchingly attested by a young
miner whose wife had died giving birth to twins, after her doctor had
refused to give information about birth control. "When I get your
monthly papers, I hand them on to married women. I wish to God my
wife was here," he wrote.

Marie was becoming obsessed by the need to publicise her campaign.
London Transport, among other organisations, refused to carry her
clinic advertisements; but why should she not advertise in theatres?
Marie had by now transferred her books to Putnam's, where Charles
Huntington proved much more sympathetic to the idea of selling large
numbers of books than her original publisher A. C. Fifield. She bombarded him with publicity ideas and in November 1921 sent him a
draft advertisement to be displayed in every London theatre:

> You are now being made happy for an hour or so. Perhaps you came
> here with a sad heart to forget your own unhappiness? Would it not
> be splendid to be happy for life and to make your dearest one happy
> also? If you love, knowledge alone is needed to make your life happy.
> That Knowledge you will find in the three great books which have
> been making public opinion in the last three years.[6]

Such energy was even more remarkable in that she had just returned
from a gruelling visit to New York, involving quarrels with Margaret
Sanger and Dr W. J. Robinson, publisher in America of *Married Love*.
Marie's love for her husband was tempered by criticism. Shortly after
leaving Southampton she wrote to Humphrey: "I'm glad to have been
a little way off of you and so to have seen you again towering above
your fellow men. But little things do so *hurt* when one is close, so close
that one sometimes forgets the big outline – and oh, *how* it hurt that
you forgot to wish me well on my birthday ... Darling – life's little
ceremonies should be made to pile up life long joyous memories not

---

* The Doukhobors were a sect that Maude had helped to emigrate from Russia to
America, where they were now so prolific that they demanded the right of infanticide.

pain." In fact, on October 10, five days before her birthday, Humphrey had already written so that she should have a letter waiting for her when she arrived in New York.

By the time she arrived, on October 24, Marie had recovered her spirits and wrote to Humphrey:

> Sweetheart darling . . . I'm just getting starved for love and want of you — I wonder if you feel the same too? I don't want ever to be in a city again — not ever — I'd like to be a private person and only love you and the flowers and a babykins and the squirrels and not be mixed up in all these horrid, horrid businesses with Sangers and Drysdales and discussings and arrangings . . .
>
> Bits of New York are impressive and beautiful, but it is exactly like being in a cinema picture, it is difficult to feel real . . . That sort of thing is *silly* but Margaret Sanger, I fear, is worse than silly.* Well, I'm not cut out for public life and I shall retire into private life on my return and not budge again. I can't bear being so disillusioned about people. Oh dearest sweetheart, don't *ever* let me feel disillusioned about you and love . . . Signed, Margorie — Tigerette — Humphlekins.

On October 17 Marie addressed a large meeting in New York's Town Hall, organised by the Voluntary Parenthood League. Bringing the battle to their own doorstep, she referred to Harding's presidential address in March of that year: "We want the cradle of American childhood rocked under conditions so wholesome and so hopeful that no blight may touch it in its development."[7] Marie was not impressed. "I thought as I passed your Statue of Liberty the other day that on her face I saw an ironical smile. She had listened to your President's fine words and she still saw passing beneath her the coerced and enslaved women from whom knowledge is forcibly withheld."

The Comstock Law, she argued, had been drafted by people who confused physiological knowledge of sex and birth control with prostitution, obscenity and vice. To put things right, Marie offered a re-written Declaration of Independence: "We hold these truths to be

---

* Margaret Sanger, rather like Marie Stopes, quarrelled with most other birth control workers. In 1921 she organised the American Birth Control League, in opposition to Mrs Mary Dennett's Voluntary Parenthood League. Mrs Dennett had been kind to Marie, who therefore saw Margaret Sanger's action as "betrayal".

self-evident – that all men *and women* are created equal; that they are endowed by their creator with certain unalienable rights; that among these are life, liberty, *knowledge* and the pursuit of *health* and happiness, *both for themselves and to control their unborn children in the interests of the race."*

Marie was delighted by her reception. She wrote to Humphrey after the meeting: "Just after 11 at night . . . Yes, sweetheart, a *real* success. I got quite 5 times more and more intense clapping than either the chairman or the other speakers . . . It all went very well – not even a whisper of protest – and they clapped and clapped and clapped till it rang when I got up to speak."[8]

Even sea-sickness on the way back to England failed to dampen her triumph. On November 4 she wrote to Humphrey from S.S. *Cedric*:

> Darlingest Tiger-Humphlekins . . . There's no doubt, *power* to feel depends partly on body-strength and when one is drefful sea sick one *can't* love at one's strongest.
>
> The truth is out! and a young man [Noel Coward] "spotted" me so I have had interesting talks all day. He is a dear and a dramatist and full of youth and enthusiasm and yet *sanity*. We agree absolutely about Aristocracy and he thinks you tremendously handsome and he is using his money success to help his mother and family and he is hoping to use his power of laughter to help in social progress and he told the people at my table that I am one of the greatest living intellects which made them sit up . . . I'm hungry for intelligent youth. Leatherhead is too grown up.

The next day, Marie wrote to Humphrey again about Noel Coward: "I have read two of the plays of this interesting young author-actor – one *very* good and one very bad – I told him it was 'putrid' and he took it ever so nicely . . . I think he is not only *real* but was sent by Providence to re-open my interest in my dear old love, the drama." Coward, though he later refused her offer to rewrite *The Vortex* on birth control lines, was sufficiently intrigued to send her a poem:

> If through a mist of awful fears
> Your mind in anguish gropes
> Dry up your panic-stricken tears
> And fly to Marie Stopes.

If you have missed life's shining goal
And mixed with sex perverts and Dopes
For normal soap to cleanse your soul
Apply to Marie Stopes.

And if perhaps you fail all round
And lie among your shattered hopes
Just raise your body from the ground
And *crawl* to Marie Stopes.[9]

If the "babykins" to which Marie referred so longingly in her letter from New York had materialised, she might possibly have carried out her threat to retire to the world of "flowers and squirrels". On November 3, as she was on her way back from New York, Humphrey wrote from Givons Grove – on *Mothers' Clinic* writing-paper – "You little Wood Nymph, Very soon now you will be with me, but as *I* keep a diary to date, it means that *I* must tell you not to overstrain yourself on or about Tuesday, 8 Nov." Humphrey's plans, however, came to nothing. Six months later, in May 1922, one of Marie's gynaecologists wrote to her. She was now nearly forty-two, and there was still no sign of the child that both she and Humphrey desperately wanted:

Dear Dr Stopes . . . You and H. have been often in my thoughts and I have been wondering how matters have progressed – Is he in any degree more vigorous? There are cases in which the special function of which you wrote to me becomes feeble at a much younger age than normal. I would like very much that the strong wish of you both to possess a healthy infant would be gratified, for your child ought to be normal in every developmental way, and to have a fine brain – It would be well if the entrance of the seminal fluid to the vagina could be managed and if you should have little or no excitement *you* might arrange to bring that about and possibly the spermatozoa might find their way to the uterus . . . H. should not be too anxious about his condition and should not try too often, but when anything is attempted he and you should do all possible to arouse him thoroughly . . . .[10]

The ironies are too obvious to be pointed out. But Marie's vast energy, deprived of the desired outlet in motherhood, was being channelled into a partly defensive arrogance, criticised even by her friends. Dr Binnie Dunlop, one of her more fervent admirers, said bluntly: "Many people consider you unbearably egotistical and some write to ask if there is not another society besides the CBC. I always say you have good grounds for being egotistical. How great you would be if you were not."[11] Marie was desperate to establish her supremacy. She complained to Dr W. F. Robie, the American writer on sexual topics, that his latest book failed to mention her work. In some puzzlement, Dr Robie replied that most of his books had been written in advance of hers, that clergymen had congratulated him on having written a fifth Gospel – "but yet you failed entirely to mention my books".[12] Back in England, she was much upset by the publication of *Wise Wedlock* by "Courtenay Beale", a pseudonym, so one of her correspondents informed her, for a Polish Nonconformist minister in the North of England, who had been defrocked for immoral behaviour within his flock. Marie complained to Havelock Ellis that Beale had stolen all her ideas and even the format of her books. Ellis gently replied that the author had stolen even more ideas from him – "But I am so used to that! I am meeting with it constantly. But ... I am pleased to see ideas to which I attach value put into circulation, whether or not they are labelled with my name."[13]

Such generosity of spirit was totally foreign to Marie. Her possessiveness may in part be ascribed to her long academic training. Many academics, after all, live by denigrating the work of others, the better to enhance their own, more "original" contributions to human knowledge. Her guarding of what she considered her exclusive preserves, however, went far beyond the spiteful footnotes with which academics usually content themselves. She threatened to sue Courtenay Beale, but was unable to find him – and also the booksellers who slipped advertisement circulars into her books.* She was also beginning to see any reported failure of the cap, plus a spermicidal, method – the combination had not been invented by Marie – as a personal attack. To the father of five children, whose wife had again become pregnant only two months after taking Marie's advice, she wrote asking him to send the cap and soluble pessaries: "I have heard of pessaries that are made without quinine in them just to put into circulation that my method fails."[14]

---

* She had good reason for this. One such circular advertised "Dr Patterson's Famous Pills, the Great Remedy for Irregularities of Every Description" (i.e. pregnancy).

It was unlikely that any manufacturer of quinine pessaries would have been a Catholic; but undoubtedly the Church was stepping up its opposition. As might be expected from an organisation that had invented the term, their propaganda was well-organised. The same names appeared over and over again in letters to the press (rather in the manner, a few decades later, of Moral Rearmament and the Campaign for Light). A typical correspondent was J. W. Poynter, a member of the Westminster Catholic Federation (the political pressure group for the Catholic church). Marie Stopes, he argued, was teaching people how to gain pleasure from a natural function without suffering its fruits. How did this differ from "secret vice"? Marie replied that if the Catholics would themselves pay for "all their own poor and degenerate children, still births and women ill through excessive pregnancies", it was all well and good: "but the public will soon tire of paying for sections of the community which wilfully hinder rational and racial progress".[15]

At a more official level, the Catholic Truth Society published a stream of pamphlets inveighing against birth control. One of the oddest was almost in favour of contraception, on the grounds that the practice might restore Britain to the True Faith: "Our faithful Catholic mothers are doing a wonderful work for God. In time, if wrong methods of birth control continue to prevail among the non-Catholics, their race will die out and the Catholic race will prevail and thus England will become again what it once was, a Catholic country."[16]

Few opponents, however, were prepared to wait that long. Father Vincent McNabb was one of Marie's more assiduous critics. In December 1921 Marie took Counsel's advice over his comments on the CBC society in the *Catholic Times*: "Its literature is almost incredibly obscene by its advocacy of unsocial and unnatural sin. No wonder that the authorities of the United States have banned its literature and its public meetings, thanks to effective Catholic propaganda."*[17] Marie was advised not to proceed with her libel action. But she could not tolerate with equanimity the build-up of the Catholic campaign. In 1922, a conference of Catholic doctors in Glasgow called for a total ban

* Shortly after Marie's public meeting in New York, Margaret Sanger's meeting on November 13 was raided by police, apparently on the direct order of Archbishop P. J. Hayes. The ensuing investigation became a *cause célèbre*, and "scores of society women, expensively gowned, divided into two hostile camps in the small room and glared at one another through their lorgnettes." – *New York Illustrated News* 24 January 1922.

on the sale or advertisement of contraceptives, and in August, the Westminster Catholic Federation succeeded in engineering a question in the House of Commons, asking the Secretary of State, "what steps, in the way of criminal proceedings, he proposes to take in order to check the seriously increasing output of obscene literature having for its object the prevention of conception".

Politicians wanted nothing to do with either side. Among her papers, Marie preserved a hastily scribbled account of her meeting with Lloyd George. She had just returned from America, and called at Number 10 Downing Street, to see Frances Stevenson, the Prime Minister's secretary, and a supporter of birth control. I reproduce Marie's account in full, since it is nowhere else available:

Saw and was chatting with Miss Stevenson: door suddenly opened and the PM came in, smiled. Miss S. at once introduced us. He shook hands very warmly, looked me straight in the eye and said he was very glad to meet me. I said "What luck" – a few friendly commonplaces and I said "I'm just back from America where I had an awfully good time."

PM Yes – row, I saw.

MCS Not *mine*: I had perfectly splendid quiet meeting. All these horrid pars about rows are a put-up job by the RC's (looking him straight in the eye) I wonder if you realise what *devils* the RC's are?

PM Oh, as bad as that? I know they cause a lot of trouble.

MCS They are faking a lot of public opposition to us – but all the time we are winning.

PM Yes, on all sides you are getting support. But I see the D. Express has gone for you.

MCS (smiling): Yes. And all because I *can't* flirt with Lord Beaverbrook. He is our nearest neighbour.

PM Then you ought to get at him.*

---

* Two months earlier, Marie had written to Beaverbrook, "with a proposition which should very materially extend your influence and circulation". She suggested advising all her followers – and she had, she said, sold over a quarter of a million of her books, "a following not to be sneezed at" – to switch to the *Daily Express* (in return, of course, for "proper publicity" – a sentence she immediately crossed out). Whether or not she flirted with him, Beaverbrook was not to be bludgeoned into increasing his circulation by courtesy of Marie Stopes. Besides, as he told her later, though a Presbyterian, he was "very much attached to the Roman Catholics".[18]

MCS But I'm not his type – and I can't flirt. It's dreadful not knowing how to flirt.

PM You'll have to flirt with Beaverbrook or you'll never get him to do anything.

The telephone rang – he gave a word or two to Miss Stevenson and went off." [19]

Following all the other attacks, and the failure of the Prime Minister and Beaverbrook to devote their full – or, indeed, any – energy to her cause, Dr Sutherland's book was for Marie the last straw. Published in March 1922 it was widely and favourably reviewed, and Marie was further disgusted by Halliday Sutherland's attempt to turn birth control into a political issue. Shortly before his book came out Dr Sutherland, as secretary of the League of National Life (an anti-contraception, mostly Catholic organisation), wrote to the *Catholic Times*. He argued that birth control was a class conspiracy against the poor, offered in lieu of better wages and housing conditions. "If the workers reduce their numbers, they reduce their voting strength," he added, a neo-Marxist argument that was not uncommon among Catholics and extreme right-wing Anglicans. Marie had obtained an advance copy of the book, and on April 12, Humphrey Roe sent Sutherland a politely worded invitation to debate the matter with Marie at one of the CBC meetings. As politely, Sutherland refused. The battle was on.

The first issue of *Birth Control News*, edited and mostly written by Marie, carried a review of Sutherland's book. It would, she said, "impose only on those who are more ignorant than he is. It is nicely calculated to encourage the biased in their prejudices, for now, when speaking against birth control, they can say 'A doctor says so!' They will probably forget he is a Roman Catholic doctor. The omissions from the book are quite as remarkable as its lies. We could fill our columns in illustration of this, but space is too valuable." A week later, on May 11, Marie issued a writ for libel against Sutherland.

For both of them, the next nine months, until the case came to trial, were worrying, to say the least. True, Sutherland had the Catholic Church behind him. He had let his relative poverty be known, and the day after the writ was issued, a message came from Archbishop's House, Westminster: "Tell Dr Sutherland that Cardinal Bourne will stand by him to the end."* If it had not been for this, Sutherland later recalled, "I would have been ruined. My attitude thereafter was that I was merely an instrument having the honour of representing the Catholic Church in a great public controversy."[20] Nevertheless, the strain of publicly representing the church must have been considerable – rather like the Inquisition in reverse.

Marie and Humphrey, though financially much better off than Sutherland, were not so rich as was generally assumed. Givons Grove was expensive to run, they paid most of the clinic's costs, and by now there were numerous secretaries to be paid to cope with Marie's vast correspondence. Even before the trial started, Marie had paid her solicitors, Braby & Waller, more than £2000. Her fears about the outcome of the case – already somewhat prejudiced by the delay in bringing the action, which indicated no very great degree of damage – presumably occasioned her extraordinary letter to Henry Ford, car manufacturer and philanthropist. In November 1922 she wrote:

> My dear Mr Ford, I am writing to you because you are the only man alive I know of who has the vision and the power to do something big the world very much needs ...
>
> Briefly put, it is that I have found as a result of the charitable and reforming efforts of my husband and myself (we founded at our own sole cost the first birth control clinic in the British Empire and we have had a very great amount of gratitude from poor and rich and learned alike) we have found ourselves up against immense forces of suppression and evil ... We are not "big rich" but are very well off in an ordinary sense, intelligent, socially rather powerful, but the forces arrayed against us are far too powerful for us to cope with. The *chief* source of evil is the political (and secret) attitude of the Roman Catholic hierarchy. I have been honoured by their saying the "great war" is less than the war against me personally! ...
>
> *... I dare not tackle the Roman Catholics as a force arrayed against world peace and individual health and happiness unless I have much more financial power than I have ...*
>
> The great strength of our movement so far has been that my

* Cardinal Francis Bourne, Archbishop of Westminster. He contributed £400 to Sutherland's defence, and guaranteed a fund to pay all his costs.

husband and I have personally entirely financed it − but we are not *big* in a financial sense as you are. So I am writing to ask you with all the earnestness of a fellow reformer to help us in what will prove the very biggest fight in history for human health, happiness and peace against the reactionary forces which would deprive the masses of these. You are so gloriously rich, and could spare a million or two pounds so easily − won't you send me that right now? *Do*: you will be rewarded. By God. [All italics are Marie's. She crossed out "By God" in this rough draft. There is no record, unfortunately, of Henry Ford's reply.][21]

By the end of 1922 even Marie's energy was beginning to wilt under the burdens she had so blithely assumed. Stung by critical references to her medical ignorance, she was writing a textbook on contraception for the medical profession.* Her work at the clinic, and as lecturer and propagandist, grew as geometrically as Malthus's population. But, at forty-two, she remained obstinately un-pregnant and, "socially powerful" though she felt herself to be, she had still not achieved her ambition of being presented at Court.† Her own life, she felt, was being drained by the demands of others. To a doctor in the Indian Medical Service, who had asked permission to send a patient for private consultation, she replied tetchily:

I am not, and do not desire to be, a professional consultant. Without doubt, I could make a fortune should I choose to do so, but I do not.

I have devoted four years of my life, pay four secretaries to answer the letters of people who do not even send stamped envelopes for reply, founded a Clinic where free knowledge is given without any charge at all, helped with advice thousands of people, including medical men . . . but I am beginning to feel that the personal burden is quite intolerable, for I am a young married woman of the social class who would naturally be enjoying herself and doing nothing else at all.[22]

* *Contraception, Theory, History & Practice*, John Bale, Sons & Danielsson, first published June 1923; the first, but not the most reliable of the modern histories of contraception.

† On 10 October 1922 the Lord Chamberlain informed her solicitors that before Marie's name could be submitted he would have to see a copy of the decree of nullity, and the official shorthand writer's notes of the nullity proceedings (divorced persons not being presentable at court, or, indeed, in the Royal Enclosure at Ascot).

Marie's private frustrations, and her worries about the forthcoming trial, undoubtedly contributed to her growing lack of sympathy with other workers in the field of birth control. In December 1922 Nurse E. S. Daniels, a health worker with Edmonton district council, was dismissed for telling women at maternity clinics where they could get information on birth control. At first Marie was indignant about the case; but, once public demonstrations against Nurse Daniels' dismissal had provoked a ruling from the Ministry of Health that such information was not to be given at maternity centres, Marie withdrew her support – on the grounds that Nurse Daniels, by ignoring the orders of a doctor, had violated her professional code.[23]

Marie's desertion of Nurse Daniels (who later set up her own birth control clinic) went unnoticed. But in January 1923, a month before her own court case, Marie's perhaps understandable unwillingness to risk her reputation to help others provoked unfavourable reaction. Guy and Rose Aldred, both communists, were prosecuted and found guilty of selling an obscene publication, *Family Limitation*, a pamphlet written some years earlier by Margaret Sanger. Bertrand Russell, as a member of the CBC, wrote to Marie asking for her help in organising the Aldreds' appeal. He could find nothing in the pamphlet, he wrote on January 13, which, if declared indecent, would save her own works from prosecution: "I feel it important that all who stand for Birth Control should hang together, if only for fear of hanging separately."[24] Marie had no intention of hanging together, particularly not with Margaret Sanger. She not only refused help. She wrote to Sir Archibald Bodkin, Director of Public Prosecutions, that the pamphlet was "prurient", especially the illustrations of sexual organs, and the suggestion that abortion was sometimes justifiable. This was rather hypocritical, since she had herself sent women to doctors when she felt an abortion necessary; but, to the DPP, she argued that it was "both criminal and harmful".[25]

Despite the *Daily Herald*'s support (contributions to be sent to the *Bakunin Press*, Shepherd's Bush) the Aldreds lost their appeal, and copies of *Family Limitation* were seized and destroyed. *John Bull*, a newspaper not noted for its championing of libertarian ideas, found it "inconceivable that the modest publications of Mr & Mrs Guy Aldred should perish in the flames of official wrath while the erotic outpourings of Dr Marie Stopes are flaunted from every bookstall".[26]

Bertrand Russell, on January 30, contented himself with resigning from the CBC. The incident did Marie a lot of harm, though not in the short term. Like others, Bertrand Russell and his wife Dora channelled their birth control zeal into movements less dependent on the glorification of one woman's ego.* Dr Killick Millard, one of the saner birth control proponents, refused to take any part in Marie's forthcoming action on the grounds that he thought it "unnecessary".

Nevertheless, Marie could call on an impressive array of distinguished medical experts, among them Sir James Barr, vice-president of the B.M.A., Sir William Arbuthnot Lane, consultant surgeon at Guy's Hospital and Sir William Bayliss, professor of physiology at University College.† Leading her case was Patrick Hastings, KC, MP (Marie found his Labour affiliations distasteful but eventually agreed to retain him).

Dr Sutherland countered with Professor McIlroy, Dr Mary Scharlieb and Sir Maurice Abbot Anderson, eminent surgeon and court inspector in nullity suits (it was he, ironically, who had signed the report testifying to Marie's virginity in 1916, thus freeing her for the activities against which he now ranged himself). And Sutherland had even higher authority on his side. The night before he went into the witness box, he said, "I had asked Blessed Thomas More, once Lord Chancellor of England, to help me." He had also spent a week in court listening to Patrick Hastings – "He did not know me in the witness-box but I knew him, his inflexions of voice and his methods in cross-examination."[27]

The case opened in the High Court on February 21 before Lord Chief Justice Hewart, a man remarkable, even among his fellows in the judiciary, for reactionary bias. The press was there in force, and the *Daily Graphic*, with its usual eye for the telling detail, picked on one man in the crowd outside the courts. "'The birth-controller!' whispered the man. Had the gentle little woman [i.e. Marie Stopes] in a

---

* It is significant that, twenty years later, Marie was still justifying her action in the Aldreds' case. She wrote to the Duke of Bedford: ". . . they were rightly prosecuted. The prosecution caused a lot of confusion in the minds of the public and led Bertrand Russell (a careless and inaccurate and pig-headed thinker) into spreading untrue statements in the press all over the world." (14 May 1941, MCS to Bedford. BL-S.)

† The stress on medical expertise was necessary, since in the recent Aldreds' appeal the testimony of H. G. Wells, Harold Cox (editor of the Edinburgh Review) and J. St Loe Strachey (editor of the *Spectator*) had been ruled inadmissible on the grounds that they were not medical men.

rather unfashionable fur coat been a husband-poisoner he could hardly have spoken in a more awesome tone."[28] Even Marie's mother was considered worthy of description: "A little grey-haired old lady with an old-fashioned Bonnet," wrote the *Sunday Times*, "she is constantly to be seen in the Public Record Office, or in the reading room of the British Museum, where she pursues her studies with unabated enthusiasm."[29]

One "human interest" angle was, perhaps fortunately, missed. Winnie Stopes, Marie's sister, was dying. For some years, Marie had paid for her ailing sister to be cared for in a private nursing home, run by nuns. On February 22, the day after the trial opened, Winnie's doctor wrote to Marie that her sister, still only thirty-eight, could not hope to survive much longer. To Marie, in the middle of her court case, the threat appeared to be yet another example of Winnie's selfish solicitation of her family's sympathy. She wrote back:

Dear Dr Robinson ... I am sorry she is in this state, but feel with her *marvellous* vitality, one not used to her may underestimate her powers of recovery. It is over ten years ago when we were told she could not live six weeks and for *years* she kept us at a daily strain of expecting her to die that very day till my mother's and my health simply broke down ... as you can imagine I am under a very great strain of *urgent* work this week.[30]

Winnie died next day, on February 27. Marie did not have time to see her before her death, but she kept a receipted bill for the funeral expenses: "To Polished Elm Coffin, Lined and Padded with best lining including Shroud also Brass fittings for same and attendance. Payment of 6 Bearers, £9 10s."

CHAPTER 13

The Great Trial

"Members of the Jury, you have now at length come
almost to the end of this rather long and disagreeable
case ... Upon you has fallen in this matter, so far as it
can any longer be controlled, the guardianship of public
morals ..."
Lord Chief Justice Hewart, King's Bench Division,
High Court of Justice, 28 February 1923[1]

THE operation of English libel law is notoriously fickle. As in the case
of Oscar Wilde against the Marquess of Queensberry, it often rebounds
on the plaintiff, when the defence offers evidence to justify the alleged
libel. Unlike Wilde, Marie was not criminally prosecuted as a result of
her action. She herself had started proceedings, and Sutherland's
defence constantly maintained that the hearing was not "a State trial of
birth control". It was, however, essentially Marie and her ideas which
were on trial.

The full passage in Halliday Sutherland's book that Marie complained
of, read:

Exposing the poor to experiment
Secondly, the ordinary decent instincts of the poor are against these
practices; and, indeed, they have used them less than any other class.
But, owing to their poverty, lack of learning, and helplessness, the
poor are the natural victims of those who seek to make experiments
on their fellows. In the midst of a London slum, a woman, who
is a doctor of German Philosophy (Munich), has opened a birth
control clinic where working women are instructed in the method

of contraception, described by Professor McIlroy as "the most harmful method of which I have had experience". (Proceedings of the Medico-Legal Society, July 7, 1921.)

It is truly amazing that this monstrous campaign of birth control should be tolerated by the Home Secretary. Charles Bradlaugh was condemned to jail for a less serious crime.[2]

Even her solicitors advised against action. Since she had taken so long to bring the matter to court, Braby and Waller argued, the alleged libel could not be all that damaging – particularly since Sutherland's book had sold only 800 copies. Marie was adamant. At last she had the opportunity to prove her worth. Her brief to Patrick Hastings, KC, pointed out that she "inherited from both sides of the house a large number of intellectual interests, among her paternal ancestors were a rather preponderating number of Clerics; she understands that Bishop Aylmer, the friend and tutor of the tragic little Queen Lady Jane Grey is among them." Of her message to the Anglican bishops in 1920, Marie informed Hastings, "She did not intend to communicate with them but, coming as she did of Quaker stock, when the Spirit moved her to communicate with them, it was impossible for her not to do so . . . This message has, she believes, been the subject of ribald comment by those opposed to progress but she has nothing to say about it more than the fact that she did not dare not to do what she was definitely instructed to do."[3] Wary at first, Cedric Braby, her solicitor, was eventually won over. At the end of January 1923 he wrote to her: "Did you see in yesterday's *Sunday Pictorial* the announcement of the suicide of a poor woman, who had previously said she was sick of having so many children one after the other?"[4]

The trial opened on 21 February 1923, before Lord Chief Justice Hewart, and lasted nine days. Marie was represented by Patrick Hastings, KC, Sir Hugh Fraser and Herbert Metcalfe; Ernest Charles, KC, H. V. Rabagliati and Harold Murphy appeared for the defendant, Halliday Sutherland; and Serjeant Sullivan, KC, and Theobald Mathew for Sutherland's publishers, Harding and More. What the jury would have to determine was, firstly, whether the alleged libel was defamatory – that is, would it expose the plaintiff to "hatred, ridicule or contempt", cause her to be "shunned or avoided" or damage her in the exercise of her profession or trade? They would then have to distinguish between

statements of fact and statements of opinion and then decide whether
the alleged facts were true and whether the opinions based upon them
were fair comment on a matter of public interest.[5]

As press coverage of the trial revealed, there was still considerable
prejudice against the public discussion of sexual matters. No newspaper
reprinted the more explicit extracts from *Married Love* that were read
out in court, and the headlines in even the popular papers were scarcely
more lurid than *The Times* of February 22: HIGH COURT OF JUSTICE.
KING'S BENCH DIVISION. BIRTH CONTROL LIBEL ACTION. STOPES V.
SUTHERLAND AND ANOTHER. In his opening speech for the plaintiff –
oddly, it might be thought, since he was representing a woman in a
matter of some concern to women generally – Patrick Hastings
betrayed the same feeling. "I am rather glad to think there are no
women on the Jury," he said. "It is a case which it is easier to discuss
with one sex alone rather than a mixture of the two."*

Given the extent of public prejudice, it was obvious that the defence
would concentrate on the sleazier aspects of the case. The first witness
was Sir James Barr, a Fellow of the Royal College of Physicians, former
vice-president of the British Medical Association, and a practising
doctor for forty-seven years. In his cross-examination, Serjeant
Sullivan, counsel for Sutherland's publisher, passed from the "utterly
demoralising" aspects of *Married Love* to the rubber check pessary, of
which, as a vice-president of Marie's clinic, Sir James was in favour:

Q. They are on sale at your Clinic, at this clinic; I call it yours because
you are one of the Patrons; they are on sale there?——A. Yes.

Q. And you approve of the sale of them?——A. Certainly.

Q. I want to know was not the sale of these rubber goods known in
London long before the place, the Clinic, where you might buy
them?——A. Yes, certainly you can buy them in any town.

Q. You know the class of shop in which they appear to have been
sold before the Clinic was started?——A. I do not know what you
mean by class, but I have seen them in most highly respectable
instrument makers in all large towns.

---

* Hastings' instinct was sounder than he probably realised. In 1926 Ernest Thurtle,
MP asked leave in the House of Commons to introduce a bill authorising local authorities to set up birth control clinics. The motion was defeated by 167–81, on a free
vote. Of the four women MPs who voted, only one – Ellen Wilkinson – was in
favour of the motion.

Q. Have you ever noticed in shops, rubber goods stores, and largely advertised, these three books displayed in juxtaposition to these check pessaries?——A. No.*6

The presence of Marie's books in the dreaded "rubber goods store" was as nothing, however, to Serjeant Sullivan's horror at her detailed descriptions in her books of the human sex organs. Was it desirable, he asked Sir James, that such information should be broadcast among the young? Every young person ought to be in possession of such knowledge, Sir James replied.

Q. That is not my question; is it desirable that it be broadcasted to be picked up at the pleasure of the young buying this book? Between ourselves, Sir James, is it not the most probable time at which young people would be tempted to spend their money on such a book, just at the very moment when sexual temptation is strongest within them? Should it not be kept from them? – Is not that so?——A. No, I do not think so; I think it is a pure matter of physiological knowledge which ought to be taught to every young person.

Q. I am not asking you about teaching a young person; letting young persons read such books for themselves is what I asked you; is that advisable?——A. I do not see that it is unadvisable.

Q. If it is not inadvisable why would not you leave that book to be read by your young servants, or, indeed, give it to your own female relatives; is there any objection?——A. If they were that way inclined, it might keep them out of trouble.

Q. At what expense, Sir James?——A. It would be very much better doing that than getting in the family way.

Q. But without the least make-weight of temptation they might have resisted altogether?——A. They do not resist; people who want these books, human nature prevents them from resisting.

Marie gave evidence on the second day of the trial, and she was in the witness box for well over three hours. The defence concentrated their attention on her books – not just her writings about birth control, but about sex generally. The emphasis on this side of her work seemed to

---

* In his particulars of defence, Sutherland had included "The exhibition for sale in the window of a London shop of *Married Love* in close proximity to both rubber pessaries and 'books of a sensual nature', namely *Five Nights*, *Thaïs, or the Monk's Temptation*, *The White Slaves of London*, *The Kinema Girl*."

Marie totally irrelevant. But part of the libel complained of lay in Sutherland's remark: "It is truly amazing that this monstrous campaign of birth control should be tolerated by the Home Secretary. Charles Bradlaugh was condemned to jail for a less serious crime." Since Bradlaugh had been sentenced, in 1877, for publishing an obscene libel (the conviction was overturned on appeal) the defence would have to imply the "obscenity" of Marie's writings, accused as she was of a crime more serious than Bradlaugh's. *Married Love* provided a rich source for mud-slinging, and Ernest Charles, Sutherland's counsel, was particularly incensed by her mention of the possibility of artificial insemination, where normal conception was impossible:

Q. When you are publishing broadcast to old and young, especially the young, have a look at the dedication of the book itself, "Dedicated to young husbands and all those who are betrothed in love." When you are writing a book of that sort dedicated in that way, why do you include a considerable amount of insemination of a woman by the seed taken from a man to whom she has not been . . . why?

A. Because I think it is a matter of great scientific and racial interest, because it has been presented to the world in a serious manner by a serious person, and I am impartial enough at any rate to give a hearing to ideas whether I approve of them or not.

Q. I am not asking, Madame, why you think; I am asking why you think it is desirable or necessary, whichever you like, to include it in a book which you dedicate to young betrothed people, and sell to anybody, even children?

A. Because I think all scientific knowledge relating to such a subject should be in the possession of all rational people.

Q. But you not only do that, Madame, you advise, at page 152; "Hence I suggest that the husband who is deprived of normal fatherhood may yet make the child of his wife's body partly his own, if his thoughts are with her intensely, supportingly and joyously throughout the whole time of the unborn baby's growth. If he reads to her, plays beautiful music or takes her to hear it, and gives her the very best of his thoughts and aspirations, mystical though the conclusion may seem, he does attain an actual measure of fatherhood." So you not only quote it, you quote it with approval as a system?

A. Perhaps because I know of homes in which the young man has been rendered sterile by an early act of careless lasciviousness, and for his life, to his regret, is rendered incapable of fatherhood. I do happen to know even amongst the English aristocracy of a child which has been brought about in this way, to bring happiness and comfort to that home.

Serjeant Sullivan joined the attack with an objection to Marie's advice in *Married Love* as to how best to arouse a woman's physical feelings.* She used "dangerous language", he said, and neatly trapped her into a damaging admission.

Q. You would not like me to read the passages in this assembly, would you?
A. I would not like the spirit in which you read it, no.
Q. The reading of a passage in this assembly you would think would be indecent, would not you?
A. Because of the way in which you read it.
Q. Do not you think it would be indecent?
A. Because of the way in which it would be read.
Q. Would you think it would be indecent for me to read page 51 of your book?
A. For you to do so, yes.
Q. Then, Dr Stopes, will you take it up and read it yourself?
A. No, sir.
Q. Why not?
A. Because of the spirit in which it would be listened to.
Q. By this assembly?
A. Yes, sir.
Q. Then may I take it that neither the reverent nor the irreverent reader could read that passage without scandal here?
A. No.
Q. Then why should not one of us be doing it?
A. Because of the atmosphere in which it would be either read or received.

* "The sensitive inter-relation between a woman's breasts and the rest of her sex-life is not only a bodily thrill, but there is a world of poetic beauty in the longing of a loving woman for the unconceived child which melts in mists of tenderness toward her lover ... her husband's lips upon her breast melt a wife to tenderness and are one of a husband's first and surest ways to make her physically ready for complete union." *Married Love*, 1st edn p. 21 (p. 51 in the edition quoted by Sullivan).

Q. The atmosphere is the atmosphere of the administration of justice; do you know any better; do you know any better atmosphere?
A. I would read it to my Lord and the jury alone, if necessary.*[7]

Serjeant Sullivan, indeed, appeared to think that any form of stimulation was tantamount to prostitution. In *Married Love* Marie had discussed the problem of the married man who might find his wife frigid because his only previous sexual experience had been with prostitutes: "They may not realise that often all the bodily movements which the prostitute makes are studied and simulated because her client enjoys his climax best when the woman in his arms simultaneously thrills."[8] Was not Marie, Sullivan argued, advocating that a woman should be taught how to experience passion? Marie appealed to the Lord Chief Justice:

> My Lord, do you understand I am being pressed about matters which are very difficult to answer. My meaning is, in prostitution, the sexual act is defiled and debased and, contrariwise, on marriage the ordinary young girl marries so ignorant that she does not know, and is not capable of the ordinary complete relationship of marriage. We are brought up so ignorant and so cold that often the nice woman fails in her part, and I tried it – it is difficult matter to do – I tried there to draw the distinction between the prostitute and the ultra-cold and ignorant girl, and to indicate the right thing in marriage is the full physiological reaction to the woman giving wholesale healthy happiness in marriage.

Q. And, carrying out your theory, is not the meaning of that original paragraph of yours that the uninstructed cold woman should be stimulated to passion; do not you advocate that?
A. I only advocate –
Q. Do you advocate that?
A. No.
Q. What do you advocate?
A. I advocate that the woman should be treated as is every feminine

* Referring to this incident in his memoirs, Sullivan later commented: "I am bound to say to her credit that she blushed and protested 'It would be an outrage for anyone to read this book aloud in this atmosphere.' I observed that the atmosphere was that of a court of justice and asked her if she could suggest any atmosphere in which this publication might be read aloud. She could not do so, coming perilously near to adopting the settled criteria of what in law is called an obscene libel." (*The Last Serjeant,* Macdonald, 1952, p. 302.)

creature in God's earth, that the male who is about to approach her, should woo her and stimulate her as all male creatures in the universe do.

Q. That is what I asked you, whether she should not be stimulated, whether this ignorant and cold woman should not be sexually stimulated; is that what you mean?[9]

A New Gospel, of course, provided the ideal opportunity to ridicule Marie. Ernest Charles, K C, read out most of the preface, with Marie's account of hearing, among the yew trees, the explicit instruction from God: "Say to my Bishops." He then asked her:

... Do you believe and represent that what follows here came direct from the Almighty to yourself?

A. As a Quaker, I believe that the spirit moves me at any moment of my daily life.

Q. I am asking you, Madame, do you believe – I have a reason for asking it, because some of the passages – that the Almighty is, I was going to say, supposed to have said, if I may say so without wrongness – do you say to my Lord and the Jury that all that follows in these pages, *A New Gospel*, came from the Almighty God as a God-given message?"

After quoting some of the more inflated prophetic passages, Charles went on:

Q. Now listen to this piece. I will read it and the Jury may see for themselves. "By some ascetic-minded Ministers 'self-restraint' is urged in simple faith in this sense, but it may be and often is misunderstood by the laity to mean what other ministers mean who advise their flock to use 'self-restraint', so as to truncate the act of union that the vital sperm from the man does not penetrate the woman." Forgive me for waiting for the moment. Does not that sound especially like an extract from one of the published works of one Marie Stopes?

A. All my works are not of my own knowledge, but of the instructions I receive of what I am to do.

Q. That is a reason, possibly, why there is a resemblance...

Under further cross-examination by Serjeant Sullivan, the exchanges became even more ludicrous:

Q. I suppose, Dr Stopes, that you recognise that at the bottom of the controversy that you attempt to raise here, there is a question of morality?

A. Profound morality.

Q. So if you are a prophet of God, of course there is an end to it. There can be no controversy. If you are not, that is a subject upon which men must differ as a fundamental conscientious conviction?

A. All the different sects of religion differ.

Q. But if in 1920 the Almighty had sent Dr Stopes to put an end to controversy on this point they may not differ from that put forward; is not that so? is not that your attitude?

A. Oh no, not at all: the Almighty sent Mahomet and still Christians differ from Mohammedans.

Q. He also sent Mahomet?

A. I say there are religions of many sorts. I instanced Mahomet and said the Mohammedans differed from the Christians.

Q. I know that, but you know in 1920, on this subject of sex relationship, you are the last word, are you not? Do you not claim to be the last word; that when you transcribe or transmit the word of God, that ends controversy, does not it? It should end it?

A. I do not think Christ himself ended controversy.

Marie was eventually forced into the position of appearing to claim that God had personally sanctioned the rubber check pessary. Quoting from *A New Gospel*, Sullivan went on:

Q. "God through Science shows how this may be done": did not you understand that to mean the check pessary?

A. Not only, or entirely; it is not my method in any case.

Q. I see, but it includes the check pessary?

A. I did not invent the check pessary.

Q. No, I was going to say the man who invented it, if the circulation of the knowledge of the check pessary is the Divine institution, what must be the moral status of the man who invented it?

A. A great benefactor to humanity.

Q. Did you understand that *Married Love* was included in the benefaction of the researches of science? – Is *Married Love* in the text or among the Apocrypha?

MR PATRICK HASTINGS: I do not think you need answer that.

SERJEANT SULLIVAN: Do you claim for *Married Love* it is similar inspiration of the message to humanity?

A. No, except my whole life is guided by Divine inspiration. I am a Christian, I believe in a living God, with whom I am in daily contact.[10]

Whatever the precise provenance of *Married Love*, Marie was not allowed to escape the imputation of encouraging unmarried love. Towards the end of her long cross-examination, Serjeant Sullivan asked her opinion on the Bradlaugh pamphlet. Using the definition of obscene libel, was it "likely to deprave or corrupt those whose minds are open to immoral influences, and into whose hands the publication might fall?" Under pressure, Marie admitted that certain sentences (the passage appears to be the mention of cantharides, or Spanish fly, as a sexual stimulant) possibly might be. Sullivan immediately reverted to her own books, thus implying a connection. At the end of three hours in the witness box, Marie's mind was at least as sharp as Sullivan's. The exchange is also revealing both of current ideas about sexual propriety and as the first instance of Lord Hewart's bias.*

SERJEANT SULLIVAN: ... Have you, in the course of your investigations considered whether the apprehension of the responsibility of parenthood might be a deterrent to acts of impropriety?

A. I consider that insulting to womanhood.

Q. I do not know that you understand the question I put to you?

A. Perfectly.

Q. I want to know have you considered that among young people, apprehension of the possibility of parenthood has acted as a restraining influence in favour of propriety?

A. I consider that an insult to womanhood; we are not moral because we are afraid, we are moral because it is right and intrinsic in our nature to be moral.

---

* Serjeant Sullivan later remarked of Hewart: "It was ... a great disappointment to his friends that Lord Hewart, the Lord Chief Justice, gradually became an intolerant little tyrant ... He had no judicial qualifications. His mind, like mine, was essentially partisan, a characteristic of my countrymen which makes them good advocates but bad lawyers ... He could not understand what impartiality meant. He made up his mind without hearing a case what justice required, and he did not care how that end might be arrived at." (*The Last Serjeant,* op. cit., p. 301.)

Q. Are you able to answer the questions?

A. You ask me: have I considered that question. I have considered it, and I consider it an insult to womanhood.

Q. Will you answer the question?

A. I understand the question to be: Have I considered that possibility and I say, Yes, I have considered it.

Q. In your opinion?

A. Might I have the question explained. I do not understand.

Q. Perhaps you do not, and your answer suggested to me that you did not understand it, though I thought it was clear. Have you ever considered that the apprehension of resulting parenthood may be a restraining influence on the conduct of young people towards one another?

A. My answer is I have considered that, and I consider it an insult to womanhood.

Q. Very well, that is formal and I pass from it.

LORD CHIEF JUSTICE: Do you mean unmarried people?

SERJEANT SULLIVAN: Yes, unmarried people.

DR STOPES: He means, does he not, that women are moral because they are afraid, and I say no.

LORD CHIEF JUSTICE: I do not think he means that.

DR STOPES: Would you explain to me what he means?

LORD CHIEF JUSTICE: I should put it the other way round. Do you suggest there are not some cases, perhaps many cases, in which persons refrain from fornication because they do not want to produce illegitimate children?

A. I do not think so, except in very rare cases. I think that women are moral because it is right to be; it is insulting to suggest that we are only good because we are afraid.

Q. That is not suggested.

A. It is implied to me.

Q. It is not suggested that is the reason, but that in some cases it may be, and in many cases, it is the reason.

A. I do not think so, no.

Q. In other words, to put it another way, I am sure you will perceive that a criticism will no doubt be made which I think you ought to have an opportunity of dealing with. If you are to teach in a book, married people how to avoid the generation of children, notwithstanding the sexual act is performed – are not you also teaching unmarried people the same thing?

A. My Lord and the Jury, since 1823, these methods of various sorts have been taught. In my books for the first time, I distinguish between what is good and what is harmful, and the method I teach cannot be used by an unmarried girl . . .[11]

Marie's appearance in the witness box created a favourable impression. From her earliest days, when her father had taught her to speak clearly and without embarrassment to his academic friends, she had enjoyed public speaking, and gave no hint of nervousness. Neither did she look at all like the sex-mad, money-seeking Jezebel portrayed by extremist magazines like *Plain English* and *John Bull*. Under the voluminous fur coat that Humphrey had given her, she wore a plain dark dress, with an innocent white Quaker collar and cuffs. Her hats were furred and feathered somewhat extravagantly, but at that period she wore no make-up, and her hair was its natural, dark chestnut colour. The *Daily Graphic* reporter commented: "You might have imagined that Joan of Arc had come to life again. With clasped hands and up-turned eyes, the woman in the box declared that she was the channel for transmission of a message sent direct from Almighty God."[12] Mary Abbott, who had not yet met Marie, wrote to her before even filing her report for the *Westminster Gazette*:

> Dear Dr Stopes, I have just come away from the Lord Chief Justice's court and feel I cannot lunch before sending you my kindest thoughts as well as my sincere congratulations on your splendid courage and wonderful bearing in the witness box . . . your personality dominated the entire Court and created an atmosphere which the cross-examining Counsel found difficult to fight. It was a joy also to see the effect your answers had on the junior members of the Bar who crowded the Court.[13]

As interest in the trial grew, Marie's home at Givons Grove and her office at the Mothers' Clinic were inundated with letters. Some – mostly from Catholics, and usually anonymous – were scurrilous, but they were vastly outnumbered by the letters of support. Lady Constance Lytton offered to help – "I am a spinster without children and not the sort to do much use . . . but it has been practised in our family and by their numerous friends for generations. It should be known, by those who crave to know it, in every class."[14] There were letters from doctors and midwives, approving Marie's stand and asking for information, and from former school friends. One of the saddest was from a woman who had married an Irish farmer. "I often think *what* a difference your Books would have made to our first year of married life!" she wrote to her old friend. "It was a year after our fourth child was born that I first came on your books and do you know it was only then we discovered that we had been wrong all the time as to position which my husband (whose chief knowledge of the subject was gained from his Farm) thought was for the woman to lie face downward. As you can imagine we had never succeeded in having unions that were comfortable . . ."[15]

The support was not limited to the upper and middle classes. George Mills of Hanwell, Middlesex, who had been brought up in a large and poverty-stricken family, wrote in some bitterness about Dr Sutherland's assertion, "The poor are the sanest people in this country about sex matters":

Dear Friends of the Poor . . . Has Dr Sutherland ever waited for his Father's Herring skins with the same eagerness as a Cat and look upon it as a Luxury like thousands of poor Children No I might mention a Cat would never stop in our Home and we were always bringing Stray Cats from the Streets, I suppose our House smelt too much like a Cemetry so they popped off . . . [16]

Marie's performance in the witness box was, perhaps, not quite so pleasing to her legal advisers as to the general public. After a brilliant opening speech, Patrick Hastings appeared to lose interest; so much so that he was not even in court to hear the verdict. Marie prided herself on her knowledge of the law, and she must have been a difficult client. No lawyer likes to be told how to conduct his case and, right at the end of her evidence, when Hastings had completed his re-examination, she demanded to be asked another question, on the grounds that too much irrelevant matter had been dragged in. Hastings, as her counsel, was obviously annoyed:

MR PATRICK HASTINGS: Do not you think you might safely leave that to me?

DR STOPES: I have not been asked about it.

MR PATRICK HASTINGS: If you want to make the speech that otherwise I should make, I shall be glad. I think you may leave it to me. I know how much irrelevant matter has been introduced.

DR STOPES: I have not been asked the question, and I want to answer.

MR PATRICK HASTINGS: I do not want in the least that you and I should part. Tell me the question you want me to ask and I will ask you.[17]

Marie's behaviour, objectionable though it was to her counsel, was far less damaging to her case than that of some of her friends. Dr George Jones, whose ideas on sexual matters were far more liberal than Marie's – he believed in contraception for all who wanted it, rather than just for the married – was quickly in trouble. A gynaecologist and venereologist, who had practised for most of his life in the East End of London, he said that he had never heard children discussing contraceptives, though they talked about sex. Perhaps, suggested Ernest Charles, cross-examining for the defence, that was because they had been reading *Married Love*? Dr Jones rose to the bait. East End children, he replied, said no more than what Quintilian had said centuries earlier.

Q. I rather forget it for the moment.
A. Then I will tell you. "I forget the time when I was a virgin," that was what Quintilian said.
Q. So do I.
A. That is what you are reproducing in a C.3. population which you are so anxious to increase, more shame to you.

Dr Jones's classical education got him into much more serious trouble later in the cross-examination. Ernest Charles questioned him about a particular passage in *Married Love*:

Q. Do you think that is a nice thing for a young person to read?
A. Yes, I do not see why they should not read it; all knowledge is interesting and all knowledge is useful.
Q. If it happens to include filth it does not matter?
A. All knowledge is interesting, filth or no filth, all knowledge –
Q. Is interesting?
A. Yes, '*Homo sum; humani nihil a me alienum puto.*'
Q. You must not talk French here.

A. It is Latin; it is the motto of my own hospital, and it is in Terence's Heautontimoroumenos, Act 1, Scene 2: you ought to have read it.

THE LORD CHIEF JUSTICE: If that is the true doctrine, Dr Jones, the law against obscene publications ought forthwith to be repealed?

A. That is in Terence: I cannot help it.

Q. I am not disputing Terence or the proper application of *Homo sum*. I am dealing with your opinion. I want to see what your opinion really is. If the true doctrine is that all knowledge is interesting, filth included, it seems a little absurd, does it not, to have a law against obscene publications?*[18]

As the case wore on, Lord Hewart's bias became more evident. Dr Harold Chappell, FRCS, gynaecologist at Guy's Hospital, a son-in-law of Arbuthnot Lane – a fact which, the defence appeared to think, revealed a lack of independent judgement – said that he could find nothing morally damaging in Marie's books, nor anything physically damaging in the check pessary. Just before he left the witness box, the Lord Chief Justice interrupted:

LORD CHIEF JUSTICE: ... Why in order to teach a young girl about sex are you to talk to her about the check pessary and why in order to teach a married woman the use of the check pessary are you to write this also about sex?

A. May I reply to your Lordship just in a few words. I happen to be, as you have possibly gathered, the gynaecologist of Guy's Hospital, and I am face to face with very serious problems and a great deal of misery. If you had a heart of stone you could not help being touched by the urgent necessity of trying to help people, but people do not want merely sympathy, but help; it is one of the commonest things. A little time ago, one came as an outpatient ...

Q. I do not want to interrupt you, but we are not dealing with hearts of stone or hearts of gold; we are dealing with a simple plain question. I will repeat it: let it be granted that it is desirable, with a good taste and a right purpose, to teach young mothers of sex. Let it be granted again that for social purposes it is desirable to teach married women,

* Dr Jones later resigned from the CBC, feeling "hopelessly discredited ... The reports of my evidence all suggest that I advocated obscene matter." (16 March 1923, to MCS. BL-S.)

and not the least, the poor married women, about the use of contra-ceptives; what is the point of mixing the two up?

A. How can you do one without the other?

Q. Do you say you cannot?

A. The whole question is merely a question of teaching people about their sex, to tell them that when they become married, under certain circumstances, they will become pregnant, and teach them that which is perfectly obvious from the medical point of view – that a woman cannot go on having a child every year.

Q. Do you really believe and say, doctor, that in order, for example, that a wise father or a prudent mother might teach their children in proper language with righteous purpose something of sex, they must talk to them of check pessaries?

A. If you are going to go into the whole problem you must talk about check pessaries; if you are going to one part of it, you will omit that part of it from the question.

Q. Very well. Thank you.

MR PATRICK HASTINGS: Would your Lordship ask the witness one question upon that, or might I ask it through your Lordship?

THE LORD CHIEF JUSTICE: Certainly.

MR PATRICK HASTINGS: It is as to whether he has found in *Married Love* any references to check pessaries?

THE LORD CHIEF JUSTICE: There are cross-references.

MR PATRICK HASTINGS: Only to the next book.

MR ERNEST CHARLES: One is the sequel to the other.

MR PATRICK HASTINGS: That, we shall see.

THE LORD CHIEF JUSTICE: And, of course, that which is being criticised here is not the one particular book, but all the books which were cited in what is called this campaign.

MR PATRICK HASTINGS: If I may call attention to what I am going to suggest about that, it is, of course, that books do not cover the whole ground of this libel: they have swept them all into one, I admit.

THE LORD CHIEF JUSTICE: I have looked at the books and read a considerable portion of them, not every word, but a good deal, and they dovetail into each other, not without a good deal of ingenuity.

To substantiate the charge of "experimenting on the poor", the defence had to prove the damaging effects of the rubber check pessary.

Since so little was known about contraception at the time, medical opinion in court was evenly divided. None of the poor, ignorant, defenceless victims of Marie's experiments was produced in court to testify against her (they had, after all, not been obliged either to attend her clinic, or to take any advice offered there). In several of her books, however, Marie had mentioned that some women left in the pessary for as long as three weeks – though always with the rider that she herself would never advise its being left in for this length of time. The poor were universally assumed to be dirty, and the defence was much concerned about the possible effects of damming back uterine secretions. The arguments led to some ludicrous exchanges. Cross-examining Sir William Arbuthnot Lane, F R C S, consulting surgeon at Guy's Hospital, Ernest Charles was worried about applying the pessary to a woman suffering from (he was too shy to use the word) "one of those uterine troubles which increases the secretion".

SIR WILLIAM ARBUTHNOT LANE: Do you mean a woman who has got acute gonorrhea? I do not follow you at all.
Q. No?
A. You mean merely some discharge like most women, or most women have?
Q. Endometritis?
A. A pessary would do her no harm, she could dust it and put it by in her pantry, or wherever it is, and use it next day.
Q. What does she do with it?
A. Dust it with a little powder and put it in the drawer; if the children or the cat have not played with it she could use it the next morning.
Q. If the children get hold of the instructions they might put it up themselves . . .

For Mr Charles, cleanliness, and even a modicum of intelligence, were not to be expected from the lower classes. In his exchange with Dr Jane Hawthorne, consulting gynaecologist at the clinic, who was called when the midwife who normally prescribed and fitted the pessaries felt that the case should be seen by a doctor, Mr Charles came off rather the worse:

MR ERNEST CHARLES: Now I want to ask you about the rules that are prescribed by Mrs Stopes in her books as to the way the women are to do it, to feel about and to sit on their heels and so forth and feel about themselves – do not you think that is a very dangerous thing with poor people that they should feel about for themselves?

A. Dangerous in what way?

Q. From the point of view, to begin with, from poor people of cleanliness; I mean to say, one is saying nothing against poor people, but in, say, a district round Holloway, the hands of women that you would see would not be very clean, would they?

A. Well I think they would know that this was a very special occasion on which they had to wash their hands very carefully.

Q. Do not you find that poor people are very careless?

A. I have found on many occasions that the poor patients are very nervous about their own anatomy, and rather reluctant; and that would lead them to be very careful about washing their hands under these conditions.

Q. I do not think I need pursue that further. You agree with me that the dirt in the nails and so forth of very poor people in a slum area or very poor area, would be very dangerous machines to be working with on a business of this sort – dangerous, not machines, but articles, whatever you like to call them, to be feeling a way in the vagina with, and so forth?

A. Well, I cannot say I think it would be very dangerous.

Q. Supposing, for example, you know how broken women's nails are with poor people?

A. Yes, they are generally very short, are not they?

Q. Sometimes.

A. Well, worn down.

Q. And very dirty?

A. Well, if they are very short, they will not have a chance to be dirty.[19]

Professor Anne Louise McIlroy, a specialist in gynaecology since 1898, and unmarried, was adamant in court about the dangers of the check pessary. It could, she said, cause haemorrhage, peritonitis, sterility and death. Supposing, Patrick Hastings asked,

. . . a woman were to come to you and suppose she says "Now I have had three or four children; it is really too much for me, coming too quickly, getting a child every year". Would you advise her to use contraceptives?

A. I would advise her not to have sexual intercourse.

Q. In other words, Dr McIlroy, are not we now getting to the crux of the question; you would advise her not to have relations with her husband?

A. Yes.[20]

Such an attitude, of course, was by no means unusual, especially among unmarried women doctors. More remarkable was the gradual eliciting from Dr McIlroy that she had absolutely no clinical experience whatsoever of the contraceptive method she had so blithely condemned. Once again, Lord Hewart's bias is evident:

MR PATRICK HASTINGS: Now I want to deal with the question of the particular contraceptive for the moment. Have you ever had a case of a woman who has worn one of these pessaries?

DR MCILROY: I have never met a woman yet who was able to fit on the pessary.

Q. I wonder whether you could answer my question: have you ever met a case yet of a woman who has worn one?

A. No.

Q. So that all you have been telling us at some little length in answer to Mr Charles about the dangers of this, is based upon practical experience which does not include one single case of that having been worn?

A. My remarks have been based on the experience of occlusion of the womb.

Q. Quite; but was my question accurate, that it is all based upon experience which does not include one single case where it has been worn?

A. It is not necessary to have a single case.

Q. The answer is that my question was accurately framed and the answer would be yes?

A. It is not necessary to have a single case.

Q. When I say it would be yes, perhaps I may say it should be yes?

A. I do not know.

Q. I do not think I will trouble you any more about that.

THE LORD CHIEF JUSTICE: But I understand the witness to say, Mr Hastings – I am sure you want to deal with the point of the answer –

MR PATRICK HASTINGS: Certainly.

THE LORD CHIEF JUSTICE: I understood her to say: "True, I have never

met a woman who wore a check pessary and had an occlusion of the womb from that cause, but I have had a large experience of the occlusion of the womb and it is upon that experience, not upon my absence of experience of the check pessary, that my evidence is based."
Is that what you say?

A. Yes, my Lord.

MR PATRICK HASTINGS: I am much obliged to your Lordship. I quite accept that, but that was not, if I may say so with respect, the point of my question. My question was – let me see if I am quite right, Miss McIlroy – that you had never had a case of a woman who has worn one of these check pessaries?

A. No.

Q. That is all I want.*[21]

Since opinion – it can scarcely be called evidence – was so evenly balanced on the check pessary issue, Dr McIlroy's admission was a point in Marie's favour. Much more damaging to her case, however, was the "gold pin" †controversy. Little known in Britain at the time, the pin had been mentioned several times by Marie in her books – though

---

* A few years later, Marie claimed a moral revenge. Hearing that Professor McIlroy was now fitting women with pessaries, she disguised herself as a very dirty charwoman and went along to the clinic: "After I was arranged on the examination couch underneath a coverlet, Professor McIlroy approached me wearing a rubber glove and told me to move my legs apart, pushing my legs in the direction desired through the coverlet. Before actually fitting the cap she did not even glance at the sex organs or even by a momentary view examine the labia or vaginal orifice for discharge. She made no examination for venereal or other germs ... A nurse supplied Dr McIlroy with a graded series of vaginal rubber caps. She took one out and without visual examination or looking what she was doing, thrust the cap in, and almost immediately withdrew it, saying 'Yes, that is your size!' While the cap was being inserted, I felt extreme discomfort amounting to pain sufficiently acute to make it a great strain not to cry out or wince ..." (13 December 1927. BL-S. Autobiographical fragment.)

Marie wrote to the Royal Free Hospital, demanding an apology and a retraction from Professor McIlroy for her earlier statements about the pessary. The secretary of the hospital wrote back: "Dear Madam, I am directed to acknowledge receipt of your letter of the 10th inst, which has been considered by the Weekly Board. They are much surprised that you should have abused the privileges of the Hospital by obtaining advice under such circumstances. They are not concerned in the dispute to which you refer and as you make no complaint regarding your treatment, my Board see no object in continuing the correspondence."

† The first of what are now called intro-uterine devices, or IUDs. Shaped like a wishbone, with a hollow stem, the device had first been introduced to promote conception by encouraging the passage of semen into the uterus, the pin being removed once conception had been achieved. Its contraceptive effects, however, were quickly noticed. Even now, the precise mode of action of the IUD is not fully understood, though there is evidence that a foreign body in the uterus may create a hostile environment to an already fertilised egg. (See J. Peel & M. Potts, *Contraceptive Practice*, C.U.P., 1969 p. 131.) In this sense, the method could be described as an abortifacient.

always with the proviso that it must be fitted by a doctor, and that its effects were not fully known. Marie was interested in the idea and, only a month after the clinic opened, asked the Surgical Manufacturing Company to make to her own specifications "a small simple pin of flexible vulcanite or celluloid medicated so as to be suitable for internal use".[22] Though the pin was not used at the clinic, it figured largely throughout the trial, and even Marie's own witnesses found it impossible to deny that its action might be that of an abortifacient.

The defence subpoenaed Norman Haire, the doctor originally in charge of the Malthusian League's clinic which had opened in Walworth six months after Marie's. In June 1921 Marie had sent along to Dr Haire one or two women whom she thought might benefit from the insertion of a gold pin pessary. Her accompanying letter, read out in court, was highly damaging:

> ... I am interested in what you say about the women who are keen on birth control and quite unbiased. Are they themselves speaking from personal knowledge of their own use of it, because I hear from American women it is entirely satisfactory. I should therefore, like very much for you, if you do not mind, to take on two or three cases, which you could watch carefully and if these yielded unsatisfactory results, we will then drop it. On the other hand, if it does have, as reported, so many advantages, I should be sorry to discard it without proper investigation. I have now on hand two or three people who desire its insertion ... In corresponding with these two women, I have stated as follows: "I would warn you that the method being a new one, we are not yet quite sure whether the result would be entirely satisfactory, but Dr Haire will watch the case carefully and remove the spring if it seems advisable ..."[23]

Dr Haire did not insert the pin largely because, as he wrote to Marie, he had heard of a case where such insertion had been followed by septic abortion. But the "experimental" implications of her letter were damning, as Serjeant Sullivan was not slow to realise. Next day, in his final address to the jury, he went through the whole letter sentence by sentence, asking at the end of each – with some justification – "Is that not experimenting?"* On the wider accusations of "experiment"

---

* In his evidence, Dr Sutherland had defined what he meant by "exposing the poor to experiment" as "The indiscriminate distribution of knowledge of contraceptives

Sullivan's histrionic talent was displayed at its most flamboyant. What, he argued, was to have been the position of the working classes if, in 1880, they had ignored the birth control advice of Bradlaugh and Mrs Besant? The poor were to be overwhelmed by their children, to sink lower and lower into misery and be reduced to a dreadful position of servitude. Yet Bradlaugh had failed in the campaign which Marie Stopes was now trying to revive, and what was the result?

> It is not altogether unfortunate that we can look back on this prog-nostication of 40 years ago. Some of you can remember your city of forty years ago, or perhaps you cannot, because the man who passes through it every day thinks that the city he sees today is the one he looked at yesterday. It is not. The stranger will come back – he has not seen your city for forty years, and therefore *he will see the wonderful progress of civilisation, the wonderful advent of capitalists and comparative prosperity to the class that was to be overwhelmed in misery by its children* ...
>
> Have the workers become slaves? Have the slums become more noisome and more pestilential? Have these people been ruined by their children? Their children have made them the rulers of your land. They have the right of the highest of the land, and their numbers have secured for them a position that in the day of Bradlaugh and Besant might have appeared to be the dream of a lunatic. So you see, when we come to consider whether this new Evangel is not itself a gigantic experiment, we can look back to its last revival and see the prophecy of evil if it was not then adopted. It was rejected, and its rejection so far from bringing in its train the dreadful misery and servitude of the poor, *has raised the humble workers of this country to that magnificent position of social and political independence that they never could have attained if they had ceased to be the fathers and mothers of their children.* (author's italics)

It was not a picture of England in 1923 that would have been immediately recognised by Britain's two million unemployed capitalists. Nor was the Lord Chief Justice totally in touch with reality. Indeed, on one point at least, he was in definite error. Summing up to the jury at the

---

amongst the poor for the purpose of attempting to redistribute the birth rate by artificial contraceptives and contrary to the law of nature." (Box, *The Trial of Marie Stopes,* Femina Books, 1967, p. 238.)

end of what he called "this rather long and disagreeable case", Lord
Hewart referred to Marie's counsel's stress upon the plaintiff's philanthropy, and the way in which she devoted her money to what she felt
to be a righteous cause. Well, said Lord Hewart:

... when I heard that the second time, I was minded to do a little
sum. *Married Love*, in the copy which is handed to me is the 191st
thousand. You see on an early page this remarkable list of re-publica-
tions and reprints – this little thing – not a great deal of paper and
typesetting in it – is 6s. net. *Wise Parenthood* in my copy is the
165th thousand; I do not know what further issues there have been,
or whether there the matter ended; but you know 191 thousand
copies at 6s. make £57,300; 165 thousand copies at 3s. 6d. make
£28,875. If you add them together, you get £86,175 – something
between £80,000 and £90,000 sterling. Well, of course, one does not
know what part of that sum has been swallowed up in printing,
paper, bookbinding; 9s. 6d. they cost together – but it is quite clear
that there must be a very large part of the £80,000 or £90,000
available for some purpose. Now, the Plaintiff says that money is
devoted to the cause. Then one begins to see what the dimensions of
this propaganda may be, or may become.[24]

Lord Hewart's elementary mistake was in assuming that Marie would
herself get most of the published price of the book. Few authors are on
a royalty, per copy sold, of more than 15%; up to this stage, Marie
would have made no more than £12,000, certainly not £80,000.

On the question of obscenity, Lord Hewart reminded the jury of the
prosecution's argument that the publications could not be obscene,
since there had been no criminal prosecution.

Members of the Jury, you probably know – if you do not know I
will ask you to take it from me – the Attorney-General and the
Director of Public Prosecutions often – not occasionally, but often
– have to consider whether upon the whole, it is or is not desirable
in a particular case to commence a criminal prosecution – not
because they have much doubt as to the strength of the case which
might be made before the Jury – but whether they may not do a
great deal more harm than good by launching the matter into the
public and the press. I speak of what I know.

The jury, he went on, may think it a calamity that such books should be widely available, but they must ask themselves the question:

What can be the legitimate purpose of the insertion in these books, to be read by married and unmarried, young and old, persons of both sexes, whoever can find, in the one case, 6s., and in the other case, 3s. 6d., passages which describes the male organ in quiescence and in erection, which describes the encouragement which a man should give to a woman and a woman should give to a man before the act of intercourse is entered upon, and which analyse the successive phases and sensations of the act of sexual intercourse?

Suppose, he went on, that the issue (of the books alone) were being tried at the Central Criminal Court, and that the defence submitted to the jury that there was no evidence on which the publication could be found obscene. "Would you not be greatly astonished if any one of His Majesty's judges held that there was no evidence?"[25] And if, for some reason, the jury should think that Dr Sutherland had gone a little too far in some slight respect, and the question of damages arose, "there is a very, very small coin of this realm which is sometimes thought suitable in such a case."

Four hours later, at eight p.m., the jury returned with answers to the four questions the Lord Chief Justice had asked them to consider.

1 Were the words complained of defamatory to the Plaintiff?——Yes.
2 Were they true in substance and in fact?——Yes.
3 Were they fair comment?——No.
4 Damages, if any?——£100.

On this confusing verdict, both sides in the case claimed judgement and Lord Hewart deferred his decision until the next day. Next morning, March 1, most newspapers had interpreted the jury's verdict as a victory for Marie Stopes. The Lord Chief Justice, however, was of a different opinion. After legal wrangles over the implications in his summing-up as to what constituted fact and what constituted opinion, he found in favour of the defendant, Dr Halliday Sutherland.

Lord Hewart's decision created a furore. Alfred Goodman, KC, obviously thought that Hewart's summing-up had been biassed, and that Marie Stopes had been robbed of her victory by legal technicalities. "After such a summing up as the jury listened to I cannot for a moment think that it was their intention to decide otherwise than that you had been unfairly treated."[26] The jury, apparently, were of the same opinion. According to Marie's solicitor, Cedric Braby, they abstracted all Marie's books from the jury room, leaving Sutherland's ostentatiously behind. The majority of newspapers, among them the *Manchester Guardian*, *Reynolds News* and the *Westminster Gazette*, deplored Hewart's decision, and the *Daily News*, which carried a leader applauding Marie's determination to appeal, gave prominence to a letter from George Bernard Shaw:

Sir – Your article in this case is headed "A Verdict and a Ruling". May I point out that there was no verdict? Instead of finding a verdict the jury allowed itself to be drawn into answering questions, which was not its business. Juries should never answer questions and never argue. What has just happened in a case quite as important in its way as the trial of the seven bishops makes it unnecessary to say anything more except that if jury men are not better instructed in their rights and duties than they are at present, the continuous pressure of the Bench to usurp their functions will end in nothing being left to the jury but the responsibility for the Judge's decision.[27]

The *Westminster Gazette* argued that if Marie Stopes was immoral, then all cinemas, theatres, shop windows, evening gowns – even spring mornings – were also immoral. "Women who desire to know how to prevent unwanted children are bad women. Such is the law as it stands. The law is not functioning usefully."[28] Evelyn Sharp, in the *New Leader*, deplored the fact that birth control was condoned "if practised by the wealthier and more instructed sort ... You could always pretend that it was a curious provision of Nature that endowed the duke's wife with three children, and the docker's wife with thirteen."[29]

Charles Huntington, Marie's publisher at Putnam's, was delighted with the result of the trial. While indignant about the verdict, he exulted in the orders for Marie's books. "I think you would have been pleased," he wrote to her on March 3, "if you could have looked in at the office any day and almost any hour during the last few days and seen the writing of invoices, addressing of labels, packing and the huge stream of parcels of your books going out constantly." From the general public, there were so many letters of sympathy that Marie had to send out duplicated letters in reply: "Dear ..... The result of the trial is indeed remarkable, but I feel absolutely vindicated as I obtained a clear finding for damages from the British public as represented by a Jury, though this is withheld as a legal technicality. Even this has worked for good and led to many public expressions of sympathy and indignation ..."[30]

One of the public expressions of sympathy caused a small riot. On March 3, two days after Lord Hewart's ruling against Marie, the Mayor of Oxford and the Vice Chancellor of Oxford University (where two days previously a Union debate had decided by 137 votes to 93 in favour of government support for birth control) banned a Town Hall meeting at which Marie was to speak. The meeting was rapidly transferred to Ruskin College – outside the university's jurisdiction – and Marie eventually appeared, to enormous applause, and the presentation of a bunch of yellow mimosa from Evelyn Waugh, then an undergraduate and not yet a Catholic.*

For Marie, such moral victory was not enough. She appealed; and five months later, on July 20 1923, Hewart's judgement was reversed in the Court of Appeal, by a majority of two to one, and Marie got her £100 damages, half the costs of the actions and the costs of the appeal. Not all judges, it appeared, were as unaware as the Lord Chief Justice of the change in public opinion as to what constituted a tendency "to deprave and corrupt". Lord Justice Scrutton pointed out that opinion had changed since 1877, when the Bradlaugh-Besant case came to trial, and when a public discussion of venereal disease would have been "almost impossible".

> ... but since the war the most respectable papers have opened their columns to the plainest discussion of these matters, and the most respectable persons have taken part in these discussions. The merits and methods of artificial birth prevention seem to me to stand in a similar position. In 1887 it would have been impossible to discuss them publicly; in 1923 there is probably a great change in public

---

* "It caused a tremendous stir," recalls George Edinger, who organised the meeting. "We broke the glass case outside the Town Hall, and removed the notice banning the meeting. I was arrested, charged with malicious damage, and released on bail. I was fined £3. The court was full of incensed undergraduates, and the Vice Chancellor refused to let me take my degree. To us, you see, Marie Stopes was a victim of the Establishment." – George Edinger, barrister and journalist, interview with the author, 20 August 1975.

THE GREAT TRIAL 239

opinion, as to the necessity for discussion, coupled with great difference of opinion as to the advisability of such methods. Whether or not the Plaintiff's book in 1923 is a more serious crime than Bradlaugh's publication in 1877, involved to my mind a series of questions of opinion . . .

Lord Scrutton's views on the "Doctor of German Philosophy" issue, which Dr Sutherland maintained in court had been meant only as a reference to his disapproval of the "materialism" of German philosophy, were also pertinent:

We do not talk about Doctor of (English) Science, or Master of (English) Arts, and the jury may have thought the expression was used to tar the Plaintiff with the German brush to an unfair extent and not have been much impressed with the suggestion that what was meant was that German philosophy was grossly materialistic, a view that does not show much acquaintance with the works of Hegel and Immanuel Kant.[31]

For Marie and her supporters, it was a famous victory, but Pyrrhic. The Catholic Church was not going to accept defeat. Their only recourse was appeal to the final arbiter – the House of Lords. Legal advisers on both sides suggested that an amicable settlement could be reached without going to these lengths. But Marie, like the Church, was unwilling to make the slightest concession. She wrote to her solicitors in December 1923: "Dear Mr Braby . . . the suggested announcement for the Press seems to me simply impertinent. I should be inclined at the moment to get you to write in the following terms: 'Our client considers your suggestion laughable, and says "go to the Lords and be damned!"'"[32]

It was Marie who was to be damned. Backed up by the Church, Sutherland decided to appeal to the House of Lords. A national fund was set up – Cardinal Bourne contributed £400 – and, under the heading, SOMEONE HAD TO STEM THE FLOOD, the Catholic newspaper *The Universe* invited every "right-thinking person" to contribute: "It has been endorsed by every Catholic Bishop in the Country. Such is the importance which Ecclesiastical Authority attaches to the case. By the immediate success of the Fund it is hoped to give the country a lesson of the solid Catholic determination to stem the flood of Pagan ideas which threatens the future of the Nation and of Christianity . . .

Every Catholic – every right-thinking person – is asked to give something – something large if possible; but at least a mite as an evidence of goodwill."[33] Catholics were not alone in their defence of Dr Sutherland. In February, 1924, a leader in the *Church Times*, the Anglican newspaper, recommended its readers to contribute to the fund.*

Three of the five Law Lords who heard the appeal on 21 November 1924 were over eighty years of age. It may possibly have been this factor, rather than Catholic opposition, that decided the issue. By a majority of four to one, they decided in favour of Dr Sutherland, with costs against Marie, including the insignificant but highly symbolic repayment of the original £100 damages. Dr Sutherland estimated that the case had cost about £10,000 (mostly paid by fellow-Catholics). Marie reckoned her own costs at about £12,000 (though she never mentioned the contributions from her publishers. In January 1924, delighted by the boom in her sales following the trial, Charles Huntington sent a cheque for £1325 towards her costs).

Who, then, apart from the lawyers, were the beneficiaries from this case, which had dragged on for two and a half years? Cardinal Bourne was in no doubt. On November 22, the day after the Lords' decision, he told his congregation: ". . . a really great victory has been gained for the cause of morality . . . it seems to me there is a particular significance in the fact that this very far-reaching decision was arrived at on the Feast of the Presentation of Our Lady."[34]

Marie's reactions were not so simple. She had plenty of support. Immediately after the appeal to the Lords, Alfred Goodman wrote to her: "My dear Dr Stopes, I am amazed and horrified at the result of the appeal! What it must mean to you – to have to face this frightful and unexpected blow – I dare not think! . . . Every right-thinking person in the country must feel sorry and ashamed at such a travesty of justice." In December 1924 Bernard Shaw wrote from Ayot St Lawrence:

My dear Marie Stopes, The decision is scandalous; but I am not surprised at it: the opposition can always fall back on simple tabu.

---

* "Many Anglicans also subscribed, although the Archbishop of Canterbury had declined to co-operate with Cardinal Bourne in this matter. As the fund was over-subscribed, the Anglican subscriptions were returned." (Halliday Sutherland, *A Time to Keep*, Geoffrey Bles, 1934.)

The subject is obscene: no lady would dream of alluding to it in mixed society: reproduction is a shocking subject, and there's an end of it ... Huxley had to have reproduction out of his textbook of physiology, and you are as helpless as Huxley. I wonder what the Lord Chancellor will say to your last appeal! And WHAT has this business cost you? ever GBS. [35]

For Marie, sympathy was not enough. She was well aware of the incalculable publicity the trial had brought her. But she could not bear to be officially in the wrong, even though that position, brought about by her "implacable" enemy, the Catholic church, was essential to her propaganda. She needed to be hated, but wanted to be loved – an impossible, but not uncommon, ambition. From now on, her cause, her enemy, and she herself became so closely identified that she was no longer able to make a rational distinction between them.

CHAPTER 14

A Son is Born

"ROE: on the 27th March to Dr Marie Stopes, wife of
H. V. Roe, of Givons Grove, Leatherhead, Surrey
– a son."
Advertisement refused by *The Times*, 27 March 1924

ON 27 February 1923, the fourth day of the libel action against Dr
Sutherland, and the day of Winnie's death, Hatchard's, the Piccadilly
booksellers, sent on to Marie a postcard from Wakefield. The card,
headed "P. Ward, Dealer in Oysters, Mussels, Cockles and Whelks,
Old Crown Yard, Wakefield", went on: "Dear Sir do you stock Dr
Stopes Book on Large Famerleys if so kindly state prise i want it for a
friend has i am over 60 & no use for me i enclose 1½ stamp for reply
please Having seen the Case in the Dailey News."[1]

Marie had at last got through to the working classes – and far more
successfully than through the pamphlets deliberately addressed to them.
With her sure instinct for publicity, she was always "good copy", and
delighted as much in providing it as newspapers revelled in reporting
her every move (for the final House of Lords appeal in the Sutherland
case, Marie wore a large black hat, trimmed with white ostrich feathers,
thus ensuring maximum front-page coverage in most daily newspapers).
As one newspaper remarked: "She is among the most photographed
ladies of the day, and the list of her achievements appears on all
occasions. In fact the fierce light that beats upon a throne is a feeble
luminary compared with that which keeps the public informed about all
that happens to Dr Stopes ..."[2] Even the *Sporting Times*, a newspaper
not noted for its interest in ladies' fashions, quoted a description of her
taste in dress: "... on the bright side of things, and faring forth to a

London garden party and arrayed in a frock of several joyous colours, she makes rather an unusual picture in the streets – the picture, as it were, of a country girl letting herself go with a cheerful complacency in the adoration of the swain who is hurrying to meet her with all his fervent might"[3]

Marie recognised the benefits that the trial had brought her. Lord Hewart's decision in favour of Sutherland, she wrote to her publisher, "has roused so much more enthusiasm for me than simple success would have done that I cannot regret it". Charles Huntington calculated that she would now make more profit from her books in six months than she normally would in a year. Given Marie's phenomenal energy and output, this would make a considerable difference to her income.* By the end of 1923, only five years after the publication of *Married Love*, she had written no fewer than ten books on sex, marriage and birth control; three stage plays on related topics; pamphlets and articles, in addition to her scientific publications, with R. V. Wheeler, on the structure of coal. But the making of money was never Marie's first consideration. It was, she felt, much more important to harness the wave of enthusiasm generated by the trial. Books, press articles and litigation were all very well, but they were no longer enough for the vast conversion she had in mind. Through the cinema, a relatively new medium, she could obviously reach a much wider audience. Within two months of her original libel action against Sutherland, Marie had written her first film.

Maisie's Marriage† was a fast-moving popular melodrama, of a kind that would now raise condescending giggles, though it was no funnier than Marie's stoutly maintained assertion that she had absolutely no propagandist intent. "It is not ours to preach nor to judge the conduct of others," ran the first caption in this silent film, before launching into what was in fact a cinematic version of Marie's ideas. The heroine, Maisie, is the eldest of the ten Burrows children, who "live in Slumland" (shot of harassed mother, squalling brats and drunken, violent father). She loves Dick, a local lad whose steady rise up the ladder of the

* By December 1923 *Married Love*, with 22 reprints, had sold in Britain alone 406,000 copies; *Wise Parenthood*, with 14 reprints, 305,000 copies.

† The film was originally entitled *Married Love*, but the British Board of Film Censors objected. *Maisie's Marriage* was produced by Samuelson's, who now possess one of the few, uncensored copies of the original version. David Samuelson kindly lent me the copy, and it was screened privately at the British Film Institute in December 1975.

fire service is, apparently, due to his being an only child (shot of beaming, white-haired mother knitting happily by brightly polished fender). Maisie refuses to marry Dick, so frightened is she of ending up like her mother, and runs away from home. Lost in Piccadilly Circus, she is befriended by some prostitutes who take her to a nightclub: "a mystic underworld," runs Marie's delightful caption, "where Aphrodite and Bacchus foxtrot to the music of a negroid band." There she is approached by a drunk who confides that it is all his wife's fault – "A man's a man, flesh and blood – can't mate with an icicle." A fight develops and Maisie, distressed by negroid music, champagne, and the thought of her nine siblings, rushes out and jumps into the Thames. She is rescued by a Mr Sterling (the actor playing the part misjudged his leap, broke an ankle and had to be replaced).

The Sterlings obviously represented Marie's ideal of the happy home. They live in a large house, with a well-kept garden, three well-kept children, a nurserymaid, cook, and an open Lagonda tourer. Why, wonders Maisie, gratefully accepting their offer of a post as under-parlourmaid, is it all so different from Slumland? Well, explains Mrs Sterling (ignoring the slight matter of a large annual income), take roses, for example. If allowed to grow unhindered, they produce sickly, weak blooms, quick to wither and die. Prune them, and you get magnificent, long-lived flowers (shot of a rose gradually turning into a baby's face). All is now clear; but, left in charge of the nursery one evening, Maisie is visited by one of her dissolute brothers, a weak and sickly bloom, who becomes so obstreperous that she has to leave the nursery to get help. Inevitably, the nursery catches fire; equally inexorably, they are all rescued by Dick the fireman and Maisie can at last look forward to a life of married love and joyous and deliberate motherhood.

Not surprisingly, the British Board of Film Censors, under its president, T. P. O'Connor (a Catholic) reacted strongly. The board wrote to the producers: "There are many scenes and sub-titles which render this film in our opinion unsuitable for exhibition before ordinary audiences; while the title, taken in conjunction with the name of the book and the authoress referred to, suggests propaganda on a subject unsuitable for discussion in a cinema theatre." He objected in particular to the shot of the rose turning into a baby's face, and also to Maisie's explanation to Dick of why she could not marry him. The caption, "It's drudgery, and then it will be children, children and we can't afford to clothe and keep them," must be replaced, the board stipulated, by "It's drudgery, drudgery from morning till night." They also insisted on the deletion of Maisie's comments, "Your father died before he did the harm mine's done," (i.e. the fathering of ten children) and "Did I ask to be created? Don't you think had I known, I should have remained unborn?"[4]

At first, Marie gave T. P. O'Connor the benefit of the doubt. "Dear Mr O'Connor," she wrote on May 15:

> You will probably recall that you and I were together on the Cinema Commission and you know how anxious we were to raise the whole tone of the Cinema, so I am sure that it was without your knowledge that when I had taken exceptional trouble to get a film of the highest moral character and absolutely unimpeachable, in which there is not one word or scene to which any reasonable exception could be taken that I am more than astonished to receive a letter dated May 11 from one of your assistants who has written that the film produced for me by Mr Samuelson, one of our best producers, is censored ... The subject of love is surely not unsuitable in a Cinema theatre and I should have thought that you would prefer to have love married rather than unmarried as it is in most of the vulgar films.[5]

On hearing, however, that T. P. O'Connor had stolen Home Office writing-paper to write to all the country's Chief Constables (decisions about whether or not to show films were taken by local watch committees, outside the board's control) Marie threatened him with legal action, and wrote to all the Chief Constables personally. Most of them ignored O'Connor's advice and – outside London, where the film did not receive a West End screening until 1925 – *Maisie's Marriage* was a success, coinciding as it neatly did with Marie's successful appeal in July against the Sutherland decision.* She remained convinced, however, that T. P. O'Connor had ruined a brilliant career as a film-writer.†

---

* One newspaper carried a big display advertisement: "£100 DAMAGES was awarded yesterday to DR MARIE STOPES, in connection with her great work MARRIED LOVE. Remember your last chance to see this wonderful story is TONIGHT, at the PICTURE-DROME, the coolest house in Burton." – *Burton Daily Mail* 21 July 1923.

† Hearing that Bernard Shaw had been offered £20,000 for what she called "one of those ancient and rather unmarketable stories", Marie in 1927 offered the film producer, W. R. Newman, one of her own films for £5000. This was too much, Newman replied,

The sheer volume of Marie's activities at this period is scarcely credible. *Maisie's Marriage* was made in a fortnight, and trade-shown in May 1923. During the next month, she gave lectures throughout the country in cinemas where the film was showing, attended a three-day central heating conference in Paris, and wrote four articles for various cinema magazines on the perfidy of Mr T. P. O'Connor. None of them was published. "It was a rather funny coincidence," one of the articles ran, "that the week I was banned in the Cinema, I spoke from the Pulpit in Portsmouth. At the Sunday evening service at which I spoke the crowds down the aisle and standing even on the gravestones were so great that I was told afterwards people were enquiring what member of the Royal Family was there."[6] In June, her book *Contraception, Its Theory, History and Practice* was published. Aimed primarily at the medical and legal professions, it was, for Marie, unusually restrained and sober in style, and was well received by the medical press (the *Law Times* refused any advertisement for it). Marie allowed herself, however, to reprint several of the more harrowing case histories from her Mothers' Clinic, which, in the middle of all her other preoccupations, she still visited daily, when not flitting about between Glasgow, Portsmouth and Paris.

The clinic records, indeed, provide the most accurate measure of the value of the publicity accruing from the trial. In 1921, when it opened, advice was given to 518 women. In 1922, the first full year of operation, there were 1019 cases and in 1923, the year of the trial, the attendance figures leapt to 2368.[7] Naturally, her very success increased Marie's burdens. Though always careful to point out to patients that she was a doctor of science, and not of medicine, she saw many of the women herself before passing them on to Nurse Maud Hebbes, the clinic's midwife, who then either recommended a contraceptive or referred the case to Dr Jane Hawthorne, the visiting consultant.

The trial also resulted in a vastly increased correspondence. The case had been reported in newspapers all over the world and one postal delivery alone at the clinic in 1923 brought 350 letters. A fairly typical plea for help came in November that year from Mrs Mary Willis, of Queensland, Australia, who wrote that the Customs had seized the

---

though he would give £10,000 for anything Shaw might produce. Furious, Marie wrote back: ". . . my books sell in far greater numbers than his do . . . I should not have thought that he would be twice the draw that I am." (13 and 23 December 1927. BL-S.)

"Pro-Race" pessary Marie had sent her: "Dear Doctor ... I have again become pregnant when my baby was only six months old ... I would to God you could write me on the subject. It sounds drastic, but unless I can get relief somehow I will leave my husband, as I am just sick and weary of being a breeder just fancy travelling as we have to do long distances 2 or 3 days by coach to the nearest railway station (with a family of little ones) then back again with another, year in and out with never a friend near you ..."[8]

Officially, Humphrey was Secretary of the Society for Constructive Birth Control, and was only too ready to take on the bulk of the correspondence. But Marie found it impossible to delegate responsibility: only she could deal adequately with the urgent human problems that came in by every post.

As if all these were not sufficient activity for one woman, Marie decided to expand her crusade further. On 14 November 1923, her first major stage production, *Our Ostriches*,[9] opened at the Royal Court Theatre in London. Even more blatantly propagandist than her film, the play features a typical Stopesian heroine, Evadne – middle-class, beautiful, and with a serious social conscience aroused by the sufferings of an East End family overburdened with children. The action alternates between the slums and the meetings of the Birth Rate Commissioners (the "ostriches" of the title). Eventually, Evadne throws over her rich, aristocratic fiancé, and finds true love with Dr Hodges, the only Commissioner who has dared to sign the minority report dissenting from the commission's condemnation of birth control. The parallels with Marie's life are too obvious to need pointing out. As the curtain fell on the opening night, some hissing was noticed by the reviewer from the *Westminster Gazette*, though the press reception was generally friendly. The reviewer found himself unable to comment on it as drama, finding it "deliberate and unadulterated propaganda".

Between *Maisie's Marriage* in May and *Our Ostriches* in November, Marie had finally managed to become pregnant. Whatever Humphrey's failings, she never hinted that her marriage was anything less than perfect. She and Humphrey, she insisted, were "still on their honeymoon", five years after marriage.[10] In addition to Givons Grove, their large house near Leatherhead, Marie had now acquired a holiday home, the Old Lighthouse on Portland Bill in Dorset, the gigantic rock jutting out into the English Channel. The area was relatively unspoiled at the time, and the lighthouse, consisting of two circular rooms one on top of the other with cottages attached, was surmounted by a platform with views over cliffs and sea grand enough to satisfy even Marie's romantic imagination. It was here, at the age of forty-two, that her only living child was conceived. Shortly after his birth, in phrases purpler than any Homeric sea, she recalled the occasion: "This baby was loved . . . loved for years before times were propitious for his advent, loved most specially on the day he was conceived, when on a stone tower high above the sea, with the sea all round it and the brilliant blue sky above, in a blaze of sunlight, he was called into being. There, as the night fell and the blue darkened into a purple curtain spangled with great stars, his mother lay under the sky, high above the world all night . . ."[11]

It was a heady beginning for any child. "A peaceful, brooding life is the one for you now," wrote a friend, "wandering about your grounds and needleworking for your coming joy."[12] Marie had no intention of following either this, or her own advice in *Radiant Motherhood* as to the importance to the developing foetus of beautiful music and improving pictures. She had enough sense, at the advanced age of forty-three, not to trust to either Nature or Art. Her child was born on 27 March 1924, by Caesarean section. He weighed, announced the birth card, $8\frac{3}{4}$ lbs, and was 19 inches tall.

Without giving any reason to Humphrey, who had taken the announcement round personally, *The Times* refused to print it.* Other newspapers were not so worried about offending their readers. "SON & HEIR FOR DR MARIE STOPES", announced the *Daily Sketch*, "Famous Advocate of Birth Control a Mother. AUTHORESS AND LINGUIST. Story of Romantic Marriage to Aircraft Pioneer."[13] The *Daily Express* interviewed Humphrey, who said he was sorry it had not been twins, "We should have liked a girl as well", and a fortnight later spoke to Marie, after her further operation following the birth: "'The

---

* *The Times* often refused advertisements for Marie's books, her clinic, and meetings of the CBC. After complaints, Mr Walter of *The Times* wrote in February 1924: ". . . let me assure you again that the Roman Catholics are not responsible, either directly or indirectly, for the exclusion of your advertisements . . . The fact is, that however one may sympathise with the object you have in view, there is a widespread difference of opinion as to the desirability of publishing broadcast detailed explanations and discussions of the methods you advocate. The advertisement of one of your books which appeared in "The Times" on a former occasion, gave rise to protests from a number of our readers." (7 February 1924, Mr Walter to MCS. BL-S.)

sister at the nursing home where he was born told me that she had never seen such a beautiful new-born baby in the whole of her career . . . That is what comes of birth control. You get your babies when you want them and at the right time. You get the good, strong babies and cut out the weaklings.'"[14]

Marie was convinced that Harry Verdon Stopes-Roe was the most extraordinary child ever born to woman (she had many a wrangle with the aged Mrs Stopes as to which of them had produced the most beautiful baby). Most mothers think this about their children, of course, but Marie pursued the feeling to obsessional lengths. A month after Harry's birth, she wrote to Professor Wheeler, her former colleague in coal research, and Harry's godfather: "I want to let you see Baby Harry, otherwise known as the infant Hercules, for he lifted his head and poked it around while lying on his 'tummy' when only one day old, a feat which is only achievable, according to Truby King's standard work, by a child two months old. He is really a remarkable baby."[15]

Her problems as a mother were rather different from those of the mothers she wrote for. Where, she complained, was she to find a cook good enough to make the kind of nourishing milk pudding suitable for her son? Where was there a nursemaid of sufficiently high standard to cope with such a paragon? When Harry was just over a year old, Marie wrote to the nursing agency who supplied her with a constant stream of replacements. The latest, she informed the agency, had many admirable qualities, but "I left her in sole charge for two weeks while I was away from home and parted with a blooming healthy baby to return to find a pale, ill child about whose condition I was so worried I had to take him at once to a specialist."

Marie's fierce possessiveness about the child – who was, after all, half Humphrey's – probably accelerated their estrangement over the next few years. Publicly, their marriage was as perfect as young Harry – perhaps too perfect to carry conviction. Mary Stocks (the late Baroness Stocks) also had a holiday home near Portland Bill and the two families spent some time together. Even on the beach, she later recalled:

there was . . . a certain flamboyance about her presentation of herself and her husband. One suspected that she was, unconsciously or not one did not know, projecting the image of her books. The terms of endearment passing between her and Humphrey Roe occasionally put a strain on the discretion of my growing family, as did the unconventional attire which her small son was constrained to wear.* He was, in her view, not as other boys. Certainly more intelligent, as well he might be, and requiring an educational regime specially adapted to the exceptional circumstances of an exceptional son of an exceptional mother. Indeed, in this, as in other respects, Marie Stopes radiated a personal vanity so uninhibited as to be positively endearing and wholly unrestrained by a sense of humour.[16]

Humphrey's role cannot have been an easy one to accept for a man with any pride. Twenty years later, Marie was still raging over a tiny incident which, because it concerned her child, had assumed monstrous proportions. "Baby Buffkins", as he was called, was eighteen months old – "a golden-curled laughing angel. Do you ever think of the day in the sunshine of Portland when in the main bay we were sitting in the middle, with several families at the sides – Buffie tiptoed up behind you and with a gurgle of happy laughter tipped your hat over your eyes. Instead of catching him to you and kissing him you swore at him and cursed him and swore at me and reviled me for the 'crime' – and all the people on the beach heard you and the child was terrified and you seared his soul and mine."

Marie was ill after Harry's birth. But, with her usual refusal to admit weakness, she had recovered sufficiently by June to achieve another of her ambitions. She was presented at Court (protesting violently, and in vain, against being announced as Mrs Humphrey Roe) in a dress of "cream net sewn with crystal and iridescent pearl over satin. Train to match fringed with shaded orange and flame coloured ostrich feathers."[17] Neither would Marie allow her physical frailty to interfere with her campaign for birth control. Dr Sutherland's final appeal to the House of Lords was pending and in May 1924 the Catholic newspapers, the *Universe* and the *Tablet*, appealed for help towards Sutherland's costs. In its editorial, the *Universe* said:

The Nation was being swept by a powerful and insidious campaign to encourage the artificial limitation of the family. It was a campaign designed to reach the masses, and it was reaching them. So successful was it that "birth control" became a normal topic of conversation.

* Forgetting – or ignoring – her own childhood miseries in the cause of Rational Dress, Marie dressed Harry in knitted breeches, sometimes skirts, and loose smocks.

From a national point of view it was a dangerous campaign. For the nation needs children. A nation with empty cradles today is a nation with a black tomorrow ...

AN ACTION FOR LIBEL, TAKEN OUT BY DR MARIE STOPES, PH.D, WENT IN FAVOUR OF THE DEFENDANTS ... THE COURT OF APPEAL REVERSED THE DECISION AND LEFT THE CATHOLIC CHAMPIONS RESPONSIBLE FOR HEAVY LEGAL COSTS. THE CASE MUST NOT BE ALLOWED TO END THERE ...[18]

In June Marie took out an action for contempt of court – the case was *sub judice* – and the editors of the *Tablet* and the *Universe*, both on holiday in the South of France, had to rush back to make an undertaking in court that they would refrain from any further mention of the case until the appeal was heard.

By September Marie had recovered her high spirits and held a dance at Givons Grove. There was an Italian cabaret, singing "Funiculi, Funicula", "Ciribiribin" and "La donna è mobile" and a dance orchestra (not negroid) played "What'll I Do", "I Love my Chili Bom Bom" and "In Pasadena".[19] But Marie was worried about her six-month-old son. The physical injuries from Harry's birth made further conception unlikely, but she did not want him to grow up without companions. Tentatively, she asked her friends if they knew of any child suitable for adoption and, when Harry was two, she wrote to her solicitor:

I do not wish it to be known that the adoption is for me and I should be much obliged if you would write to the Matron of the Claremont Central Mission, Pentonville, and also to the Foundling Hospital in somewhat the following terms:

"A Client in a very good position is desirous of adopting (complete adoption) a little boy between the ages of 20 months and $2\frac{1}{4}$ years. Illegitimacy is not objected to so long as it was a love child and not a rape, and so long as the mother was entirely healthy and normal during pregnancy and there is no inherited disease on either side. The child must be absolutely healthy, intelligent and not circumcised."

You might also say that you can add from a personal knowledge of your client that it would be an exceptional opportunity for any child; that he would be brought up in the nursery as a brother with the son and heir, and if the child's intelligence warranted it, he would receive a University education and a suitable start in life.

Her desire for secrecy was understandable. As the country's best-known proponent of birth control and joyous motherhood, her advertising for a possibly illegitimate child to counter her own conceptional deficiencies would not have been disregarded by her enemies. It is not surprising, given Marie's besottedness with her child, that a suitable companion was never found. Harry, it appears, was not only beautiful, clever and imaginative, but had also been born with a social conscience and, like his mother, a direct line to God. At the age of five, his mother wrote to Humphrey: "He is looking celestially beautiful and talks much of God and how angels come with no footsteps and talk beautifully to him and how one said 'God is coming down to love you Buffkins – be quiet for God is coming' – the view was exquisite today and BB *so* eager to paint it, lots and lots of times over so the poor people in London can have it as a picture as they can't see it."[20]

It was not until 1930 that the first of a succession of little boys arrived on approval at the Stopes-Roe household, as a companion for Harry, only to be promptly returned as unsuitable. Marie was no believer in the permissive upbringing of children.* Robin Wilkinson, about the same age as Harry, was an orphan brought up by two elderly aunts – to whose care he was quickly returned. One of the sisters wrote back to Marie: "To speak quite plainly, it pained us very much to hear you describe him repeatedly as 'a dreadful little liar' . . . I have pictured to myself many times a day, with great distress of mind, the little fellow being 'thrashed' for insubordination. Is it the only thing to do ?"[21]

Richard Scott-Foster, delivered from the National Children's Adoption Society, stayed a little longer, but was eventually sent to an orphans' home. "Dickie does make progress, but will never bloom so as to be a credit to us!" Marie told the society in 1931.† Robin was

---

* "Reverence is being exacted by some rather from the parent towards the child as a fresh, new, unspoilt being. This too often results in spoiling the child . . . The child should be taught from its earliest days profound respect, reverence and gratitude towards its parents, *and in particular towards its mother, for of her very life she gave it the incomparable gift of life.*" – *Radiant Motherhood*, 1920, p. 223 (author's italics).

† In August 1931 Marie was quoted as saying: "No one-child private nurseries should remain; the derelict children should be saved from institutional treatment and the lonely little 'onlys' given companions of their own age." *Nottingham Evening News* 22 August 1931.

brought back, but again returned to Manchester, with Marie's detailed
account of his alleged monstrous vices. Miss Wilkinson, his aunt,
again wrote back: ". . . your letter appears to have been deliberately
intended to hurt and even insult us . . . The child probably 'senses'
that he is a discordant and unwelcome member of your household . . .
Undoubtedly we cannot give him the material advantages that life
with you afford, but love and sympathetic encouragement far outweigh
these."[22]

John Bicknell was the next experiment. After giving strong hints that
she would formally adopt him, Marie sent John back to his mother with
the comment: "The truth is, he is *so* behind his age that he failed hopelessly in both the entrance exams of suitable gentlemen's schools where
I would have paid the fees . . . I shall *not* 'legally adopt' him – for
that one wants more complete likeness of interests and attitude toward
life. John's interest is mainly mechanical – not at all literary and
artistic and I think often all the beauty here is quite wasted on him . . ."[23]

Worse was to follow. At the end of 1934, Marie took in young Barry
Cuddeford, son of a former major in the Indian Army, but now living
in much reduced circumstances and unable to afford a public school. At
first, Barry was a "charming boy". But by May of next year, he had
developed into the usual "monster". Marie wrote to his father: "I
should feel inclined to say every time he is dirty he is sent home to be
thrashed. A night or two ago, for instance, after tea he was out in the
garden with Buffky and me doing nothing in particular – a little
gardening in his own plot, playing with the kitten, swinging, no compulsion or restraint in anything, but he came in so that when I looked
into his bedroom when he was having his bath, his underpants were
absolutely soaked with urine and of course smelling horribly. It is
quite inexcusable and renders him unfit for a decent household."[24] The
reply from Barry's mother two days later was, in the circumstances,
polite:

Dear Dr Stopes . . . I hope you fully realise how unhappy we have
been made to feel, and how sincerely sorry we are that you should
have had such an unpleasant time with the boy and I quite understand
that the whole affair must have disgusted you and your husband
and anyone else but a decent household . . . you need not be
quite so heavy-handed and downright with us . . . I see that you

have decided to send him home this weekend for a thrashing – well – he shall be punished and very severely – but he won't be thrashed.[25]

Perhaps she realised the probable origin of her son's "dirty habits" in his emotional disturbance – it can have been no easy matter for any child to live with a woman who so obviously doted on her own child, and saw nothing but faults in others.* At any rate, the boy's parents decided not to send Barry back, and Marie finally settled for Robin, who called Marie "Mummy" and stuck it out until old enough to join the Merchant Navy.

Marie's jealous guarding of Harry's development was not limited to choosing – or, rather, rejecting – his few companions. Like her mother, Marie did not believe in schools. Reading, she argued, developed second-hand minds, and only "the very sturdy and unintelligent" should be sent to school. "The sensitive quick child at that age is far better occupied in a home garden, or where it can be individually considered and can live out of doors. This presupposes, however, both leisure and intelligence on the part of one or both of the parents."[26] Though he had a succession of tutors, Harry was not allowed to read until he was ten,† and first attended school at the age of fifteen. Even then, Marie did not relax her grip. She later bombarded his housemaster at Charterhouse with instructions about Harry's education – he was *not*, she stressed, to be allowed to attend any lectures about sex; nor was he to be approached about Confirmation or taking the Sacrament. Even when Harry was nineteen and a science student at Imperial College, she wrote directly to the Registrar: "I am extremely perturbed about the matter of drinking water at the Imperial College. The

* Harry Stopes-Roe was whipped once by his mother, "but it was a traumatic experience for both of us". Completely dominated by her, he only gradually came to realise the unfairness of the treatment meted out to his prospective "brothers": "I remember thinking that they did things and were punished, I would do the same and not be punished. It was the same with presents. If we got suits of armour, mine was in shiny tin, his in cardboard." Interview with the author, 10 July 1975.

† He was, however, allowed to "write". At the age of six – according to Marie, who no doubt had a hand in it – he "dictated" a play, exhibiting, his mother said, "the most glorious imagination". *Buckie's Bears* was the Christmas production at the Royalty Theatre, London, in 1931. "Madam," Marie wrote to the Duchess of York in 1933 when the play was again produced, "My little boy craves the honour of presenting the little Princess Elizabeth [now Queen Elizabeth] with a box to see his play ... we feel sure she would enjoy it *really* as it is all about Sam and Barbara the polar bears at the zoo who escape into fairyland and have the greatest fun." The offer was refused.

position is that my young son has been properly trained to drink water between meals and requires to do so to keep in full health."

Her love for Harry, expressed as it partly was in her intolerance of companions and in her possessiveness, proved for him an intolerable burden. Eventually, and inevitably, Harry fought for independence – a demand that Marie found so unacceptable that it eventually soured a relationship that meant so much to her.

CHAPTER 15

Unenduring Passion

November 1918: Married Love (5th edn.): "To the adored One, from the Author, Marie C. Stopes."

January 1921: Truth About Venereal Disease: "With true love to the man who swore he had not got it; and so got love, on the Leatherhead River Meadow. HVR MCS."

October 1928: Enduring Passion (1st edn.): "To You, Hoping it's True. Marie C. Stopes."

July 1931: Contraception: "To a Proof-Reader with the gratitude of the author, Marie C. Stopes."

December 1946: The Bathe, an Ecstacy: "To Humphrey from Marie, the Author, Xmas 1946."

Inscriptions in books presented by
Marie Stopes to her husband

Enduring Passion was published in 1928 when Marie was forty-eight. She saw it as the sequel to *Married Love*, which came out in 1918, the year of her marriage to Humphrey. Meant as a reassurance to the middle-aged and elderly, it promised, instead of the inevitable decay of passion, "lifelong love and enduring monogamic devotion, romantic in youth, rapturous in early marriage and matured in a serene old age".[1] Yet her own marriage, it seemed, scarcely survived the first edition of *Enduring Passion*. Many years later, in one of his few references to the first decade of their life together, Humphrey wrote to Marie: "Before I married you I told you I would always love you, I was sure of that; and I asked you whether you would always love me. You answered yes. So we married . . . Unfortunately in about 7 or 8 years you got tired of me and remarked variations on the theme that our marriage for you was a great disadvantage, through me you were losing your friends and so on. At the time I hoped it was a temporary phase and you would get over it. But it continued worse and worse . . ."[2]

What went wrong? The birth of her much-desired son in 1924 certainly provided Marie with an alternative object for her passions, but it is hardly sufficient explanation for the rapid breakdown of a marriage embarked upon by both with such faith and idealism.

Outwardly, a few years after marriage, Marie should have had little to complain of. She was finally in possession of a husband, a child, an impressive home, and of the fame she had always sought. Thanks to the trial, her clinic was a success, and by 1925 she could publish a study of her first 5000 cases. In the same year, she started training nurses in contraceptive techniques, even setting examinations for them.* "In my opinion, you are the greatest heroine of all time," wrote one patient. As a public lecturer, she was in demand all over Britain, and was much embarrassed that year when, on her Scottish tour, the audience at a meeting in Paisley stood up at the end and sang, "Better lo'ed ye canna be, Will ye no come back again."[3] She was an attractive figure and took care with her clothes. In Edinburgh, she appeared appropriately swathed in misty pale-grey furs, reserving the salmon-pinks and oranges for the more decadent South. The railway shunter who organised a large meeting for her in the Philharmonic Hall, Liverpool, was bowled over by the enchantment of her address (despite the fact that he had to write twice: hearing that he had influenza, Marie fumigated his letters to the point of illegibility):

> . . . I would not like to meet you too often or I should fall in love with you – even if you are a Tory – because I admired your voice, your pluck and the way you handled your audience; I had figured you once or twice as too aristocratic in manner, that is to say very "stuck up" . . . Permit me too to compliment you upon your eloquence and the timbre – I mean sweetness of your voice; it carries with it all that the word "feminine" ought to mean . . .[4]

* One of the questions ran: "Write brief essays (not more than two pages each) of what you would say in answer to the following objections to contraceptives: a) that it is immoral b) that it leads to sterility c) that Dr Stopes' methods are 'no good'." (21 May 1925. BL-S.)

Her energies were not limited to the promotion of matrimonial technique and birth control. Throughout the twenties, despite her promise to devote the next twenty years to the direct service of humanity she continued to pursue her literary ambitions. Fearful of the rather *risqué* connotations now attaching to the name "Marie Stopes", she adopted several pseudonyms. In 1926 her stage play, *Don't Tell Timothy*, was allegedly written by "Mark Arundel". She took the name "Erica Fay" for her collection of fairy stories *A Road to Fairyland* and in 1928 assumed the title of "Marie Carmichael" for her only novel, *Love's Creation.* ("So help me Heaven, it is not a good novel," commented her candid playwright friend, Alfred Sutro.)

Nor could Marie sit through the General Strike without attempting to solve the country's ills. The strike started on 3 May 1926, sparked off by the coal-miners, for whom Marie, as a coal expert, had some sympathy. On May 6, though herself a Conservative, she wrote to Stanley Baldwin, the Conservative Prime Minister, in terms highly critical of his policies. What the miners needed, she argued, with a good deal of sense, was a minimum uniform wage of about £3 a week:

> At the present moment it is not exaggeration to say that some men, honestly at work, are by piece work, odd day shifts etc., rendered incapable of earning more than 25s. to 30s. per week. In these days this is sheer, cruel starvation and it is this *insecurity* which is rankling sore behind the difficulties . . .
>
> May I say, personally, that I think your insistence on the miners accepting "without any reserve" the report of the Coal Commission is misguided, as the Report is largely a well-meaning but academic expression of unrealities which the miners know would not solve the difficulties.[5]

Her impact was not limited to Britain. The new régime in Russia could not cope with its original promise of free abortion and in 1925 Professor Paul Lublinsky, of Leningrad University, asked her for help, "as anti-conceptive measures in Russia are now officially recommended".[6] Marie did not reply to his letter. She disapproved of "Bolshevism" and, even in *Birth Control News*, which desperately needed advertising revenue, she would never accept advertisements for anything to do with Communism – a form of censorship neatly contradicting her attitude to the censorship imposed by *The Times*.

India, however, was a different matter. It was still a British colony and Marie's books were published there, though usually in pirated editions. Ever mindful of her duty both to the human race and to the Empire, Marie wrote to twenty-three ruling Indian princes (many of whom had, after all, been educated at Eton, and could therefore be counted as honorary gentlemen). She pointed out to them the dangers of reckless breeding* and asked for help in financing her birth control work. None replied, though the palace surgeon at Bikaner, Rajputana, wrote asking for advice about "hasty ejaculations". Another letter came from Mr K. A. Aziz, M.A., who offered to translate Marie's books into Urdu. He had started his own married life on a foundation of *Married Love*, he wrote, and was surprised: ". . . how little female nature in these climates differed from that unfolded in your epoch-making treatise . . . My own success has generated a zeal in me to transmit the heavenly light you brought so Prometheus-like to the ignorant masses of Indian husbands . . . and thus ensure for yourself as well as for me the benediction of the suffering millions of the Indian womanhood, whom the Adam old belief of husband worship as her physical Lord and preposterous standard of feminine modesty have reduced to abject thralldom."[7]

In Africa too, apparently, Marie had attained a recognition parallel to that of the Great White Queen. "You will be interested to hear," wrote the anthropologist, Professor Malinowski, "that your name is better known right in the heart of darkest Africa than that of any other writer. The paramount chief of Swaziland, the tribal chief of the Chagga and a whole lot of other intelligent Africans spoke to me with enthusiasm of you and I was proud to be able to tell them I was your friend."[8]

It seems odd that, with this amount of public and private support, Marie should have been discontent. Yet, by 1928, her personality had changed – or, rather, rigidified into a pattern that had always been incipient. Dr Helena Wright first met Marie and Humphrey on their honeymoon in 1918 and did not see them again until 1928, after her

* Marie was one of the first to recognise India's population problem. For the rest of her life she conducted a battle, in British and Indian newspapers, with Gandhi who, as a Hindu, did not believe in birth control. Gandhi argued that it led to "imbecility and nervous prostration" and that "the husband should avoid privacy with his wife. Little reflection is needed to show that the only possible motive for privacy between husband and wife is the desire for sexual enjoyment." This, Marie replied, was complete and arrant nonsense, and betrayed such "total ignorance of the higher relations between the sexes, that I am amazed that he can retain the respect of millions of people". (Maude, 1933, op. cit., p. 187.)

return from medical missionary work in China. She went to Marie's clinic, which had by now transferred to premises in Whitfield Street, off the Tottenham Court Road, and was shocked by the change in their personalities:

> In 1918, Humphrey was a keen, independent young man; in 1928, he was a gramophone record. I remember it vividly. His wife was not there, and I wanted to know about the latest developments in birth control, so I said I would come back. "What, you are not going to wait for her?" He would have been hurt if I had not waited ...
>
> I did wait, and eventually, in *swept* this figure ... She was not really interested in other people, but I said I had come to see her especially and that pleased her enormously. ... Now comes the very very subtle change. She knew no more of medicine than in 1918, and she was suffering from two very grave pathological diseases – can you guess what they were? Yes, paranoia and megalomania.[9]

Was there no other cap, Dr Wright asked, but the small cervical "Pro-race" advocated by Dr Stopes? Certainly not, replied Marie, all other sorts caused cancer. "Then the telephone rang and I watched her face and I could hear the concentrated fury and fear when she heard the words Roman Catholics. ... By 1928, they were beyond any help – Humphrey and Marie, that is."

Long before 1928 Humphrey had felt his ignominious position. In 1924 he objected to a poster advertising a lecture he was to give: "... both Dr Stopes and I object to this description. Why not refer to me as the Hon. Sec. of the CBC or, if you would prefer it, Joint Founder... but please do not bill me as the husband of Marie Stopes."[10]

Few people can cope with paranoia in others, so firmly does the sufferer believe in the reality of the imagined persecution and in the delusions of grandeur that usually accompany the malady. Marie's case was complicated by an element of truth. The Catholics *were* plotting against her – in the sense that she herself was plotting the overthrow of Catholic dogma and Christian thinking generally.* She was also a

* "I am out for a much greater thing than birth control. I am out to smash the tradition of organised Christianity, and to enthrone Christ's own tradition of wholesome, healthy, natural love towards sex life." Marie Stopes, address at the Criterion Theatre, quoted *Daily Mirror*, 16 March 1925.

truly "grand" person, not just in her achievements, but in the possession of a personality so forceful that within a few short years she had
influenced public opinion to a striking extent and succeeded in turning
her husband into a "gramophone record" of her own beliefs and
sayings. There comes a point, however, when the recognition of
opposition and a legitimate pride in achievement pass beyond the
bounds of normality.

For Marie, the turning-point appears to have been the libel case
against Halliday Sutherland in 1923. This had increased support for her
cause, but it had also increased opposition – and not just in the
Catholic press. The extraordinary issue of the *Practitioner* in July
1923, devoted entirely to birth control, was remarkable for its prejudice. The leader pointed out that "medical men have found in popular
handbooks, written by women with no medical qualification, practical
information of which they had hitherto been ignorant and a great deal
of which they might legitimately disapprove": and Dr Norman Haire
begged the medical profession to study contraception properly: "Only
thus may it be rescued from the hands of quacks and charlatans
and non-medical 'doctors' who write erotic treatises on birth
control conveying misleading information in a highly stimulating
form."[11]

Feeling that her reputation had been besmirched, Marie persuaded
her old friend, Aylmer Maude, to rush out a quick biography. She
undertook all the costs, in return demanding a complete veto on anything she disliked – including any mention of her age, an elementary
requirement, it might be thought, in any biography. *The Authorized
Life of Marie C. Stopes* came out at the end of 1924, just in time, Marie
hoped, to correct the impression of failure created by the final loss of
her case against Sutherland in the House of Lords appeal. It was a
complete flop. "The book is a panegyric and not a biography,"
commented the *Spectator* and *The Star* observed: "... writers of
'authorised lives' are prone to bias in favour of their subjects, but Mr
Maude's acceptance of the idea that the London press has shown hostil-
ity to Dr Stopes in obedience to a secret Roman Catholic campaign
against her indicates deplorable credulity or deplorable docility ... I
am sorry to find Mr Maude, the biographer of Tolstoi, employed on
this trivial 'puff'."

The book sold only a few hundred copies, and Marie was furious.

Like most people with paranoid tendencies, she had to blame someone else for her own deficiencies. Since, it transpired, she had written most of the book herself, it was particularly unfair to blame Aylmer Maude for its lack of success. "Dear Una," he wrote, "You so impressed on me the importance of getting the *Life* out *quickly*, and I evidently rushed it to the point of scamping it and *failed to correct some of the errors in your rough draft*." Three months later, she was still attacking him for the book's failure, and he wrote again: "In fact, the three points in which I have been most severely attacked (pretentious title, a biography which does not give the age of its subject, and neglect to mention previous birth control movement) were none of them my fault."[12]

Marie could scarcely blame the Catholics for the failure of Maude's biography, just as she could not hold them responsible for Mrs Winston Churchill's refusal to have lunch with her (on the grounds that it might damage her husband's political career) or for the Abertillery Free Church's protest, after one of her meetings in Wales, "against the placarding of our streets with such posters as would bring the blush of shame to the cheeks of our mothers".[13] Nevertheless, throughout the twenties, the Catholic church provided ample food for Marie's paranoia. In 1926 the Catholic Truth Society of Ireland published its report on "evil literature".* Following the society's recommendations, the Eire government two years later brought in a Bill outlawing all books, newspapers and periodicals advocating or advertising birth control. The Irish Censorship Bill became law, eliciting a fine piece of polemic from Ezra Pound to the *Irish Times*: "... permit me to compliment your budding nation on having produced something more stupid, more asinine, more obfuscatory, more bigoted, more Protestant, more Baptist, more Ku-Klux, more Arkansas, more Tennessee, more reactionary, more degrading even than that Article 211, produced by the American Congress, which has hitherto been my standard of measure for the lowest possible point reachable by so-called human stupidity."[14]

---

* On moral grounds, the society disapproved of "almost every newspaper and periodical". The *News of the World* came in for particular attack, especially for "depraved" headlines as: "Caused by Gossip. Aged woman strangles herself with bandage"; "Young Girls' Escapades. Nights spent in Chinese laundries" and "Indicted by Family. Grave allegations against Septuagenarian". These headlines culled by the society from the *News of the World* of 14 February 1926.

It was probably this law, rather than secret cadres of Catholics infiltrating Britain's newspaper offices, that caused the refusal of many of Marie's advertisements. Newspapers do not like to lose circulation and would not risk the seizure and burning by Dublin police – as occasionally happened – of a whole issue. Marie, of course, did not see it this way. The Sutherland trial had given her a taste for the law – she even took the trouble to have lessons in court procedure from a lawyer – and for the next few years she spent much of her time in lawsuits.

Her first brush was not very rewarding. After having taken her advertisements for six years, the *Morning Post* suddenly refused them. Marie's letter of complaint to the Duke of Northumberland, chairman of the board, revealed her growing obsession with the idea of Catholic plots:

> My dear Duke of Northumberland, I am sure you would just hate to feel that a very small handful of Roman Catholics were *manipulating* your paper, the *Morning Post*, unknown to you, and I hasten, therefore, to tell you that this is going on, because I feel sure you would like to put a stop to it ...
>
> ... Now, are you going to see contracts broken by the *Morning Post* for perfectly proper and suitable advertisements in its columns at the instigation of anyone? I daresay your Manager will tell you the matter is controversial. That is the way the cunning Roman Catholics put it ...

The Duke of Northumberland forwarded her letter to his editor, H. A. Gwynne, with the comment: "I do hope we shall keep off this subject of birth control, as I feel sure it will do us a lot of harm if we help to advertise it." Mr Gwynne was not amused by this slur on his professional conduct. Marie apologised – not handsomely enough – and Gwynne issued a writ for libel. By January 1928 she was once more back in the High Court, listening with fury to the prosecuting counsel describe her as "a propagandist and author who has devoted a considerable amount of time and study to the arresting and interesting proposition of how to achieve sexual satisfaction while at the same time avoiding the attending inconvenience of having children." (Against this passage in her transcript of the trial, Marie scribbled "Dirty!") Unfortunately, she had absolutely no evidence of a plot at the *Morning*

*Post.** The jury was out only ten minutes, and gave a verdict in favour
of Gwynne, with £200 damages and costs against Marie. A further
casualty was the *New Statesman* which, though not in favour, as it
hastened to point out, of Dr Stopes's aims, labelled the verdict "a
substantial miscarriage of justice", and accused the judge, Mr Justice
Avory, of bias. Faced with an action for contempt, the editor retracted.[15]

So overwhelmed was Marie by the thought of the forces ranged
against her that she seriously considered an offer from Horatio Bottomley, a former editor of *John Bull*. Bottomley was just out of prison,
after serving a sentence for fraudulent conversion. In March 1928,
thinking of starting a new magazine, he offered Marie favourable
publicity – for the payment of £1000. Only the good sense of Aylmer
Maude stopped her accepting the offer.

Two months later, Marie sacked her lawyers and conducted her own
appeal in the Gwynne case. She had no compunction about using
feminine charm. On May 2 she wore a brown velvet coat, fur-trimmed,
and a toque decorated with pink ribbons. Lord Scrutton was a little
nonplussed when she winsomely addressed him:

DR MARIE STOPES: . . . But before taking up that argument, may I say
that I am handicapped by being so short; may I stand on this
seat?
LORD SCRUTTON: It makes an awkward precedent, but if you like to
stand I do not mind.
DR MARIE STOPES: It is such a handicap not being able to see your
lordships' faces, and I find it so difficult to speak throwing my voice
upwards.
(The Appellant addressed the Court standing on the seat.)[16]

Their Lordships, however, were proof against such wiles, and the
appeal was dismissed. Marie's action had accomplished nothing, except
to ensure that the *Morning Post* would in future refrain from giving her
any publicity. In November that year, following complaints from Marie

---

* Marie herself was not averse to a bit of plotting. Halliday Sutherland was a leading
figure in the "League of National Life", an anti-birth control movement. Trying to
create evidence of a Catholic plot at the *Morning Post*, Marie got a friend to write to
Sutherland: "I was glad to see by the splendid *Universe* this week that you are exposing
the nonsense of the Catholic plot. Can I, as a member of the League of National Life,
have the pride of feeling that it was our society that got these advertisements stopped in
the *Morning Post*, and can I thank you for it personally?" (7 February 1928, Mrs Peggy
Richardson. Copy in BL-S.) Sutherland did not bite.

about the misreporting of another of her court cases, H. A. Gwynne wrote to her solicitors: "In order to avoid anything of a similar nature in the future, I have given instructions to my staff to omit mention of any case in which your client may be a party."[17] Marie, it seemed, had been hoist with her own petard.

It was not long, however, before she had the chance of a counterblast. Like her father, Marie was full of visionary publicity ideas – not the most remarkable of which was a long and closely reasoned letter to the editor of the *Aeroplane* in 1925, arguing that war could be averted for ever by using aeroplanes to scatter birth control propaganda all over the world.[18] Some of her apparently ludicrous ideas she put into effect. In 1927 the world's first travelling, horse-drawn, birth-control caravan clinic took to the roads, sped on its way by £100 from Selfridges department store, and £1000 from an anonymous Midlands textile manufacturer. From a purely clinical point of view, it was not a great success. Women did not like to be seen entering the caravan, and one of the nurses, as well as being incompetent, was nearly always drunk.* But no one could deny its publicity value. In November 1928, while parked in Bradford, the caravan was burned down by Elizabeth Ellis, aged thirty-four, an unmarried sweetshop assistant. Having already tried to burn it a week earlier (she was let off with a warning and a ten shilling fine) her success this time could not be ignored and she was sentenced to two months imprisonment.†

Miss Ellis was also a Catholic. Once more Marie went joyously into battle. Under huge headlines – ROMAN CATHOLIC OPPONENTS TIRE OF ARGUMENT. USE ARSON INSTEAD – the January 1929 issue of *Birth Control News* accused Catholics of resorting: "to the good old medieval practice of burning, instead of enlightening the enemy. The poor dupe who acted as catspaw for the gang, the unmarried Ellis, has to take her punishment alone. There is little doubt, however, that she is not the only one who should have stood in the dock for the crime . . ."

* ". . . she drinks brandy like we drink water", wrote Nurse Shears about her colleague. "All the weekend she drinks hard. It is really disgusting and horrible and I'm fed up with bearing with her slackness and gross incompetence." (16 December 1929, Nurse Shears to E. Bootle, MCS's secretary. BL-S.)

† In court, Miss Ellis explained: "I purchased the petrol and took it along the Leeds Road after 10 o'clock and destroyed a source of immorality and venereal disease . . . There was a conflict in the mind – sort of two personalities working, one representing an effort to keep the peace which was dominated by the second. I take it that in keeping the peace is what you call the common law. The second represented a higher law, the natural law, God's law in my body and all women's bodies."

Since the article – with apparent deliberation – was placed immediately next to yet another tirade against the iniquities of Halliday Sutherland, he felt justified in suing for libel. In March 1929 the High Court was again the setting for that well-rehearsed drama, Sutherland v. Stopes, with Serjeant Sullivan as chorus. This time, surprisingly in view of the continuing prejudice against her, Sutherland lost – as he also did on appeal. As Bernard Shaw pointed out:

Dear Marie, What a lesson! You lose all the cases in which you are clearly in the right. Then you are fortunate enough to be obviously in the wrong, and instantly you have a triumph.

Moral: take care to be in the wrong always, and to conduct your own case. Congratulations! Ever, GBS.[19]

Not only did Marie have her revenge. Soon after the caravan incident, she held a large meeting about it in Bradford and got enough donations to buy two more caravans. One local reporter expressed his surprise at Dr Stopes, "whom I half-expected to find a hard-faced propagandist like some of the old fashioned Suffragettes. She is, in fact, a most gracious and winsome personality and is much misrepresented by hostile influences."[20] It was not a picture that would have been recognised by those who crossed her. At the same time as dealing with Catholic arson, she was also intent on bringing miscreants to justice. William Carpenter, a former stoker in the Navy, had the ill judgement to display the name of Marie Stopes prominently on the birth control and abortion clinic he had set up in Notting Hill. His abortion techniques consisted of intercourse (with himself, a method recommended by Casanova), pills and the insertion of a piece of elm bark. He did not offer the first alternative to Marie when she appeared one day, accompanied by a detective, claiming to be pregnant and demanding an abortion, but sent her away with some pills. Largely through Marie's efforts, he was arrested, and sentenced to five years' penal servitude on fifteen counts of rape, abortion and indecent assault.

While disposing of impostors, Marie was also engaged in her oddest legal battle – not for its forensic importance, but for the light it throws on her personality. Her chow, Wuffles, had for some years been accused of indiscriminate attacks on dogs, Protestants and Catholics. Farnham magistrates' court ordered her to keep the dog on a lead thus, she wrote in the brief to her solicitors, "giving the opportunity to a number of yapping, scurrilous curs to glory over him and to attack, or attempt to attack him, and say unforgivable things". It was all the fault of Roman Catholics. After further incidents, the court ordered Wuffles to be destroyed. Marie refused to comply, sent ten guineas to the National Canine Defence League, and employed a detective to find out how many Catholics there were among Farnham magistrates: they were all Protestants. She wrote to MPs, to J. Ramsay Macdonald, the former Prime Minister, and to the Home Secretary, who turned down her demand for a parliamentary bill "to save innocent dogs and their owners from suffering the injustice of unfair condemnation without any power to appeal". Fined a pound a day for failing to destroy the dog, she was very ungracious with the policeman sent to check on whether Wuffles was dead:

OFFICER: All I ask Madam, is "Has the dog been destroyed?"
DR STOPES: By what authority – under what clause of the Dogs Act are you empowered to ask this question?
OFFICER: I can't answer any questions.
DR STOPES: Then I refuse to answer any questions. Good morning.[21]

Even her home, it appeared, was developing into a law court. She had, meanwhile, taken the precaution of ordering another black chow, to destroy and present to the police as evidence of a dead Wuffles. It never came to this. Three days after Marie had written to the Lord Chancellor with a petition to reprieve Wuffles, the Farnham magistrates' court, baffled, adjourned the case *sine die*. They found it impossible to decide, under the 1871 Dogs Act, on whom lay the onus of proof as to a dog's being alive or dead. Marie had won again.*

Such successes did nothing to palliate her paranoia. Her insistence on pre-eminence was by 1930 as inaccurate as it was damaging to her reputation. True, she had set up the first birth control clinic in Britain. But since 1921 other clinics had opened both in London and provincial centres, and there were several societies other than Marie's Constructive Birth Control society, with equal support. In 1930 they decided to band

* Her devotion to Wuffles was extreme. In a poem addressed to "The Black Chow Companion, Friend and Protector of Dr Marie Stopes", she apostrophised him:
... Rubbing your head and making devout love,
Caressing knees and arms; your soft black tongue
Kissing me finger-tips to shoulder; all the bare arm
Caressing with slow motion up and down ... (MS about 1930, SR-Coll.)

together as the National Birth Control Council (later the Family Planning Association) and Marie was asked to join. Dr Helena Wright, then the doctor in charge at Margery Spring-Rice's North Kensington clinic, recalled Margaret Pyke's invitation to take part: "I answered that I would not join unless every existing clinic was included. Mrs Pyke answered. 'I suppose you mean Marie Stopes.' I said, Yes, I did. After a pause she wrote again and said, 'All right, if you will manage her.'"[22]

Though Marie, as doyenne of the movement, proposed the resolution setting up the association, no one ever succeeded in managing her. She resigned in 1933, being unable to agree with anyone. Even while still a member of the association, she treacherously wrote to a professor, asking him to become a vice-president of the CBC:

> With you, I enquire, why two Societies? The National B.C. Assoc. was only founded about a year ago – We, the *Constructive* B.C. Assoc were founded *eleven* years ago, just after my husband and I founded the *first* British Birth Control clinic. We have given and spent on the b.c. movement over £20,000 of our own money and sacrificed more than any could imagine in the fight: I haven't had a day free from work and anxiety for eleven years. And the newly founded National Assoc was started last year by a Society woman* who didn't even take the trouble to come to see our Clinic first! Having no fighting to do she has scooped up heaps of people (like yourself) whom I should have approached long ago had I had more time and strength from my many labours.

She had learned nothing and forgotten nothing. Though all clinics had by now adopted the diaphragm (Dutch) cap as easier for most women to use, Marie clung doggedly to the small, high-domed pessary. Her exaggerated claims for its success, based as they were on inadequate follow-up procedures, made her something of a laughing-stock in medical circles. Reviewing her notes on the clinic's first 10,000 cases, with its alleged failure rate of only 0·52%, Dr C. P. Blacker said it was "not borne out by the experience of other clinics. Dr Stopes' claim with regard to the success of her method will, of course, be received with scepticism by other workers in birth control. This is fully anticipated by

* Lady Denman, niece of Lord Cowdray.

Dr Stopes who says: 'Our detractors and those who also desire to magnify themselves will not accept as possible any such degree of success from our work.'"[23]

Marie also took full credit – quite unfairly – for the Ministry of Health's Memorandum 153, a document bearing the same relationship to birth control as Luther's theses to Protestantism. Under mounting pressure from public health authorities, Women's Co-operative Guilds, groups of Labour women, and various birth control organisations, the Ministry had finally agreed to allow information to be given at maternity and child welfare centres. On July 6 1930 Marie noted: "Today a Sec. of State visited me in my country home ... with a message to me from the Cabinet telling me that the Govt had decided no longer to oppose me." She did, however, perform a useful service in getting hold of a copy of the memorandum – which the ministry did not release either to the press or to local authorities – and printed it in full in the *Birth Control News* – after which there was no point in the Ministry's trying to keep it secret.

Marie had plenty of warnings about the likely effects of her unbridled arrogance and vanity. Aylmer Maude was as unappreciative of her attempts to meddle with his literary work as was Noel Coward (who never accepted another invitation after she tried to put on her own version of *The Vortex*) and Rudyard Kipling, whom Marie ordered to alter the last line of his well-known poem, *If*. The line – "You'll be a man, my son" – was unfair to women, she argued.* Maude, incensed by her jeers at Rebecca West's introduction (which Marie had herself wanted to write) to a volume in his Tolstoy edition replied: "I fancy that you do not realise how many people's faces you smack in business and how much harm this impulsiveness does you." Bernard Shaw managed to keep his temper when Marie publicly attacked his views on motherhood, which were not quite so "radiant" as Marie's. He refused her demand to retract his opinions, and wrote back:

I have given every possible publicity to my obligation to my mother, and have been duly reproved for not playing the conventional good son ... What I have never said, and what you must not elicit from

---

* Kipling replied: "I am sorry that I do not see my way to comply with your request to change, as you propose, the final line in my verses, 'If'. As you can easily see, if a precedent of this kind were established, one might end by sanctioning the change of every line." 23 May 1925. SR-Coll.

me in public, is that to call my mother a bad mother would be unjust only because from your point of view she really was not a mother at all. The fact that I am still alive at 78½ I probably owe largely to her complete neglect of me during my infancy ...

On reflection you will see the importance of insisting on the fact that motherhood is not everyone's vocation ... You must always assume that I am always right; and then you will never be wrong. Yours, dearest Marie, G. Bernard Shaw.[24]

On another occasion, she sent him an article turned down by the *London Mercury*, and written in reply to an article by Shaw on censorship. "Why did you disparage me," Shaw replied, "in terms which, though of course they do not offend me in the least, might possibly be supposed by the editor to do so at a moment when he is particularly anxious to keep on good terms with me? Your urgent business is to expose Catholic Action and to play for your own side, which means to back me up. Instead of which you go out of your way to declare that my plan is no use. Even if you think so does it help you to say so in the face of the enemy? ... In short, I advise you to chuck the last three paragraphs and keep your incorrigible pugnacity for someone less devoted to you than GBS."[25]

Few were as good-humoured as Shaw in face of Marie's difficult personality. There were several resignations from the CBC – often on the grounds of what one defector called "the ceaseless advertisement of one person".* The most comprehensive condemnation came from J. H. Guy, secretary of an organisation (unspecified in the correspondence) which had offered to help Marie. After undertaking several tasks – among them an attempt to find out the number of Catholics in the English press, and the compilation of a secret report on the World Population Conference in Geneva ("You did not inform us in advance that you were *persona non grata*," Mr Guy commented) – the organisation had second thoughts. "It is not for us to sit in judgment or criticism," he continued: "We merely observe as a fact that a large body of useful and devoted workers find themselves unable to co-operate under your leadership." His society would continue to devote its funds to birth control, "but membership of your society as far as we can judge,

---

* In the March 1926 issue of *Birth Control News* the name Marie Stopes is mentioned, in its four small pages, no fewer than twenty-five times.

merely means registering your decisions and judgments and assisting to pay for the same. If you desire widespread co-operation and financial assistance, it must of necessity lead to democratic control. It is quite possible that your best qualities would not be drawn out under such circumstances."[26]

There were now many workers in the field of birth control and an already vast body of literature both about its history and about modern clinical techniques. Marie's querulous complaints every time her name was not mentioned in the same breath as birth control did not endear her to any but the staunchest admirers. As Dr Norman Haire neatly and flatteringly asked, was it necessary to mention the name Lister every time antisepsis came up?[27] It was only too likely that it was Marie's behaviour rather than Humphrey's, as she claimed, that gradually depleted the ranks of her friends.

On the last day of 1930, Pope Pius IX issued *Casti Conubii*, the first papal encyclical on marriage for fifty years. It was strongly against contraception. The Catholic church, ran the rather unfortunately phrased English translation, stood "erect in the midst of the moral ruin which surrounds her, in order that she may preserve the chastity of the nuptial union from being defiled by this foul stain, raises her voice in token of her divine ambassadorship: any use whatsoever of matrimony exercised in such a way that the act is deliberately frustrated in its natural power to generate life is an offence against the law of God and of nature and those who indulge in such are branded with the guilt of a grave sin." Earlier that year, in April, Marie had written personally to the Pope (her rough draft, on thick vellum, is preserved among her papers). She and the Pope, she informed him, were really on the same side, since they were both against "the evil practice of murderous abortion". Her plea for help in promoting contraception ended: "Believe me, with Yourself, one wholly devoted to the service of humanity, Marie Carmichael Stopes."[28]

The Pope, however, was not lightly going to overturn nineteen centuries of theology even for Marie Stopes. So convinced was Marie of her own importance that she took his 16,000-word encyclical as a personal reply. The Pope, she sadly observed, had failed to understand her letter: – "or he thought himself and his world-wide organisation stronger than the forces of scientific truth for which I stand, and his answer was the reactionary Papal Encyclical".[29] In fact the encyclical was a reply to the Lambeth Conference of Anglican Bishops, which that year, by 193–67 votes, passed a resolution permitting artificial contraception. It was also a Vatican reinforcement of Fascism and of Mussolini's attempts to increase the birth rate.*

How was Humphrey to cope with a wife who saw herself as an anti-Pope? A gentle, rather indecisive man, he had been persuaded into unwise investments and, in the 1929 crash, lost most of his wealth. Incensed by his deficiencies, Marie, in 1931, persuaded him to see one of her medical friends. The report was not encouraging:

> I saw your husband yesterday and feel convinced that there is trouble in the spine ... His knee jerks are exaggerated and the difficulty he has with regard to getting up at night ... all point to a defective enervation of the genito-urinary segment of the body, arising in the lumbar region of the spinal cord.†
>
> There is something quite unusual and puzzling about his whole personality. I can express it best by the term "arrested development": his youthfulness is not that of vitality but of arrested growth; he seems to me to be living in "mid-air" as it were – skimming life; as if the shock of the "crash" had partly dissociated his personality from the physical body, so that the two are not reacting to each other ... the physical tissues age, but the lineaments do not bear the impress of internal struggle which is the usual accompaniment of inner development.

In March 1932 the same doctor wrote to Marie: "I hope Mr Roe did not find me offhand, but I am afraid I did not appear very interested in the anecdotes with which he regaled us ... I feel really rather distressed with the way things are going with him and would welcome a quiet talk with you ... although I am afraid I don't see how to help you ..."

---

* In 1931, Dr Letitia Fairfield, a Catholic convert, described one of Mussolini's receptions: "I was thoroughly astounded ... women were introduced to him not in the order of social rank but in the order of the number of children that were borne to them." *Catholic Herald* 8 November 1931.

† In *Enduring Passion*, in the chapter headed "Under-sexed Husbands", Marie had already pointed out, in her usual autobiographical vein, the possible effects of war injuries: "In men blows or other injuries to the spine (such as may be experienced through a fall in the hunting field, or wounding in warfare, or other form of accident), involving those spinal nerves which control the sex organs, may leave the man not only temporarily, but more or less permanently, incapable of a normal sex life." – *Enduring Passion*, p. 41.

Radiant Motherhood: Marie with her son Harry, 1926

Top: Harry (*left*) with a candidate for adoption, 1930

Bottom: Harry Stopes-Roe and Mary Wallis were married in July, 1948

Marie's dissatisfaction with Humphrey was not stifled by any consideration for his problems. Humphrey had never managed to find a niche for himself after he left Avro, the aircraft company he had founded with his brother. Alliott (who was now Sir A. V. Roe) was rich and respected; Humphrey's only claim to fame was that he was the husband of Marie Stopes. In 1929, to combat the combined financial burdens of the clinic, Marie's litigation, the slump, and Humphrey's incompetence, the family gave up Givons Grove* and moved to a much smaller house, Heatherbank, in Hindhead. Marie complained about the diminution in their circumstances, their new home, Humphrey's failure to appreciate poetry and the finer things of life, and his lack of physical ardour. He was deeply upset by her criticisms. He wrote to her in 1932:

> Dearest Sweetheart, I am no good at putting my thoughts into words. When a Lancashire lad says "I love you" it means far more than a Poet would get into many verses. You know I am that way. For instance, suppose I compared my love in the poetic fashion with the sky yesterday evening. It really was a beautiful show.
>
> The poet would have said his love was like that, always changing and each time more beautiful. Floating through the sky smoothly and quietly.
>
> If I had done that you would have wondered what was the matter and think I had copied it word for word from the "Girl's Friend" or "Peg's Weekly". So I must not really burst into verses of rhapsody. You must remember I am a plain spoken and dull Lancashire Lad . . . Your loving, dull, stupid Tiger.

It is difficult to assess the reality of the financial ruination which, Marie assured everyone, stared her in the face. Throughout the thirties, her income from books was considerably reduced. The subjects of sex and birth control were no longer quite so shocking, there were now many other competitors in the field and, moreover, she had nothing new to contribute. She turned her back on the new movement for the liberalisation of the laws against abortion, and in June 1933, annoyed at the lukewarm reception for her book, *Roman Catholic Methods of Birth Control*, she was driven to publicise it by chaining

* Givons Grove was later pulled down. A private housing estate now occupies the site.

a copy to the font of Westminster Cathedral. Only two reporters turned up for the non-event, and a sacristan quickly sawed through the chain.

The clinic, she said, could no longer go on paying its employees. She and Humphrey, she wrote to Lord Leverhulme, the soap magnate, had already spent £30,000 on the birth control movement, and was it not time that he contributed?[30] Lord Leverhulme declined. Even so, Marie managed to continue her London clinic and even, in the depressed thirties, set up provincial clinics, in Aberdeen, Leeds and Belfast. In addition, she supported overseas clinics affiliated to the CBC in South Africa, Australia and New Zealand.

Poverty, of course, is relative. What made Marie's protestations appear exaggerated was that in 1933, stifled by the suburban atmosphere of Heatherbank, Hindhead, she bought Norbury Park, a magnificent neo-Palladian mansion set in forty acres of the wooded hills above Dorking. The house had been built in 1778–80 for William Lock, and boasted the famous "Painted Drawing-Room", with pastoral scenes by Cipriani, Gilpen, Barret and Pastorini; even the floor, originally, was covered in a green carpet to give the impression of a lawn. When, in 1819, the house was sold, posters advertised its parklands as "so happily formed by Nature that Art would fail to give it additional effect; it possesses so much of Hill and Dale, such a constant and pleasing inequality . . . that if any highly favoured earthly spot may be assimilated to Paradise, Norbury Park can surely claim that distinction." Even allowing for auctioneers' hyperbole, it is still, today, an accurate description.

Marie's excuse for this apparent extravagance was her heart trouble – brought on, she claimed, by Dr Sutherland's libel action in 1929. Neither, at the time, was she aware of the extent of Humphrey's financial collapse, nor of the fact that Heatherbank was heavily mortgaged. Even so, living at Norbury Park could scarcely be described as "Love on the Dole".* She employed two full-time gardeners, two menservants indoors, a cook, nurserymaid and housemaid. It should have been the ideal background for Marie's experiment in providing a natural, Rousseauesque education for her only child. Yet Harry was

---

* Walter Greenwood's novel, of this title, published in 1933 when Marie moved into Norbury, was one of the few works to capture the miseries of the British working classes during the slump.

never happy at Norbury Park, perhaps because he sensed the collapse of his parents' marriage.

To visiting journalists, Marie maintained the picture of a happy household. "With her bun of jet-black hair, just beginning to thread with silver," wrote the journalist, Betty Ross in 1934, "green woolly dress with mother-of-pearl chain, and gold wedding ring, she might have been taken for a contented housewife working in her kitchen garden." Miss Ross also quoted Marie's comments on marriage: "I am incurably romantic, being in favour of monogamic marriage. It is the nucleus of human society ... A successful marriage? That means the perfect sex relation."*[31]

Publicly, she gave no hint of disappointment with her own marriage; but Marie had lost all respect for her husband. The handsome, rich, uniformed "Tiger Humphlekins" Marie had so admired in 1918 no longer had any status. Harry Stopes-Roe remembers that, when they moved to Norbury Park, his mother took the biggest, central, bedroom: "I had the second main room, which should have been the master's room, and father had the third room facing North. They both had double beds but probably separately occupied. My father, it seemed to me in the 'thirties, was a very much despised and inconsequential person. One April Fool's Day, I pinned a 'Kick Me' notice on his back and he was hurt and angry, perhaps indicating his awareness that my feelings had been generated by her. I was at that time completely identifying with my mother."[32]

Harry was not the only one to notice his father's diminution. Lady Jeans (Susi Jeans, the musician) then recently married to Sir James Jeans, the astronomer, lived only a few miles away and first met Marie in 1935: "She was a very powerful person – lively, outspoken, nearly dictatorial, I would say. She was not too popular locally – she *would* make remarks to mothers at children's parties, 'You don't know how to feed children' – but you knew you were in the presence of someone great. H. V. Roe looked much younger. She would always sit separately and eat separately from him. He went his own way, not taking part in anything. I had the feeling she was the fighter – jolly difficult for a man to accept that."[33]

---

*In this, as in much else, Marie was never consistent. "I do not think that love ought to depend entirely or in any great degree on sexual intercourse," she wrote to a correspondent on 26 February 1926. (BL-S.)

The only certainty about Marie's impact on others was its violence. Some found her lively, utterly charming and full of humour. Barnes Wallis, the inventor, aeronautical engineer and father of Harry Stopes-Roe's future wife, Mary, was one of those who disagreed. In his biography of Wallis, J. E. Morpurgo tells the story of what appears to have been a monumental clash.[34] In 1935, Molly Wallis took her daughter Mary, then aged eight, to a children's party:

> From the mob of neatly-bowed girls and scrubbed boys one stood out for rare beauty and for eccentricity of dress, but whether this handsome young creature, long-haired and wearing a knitted and pleated woollen skirt, was boy or girl even Molly, the mother of both boys and girls, could not tell. Molly Wallis had a quick way with a mystery: she put the question direct to her hostess. To the answer that this was Harry Stopes-Roe, the 11-year-old son of Marie Stopes, there was added the gratuitous explanation of the odd garment. The great pioneer of birth control would not suffer her son the risk to his genitals that she foresaw in the wearing of trousers.*

The marriage of Barnes and Molly Wallis was founded on *Married Love*, and Molly enthusiastically supported the birth control movement. However, continues Morpurgo:

> If Wallis shared his wife's admiration for Marie Stopes's crusading work for women, he was unlike Molly in that he was aware of her other attainments and cared for them not at all. Her claim to creativity as palaeontologist, biologist and coal-chemist he knew to be no more than pretensions; as for her literary efforts, he saw them for what they were, affected drivel made even more sickening by her out-of-character obsequiousness to men of real authority in the world of letters.

This may be an accurate reflection of Barnes Wallis's feelings, but it was scarcely fair to Marie, whose scientific reputation was genuine, and merited. Her attitude to some men of letters – in particular Maurice Hewlett and Thomas Hardy – was certainly unctuous; but this could

---

* Marie believed that men should wear a kilt, "instead of the ugly and heating-in-the-wrong-place garment which most men are now condemned to wear". (20 August 1940, MCS to Commander F. Hall, RN. BL-S.) However, Harry Stopes-Roe denies that he was obliged to wear the kilt. He recalls that as a child he mostly wore knitted trousers. (Interview with the author, 23 September 1976.)

never be said of her spiky relationship with George Bernard Shaw. Marie was, however, invited to the Wallis home, there to meet a personality as powerful as her own. As topics of conversation, birth control and music were speedily disposed of, and an evening of disaster loomed ahead:

> Wallis, in his own home, was at a disadvantage because the severe rules of courtesy which he set for himself could not make him into a patient audience, but would not allow him to contradict a guest, but when finally and with her unshakeable conviction of divine authority she came to aeronautics, an end to politeness was close . . .

> Wallis knew that his knowledge and experience was, in this one subject at least, so far beyond that of his guest as to make argument between them ridiculous, but the misconceptions and heresies that she was mouthing demanded correction. He would have exploded with forthrightness had not Marie Stopes mistaken his angry expression for bewilderment and decided that a man who could not so much as appreciate the finer points of what was supposed to be his own profession made an audience unworthy of her talents. She could not leave until her husband came for her with a car and so, as with a child who is beneath the possibility of intelligent conversation, she decreed games. Chess it was to be, but even this to rules of her own devising – "quick chess", with no pauses for thought . . .

Humphrey eventually arrived to end the nightmare, and Marie "swept out of the house screeching over her shoulder that she had let him win the chess game only because she had to leave . . . She and Barnes Wallis never exchanged another word in conversation."

If Barnes Wallis could not deal with such a termagant, what hope had Humphrey? His financial bankruptcy had resulted in a total loss of self-confidence. A complaisant man, always ready to take the blame, he retreated under Marie's attacks. It is not surprising that his sexual prowess, whatever the contribution of his war injuries, diminished as rapidly as his drooping confidence. Their marriage had been dead for several years when in July 1938 Humphrey wrote for Marie his most remarkable letter. Headed "The Old Lighthouse, Portland Bill, Dorset", it was more of a statement than a letter. There is no appellation:

> Five years ago when here I told you I wanted no more sex union and that I should not object if you decided to have a lover to replace my

deficiency – you were very hurt and answered that it was unthinkable. Now that you have suffered sex deprivation for all these years
you may feel differently, and I wish to put it on record that if you did
it would not in any way alter our existing relations and I should
never reproach you or take any steps about it, as I have long considered a wife whose husband is incapable of coitus has every right to
supplement his deficiency without breaking up the home. H. V.
Roe.[35]

Coming from Humphrey who, unlike Marie, did not feel compelled
to put everything on record, it is an extraordinary document. Written
with none of his usual mis-spellings and crossings-out, it gives the
impression of being a pupil's "fair copy". Marie was in the house at the
time, so why did he have to write? Could he not just have told her?
The obvious implication is that Marie either dictated, or asked him to
write, the statement. Her puritanism was as strong as ever, whatever
her opponents might say of her. For twenty years she had propounded
the virtues of monogamy, the holy and enduring nature of marriage,
and the sinfulness of unmarried love. Now, at the age of fifty-eight, and
possibly with a suitor in mind, she felt the need to justify herself to
posterity and to palliate her own conscience by extracting a *nihil obstat*
from her husband.

Despite the protestations about not altering "existing relations",
their marriage crumbled. In August 1939 Humphrey wrote from
London that he would like to visit Norbury Park on Sunday, September
3, but would be even more pleased to arrive on the Saturday: "I can
sleep in the Lounge that night if somebody else is in my room."

From now on, he was never more than an unwelcome guest in what
he still considered his own home. In 1940, with her husband once more
in the Royal Air Force, which he had rejoined at the outbreak of the
war, Marie refused his request to come to Norbury for the weekend:

Dear Humphrey, Forgive me typing but I am so busy. I have got
your note to say you are coming . . . I must seriously request you not
to do so. I cannot cope with you this Friday and there are no servants.

I wish also to say a word about the way you behaved last Friday,
blustering and bullying without having the elementary intelligence
to mention that Miss Johns wished to leave at 5 o'clock . . . I repeat

the request that you do not come on Friday. There will be no food and no attendance if you do. Yours, MCS.[36]

In handwriting, Marie added, "You made me frightfully ill with your abominable behaviour and I will have no more of it." In 1942 Humphrey begged to be allowed to come home for Christmas, and forestalled her objections by reducing himself to servant status: "As regards SERVICE. I can easily prepare BREAKFAST and COOK the Porridge and Bacon etc. I know all about it. Then you can leave the clearing and washing up to me. DINNER, I can peel the Potatoes etc lay the cloth etc and again clear up and wash up . . . Please let me know when I can come to help in the house for a fortnight."[37]

Two months later, Humphrey bared his heart. "My dear Marie," he wrote from London: ". . . Here I am, 65 next month and I have nothing. A husband who writes to his wife for permission to be allowed to come home for a few days and invariably receives the answer No! To me the reasons are never adequate . . . I hope also you will allow me to see Harry sometimes. Now, you always appear to want to keep us apart, just as when he was a Baby you gave reasons why I should not play with him. Yours, as ever, Humphrey."[38]

Marie and Humphrey never lived together again. The sexual *carte blanche* extracted from her husband in 1938 was not so much an insurance policy against future involvements, as a justification for one that was already there. It symbolised for Marie, and not just sexually, the start of a new life – and a life in which H. V. Roe could play no part.

CHAPTER 16

"Remember My Sweet Youth"

Remember my sweet youth and not my age
Remember me as I was young and fair
With eager life rippling through all my hair
When brow and cheek were smooth as unwrit page . . .
Marie Stopes, *Love Songs for Young Lovers*[1]

AT the age of fifty-eight Marie Stopes still believed that she was a young
woman. Asked by the magazine *Housewife* for an article on "How to
Face the Forties", she indignantly replied: "I am not too flattered to be
put among the Forties, for my psychological age is twenty-six and will
be for many years to come. I am told by scientific diagnosis that I
should live for 200 years, so I shall not be feeling middle-aged until I
am a hundred."[2]

It was in the previous year, 1938, that Keith Briant, just down from
Oxford, with some reputation as editor of *Isis* and budding poet, first
met her. She was, he recorded in his biography of her, "A vigorous
woman in her fifties, but with her clear complexion, vivid sparkling
eyes and chestnut hair she might well have been in her early forties."
Briant's biography was published in 1962, only four years after Marie's
death, and he added delicately: "Sexually promiscuous people she
abhorred. She was often at pains to make inquiries about people before
inviting them to Norbury Park. She enjoyed the company of younger
men who were mentally and physically attractive, and she was not
unaware of the power she possessed as a famous woman to command
their admiration; perhaps there were occasions when she placed herself
in an invidious position." Perhaps, indeed, there were – and Briant
himself was the first to be placed in such a position.

In 1938 the birth control movement no longer commanded for Marie the interest it had once possessed. The issue was now fought not in the High Courts of Justice, but in the dingy rooms of local councils or the fund-raising salons of Society sympathisers. Among the prizes at the CBC's annual ball at Claridge's in 1938 were a weekend for two (married), a dozen apostle spoons, a bottle of passion fruit juice and a cake of floating Mickey Mouse soap.[3]

It was no life for a prophet. In July, the same month that yielded Humphrey's sexual *carte blanche*, Marie wrote one of her worst poems:

> Keith, Keith, Keith, sheeny wood pigeons are calling.
> Keith, Keith, Keith, sweet rain drops are calling and falling,
> The thunderous clouds are dissolved in swift curtains of rain ...
> Peace is achieved in the bosom of love once again.[4]

For some years, Marie had been toying with Theosophy, and the Nature of Prayer, subjects that involved long correspondence with spiritualists and with Franciscan theologians. Such preoccupations, with Marie, usually indicated deep dissatisfaction. Sexually, her life with Humphrey had failed. Contraception was – more or less – accepted, her son was gowing up, and she was growing older – without, she felt, having experienced what she termed true "erogamic" love, an enduring combination of the physical and spiritual. In October 1938 she described a night worrying about the twenty-five-year-old Keith, who had been ill: "... I found myself picturing him in bed and his mother near, in tears, and myself calming her and giving him my electric treatment and other things ... On waking or more completely waking, I scolded myself for the dreams thinking they must merely represent a suppressed desire to help him in some way."

This was not good enough for Marie's scientific training. While still dark, she recorded, her mind became filled not just with anxiety, but with longing: "For the first time the thought of him and the desire to be with him was accompanied by definite physical pain in small spasms, not localised but general ... Hitherto (since our dinner at the Ritz when he came quickly up the stair after me and I felt his pulsing hand on my arm so softly and insistently and he kissed me so sweetly and softly goodnight) hitherto every time I have thought of him it was with a sense of happiness and sometimes a little throb of quivering physical pleasure ..."[5]

Marie's indulgence in literature was not entirely, as she liked to think, her reward for having completed twenty years' work in the service of humanity. The thought of literary fame had always been at the back of her mind, and in 1928, when her novel *Love's Creation* was so badly reviewed, she took a full-page advertisement in the *Morning Post* to announce that its author, Marie Carmichael, was none other than Dr Marie Stopes. Under another pseudonym, "Gordon Mortlock", she addressed hymns to God in the *Birth Control News*:

> Grant us Thy wisdom to extol
> To tell man's world of petty strife
> That Peace equipped with birth control
> Opens Thy gates to glorious life![6]

She had a penchant for famous people, and the purchase of Norbury Park gave her the opportunity to recreate the salon atmosphere of earlier days, when William Lock had entertained Fanny Burney, Madame de Stael and Talleyrand. She collected at Norbury – in addition to handsome young poets – such diverse literary lions as H. G. Wells, Hugh Walpole, and Lord Alfred Douglas, the "Bosie" of Oscar Wilde's downfall. They had little in common, except the foibles of Marie. (She kept all the nudes in the painted drawing room covered in green baize – an action seized on by visitors as an example of her paradoxical prudery.)*

Bosie was now sixty-eight, a lonely, rather embittered man, with no trace left of the beauty that had captivated Wilde. Separated from his wife, Olive, and with his only son in a mental home, he eked out the £400 his wife allowed him annually with poetry, articles and reminiscences about Wilde. Marie admired his poetry but, as Bosie was a Catholic who had several times attacked her work in print, she had been chary of approaching him. Her solution was typically devious. Posing as "Mrs Carmichael", the mother of a young family, she sent him a sonnet, humbly asking for advice about publication. The poem was "quite pleasant, but I cannot hail it as a masterpiece," he replied. Over the next few months, by a combination of flattery and genuine solicitude – "You are indeed one of our great poets and I really yearn to discuss poetry with you," she wrote, sending a bottle of her favourite

---

* Her son claims that the explanation was simpler – she just did not like the paintings aesthetically.

tonic, Syrup of Hypophosphites,* – Marie gradually infiltrated his life. It was not until February 1939, five months after their correspondence started, that Marie finally admitted her identity. "Dear Mrs Carmichael," Bosie replied, "I was astonished to see the signature on your letter received this morning. I had not the remotest idea that you were Marie Stopes. It is really very extraordinary because (as perhaps you know) I have in the past criticised you rather strongly. Naturally as a Catholic I disagree with your views about 'Birth Control'." (Against this, Marie pencilled in: "later on he *agreed* with me about b.c. and my whole work"): "But now that you have written me so many kind letters and shown so much interest in me and my poetry and my health and my worldly condition, I feel remorseful to think that I have had unkind thoughts about you."[7]

After this, their friendship developed rapidly. Marie spent a lot of time and energy trying, unsuccessfully, to secure a Civil List pension for Bosie; in return, he criticised her poetry and, on frequent visits to Norbury Park, provided a tasty morsel for the other guests. Marie gave a description of his first visit to Norbury:

> I had been rather afraid of having Lord Alfred Douglas knowing that he is reported to be very quarrelsome and uninterested in anything except poetry. I took an early opportunity of telling him laughingly that my husband was very illiterate and laughed at poetry, and that my son despised it. He responded charmingly and developed an amusing geniality and wide interest, talking about hunting and shooting, a number of well-known people he had stayed with or who were related to him and was full of humorous anecdotes and very much the man of the world, appreciating good food and wine and making altogether very entertaining company.

What the "illiterate" and teetotal Humphrey made of all this has not been recorded; but not everyone was as charmed by Bosie as Marie appeared to be. The novelist Hugh Walpole recorded in his journal, after a weekend at Norbury: "She [Marie Stopes] has real honest goodness and incredible pluck. There is something so honest in her

---

* Syrup of Hypophosphites was, at the time, a popular patent medicine. There was always a bottle on the sideboard in the grand dining room at Norbury Park, incongruously adjacent to an ornate paper swan. Marie had great faith in it as a universal panacea, recommended it to everyone, and took it religiously, along with her daily glass of sea water.

that you feel warm in her defence. Lord Alfred Douglas, however, was something of a shock. How astonished was I when this rather bent, crooked-bodied, hideous old man came into the room. How could he ever have been beautiful, for he has a nose as ugly as Cyrano's with a dead-white bulbous end?" He talked incessantly, Walpole complained, in a shrill, agitated voice. "When someone he hates like Wells is mentioned, he gets so angry that all his crooked features light up and his nose achieves a sort of sombre glow. In the afternoon he had before all of us a first-class row with young Briant of the *Sunday Chronicle* about the Russians, listening to no argument, screaming like a parrot, repeating phrases again and again. At last he shrieked 'Oh go to Hell!' Upon which the young man went."[9]

H. G. Wells, though famous, was also troublesome. Not only did he have the temerity to argue; he also, though a notorious "philanderer", as Marie called him, failed to respond to her own sexual charms. Keith Briant remembered a lunch party in 1938 during which she and Wells both with high opinions of themselves, clashed violently. Though Wells was a fervent supporter of birth control, he dared to suggest that the medical profession was not quite so backward as Marie claimed:

This was like a red rag to a bull and a pink flush began to suffuse Marie Stopes' face. It was intolerable that anyone should in the least degree question the vital necessity of her crusade for the sex education of women, to which she had devoted the main energies of her life . . .

After lunch we withdrew to the Painted Drawing Room and settled to drink coffee. But Wells had forgotten that, apart from the possible effect of smoke on the historical and artistically valuable painted walls and ceiling, his hostess abhorred smoking. Although he was prepared to be a good week-end guest and to concede some mutually embarrassing debating points, he was certainly not prepared to concede his after-lunch pleasure in his cigar.

He and Briant crept upstairs to enjoy the Havanas that Wells fished out from his suitcase. "Wells brooded for a few minutes, gazing out of the window. 'Extraordinary woman,' he finally said, lighting his cigar. 'Brilliant in her way, but trying, very trying.' Later that evening I was alone for a few moments with Marie Stopes when she delivered herself: 'Brilliant man, H. G., but how tiresome and didactic he can be. And he is what I would call rather a gross man!'"[10]

In the evenings Marie would entertain her guests with readings from her own poetry. Dressed in her home-made, low-cut gowns, uncorseted and without a bra ("A butterfly should be able to fly up between yourself and your dress without so much as brushing the powder from its wings," she once said*) Marie cut an extraordinary figure against the highly erotic poetry she was now writing. Such poems as "The Stream," about naked bathing – one of Marie's favourite pursuits – must have been highly embarrassing in the cold, dimly lit painted drawing room at Norbury.

> When my lips your nipples touch
> Am I pleading over much
> That the rhythm thus begun
> Should continue in the sun ...
>
> Life's hot stream of love in me
> Floods into the love of thee
> Till our throbbings gently cease
> Till our breathing is at ease ...[11]

"*All* your poetry is about 'Love'," complained Lord Alfred Douglas, "which (strange as it may seem) I cannot accept as the proper subject for the highest poetry. Shakespeare wrote 'Call it no love, for love to Heaven has fled since sweating lust on earth usurped his name.' That gives a sort of hint about what I feel. All your poetry is about physical passion." In *Love Songs for Young Lovers*, published three months later, Marie was at pains to establish the generalised nature of her love poetry. Britain's greatest poet, she said (i.e. Lord Alfred Douglas) had complained that her poems were "too intimate personal accounts of your own experiences with your lover". This was not the case, Marie replied, resorting to a Jungian interpretation of her poetic inspiration. "Many of the most personally worded have no basis in any physical experience of my own, but came swiftly transmitted from the storehouse of human emotion ... Nowadays nothing is too personal for expression in prose, so surely there can be no good reason why the deep pools of the love experience of the human heart should be denied a poet because of the particularity of the radiance that may flash from the surface ripples."

* To Dr Evelyne Fisher, a frequent visitor to Norbury Park in the 1930s. (Interview with the author, 24 October 1974.)

There is little doubt, however, that the inspiration for *Love Songs* came more from Keith Briant than from the deep pools of human experience. In her acknowledgments, Marie mentioned Briant, "whom, though last, I place first in my gratitude, for he is of the generation for whom the poems are written". Her protestations that the poems were not autobiographical appears to have reassured Keith's mother, who wrote some years later, after Marie had published, without her permission, a sonnet on the death of Keith's father: "One swallows a lot in life . . . but I will tell you now that it will always be an everlasting regret that you singled out my son in a preface to your column of love poems, many, you say, when you felt the inspiration of them and yourself never having experienced all those sensations. Thank God you said that . . . Some of your poems in that volume are disliked intensely by many, including myself. My son is very happy with his beautiful young wife and children, long may they go on as they are doing."[12]

In her introduction to *Love Songs* Marie protested that the poems had been written over a long period. The manuscripts in the Stopes-Roe collection, however, reveal that the majority were written between July and December 1938, and several of them are marked "To K". It is easy enough to understand Mrs Briant's distress if the poems are taken as autobiographical, and as referring to Keith Briant. In "A Poet's Offspring," for example, Marie sees her own poems as the children she was no longer able to conceive:

> You impregnate me with immortal young!
> Your wingèd brood born springing to the skies
> Entered my lips where your lips burning clung.
> They need no mortal flesh, each swiftly flies
> Singing down all the ages your sweet name . . .

It is as well that Mrs Briant did not see another poem, "The Mother-in-Law". On her manuscript, Marie scribbled "cut out of book":

> . . . O, sacred mother of my love
> My eyes are veiled with misty tears
> Yearning for those past years.
> Now in the night it is not your dear name
> He whispers, as he sleeps in flame
> Of man's desire fulfilled in me . . .[13]

Possibly in an attempt to make light of the disparity in their ages – Marie could easily have been Keith's mother – she saw their love as a reincarnation of past lovers. In *Oriri*, a long love-poem published in 1940, the opening "Argument" runs: "He and She have a background aeons long, in which they have repeatedly met and loved. They are due to meet and love in the present time of world chaos, nevertheless they are led to this meeting in peace and understanding. Thus they are the advance guard of the human race, all of whom must ultimately learn true love." Marie's belief was not limited to poetic fantasy. Though she had turned down Theosophy as a way of life, she had obviously mentioned the idea of reincarnation to her theosophical friend, Dr Beddow Bayly, who had earlier been so dismissive about her husband's sexual and spiritual flaws. In July 1939 Dr Bayly wrote: "Dear Dr Stopes . . . Now with regard to what I told K-B (i.e. Keith Briant); I said nothing about reincarnation in general or in particular as to his relationship to you, and I don't think we discussed anything at all above material things . . ."[14]

In the same way, her feelings for Keith are paralleled in both poetry and correspondence. All lovers, of course, think their present love unique, no matter how many times they have already experienced uniqueness. "True Love", written in October 1938 might be taken as a generalised expression of this idea:

> What did we do for love before we met
> What did we do, my love, for love?
> Until we met and loved, what did we do? . . .
>
> All that proceeded meeting I forget
> What I thought love before was no real love
> I lived, I loved just when I first loved you.[15]

But in 1942, over three years after first meeting him, Marie wrote to Keith Briant: "Dear one . . . I'm delighted you've found out what I found out as a University lecturer, that the only way to learn anything is to teach it. That's why I know so much about love, I've been teaching it to thousands by correspondence and Clinics, every day for seven thousand days. And only you have taught me."[16] Even in 1943, when Keith Briant was married she was still garnering scraps of comfort from the liaison. In February of that year, she wrote on a scrap of paper:

Keith here to tea and dinner after Court Martial in wh. he was witness at Leatherhead – 100 officers took part – He was heavenly sweet and so smart in his Guards uniform, but looked v. tired. After tea wanted to see all over the house, on roof, into Harry's nursery where we blew trumpets and he looked at the dolls house, he loved the Mimosa flowers on the tree. We had a fire bath.* He loved my white lace dress making me turn round to examine it and said "perfectly beautiful", "lovely", "it suits you to perfection", etc. He was utterly enchanting all the time.[17]

A month later, in March 1943, Marie wrote to her husband, who could not understand why he was not allowed to visit Norbury Park: "My dear Humphrey ... You don't realise at all how day and night I *slave* far beyond my strength for lack of service in essentials. You say you see no sufficient reason when recently I've said you simply *can't* come home till I get some domestic worker to help Ivy: that is selfish and unimaginative."

The world of fire baths and love poetry obviously excluded Humphrey. Why, Marie asked, could he not find for her the extra domestic help she needed? "You've done *nothing* but make work for ages and ages and if you really do care for the home, put your back into finding someone to work with Ivy ... Directly you can find anyone old or young you can come for a bit here – it is always I who have to do the extra things and I'm near breaking point. Find someone to work in the home then you can come to it."[18]

This letter – one of the few preserved from the period, probably because she saw it as self-justification – is doubly hypocritical. She wanted privacy at Norbury Park. And she was never near "breaking point". From the outbreak of war, in September 1939, Marie's private life had never precluded her from the possibility of saving Britain. Occasionally anti-Semitic,† as many were in the thirties, she yet had no time for Hitler who, among other enormities, had closed all Germany's birth control clinics, turning them into what were euphemistically

---

* Marie Stopes believed in the beneficent effect of coal fires on the naked human body.

† One of her unpublished verses, written in 1942, ran:
  Catholics, Prussians,
  The Jews and the Russians,
  All are a curse,
  Or something worse ... (SR-Coll.)

Top left: Marie leaving the Law Courts during the Stopes–Sutherland case, 1923
Top right: On the National Birth Rate Commission, with the admiring Bishop of Birmingham fourth on her right
Bottom: An undated photograph of Marie with a group of nurses at the Mothers' Clinic in Holloway

Keith Briant

Marie with Avro Manhattan, 1957.
He had just rescued her from being
carried away by a strong current
while swimming off the island of
Portland

called "centres for eugenic advice". In April 1940 when it had become obvious that the war with Germany was no longer "phoney", Marie offered to serve as a member of the Cabinet. She wrote to Lord Halifax, then Foreign Secretary:

> Dear Lord Halifax ... re the other matter: attached is a brief summary of a few of the salients which indicate a breadth of contact and variety of expert qualifications which might make me of real use as a woman statesman (*not* politician). I am convinced there ought to be a woman in the Cabinet and very soon she would be of value.

Halifax turned down her offer and Marie concentrated on Winston Churchill – a person she could not approve of, his motto about birth control being "Tell them to breed up to quota or they'll all be wiped out." In July 1940 Marie wrote:

> Dear Mr Churchill, May I give you a slogan – Fight the Battle of Britain in Berlin's Air! Our R.A.F. are so splendidly superior – Lord Beaverbrook has now got the machines – the German's mentality is that of a bully who will squeal if hit between the eyes; please win the war in a few weeks by releasing the order to fight the Battle of Britain in Berlin's air.*[19]

Rebuffed by Churchill, Marie turned her attention to the land, in particular the problems of milk and apples. The suggestion that all milk should be compulsorily pasteurised brought upon the Minister of Health, Malcolm MacDonald, a barrage of letters, pamphlets and personal visits from Dr Marie Stopes. Like her mother, Marie believed in letting Nature take care of itself (except, of course, for birth control). In July she wrote a memo about her visit to the Minister of Health ". . . Spoke of eggs, with which all agreed and promised to do something." Marie extracted from the Minister a solemn promise that no compulsion would be used. "I left him with Sir Frederick Keeble's lecture, *The Foster Mother of Mankind* and Goodfellow's pamphlet *Hands Off Our Milk*, both of which he promised to read." As for

---

* At the time, Marie's proposal would have attracted little support. Kingsley Wood, secretary for air, replied to the proposal that all Germany's forests should be burned down with a horrified: "Are you aware it is private property? Why, you will be asking me to bomb Essen next." (Taylor, op. cit., p. 459.)

apples, Marie thought the nation was deprived. It must have been with some relief that Lord Woolton, Minister of Food, received his Christmas present from Norbury Park: "Dear Lord Woolton, re Apples ... I realise it is a specially difficult time and Christmas is upon you. The people should be able to keep going on what is available till early in the New Year. Things should be better then and I'll start worrying you about apples seriously in 1941."[20]

Rubber was another problem. As the war continued, allocations dwindled to nothing, and the North Kensington clinic was reduced to buying up a large consignment of decorated rubber flooring intended for the bathroom floors of a Paris hotel. "Those gay caps almost became heirlooms," wrote Dr Helena Wright in 1972. "No two were alike. Marbled patterns of all colours appeared and the rubber lasted so well that even now, here and there, a specimen survives."[21] For Marie, the supply of rubber for caps was of much greater importance than merely equipping an army. "In the 20 years of my campaign to lift sex matters out of the gutter and Charing Cross road 'rubber' shops," she complained to the Ministry of Supply, "we have established beyond doubt the unique value to women of occlusives and diaphragms ... if we do not get supplies, abortion will rise to a nightmarish degree. Abortion not only causes temporary ill-health, but often corrupts the woman's potential motherhood for the rest of her life, and is so bad for the race that it is a disaster greater than any German bombing of this country ..."[22] On the walls of her London clinic, she pinned up a notice: "Every kind of worker doing any work of importance has been specially asked to carry on during an air raid ... only when the sound of actual gunfire or bombs is very near is danger point considered to have been reached." Marie stayed at Norbury Park during the war, but not even there was she safe from those who tried to hinder her work. On their way back from London raids, German bombers were in the habit of ditching their remaining bombs indiscriminately. The grounds of Norbury Park were hit several times, and two bombs fell directly on the house, shattering all the glass and damaging the Painted Drawing Room (later repaired by the War Damages Commission). Marie was convinced that Goering himself had given special orders to the Luftwaffe to attack her home.[23]

Goering and the rubber shortage were not her only enemies. Christianity was also a problem. It was the "pacifist and Christian attitude",

Marie wrote in 1941, that had caused the war by encouraging Hitler to think that Britain was weak.[24] In 1943, the Bishop of St Albans made matters worse by calling for parliamentary action to ban the sale of contraceptives to all but married people, and then only on production of a medical certificate. Marie replied on June 7 with *An Open Letter to the Bishop of St Albans*. Part of the rough draft (understandably, in view of its rather extreme expression, the letter appears not to have been published) ran:

> ... Take one point only: the best contraceptive in the world is olive (ordinary salad) oil. Is your Lordship proposing to have a Bill passed that olive oil shall only be sold to married women on the production of a medical certificate? In these fantastic times you may succeed, but you won't be able to stop me telling women that castor oil and margarine remain ... One notes with revulsion the inherent cruelty in your effort to force women against their wills by coercive ignorance to bear children they do not feel physically fit to or do not want to bear. It is without doubt the most blasphemous form of slave driving, for we should be made in God's image and begotten in love. The slavery of a woman who carries in her womb day by day a child not begotten in love she did not wish to conceive, is the most insidious and horrible of all forms of slavery; and before Man and before the Throne of God I arraign your cruelty. Answer my Charge. Yours faithfully, MCS.

Her concern about birth control was not limited to wartime Britain. Genuinely terrified of being, as she put it, "swamped by hordes of Indians and Chinese", she conducted a fierce campaign for the provision of birth control clinics in India. In June 1942 she wrote to Clement Attlee, then deputy prime minister and Dominions secretary:

Dear Mr Attlee ... The whole peace of the world depends on my work being available and rightly presented to the backward peoples. The trouble in India is that Gandhi's *lying* folly is given publicity in this country and my exposure of him is suppressed. Do you realise that as a result more Indians have been added to their miserable over-population *in the last ten years* than our *total* population? ... I want to see you about this and some other things of urgent national importance.

Wearily, Clement Attlee wrote back: "I am very well acquainted with the population problem in India. Perhaps, if you have some particular point you wish to raise, you will write to me."[25]

The clinic at Whitfield Street was hit several times during the blitz. It stayed heroically open, but Marie transferred her secretarial staff to Norbury Park. There she kept up her vast correspondence. She was still incapable of delegating responsibility, and insisted on detailed weekly reports and case histories from the nurses at her provincial clinics in Leeds, Aberdeen, Cardiff, Swansea and Belfast. Nor were her ideas any more liberal than they had been twenty years earlier. To the man who wrote, in 1939, "I am one of those who suffer from being Hot Natured. I have noticed it more in the last 18 months since I have taken Dancing seriously, while dancing I find it most embarrassing," she replied, briefly, "Get married! Best wishes, MCS." And to the twenty-eight-year-old unmarried woman, whose psychiatrist had advised her to indulge her sexual urge, since men could no longer afford to marry, Marie commented: ". . . shockingly bad advice. I may tell you if I knew who the man was I should draw the attention of the police to his wicked practice . . . when you do in the end meet the man destined for you by fate, you are likely to lose him if you have played fast and loose with such a serious thing as your sex life." (Marie's case was different – she had, after all, a document from her husband expressly permitting non-marital relationships.)

Only a person of extraordinary vitality could have withstood the pressures of Goering's vendetta, political propaganda, running clinics and organising India – while at the same time devoting much of her time to writing poetry. Undeterred by her lack of success, she versified throughout the war years to a largely unappreciative audience. "The only consolation," she wrote in 1945, "is that I know I am a great poet and that people will be allowed to know that after I am dead."[26]

Even for this, she tried to blame the Catholics – but the sad truth is that her poetry was totally out of tune with contemporary taste. She had as little time for T. S. Eliot, Auden and Spender as she had for artists like Henry Moore, whose work she categorised as "contagiously abnormal, just as is homosexuality".[27] Marie believed in Beauty. She never altered her list of "Words to Use", compiled in 1912 – among them, rosemary, sapphire, beryl, amethyst, amber, roseate, ripple, valour, virginal and vervain. Among the older generation, Marie had her admirers. About *Love Songs*, Bernard Shaw wrote in 1939: "My dear Marie, You see I was right at our first meeting when I laughed at your scientific pretensions and diagnosed you as an ardent dancing girl from the tropics ... You are a poet all right. It can't be helped ..." More typical of critical reaction was Llewellyn Powys. In October, 1939, dying in Switzerland of tuberculosis, he sent a critique of *Love Songs*.

> Perhaps if I were fortunate enough to see more of you I would find it easy to overcome a certain resistance against the kind of idealism that seems characteristic of your mind ... We are, however, too different – I often like what is "ugly" – *you never do*; so it comes about that my enthusiasm for your ability, good sense, public service and life-passion is continually being discouraged ...
>
> I am sure you use the word "rosy" too much. It seems to me a significant little word ... I sometimes feel my enthusiasm and admiration a little daunted by this "rosy" quality. You are like some splendid heroine of Northern mythology, but your Freyja turns not to the hard and sun-blessed substance of amber but to a new kind of "rosy" amber.[28]

With characteristic obtuseness where her poetry was concerned, Marie wrote back that he would be thrilled and pleased to know that "rosy amber" actually existed – "in verity the ancient hard and sun-blessed substance – true amber, but in a *very rare* form; and at the moment of reading your letter ... I was wearing my marvellous ring of it – a huge hard drop of the world's blood – rich rose as a ruby *but* with far more mellow lights ... the great globe-like drop shimmers and quivers with all the joy and sorrow of the living world." The actual existence of rosy amber was, of course, not the point. Still, Marie expressed gratitude for his criticisms – "so valuable and so cheering to a lonely writer to be read by one who too can write." The trouble was, she went on, "I have had to accustom myself to the fact that people care not at all what's *in* me – mostly only for what they can get *from* me. The world seems to think I was made for its service and would have clawed me to pieces long ago had I not been rooted in rock – and as lonely as a lighthouse."[29]

During the war, Marie let the lighthouse at Portland Bill to three young naval lieutenants. At first she approved of them, since they all had literary or artistic ambitions and were personable. One of the three, Lieut. William Rose, went down with HMS *Cossack*, eliciting from Marie the elegy "Instead of Tears", using her latest poetic invention, the "mirror" or returning rhyme scheme.

> Brown berried sea-wrack tangles round your throat
> In festive chaplets where no fresh wreathed flowers
> Will reach you, and your resolute white limbs
> Are draped with laminaria's crinkled strands
> Swaying about the stillness of your thighs.
> Your eyes are closed to all the hurrying fleet
> Of fin-borne flocks darting between your feet.*
> Your breath gives no response to wave-swept sighs.
> The pearl-sailed Nautilus curves to your hands.
> Lucent green water takes the light and dims
> Your lips now fading with the passing hours
> That sang and laughed with an Elysian note.

The other two naval officers remained obstinately alive. In 1942 Lieut. Warren Tute sent Marie his play *Jack o' Lantern*, set in the lighthouse and with an inadequately disguised Marie Stopes as its female lead – a spy. "Dear Lieut. Tute," she wrote from Norbury Park in January 1942, "I have read your play with more, and more various distresses than I can put into words, for I can't express how much I dislike it." She asked him to change the setting, which would remove her worst personal objections "and save me the horrible business of getting my solicitors to go to the Courts and ask for an immediate injunction to call in all copies and stop it for further circulation."[30] Furious at her censorship – she had cut out large chunks of the manuscript with scissors, and scribbled over the rest – Lieut. Tute was not to be intimidated. He pointed out that the manuscript had been "wilfully damaged beyond repair, without justification and without a shred of authority. I reserve the right of taking further action in this matter and should in the meantime be glad of any explanation you may have of this display of impertinence and bad manners."

Warren Tute's memories of Marie are as unflattering as her comments about his play: "She was infatuated with young, creative people. I

---

* Robert Graves, to whom Marie had sent the poem for his criticism, replied that it "failed to make him weep, or wish to weep: where fin-borne flocks intrude, there is no grief." (25 April 1950. BL-S.)

remember driving up to Norbury Park. Everything appeared very phallic – now, it would not rate a mention in *Private Eye*. She looked wild – hair all over the place, no bra. She was an eccentric – *not* an attractive woman, absolutely not, physically, but attractive because she was bursting with ideas. She was always the expert – it was Moses handing down the tablets. Charming? There was the pleasure which came from meeting a world figure. She had all the charm of a viper."[31]

Marie's conviction that people were battening on her did not destroy her generosity – and not just to starving young poets. Since the failure of her campaign to get a Civil List pension for Lord Alfred Douglas, she herself frequently paid his rent and set up a covenant to give him twenty pounds a year for seven years. All she asked in return – possibly thinking, as she had with Noel Coward, that his name might add lustre to her own – was his collaboration on a play. Bosie replied petulantly:

> My dear Marie, Why do you torment and goad me? *No, no, no, no,* I will *not* collaborate with you or anyone else. How *can* you so completely misunderstand me and my processes of thought and all my views about life and art? Doesn't it occur to you that if I had ever felt I could write a play I would have done it of my own volition and off my own bat years ago? . . . I return your Ostrich title page. I read the play when I was staying at Norbury. As you yourself say I would "hate it" there can't be any harm in saying that I did.[32]

Bosie's wife, Olive, died in 1944 and Marie was insensitive enough to send a letter of sympathy telling him not to worry, as it did not matter at all that his wife had left the Catholic church. "It does not help a man who is a devout Catholic to be told that his wife's apostasy from the Faith is a matter of no importance and that 'God' doesn't care two pins whether or not a man or a woman belongs to the Church founded by Christ . . . is it not rather 'governessy' on your part to fire off that kind of trite rubbish at me? I suppose if you had met Hamlet when he was lamenting that his father had died 'unhouseled, disappointed, unanealed' you would have told him that he was making a great fuss about nothing."

Bosie died in 1945 and, despite his occasional outbursts, Marie remained loyal to him. In 1950, five years after his death, she wrote to the *Listener* about Herbert Read's contention, based on Wilde's writings in prison, that Lord Alfred emerged "as the most complete cad in history". "One has only to look at the portrait of the gross middle-aged man in his forties beside the exquisite young man in the early twenties who is supposed to have ruined the experienced elder to realise that Herbert Read has a curious sense of values."[33]

On 15 August 1945, the day after Japan's surrender, Marie sent a telegram from Portland Bill to George VI at Buckingham Palace. "Sire," it ran. "Pray graciously accept heartfelt congratulations and thankfulness for triumph of your peoples and empire and loyal appreciation of your own noble part and inspiration to all." Marie herself was feeling far from triumphant. She detested practically everything about modern life. At the international level, she approved neither of Russia nor of America's growing influence and involvement in Europe. She wrote a poem (again in returning rhyme) "To Roosevelt and Churchill on their Atlantic Charter":

> Staged in a battleship with showman's skill
> To feed the vanity of two fat men,
> Th'Atlantic Charter, writ with flourished pen,
> Sop to the stupid, is the common will.
> Who can these guiling promises fulfil –
> Freedom and food for all? When every ten
> Brief years but doubles the great social wen
> Of weakling mouths the strong must stint to fill . . .[34]

With the return of a Labour government and the promise of a welfare state, Marie, as one of the strong, would have to stint to fill the weakling mouths of the lower classes. Being unable personally to bring down the new government, she contented herself with a letter to the new Prime Minister, Clement Attlee. The whole nation, she told him, was overstrained and under-nourished: she strongly advised the bulk purchase, with American dollars, of Fellowes Syrup of Hypophosphites, and Valentine's Meat Juice.[35] She felt badly let down by the rest of the world, and wrote to a friend in Cape Town: "You, in the well-fed peace of South Africa can have no conception of the strain and misery of the half-starved people of this country . . . the British stock is being weakened so fundamentally the effect will show for centuries. We, who saved the world, are worst treated of all it seems! The paper shortage is also very serious for the intellectual life of the country and gives the lower-grade U.S.A. weeds a great impetus while our best minds are being gagged."[36] (Due to the paper shortage, Marie's own books had been out of print for some time – though their sales were declining even before the war.) The redistribution of wealth was ruining the English countryside. Though she herself ran a car, Marie could only deplore the growing numbers of motor cars, once the prerogative of the rich:

> ... Whirring and buzzing in their petrol-fed
> Chariots of tin, exhausted myriads flee.
> Aimlessly whirl to Oxford's sonorous towers;
> Leave bottles high on Snowdon; miss a scree,
> Hoot on through Stirling, crushing moorland flowers ...
> Speed throws us gifts, but scattered in their place
> Deep wrinkles lie on a once lovely face.[37]

At a more personal level, the war had meant heavy losses for Marie. Bosie was dead, and two of her more promising poetic protégés, Bill Rose and Raoul Pugh, had been killed in action. Keith Briant was still alive – but married, with children. To whom, now, could she address her sonnets? To cap it all, her husband was still hopelessly indigent in North London, and her son Harry was away at university. Surely, given his mother's closest attention from birth, nothing could go wrong in that quarter? Over the next few years, Marie's other problems – with India, the BBC, bomb damage, lazy servants and dishonest gardeners – were as nothing in comparison with the future of her only child.

CHAPTER 17

Intimations of Mortality

"My own opinion is that your work will pass away and be forgotten and that you will lose your position save incidentally in the history of the movement and that your writings will before long disappear."
Sir James Marchant to Marie Stopes, 7 June 1929

To Marie, postwar Britain was acutely distasteful. At heart a convinced élitist, she despised the grey egalitarianism which, she was convinced, socialism would inevitably produce. The old social hierarchy was dying and, with it, her hopes of perfecting the human race by encouraging only the better stock. In 1950, returning from a visit to Germany, where Keith Briant was stationed with BAOR, she wrote to Walter de la Mare: "I feel in a sad way the life of our army officers there is the last islet of the civilisation that we knew and that matters so much."[1] This destruction of the old order was paralleled for Marie by the deaths, actual and metaphorical, of her closest relationships.

Humphrey, her husband, died on 27 July 1949, at the age of seventy. They had been estranged for well over a decade, but Humphrey had never lost his loyalty to Marie, and to the ideas that first brought them together. Only a few years before his death, living in seedy lodgings in North London, he was still writing to Marie's publisher: "I do not know if you realise the misery, illness and distress caused to countless women all over the country by Dr Stopes's books being out of print . . . Will you please make a great effort and put the matter as absolutely first priority to get her books in print, for they are the foundation work of the health of the nation."[2] His loyalty to Marie was not reciprocated. Humphrey's finances had never recovered from the 1929 crash, and he had long been unable to contribute to the upkeep of Norbury Park. Marie lent him money – in December 1948, six months before his death, he sent her £50, "thus reducing the loan to £9950" – but she would not let him live at Norbury Park, which he persisted in thinking of as his home. At one point, he even took a room with Ethel Burgess, the woman from whom Marie had "rescued" him in 1918, and who was now married and living in North London. Marie visited Humphrey as he lay dying in a Croydon nursing home and, a few weeks after his death, wrote a poem. It is a sonnet which needs to be read with a good deal of charity if it is not to appear as a rather heartless thank-offering for Humphrey's timely release from the housing shortage:

> Farewell, dear heart, they tell me you are dead:
> I see you lying silent on a bed
> With youth's nobility returned to grace
> What long had been your weary pain-crossed face
> So I am glad for you, profoundly glad
> That you escape the fate you might have had
> The cruellest of poor humanity's doom,
> Long years' enchainment in a single room.[3]

Before his death, Marie's excuses for rejecting Humphrey had been strengthened by his moral stand on behalf of Harry, who was desperately fighting for independence. Harry's social contacts had always been carefully vetted and in 1942, when he was eighteen, Marie wrote to the friend with whom he was staying: "He will eat and enjoy *anything* you give him (except only lobster, crab and codfish which I do not permit him to have for very good reasons). I like him to have a grated raw carrot for breakfast . . . Please remind him to take his Hypophosphites each morning."[4]

Her possessiveness stretched beyond the merely physical. Harry was tall, handsome, with a sweet, gentle disposition that – if personality can be said to be inherited – he owed more to his father than to his mother. Marie was terrified that Harry might be "seduced" before the time was ripe. In 1935 she had written an article for the *Daily Mirror*. Headed "A Frank Letter to My Son", it was addressed to Harry, "aged seven" (Harry was, in fact, eleven at the time, but Marie liked to minimise her age). "You want to marry, my son, in your early twenties?" she wrote. "Do so, with my blessing. YOUR MOTHER." Her only stipulations were that her putative daughter-in-law should be about twenty years of age, "lovely and slender but with broad hip bones and broad breasts and broad brows, with eyes sweet and penetrating, deep and wise enough to see into the hearts of your babies and rear them with love".[5] Having met this ideal, child-rearing paragon, her son should ignore convention, waive the idea of "settlements", and start an early marriage, using contraception, before embarking on the domestic, child-rearing stage. "You will at least have this good fortune," she said, "your own mother will not demand the conventional establishment." Unfortunately, as Harry grew up, it became obvious that Marie demanded rather more than a settlement, broad hips, or an establishment; what she wanted was nothing less than the right to choose Harry's wife.

The choice was denied her. Harry had the misfortune – from his mother's point of view – to fall in love with Mary Wallis, one of the six children of Barnes and Molly Wallis. Between Barnes Wallis, the aeronautical genius, and Marie Stopes, a mutual antipathy had already been established. Worse still, far from possessing the deep, penetrating eyes that Marie deemed essential, Mary Wallis was myopic and wore glasses. Such a marriage, Marie thought, would be a eugenic disaster: were all her grandchildren to be born wearing spectacles?

After their first meeting some years earlier at a children's party – when Mary, like her family, had been unable to decide whether Harry was male or female – the two had met occasionally, though always with Mary as the unwelcome hanger-on to her brothers, who might, Marie Stopes thought, provide suitable social fodder for her only son. It was not until Harry and Mary, as students in London, saw a lot of each other, that Marie began to worry. "She terrified me," Mary recalls. "She had very piercing eyes – light hazel. Her hair was always untidy, she used to make her own clothes – cobble them up – fairly loosely corseted, to put it mildly. I suppose I was a mousy little thing – I should have stood up to her, but I was too shy." Mary was invited to Harry's twenty-first birthday party at the Dorchester. Still at boarding school, and coming from a very religious Protestant family, Mary asked Harry if he could not delay the celebrations until Holy Week was over. "He, innocent, naive boy, showed this letter to his mother. Until then, she had ignored me – but after that, she took more interest – and a dislike to me." They became engaged in October 1947. In December that year, for her annual Christmas party at Norbury Park, Marie crossed out all invitations to the Wallis family – including that to her son's fiancée. Harry helped with the organisation for the party, "but, as the first guests arrived at the front door, Harry walked out at the back. It must have been a ghastly shock when we married."[6]

It was, indeed. Marie did everything she could to stop the marriage. She wrote to Barnes Wallis about his daughter's unsuitability as a wife – and sent carbon copies of the letters to Mary:

Dear Mr Wallis . . . I am greatly distressed by the news from Harry this morning that . . . he has entered into a formal engagement with your daughter Mary . . .

He has *no* prospects from me . . . The income he has is small and is his own as his father and I gave it to him outright and with taxes and essential disbursements it amounts to no more than three hundred a year. It is enough only to free his mind to devote it to his scientific work and develop unhampered his special scientific genius . . .

. . . I may add that my extensive experience from my clinics makes my opinion on sex matters more than a personal one, and it is that Harry is physiologically ten years Mary's junior and they are sexually unsuited to each other and on Eugenic grounds I should advise against the marriage were they strangers to me. My personal observation of the children makes me sure they cannot give each other lasting happiness. Your precipitation of events is a tragedy for all, and the engagement a profound blow to my own happiness and our hopes for Harry's future. Yours sincerely, Marie C. Stopes.[7]

Marie tried to enlist Humphrey on her side, ill though he was. Mary, she wrote, was so "plain and socially dreary" that Marie herself felt humiliated by what she imagined to be society's contempt for Harry's choice of a wife. His marriage to Mary, she argued, would be a threefold crime, as well as a personal folly:

1 a crime against his *Country* – which increasingly needs fine and perfect people (those with defects at present breed so fast that in 50 years below-par stock will be doubled and first class halved). Mary has an inherited physical defect and morally should never bear children. Harry is exceptionally fine and should marry his peer in looks, inheritance and health.

2 a crime against his family: for both his father's line and mine are free from all defect. It is *awful* to both my husband and me that he should contaminate his splendid inheritance and make a mock of our lives' work for Eugenic breeding and the race.

3 a crime against *his children* (& posterity) it is cruel to burden children with defective sight and the handicap of goggles. I will not in any way take a part in or condone the planning of these crimes.*[8]

What Marie did not realise, in her campaign against Mary, was that she had bullied everyone for too long. Barnes Wallis himself disaproved of the marriage – he found Harry a little wild and unconventional – but by now he detested Marie Stopes so cordially that he automatically took the opposite line to anything she said. Even her appeal to Humphrey failed. He wrote back, in reply to her plea for help in averting the eugenic crime: "... Harry is still desperately in love with Mary. Personally, I don't think it is much good opposing it and that the more we do the more awkward the position will be if he does finally do as he wants and marries her, for then we shall have to completely change our conduct towards her. It is all a puzzle ..."[9]

For Marie, it was no puzzle at all. All she needed to do was to explain his racial duties to Harry, persecute the timid Mary, and all would be well. Unfortunately, neither Harry nor Mary were the unworthy opponents that Marie imagined them to be. Harry had begun to detach himself from his mother in early adolescence, when he realised how unfairly his adopted "brothers" were treated. "If he hadn't toughened his skin," Mary says, "she would have eaten him." Under the influence of Mary, and of his own feelings for her, Harry refused any longer to listen to his mother. Their joint stand was further strengthened when Marie wrote to Barnes Wallis suggesting that a group continental holiday the engaged couple had shared with other students was deliberately engineered by Mary to trap Harry into marriage. Barnes Wallis threatened to sue for slander, and the marriage went ahead – though without the name "Stopes" in the *Times* announcement. Humphrey, acting independently for once, attended their wedding on 27 July 1948. Marie did not. Neither did she send a wedding present, though some

---

* Of the four children of Mary and Harry Stopes-Roe, two suffer from slightly defective eyesight. This has not impeded their careers. The eldest is a civil servant, specialising in social problems, the second is teaching in Nigeria for Voluntary Service Overseas, the third is at a teacher training college in Manchester, and the youngest is still at school.

time later she sent Harry a hundred pounds, with instructions to spend it entirely on himself. He bought a piano, and Mary took lessons.

Harry's obvious happiness was additionally galling. Marie was furious when Mrs Briant, Keith's mother, sent an account of the wedding. ". . . Mary helped him all the time with his packing, etc. they were never separated, were most loving to one another . . . she will, I think, be a devoted wife. I asked her if she was domesticated. She replied, 'Rather, *she was one of six*' . . . They are buying nice things for the home . . . She suits him well in that she likes to be unconventional – bare feet, etc. He likes her even when her hair is wet."[10]

Probably any daughter-in-law chosen by Harry would have attracted the same dislike; but, in Mary's slightly defective eysight, Marie found the perfect excuse for her continued coldness. Eighteen months after the marriage, she was still nursing her grievance. "You don't seem at all to understand about Mary," she wrote to a friend. "It is not that she is 'nice' or not – niceness doesn't matter. The *essential* is health as a potential mother and she has an inherited disease of the eyes which not only makes her wear hideous glasses so that it is horrid to look at her,* but the awful curse will carry on and I have the horror of our line being so contaminated and little children with the misery of glasses. Mary and Harry are quite callous about both the wrong to their children, the wrong to my family, and the eugenic crime."[11]

Harry did his best to smooth things over, but it was no use. Marie refused to address directly her new daughter-in-law. So intense was her disapproval that Mary – not normally a neurotic person – became convinced that Marie was trying to poison, literally, both her and Harry. After their marriage, Harry and Mary lived in Cambridge. Marie was often pressed to stay with them and Harry had no hesitation in throwing back at her the ideal sexual "duity" between man and woman that for the past thirty years she had been trying to inculcate in both him and the rest of mankind:

> . . . Are you interested in US (by which I mean together and each in one)? Otherwise why do you want to come here? Yet you have made no references to US. The basis of your visiting US is Our (here the 3 of us) mutual enjoyment. But would you be nice to

---

* Mary wore perfectly ordinary glasses and, though not the outstanding beauty that Marie Stopes wished, she was certainly attractive.

Mary? By which I mean *positively* nice. I feel you would probably make her unhappy and she is such a sweet and wonderful wife *I will not have her made unhappy* ... I am always believing that you will someday realise what Mary and I are doing for each other and join in OUR happiness – then you will be welcome in OUR home ... Your loving Harry.[12]

The appeal to her own ideals counted for nothing in face of her son's "betrayal". He had dared to go against her wishes, and she never overcame her bitter jealousy. Six years after Harry's marriage, her poem, "The Mother", was published. It related the life history of a mother and her son, and the eighth stanza was an obvious reflection of her feelings towards Mary:

> A girl with moonlit face is found
> Soon she has caught his empty heart
> Toys with his will to play man's part
> Then plunges deep her poisoned dart:
> He lies a captive in her ground . . .[13]

The hated girl has a dying pet dog, the only cure for which is to be fed with the heart of her lover's mother. The once-loving son blithely cuts out his mother's heart, feeds it to the dog, and the dog recovers. The symbolism scarcely needs pointing out. Marie never forgave Harry for his defection. After the birth of her first grandchild, Jonathan, a slight social relationship was established, but Harry, her adored son, was cut out of her will. To all Marie's intents and purposes, he was as dead as Humphrey.

It is not easy to understand Marie's defiantly unforgiving response to any thwarting of her will particularly as, in this case, it acted against her own interests. Yet for thirty years she had lived with the conviction of her unique stature, a position to which, for a time, the whole world had generally subscribed. Sensitive as she was to the waning of her power and reputation, she reacted with increasing violence to any contradiction, which by now merely emphasised her decline.

In 1950 Marie Stopes was a figure from the past. By her refusal to co-operate with other branches of the birth control movement, she had forfeited her supremacy. The initiative now lay with the Family

Planning Association, which numbered its clinics in hundreds. Marie had only five clinics, most of which were absorbed by local health authorities when the National Health Service came into operation in 1948. Unlike her American rival, Margaret Sanger, she took no part in the international organisation of birth control, nor in the development of new contraceptive ideas. She maintained her aversion to the pre-marital fitting of cervical caps. A young woman who had just been appointed divinity mistress at a Leeds grammar school visited Marie's clinic there in 1951, and was refused help on the grounds that she might be "just a woman of the streets". After a complaint from the woman's local minister, Marie wrote back supporting the clinic's decision. Fitting a cap in a virgin, she explained, was tantamount to rape. Annoyed by such casuistry, the vicar replied:

> ... I was very much surprised by the tone of your letter. To describe as "Rape" the pre-marital fitting by a competent woman doctor of a patient who has expressly asked for this to be done is rather like the character in "Alice in Wonderland" who "made words mean what he wanted them to mean" ... You seem to attach some mystical and magical significance to the hymen and to the importance of its being broken by the husband. I confess that I thought this idea had long been replaced by the point of view which regards the hymen as a vestigial organ which is rather a nuisance.[14]

Marie was probably not aware of the irony implicit in an Anglican vicar's accusing her of reactionary ideas. Since 1920, when her *New Gospel* fell on stony ground at the Lambeth conference of bishops, the Anglican Church had gradually caught up. By 1958, the Lambeth conference expressed approval of birth control, in language rather similar to Marie's: "The procreation of children is not the sole purpose of Christian marriage; implicit within the bond of husband and wife is the relationship of love with its sacramental expression in physical union." Her own ideas had remained static; their acceptance by the church was no more than a belated recognition, and one that she had always prophesied as inevitable. It did little to alleviate the constant sense of failure she felt throughout the last decade of her life.

In the first Marie Stopes Memorial Lecture, given in 1971, Professor Laurie Taylor attempted to solidify the rather vague idealistic philos-ophy underlying her original campaign. Her dissatisfaction in later life, he argued, stemmed from the realisation that society had failed to transform itself through the sexual liberation she advocated. "There was no evidence that men loved each other better or more for all her ideas and her technology,"[15] he added, concluding approvingly with a quotation from Ronald Blythe's *New Statesman* article describing one of her last lectures: "She saw the world divided up between midgets and giants – and there were few giants these days. It was pure emotion which made the giants, the throbbing, rapturous chosen ones, and fear of emotion which ordained the midgets. She was sick to death of us all. She had taught the man in the street to heave overboard the prurience and taboos of centuries, so that he might soar up into the ultimate fulfilment of bliss and what had he done? The oaf had used the gift like an extra gadget in the lavatory."[16]

I would like to believe this explanation – at least it is touched with the romantic grandeur that formed so large a part of Marie's personality. Unfortunately, there is not the slightest evidence to support it. Apart from the fact that Marie herself had always looked forward to the day when contraception would be used with the same nonchalance as "an extra gadget in the lavatory"* all her complaints of disillusionment – and there were many – were to do not with mankind's failure to perfect itself through the exercise of "erogamic duity", but with the dwindling number of her supporters.

Paradoxically, it was Marie's very success that created her feeling of failure. As Shaw Desmond, the Irish author, and a member of the CBC, put it, "Dear Marie Stopes ... Birth control has killed birth control ... if we don't get another angle in line with the times and *newer thought* we shall vanish."[17] Marie would not listen. Others might meddle with oral contraceptives and agitate for abortion law reform and pre-marital counselling. But, rather in the manner of those British generals who were still fighting the battle of Waterloo forty years later in the Crimea, Marie persisted in engaging yesterday's enemies. She could not understand why she was no longer esteemed as the Wellington of the birth control campaign.

This is not in any way to denigrate her achievements. In 1951 Shaw Desmond wrote to her again, reprovingly: "Dear Marie Stopes ...

---

* Contraceptive measures, she wrote in her brief for Patrick Hastings before the libel action in 1923, were "as much simple hygiene as brushing your teeth". (December 1922. BL-S.)

Never let me again hear you say you feel yourself a failure – you who
….are the saviour and releaser of woman from her womb-shackles
into the larger air."[18] If, in Simone de Beauvoir's phrase, "la liberté
pour les femmes commence au ventre", then Marie had, indeed, contributed more than any other single person to freeing women from the
threat of unwanted pregnancies. In fact, she accomplished much more
than this.

Birth control, with which her fame became largely associated, was
only one aspect of the wider reform she initially envisaged. This was
nothing less than the total transformation of the apparently immutable
nature of the sexual relationship between men and women. In *Married
Love*, she argued that women must be taught how to regain the "instinctive" delight in physical passion that society had succeeded in repressing;
and that men must learn to recognise these unacknowledged needs and
to substitute, for immediate sensual gratification, a greater understanding and sensitivity. It was in vain that George Bernard Shaw, in 1928,
protested to Marie that she should insist "on the separation in the public
mind of your incidental work as a scientific critic of methods of
contraception with your main profession as a teacher of matrimonial
technique … You are really a matrimonial expert, which is something
much wider and more needed than a specialist in contraception."[19] To
Marie, such a separation was ludicrous. Birth control and sexual
technique were indissolubly linked and it was foolish to argue otherwise.

It is important to see these ideas in their context. As Juliet Mitchell
pointed out in her Marie Stopes Memorial Lecture in 1972, many of
Marie's ideas would not be tolerated by modern proponents of the
women's liberation movement – in particular, her restriction of sexual
activity to those bound in holy matrimony, and her disapproval of
abortion, masturbation and lesbianism.[20] Though this is certainly true,
it does not diminish the impact of Marie's ideas in 1918. Though she
did not extend her libertarian ideas so far as to dispense entirely with the
male principle in favour of the self-induced clitoral orgasm, Marie pre-
echoed in 1918 the central tenet of the modern movement for women's
liberation – that a woman should be allowed to exercise "control over
her own body". In *Married Love* she said quite firmly (admittedly, in
the context of advocating separate bedrooms for man and wife): "A
married woman's body and soul should be essentially her own."[21]

It is impossible to quantify the extent of Marie's influence. To say that by 1930 her clinic had advised 10,000 women, means little; what were 10,000 against the millions of the unthinkingly procreative? What were a million copies of *Married Love* (translated into thirteen languages) against the tens of millions of the sexually ignorant? And yet, within that decade, there had taken place a radical change in public opinion, and there were few who did not ascribe the change to Marie Stopes. Good Freudians, said the *New Statesman* in 1933, would argue that early feelings of inferiority had dictated Marie's need to prove that she was more gifted and powerful than the mass of her fellows. "But, gibe as we might at her inordinate vanity, her belief that she is directly inspired from heaven, her bitter and relentless ferocity towards her adversaries, there can be no denying that it is she, above all others, who has brought to women the right to be mistresses, and not slaves, of their own fertility."[22]

None of Marie's ideas was original. Her thinking was compounded of Havelock Ellis, Edward Carpenter and Olive Schreiner, with genetic overtones from Darwin and Galton, and a dash of Empire from Kipling. Her uniqueness consisted in her ability to combine them all together into a message irresistible to any of the media. She had no hesitation in saying out loud what few doctors and writers had only hinted at. Her apparently foolhardy libel action against Dr Sutherland in 1923 attracted some public obloquy, but even greater support. As early as 1925, a medical man wrote to her: "You will be remembered not for any contraceptive you may devise . . . but for the publicity you have given to the most important problem of the day."[23]

What appeared to many as her vanity, lack of humour, paranoia and aggressiveness were perhaps an inevitable counterpart to the obstinacy, courage, and pertinacity that gave her the strength to go on fighting for what she believed in. Dr C. P. Blacker, secretary of the Eugenics Society, was one of the few who recognised the paradox. He wrote that, before her advent:

. . . the birth-control movement had been the preserve of a group of "Neo-Malthusian" intellectuals, preoccupied chiefly by a rather academic concern about the balance between population trends and economic resources . . .

. . . Her frontal attacks on old taboos, her quasi-prophetic tone, her flowery fervour aroused strong opposition from those who disagreed with her . . . In later life, after most of the separate birth-control societies had united and achieved acceptance and respect-ability in the Family Planning Association, the defects of her qualities became apparent. She remained aloof, for she could not co-operate on equal terms with others. Her dogmatism in scientific matters lost her the support of most doctors sympathetic to her aims. The shortcomings of her exuberant style and literary imagination (which could not readily transcend the plane of private bodily rapture) marred the verse she occasionally published . . .[24]

Old-fashioned though some of her ideas now appear – if not down-right wrong-headed – Marie was both a pioneer and a prophet. In the 1920s, the medical profession sneered at her scientific pretensions. Why listen to a woman who employed mere nurses to advise on contracep-tive practice? Fifty years later, medical opinion has come round to her way of thinking. There is no point in wasting a doctor's time – and possibly alienating the patient – when a nurse can do the job equally well, and establish a more sympathetic, less deferential relationship.* Similarly, with population control. It is no use just opening a birth control clinic and waiting for people to turn up. The many modern attempts to bring contraception directly to those who need it, in India and elsewhere, are a development of Marie's travelling birth control caravan.

Though in the 1950s Marie no longer enjoyed pre-eminence in the field she considered her own, the general public remained grateful. In 1953, a woman wrote to her from the East End of London: "Dear Marie Stopes . . . When I first saw you at a meeting about 25 years ago you looked to me like a beautifull Goddess, preaching a sermon of hope to a girl like myself 25 and allready a mother of 5. Now as a grandma of 50 odd . . . my gratitude goes out to you. I might easily have been the mother of 12 and how much worse that would have been."[25]

For Marie, now over seventy, neither present gratitude nor the prospect of a niche in posterity's pantheon were sufficient to overcome

---

* "The idea that a nurse or a medical auxiliary should perform, fit or prescribe is considered profane, despite ample empirical and scientific evidence of their ability to achieve comparable medical results." "Institutional Checks to Family Planning", Dr Timothy Black, *Family Planning* July 1972.

what she described to E. M. Forster as her "total depths of despair". Surely, she thought, this was not all? Where was the passion she prescribed for others, and helped them to achieve? Where was the intensity, burning with a hard, gem-like flame, that she had always sought? "Dear Avro Manhattan," she wrote in 1952, "I'm looking forward to making a bonfire with you on Sat 13 . . . It will be nice to have a little adult conversation, my world seems to consist of many aged infants, mostly."[26] It was time to start a new life.

Chapter 18

Surprised by Death

TO THE OLD
Weep from your depths no drizzling red-eyed tears
Nor wail within a house of shuttered doors;
Do not thus slay young hope with your harsh years
Nor petrify our quickened hearts with yours.
Do not deck outward witherings in rags
Nor fritter frumpish tawdriness on dress;
Vaunt no drink-sodden men, nor blear-eyed hags,
Nor with the hand of brittle power oppress,
Age nobly! clad in velvet bloom, and shine
Upon life's banquet with creative eyes;
Rise every morning making each day fine,
Lead grandly homeward to serener skies.
    Youth has its joys, but rapture of the soul
    Grows with sweet age as life nears heaven, its goal.
                  Marie Stopes, 1944[1]

CLAD in velvet bloom, Marie was determined to age nobly, if at all. At sixty, she had considered herself in the full bloom of womanhood; at seventy, since she firmly believed she would live to be at least one hundred and twenty, she felt herself to be no more than on the verge of early middle age. Her conviction of indestructibility was no affectation. She spent much time and money travelling about Britain in search of the extremely old, whom she would then quiz as to their secret formulae for a long and healthy old age. In 1953 she wrote to *The Times* (the letter was unpublished) suggesting that the pensionable age should be raised. Why waste the country's money on mere striplings of sixty-five, she argued, when man's natural lifespan was 140? Only those suffering from bad heredity (due to the failure to apply proper birth control measures) or bad living (alcohol, tobacco, and a refusal to realise the merits of fresh air, sea water and Syrup of Hypophosphites) could be said to be old at sixty-five.[2]

Certainly, the years had failed to diminish her remarkable vitality. She gardened, swam in the heavy seas off Portland Bill, and boasted that she could still put her big toe in her mouth – an ambition to which few would aspire at any age. Neither was her campaigning spirit much affected by the extravagant despair in which she occasionally indulged. In 1947, the recently married Princess Elizabeth and Prince Philip, on their honeymoon in Aberdeenshire, were pursued by a copy of *Married Love*, with a covering letter from Marie: "Your Royal Highnesses," she wrote. "May I now send a small gift with my deepest respects and good wishes for your lasting happiness. The little gift is a special copy of my book, which more than 20 years ago led the modern movement for a then deeply needed reform. It seemed to me best to wait until you were married and I now send it in the hope that you may be able to read it together."[3]

On one of his rare visits to England, the Duke of Windsor, who had earned Marie's lifelong admiration (despite his abdication) by sending small donations to her clinics, received a long enraged outburst, modified by the respect Marie always evinced when confronted, if only postally, by Royalty:

Sir, May I first say how deep my feeling of gladness is that you are breathing English air.

In these last awful years since you so graciously wrote to me, my home has suffered war damage *seven* times and my London Mothers clinic four times ... It is now 25 years since I founded and opened the first Mothers Clinic in the world and I am no nearer than on that day to *establishing* them so that they will carry on after my death. I have to be at the wheel without cessation.

I went to see Lord Nuffield, but he told me it is "my pigeon". He wants to cure while I want to prevent people being born to inevitable disease and misery ... In all ways now things are more difficult for me than they were years ago, e.g., The Times, D. Teleg., S. Times etc which used to publish my society's modest paid-for little 3 line ads in the personal col. now refuse that and all other advertisements of my society and even those of my world-accepted books which contain no mention of birth control. At the same time the Times and other papers publish advertisements of sex books by other people substantially cribbed from my work spiced up with abnormalities . . .

This is not asking you for a subscription, but just begging, imploring you to let me come and talk with you. You are the only person in the world I feel to be wise, kind and experienced enough to give me the counsel I need."[4]

The Duke politely declined his help; but shortly afterwards Marie had a chance to take on single-handed the iniquities of the British press. The Royal Commission on the Press in 1948 invited her to give evidence, though not in person. This protected them from the obligation to publish her evidence, suspecting, quite rightly, that Marie would respond with a violent denunciation of Catholic pressures. The commission's report came to the anodyne conclusion that the British press was "free from corruption; both those who own the Press and those who are employed on it would universally condemn the acceptance or soliciting of bribes . . . the public can dismiss from its mind any misgiving that the Press is mysteriously financed and controlled by hidden influences and that it is open to the exercise of corrupt pressure from self seeking outside sources."[5] This, as Marie knew, was not true. She had ample evidence that advertisements, even for her poetry, were frequently refused by newspapers fearful of losing Catholic readership in Britain and of having whole issues seized by the Eire police. In a fury she wrote to the members of the Commission:

Ladies and Gentlemen . . . My Evidence gives you "hard facts" about grave matters not revealed by any of the other witnesses. If it is not published in full rumours and distortion about it will inevitably arise. Much of the Evidence you have published is so trivial as to lend colour to the often-expressed view that the Commission is discovering nothing – yet when you *have* serious evidence you do not publish! . . .[6]

Complaints to MPs and newspaper editors met with little success. The *New Statesman* was one of the few that agreed she had "concrete evidence of successful pressure put on newspaper proprietors";[7] much more typical was the response of Cecil King, then deputy chairman of the *Sunday Pictorial*. "I cannot offer to help you to conduct a ferocious attack on the Roman Catholic Church," he wrote. As late as 1955, *Family Doctor*, published by the British Medical Association, was still refusing her advertisements, freely admitting that the ban was "dictated by our large Irish and Catholic readership".[8]

The press was as little interested in her new career as a great poet as in her campaign against the Catholic church. Shortly after the war Marie had taken over the publishing firm of Alex. Moring Ltd. and in 1949, under that imprint, published *We Burn*, a selection from her four volumes of poetry. Her verse was as erotic as ever, and as firmly rooted in tradition. One stanza from "The Bathe" ran:

> The still air sleeps. When a young playful breeze,
> A tender zephyr, warmly soft, slips, curls,
> To burrow in the hair, it slides and furls
> Its waving light to play on bending knees.
> The errant zephyr, skimming down the back
> Touches the spine like music's potent tones
> Makes every nerve dance, penetrates the bones
> With such sweet melody along its track
> As lifts dumb sorrow from her grief; then flees.[9]

Her verse was rather more engaging the less she strove for aesthetic effect. At Norbury Park Marie kept a cow, Daffodil, to provide butter for herself and other poets who believed in Beauty – in particular, her most admired poetic hero, Walter de la Mare. De la Mare's acknowledgment of his pound of butter ran:

> Dear Daffodil, I wept to see
> Another gift to me –
> Tears not of injocundity
> But simply gluttonous glee.
> And Oh, how kind Your Mistress is;
> I mean of course Marie
> Please moo affection's thanks to her
> From Walter d.

In the person of her cow, Marie replied:

> My mistress sends her love with mine,
> And writes for me a grateful line.

I bid her say that we both ask
Your thanks should not become a task,
For not a *ton* of the best butter
Is worth one line that you could utter.[10]

Loyalty was one of Marie's more likeable qualities. In 1950 she was approached for financial help by J. W. Poynter, a renegade Catholic who had acted as a spy for her in the twenties and thirties. Towards the end of his life Mr Poynter returned to Catholicism – an act Marie deplored, but which did not prevent her sending him five pounds (though she hastened to point out that it would have been ten pounds, had he not returned to Rome). In the same way, she tried to protect Walter de la Mare from the change in poetic fashion. In 1950 T. S. Eliot, by birth an American, was awarded the Order of Merit. Furious at this insult to British poetry, Marie wrote to the *Sunday Times*:

Dear Sir . . . T. S. Eliot misled a number of miniature men by novelty out of harmony with the essence of our national speech. He has not affected the lasting poets, Walter de la Mare, Masefield and several young ones now showing some stability of poetic character. When I state that to have passed over our wonderful Walter de la Mare and given the O.M. to T. S. Eliot is profoundly deplored, I speak for multitudes too timid or unable to make their views felt. Yours faithfully, Marie C. Stopes, F.R.S. Lit.[11]

Her sense of failure, both as poet and as social and racial* reformer, drove her to expensive methods of restoring her self-esteem. If she could not achieve poetic immortality she might at least achieve it facially. In 1948 she commissioned a sketch portrait of herself from Augustus John and – a measure of her need to garner any scraps of comfort to feed her starving vanity – kept a scribbled account of a telephone conversation with Dorelia John: "Mrs Augustus John told me over the telephone tonight, 'Augustus thinks you're a witch, your power over words is so wonderful'."[12] Four years later, in 1952, possibly feeling that John's sketch was not an adequate memorial,

---

* Dr C. P. Blacker, in his study of Family Planning Association clinics from 1938 to 1947, found that though the total attendance had risen substantially there had been an absolute *decrease* in the numbers of working class women attending the clinics – the very class which Marie most wanted to reach. – Audrey Leathard, *The Development of Family Planning Services 1921–1974*.

Marie approached Sir Gerald Kelly – with some trepidation since, as President of the Royal Academy, he commanded very high fees. Marie liked his touch with skin better than anyone else's, she assured him, but might not be able to afford it, "for tho' I am supposed to be rich I am really quite poor as my career has been one of trying to save humanity from its excess of folly".[13] Unswayed by such blandishments, Sir Gerald demanded five hundred guineas for head and shoulders only; by return of post Marie replied, "I'll just have to find the five hundred guineas which, after all, isn't so much for the immortality you give."

In that year, at the age of seventy-two, Marie could no longer be objectively considered as a sexually attractive women. Her friends remained enchanted by her vigour of mind, her original ideas and – provided no rival was in the vicinity – a charm of personality that, it must be confessed, is not often evident in her vast public correspondence. But, though she may have thought of herself as a woman whom age could not wither, outsiders saw her differently. In his poem, "In the New Statesman Office", written at about this time, the Irish poet, Austin Clarke, described his meeting with Marie:

> She waited humbly at the counter,
> Beside me, stout, motherly, plain-faced,
> "What name, please?"
> > "Dr Marie Stopes."
> Though Ireland shook in my veins, denouncing
> The poor man's friend, I futured. Popes,
> Far-seen in total white and lace,
> Will pity our overbearing creed,
> Somehow prevent the loss of grace –
> And fewer orphanages need
> Those begging letters (Mercy's fount)
> Dispatched in plain envelopes.[14]

Marie would have been horrified by the description. Until the end of her life – at least for public appearances – her clothes sense remained histrionic. Ronald Blythe, the author, gave in the *New Statesman* a delightful description of one of the literary lectures she gave towards the end of her life: "She was more embroiled than dressed in quantities of luxurious russet fur, out of which her head rose, arctic and imperious. Her hair was plentiful and was dyed a rich conker red. In spite of her furs and her jewelled chains, her throat remained emphatically naked."[15] For the actual lecture, she changed to a long gown, even more décolleté, of slithery crêpe, with satin slippers and yet more beads.

At the age of seventy-three, only a year or two after the failure of her campaign against her son's marriage, rejection by the Royal Commission on the Press, and disappointment over the reception of *We Burn*, Marie had recovered her natural ebullience. In March 1954 she wrote to her son, Harry (by now partially reinstated in favour, though not in her will): "All I ask is more time for both work and for the ever enriching interests and delights of life." Life, she enthused two months later, "is incredibly rich and wonderful".[16] Marie was in love again.

Baron Avro Manhattan was thirty-five years younger than Marie. At least to Marie, who still maintained that her real age was twenty-six,* such an age gap was of no possible consequence in her search for that grand, eternal, all-consuming passion whose beauties she never ceased to extol but which in real life had always proved illusory. Surley this time, there could be no doubt?

Manhattan, a writer and painter, was a protégé of H. G. Wells, who introduced him to Marie shortly before the Second World War. Beyond noting that, like herself, Manhattan had greenish-hazel eyes, and was therefore "very special", Marie made no attempt to put their relationship on a more intimate level. At the time, anyway, her attentions were concentrated on Keith Briant. During the war, while Manhattan was running a propaganda radio service to occupied Europe, and Marie was dodging Goering's personal air raids on Norbury Park and the Mothers' Clinic, the two quarrelled rather bitterly – partly because Marie felt that H. G. Wells was turning Manhattan into a communist,† but largely because one of Manhattan's women friends had an abortion, whereupon Marie accused him of being a "murderer". The friendship was not resumed until 1952, when Marie decided to forgive him his multiple sins. Her motives are not entirely clear. At one

---

* A fantasy charmingly supported by her son, Harry, who on her seventieth birthday wrote to her: "Darling Mummy, Very many happy returns on your 26th birthday. Isn't it funny that never again will we be the same age, and that from next March on I will be older than you." (13 October 1950. SR-Coll.)

† Most of the information here from Avro Manhattan in interviews with the author, January 1976. After this initial flirtation with the Left, Manhattan's opinions became increasingly right-wing. He now calls himself (half-jokingly) a Nazi, and admires Enoch Powell, Rev. Ian Paisley, and the National Front.

level, this last attachment could be seen as an affair deliberately embarked upon as a way of restoring her flagging self-esteem. As in 1913, when Aylmer Maude had provided consolation after the failure of her first marriage, or in 1938, when Humphrey's self-attested deficiencies provided a justification for her romantic yearnings for Keith Briant, so, in 1952, could Avro Manhattan be seen as a sop to wounded vanity. But this would be too crude an explanation for such a highly complex personality. Manhattan had obvious attractions. He was young, handsome and had by this time achieved some celebrity as the author of a bestseller, *The Vatican in World Politics*. Though she admired success and physical beauty, however, Marie demanded something more. Ever at the back she heard, not Time's wingèd chariot, but the call for a marriage of true minds.

In this, she was not disappointed. They had much in common. Their various writings had been banned in several countries where Catholic pressures still successfully operated. Both were heartily against established religion, in favour of a vague immanent Reality with which they were personally in touch. They agreed about most things, including the necessity for birth control, the utter mediocrity of most of the human race, the necessity to encourage the élite, and to discourage microbes. (Manhattan was once locked for four days in his room at Norbury Park, his trousers confiscated, until his cold had passed the infectious stage.)

As usual, Marie had to convince herself of the unique quality of her new love. In 1952 their rapprochement had been decidedly frosty, particularly since Manhattan had criticised adversely some of her poems. But in December 1953, after seeing some of his paintings, Marie wrote to him:

Dearest and most precious Avro. My heart is still beating extra hard with the joyous excitement of all the beauty you showed me. Within me there is the sense of excitation and exultation and a vast panorama, clear, fresh, sun swept.

Truly I was more than a little *afraid* to see your pictures, in case they had in them something I could not find harmonious; and yet I should have had to speak the truth and it would have been terrible for me ... Dearest – the reality was so *glorious* I am singing with joy ... You are a genius ... Thank you from the depths of my being for such a cascade of fresh beauty ... Make no mistake, you are a *great* artist, with a touch unequalled by any current painter – pictures by you will be treasured hundreds of years hence ... Dearest, most precious one, all the Gods and angels guard you. Marie.[17]

Though current gossip naturally portrayed Manhattan as a fortune-hunter, so great was the disparity in their age, Marie stuck to her intuition. In February 1954 they visited the Royal Academy exhibition together and made a secret note of the painting – out of several hundreds – that each found most impressive. Their choice coincided, and on 4 February 1954 Marie wrote to Manhattan: "Twin of my soul, The delightful incident at the Academy this afternoon (another of those many flashes of light so mysterious and stirring) left me as tho' I'd drunk champagne made of bubbles of eternity sparkling through the waters of life – I can't describe it, Are you feeling the same vertigo?..."[18]

The resumption of her friendship with Manhattan gave a much-needed stimulus to her literary ambitions. Despite perpetual discouragement from rather more eminent playwrights – Galsworthy, Shaw and Pinero all told her frankly that she had little talent for the stage – Marie never gave up her dramatic ambitions. Soon after the excitement of meeting her "twin soul", she started work on a new play. "I know it is too bad of me," she wrote to a friend, refusing an invitation, "but I am completely in the hands of my Muse, who does things with me at her own will and not mine, and I am enjoying this three-act drama more than anything I have ever done."[19] The play, *Venus and Methuselah*, was an attack on Shaw's ideas about the supremacy of intellect. Methuselah, of course, is Shaw, whose plays are invading the universe with evil spirits. Ranged against his "destructive, poisonous Thought" there is only the Power of Love which, in the persons of Venus and Athene, inevitably wins the battle. The play is interesting only for the insight it gives into Marie's temperament – in particular, her yearning to be still thought of as a physically attractive woman. She identified with both Venus and Athene, and in one of the play's long debates about evolution betrays her own preoccupations:

> Look! Evolution hastes the other way.
> Now late-maturing women frequently
> Are twenty-seven ere their sex is ripe

As in the past it was at seventeen.
Some few have ev'n been noticed who are ripe
For full sex life only when sixty years ...

The casual reader of Marie's papers at this period might be forgiven for thinking her mind a little disturbed. In October 1953, the same month in which she finished *Venus and Methuselah*, Marie recorded a visitation from her husband's ghost. She woke up at midnight to see Humphrey "in the centre of this area of light, easily and naturally and as I knew him early in our first acquaintance, upright, slender, his black hair smoothly brushed, walking perfectly ... The date is not an anniversary in my husband's or my life so far as I know nor in that of my son. I know of nothing in any of our three lives to make it an anniversary in any way. It *may*, however, be connected with some current feelings and events."[20] Two months later, on December 1, Marie saw a blue light in the sky, which she identified as a flying saucer travelling from Dorking. Probably, however, Marie's mind was not so much unhinged as inebriated with her feelings for Manhattan. A member of the British Interplanetary Society, he shared with Marie a penchant for cosmic mysticism, for a universe in which anything was possible were we not too blinded by convention to see it. But, as Marie herself hinted, the appearance of Humphrey's ghost could also be seen as a reflection of her need for marital benediction of her new passion.

It was the culminating tragedy of Marie's life that, having at last found, she was convinced, a true soul-mate, there was no possibility of consummation. Though there was much fine talk of reincarnation, and of having known each other aeons earlier, the sad truth remained that Marie was seventy-three and Manhattan thirty-nine. "It was the greatest regret of her life," Manhattan says, "that she was not thirty years younger, or I, thirty years older."* Commune though they may on the astral plane, Marie's yearning for a spiritual and physical conjunction resulted in an all too earthly jealousy and possessiveness. Like Marie, Avro Manhattan was an idealist, equally capable of turning human beings into gods, or falling in love with a statue. On several of his visits to Norbury Park, he had expressed an interest in a statue of whose smile, in a certain light, he found most beguiling. In 1957, a year before her death, Marie had the statue removed to a distant part of the

* Avro Manhattan, interview with the author, 14 January 1976.

grounds, while Manhattan was in France. Her letter to him in June that year reveals the frustrations imposed by this unlikely liaison:

> Avro, dearest . . . You say you read my letters "with joy because they bring me close to you" − But why not *be* close to me? You say it's now too hot on the beach − and here am I in a neglected Norbury now nice and flowery and sunny . . .
>
> You say that if one is truly in love, there must be some outlet of expression, like the vent of a volcano for lava − and that you have deep love for me − and yet you treat me as though you care nothing for what I feel. Tomorrow begins the shifting of Diana, so you will never again see her on her island . . .[21]

Marie's possessiveness was so great that she seriously considered marrying him − not so much for the sake of the marriage itself, Manhattan claims, but to stop him falling into the hands of another woman. Such a marriage, of course, would have further fuelled the gossip about fortune-hunting. But if anything such a matter was on the other side. Convinced that she would live to at least 120, and thus outlive Manhattan, Marie herself wrote out his last will and testament, leaving everything to her. He refused to sign it, and the projected marriage did not take place.[22]

It was in the autumn of 1957 that Marie began to be seriously worried about her health. She had been feeling weak and ill for some time, but, characteristically, refused to admit it, maintaining − at least on the surface − her reputation for hard-hitting, controversial, if increasingly unfashionable, comments on the follies of the human race. Only in the last three years of her life did the BBC lift its ban on Marie's broadcasting. In September 1957 she was invited to take part in a programme about one of her heroes, Field-Marshal Smuts. She managed to get in an advertisement for birth control, a condemnation of modern life, and a statement of her belief in reincarnation − topics not immediately germane to the subject of General Smuts:

> It doesn't matter to me in the least how many people there are in the world so long as they're first-rate in quality. We wouldn't have any of the troubles we have at present if everybody was first-rate in quality and you can only get first-rate quality by having proper application of birth control . . .

... I myself am very strongly inclined to believe in the reincarnation of the soul ... people are born with extraordinary gifts; sometimes very young children with very specialised gifts, and there doesn't seem any justice or logic unless the soul is reincarnated ...

I do feel that we could in our education greatly assist the increase in the number of great people by having a much sterner discipline with the young than we have at present. We are breeding rubbish ... we are educating rubbish, and this lack of self-discipline, the lack of common honesty in young people – appals me. They should be made to have the elementary honesty of truthfulness, absolute obedience to authority, absolute respect for other people's property ...

Finally cornered by the interviewer on the topic allegedly under discussion, Marie revealed some progression from the conventional Christianity to which, for most of her life, she had professed adherence. Did she think, the interviewer asked, that Smuts possessed humility as a man?

STOPES: I don't think much, no.
INTERVIEWER: Because that is important in the build-up of personality.
A: Why should he have humility?
Q: Well, humility is a Christian virtue.
A: Well, why should he be a Christian?
Q: Well, d'you think he was a Christian?
A: I have no idea.
Q: Well – You don't think that that is a necessity in the Western civilisation – to be a Christian?
A: No, I don't – I don't.

While recording this programme, Marie had been seeing several medical specialists. Their independent diagnoses were unequivocal. She had cancer of the breast, so far advanced that no operation was recommended. This probably meant that the tumour had reached what is now known as Stage IV, when it has become so large that there is no possibility of healing after its removal, a stage often associated with the formation of secondary tumours in other parts of the body. Ironically, some of the very qualities which led to Marie's success as social reformer – intellectual arrogance, a total conviction of her rightness and a hatred of conformist opinion – hastened her own death. After the birth of her first, still-born child, she had always distrusted doctors, and their bigoted attitudes to birth control in the 1920s had done nothing to recommend the intelligence of the medical profession. By the time she sought advice, it was too late.

Naturally, Marie did not believe the prognosis. With her usual research techniques, she investigated, from China to Peru, the various "cures" for cancer. She eventually settled for a clinic in Bavaria, unorthodox homeopathic treatments for cancer have been long, and inconclusively, debated. In November 1957 she wrote to Keith Briant: "The doctors say I am dying but I refuse to believe it, I am going to Germany to a clinic where I will have an operation." Briant, his biography records, did not believe her: ". . . it seemed inconceivable that the doctors' verdict could be true because Marie Stopes had so persuaded all of her closest friends that, although she might not be immortal, at least she would live to make a centenarian seem a youngster."[23]

Her treatment was painful in the extreme. In November 1957 she described her arrival at the clinic: "This is the first day I am able to write. On my arrival I was given the first treatment at once before I had even unpacked. I was asked if I wanted a pain-reducing tablet. I did not. The pain was a continuous increasing torture. I spent an absolutely agonising night and was reduced to a wreck by the next morning. When the doctor came in he was shocked: 'Why hadn't I asked for a drug? Rung for it?' But I couldn't find a bell in my room."[24]

After six weeks in the clinic, Marie returned home to Norbury Park. She still refused to admit her illness, and told everyone she was the victim of radioactive fall-out. She did not even tell her son, or such close friends as Avro Manhattan, that she might have a terminal illness. By now, with her usual intellectual thoroughness, Marie had made herself something of an expert on cancer. Possibly for this reason, she refused further medical treatment. Her awareness of approaching death, however, did nothing to subdue her fighting spirit. At Norbury Park, a house now virtually devoid of life – except for Cherry, her ageing Chow, and a decrepit servant, so confused that she frequently had to be reminded where the kitchen was – Marie continued the management of her London clinic, her worldwide correspondence, and the pursuit of the literary fame which had always eluded her. Two months after returning from her treatment in Germany, she also embarked on a last battle with her old enemy, the Catholic Church.

In March 1958 Marie became much incensed by the Rouncefield case. Brian Rouncefield was a British seaman who had married – but only in a registry office – a Maltese Catholic girl. On returning to Malta, his wife – under the influence, he claimed, of Catholic priests – claimed that the marriage was invalid under canon law, and Rouncefield's money in Malta was "frozen". Marie immediately went into action, writing to politicians, and to Dom Mintoff, Prime Minister of Malta, asking him to take care of Rouncefield's money, "in view of the tenacity and unscrupulousness of the Roman Catholic Church", and to the Archbishop of Canterbury, enclosing press cuttings about the case. "Will you read the enclosed," she asked him, "where you will see that the seaman Rouncefield is fighting the Protestant battle for us all. I have today sent £10 to Lloyd's Bank, Leatherhead, to open a Rouncefield Defence Fund, and am writing to the Times." The *Times*, as usual, did not publish her letter; but the Archbishop replied: "Dear Dr Stopes . . . What you tell me of his treatment horrifies me. It is good of you to take steps to raise some funds to help him. If the Times refused to publish your letter that in itself is a shocking thing. I am afraid it would not be possible for me to subscribe to a fund, but I am at once taking action to bring this scandalous state of affairs to the notice of the Colonial office."

Rather unwisely, perhaps, Marie gave his letter to the *Daily Express*, who ran a story under the headline "The Primate and the Maltese Girl". Much pained, the Archbishop wrote to her from Lambeth Palace on March 14: "Dear Dr Stopes, My Chaplain tells me that you have communicated my letter of March 12 to the Press. If I may say so, this shocks me. It is, I think, generally recognised that correspondence is private, and is not to be communicated to the press except by leave of the writer . . . Yours sincerely, Geoffrey Cantuar."[25]

The Rouncefield case dragged on through the summer of 1958 and in August Rouncefield wrote a long letter thanking Marie for her help, but reporting a total lack of progress. She was by now too ill to reply. Two months previously she had overcome her lifelong prejudice against the French Riviera and joined Avro Manhattan for a holiday at Èze Plage.

Suddenly, with no explanation or farewell, she disappeared. She asked help of no one. The cancer had now metastasised, forming a secondary tumour in the brain, and leaving her half-paralysed and semi-speechless. To a woman of Marie's pride and intellect, it was unthinkable that anyone should see her in this state. Harry, her son, saw her only when she became almost unconscious. She died on 2 October 1958, a few days before her seventy-eighth birthday.

In her will, dated 11 October 1957, Marie had written, with her usual vigour, "I most emphatically wish to be cremated – at Golders Green, and to have my ashes scattered on the sea as near the Race as a fisherman can safely go, at Portland Bill, Dorset." She had never forgiven Harry for marrying "the untidy Mary". She left Norbury Park and the residue of her estate, after some small bequests, to the Royal Society of Literature.* To Harry, she left only her copy of the OED, and the freehold of a small Richmond house, in trust for her eldest grandchild, Jonathan.

Generous, as his mother occasionally was, but of a more forgiving disposition, Harry ignored the loss of the bequests to which he should, at least by common usage, have been entitled, and to which he could have laid claim (only the outer two pages of the will were witnessed). In company with Avro Manhattan, he took his mother's ashes to Portland Bill. From a high rock, not a boat, and with Mary standing on a rock below, holding their newly born fourth child, her ashes were scattered into the sea. On 15 October 1958, which would have been her seventy-eighth birthday, a memorial service was held at St Martin-in-the-Fields. "Blest are the pure in heart" was sung, and Dr Adam Fox, archdeacon of Westminster, gave the address. "It fell to her," he said, "what falls to few of us, to espouse a cause which was strange to most, and shocking to many, and to see it at last generally accepted without protest and widely adopted as a matter of practice... Those who felt the impact of that personality will find themselves missing her ever and anon, believing it impossible so much vitality should be lost or wasted."[26] The *Catholic Times*, rather less generously, acknowledged her death

---

* The society sold the house in 1960 for £8,000 to a businessman, Mr Philip Spencer. He undertook considerable restoration work, installing adequate water and electricity supplies, and burning what was left of Marie's furniture – "broken down old beds and filthy mattresses" – in the garden. (Interview with the author, January 1975.) In 1975, Norbury Park was again on the market at a price in the region of £150,000. It was later withdrawn from auction.

only by an article re-hashing the 1923 Stopes-Sutherland court case, which Marie had eventually lost. It was headed, "Birth Controller Blushed in Court".[27]

Posterity, since 1958, has been little kinder. One of Marie's ambitions had always been to see the State accept responsibility for the provision of birth control services. Posthumously, her ideal has been accomplished. Since 1975 every woman in Britain has had the right to free contraception. But Marie would not have been satisfied.

Her central belief – that the human race could be improved by the eugenic application of birth control – is now shunned. In October 1974, Sir Keith Joseph, then regarded as a likely next Leader of the Conservative Party, made a speech about the "remoralisation" of the nation. It contained as a postscript, a mild echo of the views that Marie had championed throughout her crusading life. "Our human stock is threatened," he said. "A high and rising proportion of children are being born to mothers least fitted to bring children into the world and bring them up." The resultant furore was not about the expedients he proposed – like Marie Stopes, to extend birth control facilities for "classes 4 and 5", and, unlike her, for "young unmarried girls" – but about the eugenic overtones of his remarks, the implied genetic inferiority of the working classes. Try as he afterwards might to shift the emphasis of what he had said from genetic to environmental considerations, his few sentences had cost him his chance of becoming party leader. The paradox was that the birth control movement, the greatest liberalising force of the twentieth century, and Marie Stopes, its arch-prophet, had each fed off a philosophical base that by the seventies was regarded as too "illiberal" to be hinted at even by a right-wing Conservative.

There was an equally ironic contrast between means and ends in the fate of Marie's clinic. "What will be the end of this remarkable woman," asked the *New Statesman and Nation* in 1933. "Will some English Hitler have her beaten up, or imprisoned, or exiled for her liberal opinions?"[28] The end of that remarkable woman was not nearly so dramatic as either the *New Statesman* or Marie Stopes envisaged. She left her Whitfield Street clinic to the Eugenics Society which, in common with other organisations and in tune with changing opinion, gradually added to its services pre-marital contraception and abortion counselling – a policy continued by the present lessees of the clinic, but certainly not one to which Marie's "liberal opinions" would have extended.

"Will posterity consider her," the *New Statesman* concluded, "as many consider Joan of Arc, a self-deluded megalomaniac, or will Marie Stopes find a place in the Calendar of Saints?" Forty years later, it appears likely that posterity will give a qualified "yes" to both questions.

REFERENCES

In addition to the scientific, literary and sociological works of Marie Stopes (published sometimes under her full name, Marie Carmichael Stopes, sometimes under M. C. Stopes and sometimes under Marie Stopes) the main sources for this book have been:

1) The British Library Stopes Collection housed in the Manuscript Department and the State Papers Room of the British Museum. This collection is still not finally catalogued and, for this reason, no more precise reference can be given (other than dates, of course) than BL-S.

2) The collection belonging to Dr Harry Stopes-Roe, referred to here as SR-Coll. This consists of Dr Stopes-Roe's family letters, photographs and documents; papers which the British Library felt unable to accommodate, so vast was the collection left by Marie Stopes; and literary fragments and manuscripts from the Royal Society of Literature, to which Marie Stopes left the bulk of her copyrights and manuscripts. Both collections include many drafts and copies of her own letters to other people, which Marie Stopes often preserved.

CHAPTER I

1 Undated, C. C. Stopes to MCS. BL-S.
2 Charlotte Carmichael Stopes, *British Freewomen*, Swan Sonnenschein, 1894.
3 Bernard Shaw, *Sixteen Self Sketches*, Constable, 1949.
4 Quoted by F. S. Boas in "Charlotte Carmichael Stopes", a paper read before the Royal Society of Literature, 21 May 1930.
5 26 Sept 1889, Oscar Wilde to MCS. BL-S.
6 *Woman's Herald*, 26 Sept 1891.
7 20 Feb 1929, unsigned letter to MCS. BL-S.
8 1 Feb 1924, C. C. Stopes to MCS. BL-S.
9 30 July 1886, Henry Stopes to C. C. Stopes. SR-Coll.
10 3 Nov 1902, C. C. Stopes to Henry Stopes. SR-Coll.
11 Marie Carmichael Stopes, *Marriage In My Time*, Rich & Cowan, 1935, p. 46.
12 Aylmer Maude, *The Authorized Life of Marie C. Stopes*, Williams & Norgate, 1924, p. 186.
13 ibid., p. 192
14 1 Feb 1924, C. C. Stopes to MCS. BL-S.
15 30 July 1886, Henry Stopes to MCS. BL-S.
16 BL-S.
17 Diary, October-December 1892, MCS. BL-S.
18 M. C. Stopes, *Man, Other Poems, and a Preface*, Heinemann, 1914.
19 31 Dec 1899, Henry Stopes to MCS. BL-S.

CHAPTER 2

1 M. C. Stopes, *Ancient Plants*, Blackie, 1910, p. 5.
2 Maude, *The Authorized Life of Marie Stopes*, p. 39.
3 *North London Collegiate School Magazine*, 1899.
4 11 Aug 1900, MCS to C. van Wyss. BL-S.
5 Marie Stopes, *Sex and the Young*, p. 41.
6 Marie Carmichael Stopes, *Sex and the Young*, Gill, 1926, this edition, Putnam's 1929, p. 550.
7 3 Dec 1901, Guy Pilgrim to MCS. BL-S.
8 3 Dec 1901, MCS to Guy Pilgrim. BL-S.
9 10 Nov 1901, C. van Wyss to MCS. BL-S.
10 30 Mar 1904, MCS to Winnie Stopes. BL-S.
11 13 March 1904, MCS to C. C. Stopes. BL-S.
12 Undated, Munich, MCS to Winnie Stopes. BL-S.
13 3 Dec 1903, MCS to Winnie Stopes. BL-S.
14 30 Sept 1905, Alvara Humphrey to MCS. BL-S.
15 1 Jan 1926, Professor T. Resvoll to MCS. BL-S.
16 15 June 1904, MCS to Winnie Stopes. BL-S.
17 M. C. Stopes, *Black Breeding*, Hutchinson, 1942.
18 10 March 1904, MCS to C. C. Stopes. BL-S.
19 20 April 1904, MCS to Winnie Stopes. BL-S.
20 5 July 1904, Alvara Humphrey to MCS. BL-S.

CHAPTER 3

1 14 July 1904, Professor F. E. Weiss to MCS. BL-S.
2 31 Jan 1905, Mrs Evelyn Weiss to MCS. BL-S.
3 8 May 1906, C. C. Stopes to MCS. BL-S.
4 3 Nov 1906, MCS to C. C. Stopes. BL-S. The review referred to her first book, *The Study of Plant Life for Young People*, Alexander Moring, 1906.
5 13 Oct 1904, MCS to K. Fujii. BL-S.
6 December 1904, MCS to K. Fujii. BL-S.
7 9 Nov 1904, MCS to Winnie Stopes. BL-S.
8 *Beihefte zum Botanischen Centralblatt*, Vol 20, 1906.
9 M. C. Stopes and D. M. S. Watson, "On the Present Distribution and Origin of the Calcareous Concretions in Coal Seams, Known as 'Coal Balls'" *Philosophical Transactions of the Royal Society*, Vol 200, 1908.
10 G. N. Mortlake (pseudonym for Marie Stopes) *Love Letters of a Japanese*, Stanley Paul, 1911.
11 ibid., p. 49.
12 ibid., p. 62.
13 25 April 1905, K. Fujii to MCS. BL-S.
14 "G. N. Mortlake" *Love Letters*, p. 74.
15 ibid., p. 81.
16 ibid., p. 78.

17 1 Aug 1905, MCS to K. Fujii. BL-S.
18 19 Nov 1905, MCS to K. Fujii, rough draft. BL-S. Letter of same date with longer text in *Love Letters*, p. 160.
19 12 June, 1907, MCS to K. Fujii, *Love Letters*, p. 337.

CHAPTER 4

1 The best contemporary account of Japan at this period is by B. H. Chamberlain, *Japanese Things*, 1905, reissued Charles E. Tuttle, 1971.
2 Marie Carmichael Stopes, *A Journal From Japan*, Blackie, 1910, p. 86.
3 ibid., entry dated 29 May 1908.
4 19 Aug 1907, MCS to Winnie Stopes. BL-S.
5 Marie Stopes, *A Journal From Japan*, entry dated 24 Aug 1908.
6 27 November 1907, MCS to Winnie Stopes. BL-S.
7 Isabella L. Bird, *Unbeaten Tracks in Japan*, 1880, reissued by Charles E. Tuttle, 1973.
8 *A Journal From Japan*, entry dated 15 Nov 1907.
9 30 Jan 1908, MCS to C. C. Stopes. BL-S.
10 29 March 1908, MCS to C. C. Stopes. BL-S.
11 28 May 1908, MCS to C. C. Stopes, BL-S.
12 29 April 1908, MCS to F. W. Oliver. BL-S.
13 21 May 1908, MCS to Professor Weiss, rough draft. BL-S.
14 Marie Stopes, *A Journal From Japan*, entry dated 5 Feb 1908.
15 ibid., 11 April 1908.
16 ibid., 19 Aug 1908.
17 11 Aug 1908, MCS to C. C. Stopes. BL-S.
18 Marie Stopes, *A Journal From Japan*, entry dated 24 Nov 1908.
19 ibid., 24 Oct 1908.
20 16 Nov 1908, MCS to Claude McDonald, rough draft. BL-S.
21 17 Nov 1908, Claude McDonald to MCS. BL-S.
22 D. H. Scott, *The Evolution of Plants*, Williams & Norgate, 1911, p. 39; William C. Darrah, *Principles of Palaeobotany*, Ronald Press, 1960, pp. 208, 218.
23 Marie Stopes, *A Journal From Japan*, p. 247.
24 5 Oct 1936, MCS to K. Fujii, information from Dr Yosito Sinoto, Tokyo, 1975.

CHAPTER 5

1 Marie Stopes, *A Journal From Japan*, entry dated 25 Feb 1908.
2 Feb 1909, Dr Helen McMurchy to MCS. All this sequence of letters, previously unpublished, in BL-S.
3 22 Aug 1909, C. G. Hewitt to MCS. BL-S.
4 25 April 1910, C. G. Hewitt to Edith Garner. BL-S.
5 10 May 1910, Henry Bassett to MCS. BL-S.
6 12 May 1910, MCS to Henry Bassett. BL-S.
7 Maurice Hewlett, *Open Country*, Macmillan, 1909.
8 ibid., p. 82.

9 M. C. Stopes and K. Fujii, "Studies on the Structure and Affinities of Cretaceous Plants", *Philosophical Transactions of the Royal Society*, Vol 201.

10 The opinion of Professor W. G. Chaloner, Professor of Botany, Birkbeck College, London University, interview with the author, 19 Sept 1975.

CHAPTER 6

1 Edward Carpenter, *Love's Coming of Age*, this edition Swan Sonnenschein, 1902, p. 4.

2 ibid., p. 11.

3 ibid., p. 78.

4 12 Aug 1911, C. G. Hewitt to MCS. BL-S.

5 Marie C. Stopes, *A Banned Play and a Preface on the Censorship*, Bale, Sons & Danielsson, 1926.

6 7 Nov 1927, MCS to Alfred Sutro, rough draft. BL-S.

7 Marie Stopes, *A Banned Play*, p. 127.

8 ibid., p. 135.

9 10 Aug 1913, MCS to Aylmer Maude. BL-S.

10 14 Aug 1913, MCS to Aylmer Maude. BL-S.

11 Maude, *The Authorized Life of Marie C. Stopes*, p. 71.

12 Havelock Ellis, "The Sexual Impulse in Women", *American Journal of Dermatology*, March 1902.

13 Arthur Calder-Marshall, *Havelock Ellis*, Hart-Davis, 1959.

14 Marie Stopes, obituary of Havelock Ellis in *Literary Guide*, September 1939.

15 21 Feb 1914, MCS to Aylmer Maude. BL-S.

16 *The Times*, 6 April 1914.

17 MS of poem, "Transmutation", dated May 9 1914 and signed "MCS". BL-S.

18 10 July and 13 July 1914, correspondence between R. R. Gates and MCS (rough draft). BL-S.

19 Petition drawn up by Braby & Waller, solicitors, October 1914. BL-S.

20 12 January 1915, MCS to Mr Gates. BL-S.

21 "Wine That Turned to Vinegar", from *Man, Other Poems and a Preface*, Marie C. Stopes, Heinemann, 1914.

CHAPTER 7

1 Marie Carmichael Stopes, *Married Love: A New Contribution to the Solution of Sex Difficulties*, Fifield, 1918.

2 Marie Stopes, *Man, Other Poems and a Preface*.

3 M. C. Stopes, *The Race*, Fifield, 1918.

4 Oct 1915, "Tante Tina" to MCS. BL-S.

5 Francis Galton, *Hereditary Genius*, quoted by Oliver Gillie, *Who Do You Think You Are?*, Hart-Davis, McGibbon, 1936.

6 Quoted by Lovat Dickson, *H. G. Wells*, Pelican, 1972, p. 111.

7 19 Oct 1912, *Daily Chronicle*, interview with MCS.

8 1911 (no other date) Maurice Hewlett to MCS. SR-Coll.

9 17 April 1915, MCS to Aylmer Maude. BL-S.

10 Margaret Sanger, *An Autobiography*, Gollancz, 1939, p. 97.

11 Margaret Sanger, *My Fight for Birth Control*, Faber, 1932, p. 101.

12 Sept 1915, MCS to President Woodrow Wilson (rough draft, no date). BL-S.

13 23 Aug 1917, Winnie Stopes to MCS. BL-S.

14 9 Dec 1916, poster advertising production of *Sumida River* at Birmingham Repertory Theatre. BL-S.

15 24 Sept 1917, G. B. Shaw to MCS. BL-S.

16 28 Sept 1917, MCS to G. B. Shaw, rough draft. BL-S.

17 13 July 1915, Walter Blackie to MCS. BL-S.

18 26 May 1916, Edward Carpenter to MCS. BL-S.

19 20 June 1917, R. V. Wheeler to MCS. BL-S.

20 1 Oct 1915, R. Buckley to MCS. BL-S.

21 MCS, undated, unsigned, but probably September 1916. BL-S.

22 30 Aug 1917, MCS to Aylmer Maude. BL-S.

23 25 Feb 1917, T. H. Holland to MCS. BL-S.

24 28 Oct 1917, T. H. Holland to MCS. BL-S.

25 20 Jan 1940, MCS to Lord Alfred Douglas. BL-S.

26 20 June 1917, Russell Wakefield to MCS. BL-S.

27 As quoted by Briant, *Marie Stopes*, pp. 97–8.

28 26 Jan 1918, Dean W. R. Inge to MCS. BL-S.

29 15 Nov 1917, Dr B. Dunlop to MCS. BL-S.

CHAPTER 8

1 Quoted by Peter Fryer, *The Birth Controllers*, this edition, Corgi, 1967, p. 252.

2 Edward Weeks, *This Trade of Writing*, 1935.

3 Marie Stopes, *Married Love*, p. 104.

4 ibid., p. 28.

5 ibid., p. 20.

6 Marie Carmichael Stopes, *Marriage In My Time*, Rich & Cowan, 1935, p. 9.

7 Marie Stopes, *Married Love*, p. 106.

8 ibid., p. 70.

9 ibid., p. 21.

10 ibid., p. 77.

11 ibid., p. 99.

12 15 March 1918, rough draft, MCS, possibly to Bishop of Birmingham. BL-S.

13 Marie Stopes, *Marriage In My Time*, p. 44.

14 29 January 1919, MCS to Walter Blackie. BL-S.

CHAPTER 9

1 *The Times* 1906, quoted by L. J. Ludovici, *The Challenging Sky*, a biography of A. V. Roe, Herbert Jenkins, 1956.

2 A. V. Roe, *The World of Wings and Things*, Hurst & Blackett, 1939.

3 Ludovici, *The Challenging Sky*.

4 15 February 1918, II. V. Roc to MCS. BL-S.

5 *The Star*, 4 Nov 1922, article by Marie Stopes.

6 21 Oct 1917, H. V. Roe to St Mary's Hospital. BL-S.
7 20 Feb 1918, H. V. Roe to MCS. BL-S.
8 4 April 1918, MCS to CO., R.F.C. Officers' Hospital. BL-S.
9 21 April 1918, Margaret Ashton to MCS. BL-S.
10 16 April 1918, H. V. Roe to MCS. BL-S.
11 3 May 1918, Aylmer Maude to MCS. BL-S.
12 17 May 1918, MCS to Aylmer Maude. BL-S.
13 19 May 1918, MCS, Land's End Hotel, Cornwall, to Aylmer Maude. BL-S.
14 19 June 1918, C. C. Stopes to MCS. BL-S.
15 6 Aug 1918, MCS to H. V. Roe. BL-S.
16 24 Oct 1918, H. V. Roe to MCS. BL-S.
17 2 Oct 1918, MCS to H. V. Roe. BL-S.
18 A. J. P. Taylor, *English History 1914–45*, O.U.P., 1965, p. 114.
19 William C. Darrah, *Principles of Palaeobotany*. pp. 144–5.
20 28 Aug 1918, G. B. Shaw to MCS. BL-S.
21 May 1918, Dr Armand Agate to MCS. BL-S.
22 19 Aug 1918, Dr Binnie Dunlop to MCS. BL-S.
23 23 Nov 1917, Professor Starling to MCS about *Wise Parenthood*, well before the
   publication of *Married Love*. BL-S.
24 Marie Carmichael Stopes, *Wise Parenthood*, Fifield, 1918, p. 21.
25 ibid., p. 26.
26 ibid., p. 37.
27 *Eugenics Review*. Vol XI, No. 2., unsigned article.
28 *News of the World*, 8 June 1919.
29 *New Witness*, 12 Sept 1919.
30 Dr Helena Wright in an interview with the author.
31 23 Sept 1919, MCS to H. V. Roe. BL-S.
32 11 Feb 1919, MCS to H. V. Roe. BL-S.
33 16 May 1919, Mrs Mollie Wrench to MCS. BL-S.
34 Extracts from notes taken at the time by H. V. Roe. BL-S.
35 26 Jan 1920, Dr J. Cox to MCS. BL-S.
36 8 Oct 1919, MCS to Birth Rate Commission, rough draft. BL-S.

CHAPTER 10

1 Fragment in H. V. Roe's handwriting, undated, BL-S.
2 Dr Evelyne Fisher, in an interview included in the third Marie Stopes Memorial
   Lecture, 1974, *Journal of Biosocial Science*, Vol 6, No. 2, pp. 163–82, Alan S.
   Parkes and Dee King.
3 23 Oct 1918, MCS to H. V. Roe. BL-S.
4 W. R. Inge, *Vale*, Longmans, Green, 1934.
5 W. R. Inge, *Outspoken Essays*, Longmans, Green, 1919, p. 73.
6 Lambeth Conference Report, 1920, Resolution 70, p. 161.
7 All these letters from BL-S.
8 *A New Gospel to All Peoples, First Delivered to the Bishops in Session at Lambeth,
   1920, Through Marie Carmichael Stopes*, Humphreys, 1922, pp. 16–17.
9 ibid., p. 26.

10 13 July 1920, Dr C. Killick Millard to MCS. BL-S.

11 *The Star*, 25 Jan 1922.

12 Marie Stopes, *Roman Catholic Methods of Birth Control*, Peter Davies, 1933.

13 *New York Times*, 18 Dec 1921.

14 12 July 1920, F. M. de Zulueta, SJ, to MCS. BL-S.

15 Dr C. Killick Millard, *Presidential Address to the Leicester Literary and Philosophical Society*, 1917.

16 31 Oct 1921, Dr George Jones to MCS. BL-S.

17 Dr Amand Routh, *The Birth-Rate*, pamphlet, October 1919. BL-S.

18 All these hitherto unpublished letters from BL-S, late 1922.

19 All these previously unpublished comments from replies to MCS's political questionnaire, November 1922. BL-S.

20 Taylor, *English History*, p. 120.

21 26 Sept 1922, Pearkes Withers to MCS. BL-S.

22 14 Sept 1921, Mrs Caroline Bracken to MCS. BL-S.

23 *Rochester & Chatham News*, 27 July 1920, signed "Economy".

24 25 Sept 1919, S. J. Clift to MCS. BL-S.

25 *Daily Mail*, 13 June 1919. In her list of press articles, Marie Stopes commented "large demand for books followed".

26 *Medical Press*, 27 Oct 1920.

27 May 1920, correspondence between MCS, Bishop of Birmingham, Dean Inge etc. BL-S.

28 Marie Stopes, *A Letter to Working Mothers; on how to have healthy children and avoid weakening pregnancies*, pub. M. C. Stopes, Leatherhead, 1919.

CHAPTER II

1 From a chapter contributed by MCS to *The Control of Parenthood*, ed. Sir James Marchant, Putnam, p. 202.

2 Francis Galton, *Inquiries Into Human Faculty and Its Development*, 1908.

3 *Westminster Gazette* ("Across the Tea Table", by Penelope) 7 April 1922.

4 6 March 1920 and 7 July 1920, Aylmer Maude to MCS. BL-S.

5 1 May 1924, Mrs Twine to MCS. BL-S.

6 ed. Marchant, *The Control of Parenthood*, p. 202.

7 Marie Carmichael Stopes, *Radiant Motherhood*, Putnam, 1920, p. 221.

8 ibid., p. 231.

9 *Australian Women's Weekly*, 19 April 1934, interview with MCS by Muriel Segal.

10 10 Oct 1924, MCS to V. A. Dickinson and Rev. A. Smither. BL-S.

11 *Sunday Chronicle*, 15 Feb 1920.

12 W. N. Willis, *Wedded Love*, 1920, p. 74.

13 ibid., p. 63.

14 David M. Kennedy, *Birth Control in America, The Career of Margaret Sanger*, Yale University Press, 1970.

15 Marie Stopes, *Radiant Motherhood*, p. 215.

16 13 Feb 1921, Mrs Florence Booth to MCS. BL-S.

17 13 March 1921, MCS to Chief of Police, Scotland Yard. BL-S.

18 *Sunday Chronicle*, 27 Feb 1921.

19 *The Star*, 9 June 1921. "A Great Social Campaign" by Helen R. Macdonald.

20 14 March 1921, Michael Jennings of the *Daily Mirror*, to MCS. BL-S.

21 Maude, *The Authorized Life of Marie C. Stopes*, p. 140.

22 Briant, *Marie Stopes*, p. 135.

23 MCS's own figures. BL-S.

24 12 April 1921, Dr J. J. Buchan, M.O.H., Bradford to MCS. BL-S.

25 14 April 1921, Dr Mary Kidd to MCS. BL-S.

26 12 April, probably 1921, MCS to Lloyd George, rough draft. BL-S.

27 1 June 1921, Mrs E. Thomas to MCS. BL-S.

28 *Queen's Hall Meeting*, a collection of speeches, Putnam, 1921.

29 ibid.

30 *Woman's Pictorial*, 11 March 1922, article by MCS.

31 All extracts from a typed transcript of *Transactions of the Medico-Legal Society*, 1921–22, BL-S. Dr McIlroy's reference to the check pessary does not appear in the society's official transcript, where her summing-up was not reported.

32 Halliday G. Sutherland, *Birth Control: A Statement of Christian Doctrine against the Neo-Malthusians*, Harding & More, March 1922.

33 ibid., p. 101.

CHAPTER 12

1 Quoted by Francis Watson in *Dawson of Penn*, Chatto & Windus, 1950.

2 12 January 1922, MCS to *The Times*, copy, unpublished. BL-S.

3 Audrey Leathard, *The Development of Family Planning Services in Britain, 1921–1974*, Ph.D thesis to be presented to the London School of Economics, 1977.

4 27 June 1922, MCS to B. H. Tubbs. BL-S.

5 30 June 1921, G. B. Shaw to MCS. BL-S.

6 12 Nov 1921, MCS to C. Huntington. BL-S.

7 *The Times*, 5 March 1921.

8 All these letters in BL-S.

9 Unpublished MS, Noel Coward to MCS, undated, probably 1922. BL-S.

10 29 May 1922, Dr J. Cox to MCS. BL-S.

11 28 Nov 1922, Dr Binnie Dunlop to MCS. BL-S.

12 1 Dec 1921, Dr W. F. Robie to MCS. BL-S.

13 22 Nov 1921, Havelock Ellis to MCS. BL-S.

14 14 Nov 1922, MCS to Mr Cooke. BL-S.

15 Correspondence in *Harringay and Muswell Press*, June 4 and 18, 1921.

16 *A City Full of Girls and Boys*, by "A Catholic Woman Doctor", Catholic Truth Society, 1923, p. 19.

17 *Catholic Times*, 17 Dec 1921.

18 30 Sept 1921, MCS to Beaverbrook, rough draft. 13 May 1933, Beaverbrook to MCS. BL-S.

19 22 Nov 1921, MCS. BL-S.

20 Halliday G. Sutherland, *A Time to Keep*, Geoffrey Bles, 1934.

21 16 Nov 1922, MCS to Henry Ford, rough draft. BL-S.

22 18 Oct 1922, MCS to Dr J. B. Hance. BL-S.
23 Dec 1922–Feb 1923, long correspondence between MCS and Nurse Daniels. BL-S.
24 13 Jan 1923, Bertrand Russell to MCS. BL-S.
25 Undated rough draft, MCS to Sir Archibald Bodkin. BL-S.
26 *John Bull*, 27 Jan 1923.
27 Sutherland, *A Time to Keep.*
28 *Daily Graphic*, 22 Feb 1923.
29 *Sunday Times*, 4 March 1923.
30 26 Feb 1923, MCS to Dr Robinson. BL-S.

CHAPTER 13

1 All extracts from the trial are taken from the only freely accessible transcript, *The Trial of Marie Stopes*, edited and with an Introduction by Muriel Box, Femina Books, 1967, pp. 357, 377.
2 Sutherland, *Birth Control*, pp. 101–2.
3 1922, MCS's brief for Patrick Hastings, KC. BL-S.
4 29 Jan 1923, C. Braby to MCS. BL-S.
5 This is based on Lord Hewart's explanation of the law of libel, as presented in *The Trial of Marie Stopes*, pp. 359–61.
6 *The Trial of Marie Stopes*, p. 117.
7 ibid., p. 115
8 Marie Stopes, *Married Love*, p. 23.
9 Box, *The Trial of Marie Stopes*, p. 117.
10 ibid., p. 112.
11 ibid., p. 127.
12 *Daily Graphic*, 23 Feb 1923.
13 22 Feb 1923, Mary Abbott to MCS. BL-S.
14 24 Feb 1923, Lady Constance Lytton to MCS. BL-S.
15 2 March 1923, Mrs E. Budgen to MCS. BL-S.
16 Feb 1923, George L. Mills to MCS. BL-S.
17 Box, *The Trial of Marie Stopes* p. 130.
18 ibid., pp. 197–200.
19 ibid., p. 185.
20 ibid., p. 218.
21 ibid., p. 220.
22 12 April 1921, MCS to the Surgical Manufacturing Company. BL-S.
23 Box, *The Trial of Marie Stopes*, p. 294.
24 ibid., p. 364.
25 ibid., pp. 376–7.
26 1 March 1923, Alfred Goodman to MCS. BL-S.
27 *Daily News*, 3 March 1923.
28 *Westminster Gazette*, 3 March 1923.
29 *New Leader*, 9 March 1923.
30 5 March 1923, MCS, duplicated letter. BL-S.
31 Box, *The Trial of Marie Stopes*, p. 388.

32 31 Dec 1923, MCS to Braby & Waller. BL-S.
33 *Universe*, 23 May 1924.
34 *Universe*, 23 May 1924.
35 2 Dec 1924, G. B. Shaw to MCS. BL-S.

CHAPTER 14

1 25 Feb 1923, P. Ward to Hatchard's. BL-S.
2 *Dundee Advertiser*, 25 Oct 1924.
3 *Sporting Times*, 29 Oct 1924.
4 11 May 1923, British Board of Film Censors to MCS. BL-S.
5 15 May 1923, MCS to T. P. O'Connor. BL-S.
6 MS of article by MCS, June 1923. BL-S.
7 MCS's own figures (no date, probably 1925). BL-S.
8 19 Nov 1923, Mrs M. Willis to MCS. BL-S.
9 Marie Stopes, *Our Ostriches*, Putnam, 1923.
10 7 June 1923, MCS's publicity notes for Glasgow Coliseum. BL-S.
11 *Daily Express*, 16 April 1924, article by MCS, headed "My Baby".
12 17 Feb 1924, Mrs Maud Braby to MCS. BL-S.
13 *Daily Sketch*, 28 March 1924.
14 *Daily Express*, March 28 and 14 April 1924.
15 28 April 1924, MCS to Professor R. V. Wheeler. BL-S.
16 Mary Stocks, *Still More Commonplace*, Peter Davies, 1973, p. 24.
17 *Westminster Gazette*, 28 June 1924.
18 *Universe*, 23 May 1924.
19 20 Sept 1924, programme for dance at Givons Grove. BL-S.
20 29 March 1929, MCS to H. V. Roe. BL-S.
21 3 July 1930, Miss Ethel Wilkinson to MCS. BL-S.
22 18 March 1933, Miss Wilkinson to MCS. BL-S.
23 28 Dec 1933, MCS to Mrs M. B. BL-S.
24 27 May 1935, MCS to Major C. BL-S.
25 29 May, 1935, Mrs H. C. to MCS. BL-S.
26 Marie Stopes, *Sex and The Young*, p. 175.

CHAPTER 15

1 Dr Marie Stopes, *Enduring Passion*, first published Putnam London, 1928; this
   edition, Hogarth Press, 1953, p. 20.
2 21 March 1943, H. V. Roe to MCS. BL-S.
3 19 April 1925, MCS to C. Huntington. BL-S.
4 23 Oct 1925, H. Neilson to MCS. BL-S.
5 6 May 1926, MCS 50 Stanley Baldwin, rough draft. BL-S.
6 5 April 1925, Professor Paul Lublinsky to MCS. BL-S.
7 K. A. Aziz to MCS. No date, probably 1925. BL-S.
8 7 Nov 1934, Professor B. Malinowski to MCS. BL-S.
9 Dr Helena Wright in interview with the author, 24 June 1975.
10 16 May 1924, H. V. Roe to L. A. Oliver. BL-S.

11 *Practitioner*, July 1923, p. 90.

12 3 Feb and 25 May 1925, Aylmer Maude to MCS. BL-S.

13 *South Wales Gazette*, 27 Nov 1925.

14 Reprinted in *Birth Control News*, January 1929.

15 *New Statesman*, 31 January 1928.

16 3 May 1928, transcript of Gwynne v. Stopes action. BL-S.

17 27 Nov 1928, H. A. Gwynne to Braby & Waller. BL-S.

18 25 Jan 1925, MCS to *The Aeroplane*. BL-S.

19 16 Aug 1929, GBS to MCS. BL-S.

20 *Leeds Mercury*, 15 Jan 1929.

21 28 Jan 1929, note by MCS. BL-S.

22 *Family Planning*, January 1972, article by Dr Helena Wright.

23 *Report of the International Medical Group for the Investigation of Contraception*, September 1930.

24 27 Nov 1934, GBS to MCS. BL-S.

25 21 Nov 1936, GBS to MCS. BL-S.

26 28 Jan 1929, J. H. Guy to MCS. BL-S.

27 17 Feb 1931, Dr Norman Haire to MCS. BL-S.

28 14 April 1930, MCS to Pope Pius IX, rough draft, BL-S.

29 Marie Stopes, *Roman Catholic Methods of Birth Control*, Peter Davies, 1933, p. 107.

30 9 Jan 1933, MCS to Lord Leverhulme, rough draft. BL-S.

31 Betty Ross, *Heads and Tales*, Rich & Cowan, 1934.

32 Harry Stopes-Roe in an interview with author, 10 July 1975.

33 Lady Jeans in an interview with the author, January 1975.

34 J. E. Morpurgo, *Barnes Wallis*, Longman, 1972, p. 207.

35 23 July 1938, H. V. Roe to MCS. BL-S.

36 5 Nov 1940, MCS to H. V. Roe. BL-S.

37 December 1942, H. V. Roe to MCS. BL-S.

38 21 March 1943 H. V. Roe to MCS. BL-S.

CHAPTER 16

1 Poem by MCS, "Remember My Sweet Youth" from *Love Songs for Young Lovers*, Heinemann, 1939.

2 17 April 1939, MCS to *Housewife* magazine. BL-S.

3 18 May 1938, programme for CBC Spring ball. BL-S.

4 July 1939, MCS, unpublished MS. SR-Coll.

5 4 Oct 1938, "Diary of One Day", autobiographical unpublished fragment by MCS. BL-S.

6 Undated fragment, MCS. SR-Coll.

7 14 Feb 1939, Lord Alfred Douglas to MCS. BL-S.

8 18 March 1939, unpublished typescript, MCS. SR-Coll.

9 Quoted by Rupert Hart-Davis in *Hugh Walpole*, Macmillan, 1952, p. 412.

10 Briant, *Marie Stopes*, pp. 246–7.

11 Marie Stopes, *Love Songs for Young Lovers*, p. 34.

12 31 March 1947, Mrs A. Briant to MCS. BL-S.

13 MS, undated. SR-Coll.
14 10 July 1939, Dr B. Bayly to MCS. BL-S.
15 3 Oct 1928, MS poem by MCS. SR-Coll.
16 10 April 1942, MCS to K. Briant. BL-S.
17 17 Feb 1943, autobiographical fragment, MCS. BL-S.
18 22 March 1943, MCS to H. V. Roe. BL-S.
19 12 July 1940, MCS to Winston Churchill. BL-S.
20 7 Dec 1940, MCS to Lord Woolton. BL-S.
21 *Family Planning*, January 1972, Dr Helena Wright.
22 26 May 1944, MCS to Ministry of Supply. BL-S.
23 Information from Dr Serge Mamay, U.S. Geological Survey, who visited Marie Stopes at Norbury Park during the war. (Telephone interview, September 1975.)
24 7 Aug 1941, MCS to J. W. Poynter. BL-S.
25 June 18 and 22, 1941, MCS to Clement Attlee and reply. BL-S.
26 15 Oct 1945, MCS to G. Bryer-Ash. BL-S.
27 3 Dec 1941, MCS to Francis Howard. BL-S.
28 30 Oct 1939, Llewellyn Powys to MCS. BL-S.
29 15 Nov 1939, MCS to Llewellyn Powys. BL-S.
30 11 Jan 1942, MCS to Warren Tute. BL-S.
31 Warren Tate in an interview with the author, 15 Aug 1975.
32 30 Oct 1942, Lord Alfred Douglas to MCS. BL-S.
33 5 Jan 1950, MCS, letter published in the *Listener*.
34 16 Nov 1943, MS of MCS poem. SR-Coll.
35 20 July 1946, MCS to Clement Attlee. BL-S.
36 9 May 1947, MCS to Mrs Scott. BL-S.
37 Undated MS by MCS. SR-Coll.

CHAPTER 17

1 15 June 1950, MCS to Walter de la Mare. BL-S.
2 16 June 1944, H. V. Roe to C. Huntington. BL-S.
3 Unpublished MS, August 1949, MCS. SR-Coll.
4 18 April 1942, MCS to Mrs A. Briant. BL-S.
5 *Daily Mirror*, 21 Oct 1935, article by Dr Marie Stopes.
6 Mary Stopes-Roe in an interview with the author, 6 June 1975.
7 1 Oct 1947, MCS to Barnes Wallis. SR-Coll.
8 14 Feb 1948, MCS to H. V. Roe. SR-Coll.
9 February 1948, H. V. Roe to MCS. BL-S.
10 23 Aug 1948, Mrs A. Briant to MCS. BL-S.
11 30 Dec 1949, MCS to "May". BL-S.
12 12 Nov 1948, Harry Stopes-Roe to MCS. SR-Coll.
13 *Poetry Review*, October 1954.
14 July 1951, Rev. G. Lloyd to MCS. BL-S.
15 Laurie Taylor, "The Unfinished Sexual Revolution", the first Marie Stopes Memorial Lecture, 12 March 1971, *Journal of Biosocial Science*, 1971, p. 491.
16 Ronald Blythe, *New Statesman*, 31 Jan 1959.

17 30 Nov 1946, Shaw Desmond to MCS. BL-S.

18 26 Oct 1951, Shaw Desmond to MCS. BL-S.

19 17 Nov 1928, G. B. Shaw to MCS. BL-S.

20 Juliet Mitchell, "Female Sexuality", the second Marie Stopes Memorial Lecture, 13 March 1972, *Journal of Biosocial Science*, 1973, pp 123–36.

21 Marie Stopes, *Married Love*, p. 71.

22 *New Statesman*, 9 Dec 1933.

23 19 Jan 1925, Dr R. Sandilands to MCS. BL-S.

24 *The Times*, 3 Oct 1958, obituary of MCS by C. P. Blacker (unsigned).

25 1953, Mrs M. E. Ryan to MCS. BL-S.

26 6 Dec 1952, MCS to Avro Manhattan. BL-S.

CHAPTER 18

1 "To the Old" published in *We Burn, Selected Poems of Marie Carmichael Stopes, D.Sc., FRS. Lit., etc.*, Alex Moring, 1949.

2 30 Dec 1953, MCS (rough draft) to *The Times*. BL-S.

3 27 Nov 1947, MCS to HRH Princess Elizabeth. BL-S.

4 27 Oct 1946 MCS (rough draft) to Duke of Windsor. BL-S.

5 *Britain Today* September 1949.

6 14 Nov 1949, MCS to Royal Commission on the Press. BL-S.

7 *New Statesman*, 27 Aug 1949.

8 5 April 1955, *Family Doctor* to MCS. BL-S.

9 Marie Carmichael Stopes, *We Burn*, with illustrations by Gregorio Prieto, Alex. Moring, 1949.

10 5 May 1950, MCS to Walter de la Mare. BL-S.

11 6 Sept 1950, MCS to *Sunday Times* (rough draft). BL-S.

12 14 Nov 1948, pencil scribble by MCS. BL-S.

13 24 June 1952, MCS to Sir Gerald Kelly. BL-S.

14 Austin Clarke, *Collected Poems*, Dolmen Press with OUP, 1974, p. 227.

15 Ronald Blythe, *New Statesman*, 31 Jan 1959.

16 1 March and 31 May 1954, MCS to Harry Stopes-Roe. SR-Coll.

17 22 Dec 1953, MCS to A. Manhattan (in A. Manhattan's collection).

18 ibid., 4 Feb 1954.

19 7 Oct 1953, MCS to Thomas Moult. BL-S.

20 Autobiographical fragment by MCS, headed "My Experience on the night-morning of 28–29 October, 1953, at Norbury Park". BL-S.

21 30 June 1957, MCS to A. Manhattan (Manhattan collection).

22 Avro Manhattan in an interview with the author, 14 Jan 1976.

23 Briant, *Marie Stopes*, p. 259.

24 ibid., p. 261.

25 14 March 1958, Geoffrey Cantuar to MCS. BL-S.

26 Briant, *Marie Stopes*, p. 267.

27 *Catholic Times*, 21 Nov 1958.

28 *New Statesman and Nation*, 9 Dec 1933.

SELECT BIBLIOGRAPHY

Of the many hundreds of books, pamphlets and articles that contributed to the preparation of this book (most of which are noted in the reference section), I list here only those which might be of interest to the general reader. Similarly, with Marie Stopes's own writings, I have concentrated on those works most relevant to her career (a full list is readily available in Peter Eaton's recently published bibliography of Marie Stopes). Since all her writings, apart from her botanical work, shared a common inspiration, I also felt it useful to ignore previous classifications into poetry, drama, sociology, etc., and to list her publications chronologically, thus giving a clearer idea of her development.

WORKS BY MARIE STOPES

1910   *Ancient Plants*, Blackie & Son
      A Journal From Japan: A Daily Record of Life as seen by a Scientist, Blackie & Son

1911   *Love Letters of a Japanese* (under the pseudonym, G. N. Mortlake), Stanley Paul & Co

1913   *Plays of Old Japan* (with J. Sakurai), William Heinemann

1914   *Man, Other Poems and a Preface*, William Heinemann

1917   *Conquest, or a piece of jade*, Samuel French

1918   *Married Love*, A. C. Fifield; 1920, The Critic and Guide Co., N.Y.
      Gold in the Wood and The Race: Two new plays of life, A. C. Fifield
      Wise Parenthood, A. C. Fifield
      The Constitution of Coal (with Dr R. V. Wheeler), H.M.S.O.

1919   *A Letter to Working Mothers: on how to have healthy children and avoid weakening pregnancies*, pub. M. C. Stopes
      "The Four Invisible Ingredients in Banded Bituminous Coals", *Proceedings of the Royal Society*, Vol. 90, No. 1

1920   *Radiant Motherhood*, G. P. Putnam's Sons; 1921, Putnam, N.Y.

1921   *The Truth About Venereal Disease*, G. P. Putnam's Sons

1922   *A New Gospel to All Peoples: A revelation of God uniting physiology and the religions of man*, A. L. Humphreys
      Early Days of Birth Control, G. P. Putnam's Sons

1923   *Contraception, Its Theory, History and Practice*, Bale, Sons & Danielsson
      Our Ostriches, a Play of Modern Life, G. P. Putnam's Sons
      "The Spontaneous Combustion of Coal" (with R. V. Wheeler), *Colliery Guardian*

1925   *The First Five Thousand* (first report of the Mothers' Clinic for Constructive Birth Control), John Bale & Co
      Don't Tell Timothy (under the pseudonym Mark Arundel) G. P. Putnam's Sons

1926 *The Human Body*, Gill Publishing Company; 1932, Blue Ribbon Books N.Y.
Vectia: A Banned Play and a Preface on the Censorship, Bale, Sons & Danielsson
A Road to Fairyland (under the pseudonym, Erica Fay), G. P. Putnam's Sons; 1927, Putnam N.Y.
Sex and the Young, Gill Publishing Company; Putnam N.Y.

1928 *Love's Creation* (under the pseudonym Marie Carmichael), John Bale & Co
Enduring Passion, G. P. Putnam's Sons; 1931, Putnam N.Y.

1929 *Mother England* (letters to Marie Stopes, edited by her), Bale, Sons & Danielsson

1933 *Roman Catholic Methods of Birth Control*, Peter Davies

1934 *Birth Control Today: A Practical Handbook for those who want to be their own masters in this vital matter*, John Bale & Co

1935 "On the Petrology of Banded Bituminous Coal", January issue of *Fuel in Science and Practice*
Marriage In My Time, Rich & Cowan; 1936, Ryerson Press N.Y.

1936 *Change of Life in Men and Women*, Putnam's Sons; Putnam N.Y.

1939 *Love Songs for Young Lovers*, William Heinemann; Putnam N.Y.

1940 *Oriri*, William Heinemann; 1941, Putnam N.Y.
"A Poetical Autobiography", printed in the quarterly magazine *Kingdom Come*, vol. 1, No. 3

1944 *Wartime Harvest*, Alexander Moring

1946 *The Bathe, an Ecstacy*, Alexander Moring

1949 *We Burn: Selected Poems*, with illustrations by Gregorio Prieto, Alex. Moring

1950 *If I Had My Time Again* (collection of essays with a chapter by Marie Stopes) ed. Sir James Marchant, Odhams; Ryerson Press N.Y.

1952 *Joy and Verity*, Hogarth Press

1953 *The Evidence of Dr Marie C. Stopes to the Royal Commission on the Press*, published by Marie Stopes

1956 *Sleep*, Hogarth Press; Philosophical Library N.Y.

BOOKS AND ARTICLES RELATING TO MARIE STOPES

BOX, Muriel *The Trial of Marie Stopes*, Femina Books, 1967. (The only published transcript of the Stopes-Sutherland libel action, 1923–4, edited and with an introduction by Muriel Box.)

BRIANT, Keith *Marie Stopes, a Biography*, Hogarth Press, 1962; Norton & Co., 1962

DAVIS, Henry, S.J. *The Fallacies of Dr M. Stopes*, Burns, Oates & Washburn Ltd., 1928

EATON, Peter, and WARNICK, Marilyn *Marie Stopes. A Preliminary Checklist of Her Writings*, Croom, Helm, 1976

MAUDE, Aylmer *The Authorized Life of Marie C. Stopes*, Williams & Norgate, 1924
Marie Stopes, Her Work and Play, Putnam 1933 (An updated version of Maude's earlier book, but with little new material.)

MITCHELL, Juliet "Female Sexuality" The second Marie Stopes Memorial Lecture, *Journal of Biosocial Science*, January 1973

PARKES, Alan S., and Dee King "The Mothers' Clinic", Third Marie Stopes Memorial Lecture, *Journal of Biosocial Science*, April 1974

ROSS, Betty *Heads and Tales*, Rich & Cowan, 1934 (A series of interviews, with a chapter on Marie Stopes.)

STOCKS, Mary *Still More Commonplace*, Peter Davies, 1973 (Chapter 3 on Marie Stopes.)

STOPES-ROE, H. V., with Ian Scott *Marie Stopes and Birth Control*, Priory Press, 1974 (A concise biography aimed at younger readers.)

TAYLOR, Laurie "The Unfinished Sexual Revolution", First Marie Stopes Memorial Lecture, *Journal of Biosocial Science*, July 1971

CONTRACEPTION, ETC.

Birth Control News, the journal of the Mothers' Clinic and the Society for Constructive Birth Control, ed. Marie Stopes, published at variable intervals, 1922–1946

CARTER, C. O. *Human Heredity*, Penguin, 1970

CHACHUAT, M. *Le Mouvement du 'Birth Control' dans les pays anglo-saxons*, M. Giard, 1934

CIPOLLA, Carlo M. *The Economic History of World Population*, Pelican, 1970; Penguin N.Y., 1960

DRAPER, Elizabeth *Birth Control in the Modern World*, Allen & Unwin, 1965; revised edition Penguin, 1972; Penguin N.Y., 1966

ELLIS, Havelock "Sex Impulse in Women", *American Journal of Dermatology*, March 1902

The Problem of Race-Regeneration, Cassell & Co, 1911

My Life, Neville Spearman, 1940; Houghton Mifflin (Boston), 1939

GATES, R. Ruggles *Heredity and Eugenics*, Constable, 1923; Macmillan N.Y., 1946

FRYER, Peter *The Birth Controllers*, Secker & Warburg, 1965; Corgi, 1967; Stein & Day, N.Y., 1966 (An invaluable survey of birth control history over the last century via its main protagonists, including Marie Stopes featured in chapter 20.)

GLASS, D. V. *Population Policies and Movements in Europe*, Oxford (U.K. and Toronto), 1940

HIMES, Norman E. *A Medical History of Contraception*, 1936; Wood, 1936

KENNEDY, David M. *Birth Control in America, The Career of Margaret Sanger*, Yale University Press, 1970

LUDOVICI, Anthony M. *The Night-Hoers*, Herbert Jenkins, 1928

MARCHANT, Rev. J. (ed.) *The Control of Parenthood*, G. P. Putnam's Sons, 1922. (A collection of essays revealing widely different attitudes to birth control, with a chapter by Marie Stopes.)

MARCUS, Steven *The Other Victorians*, Weidenfeld & Nicolson, 1966; Basic Books N.Y., 1966

MILLARD, C. Killick *Population and Birth Control*, Leicester, 1917

PEEL, John and POTTS, Malcolm *Textbook of Contraceptive Practice*, C.U.P.,

1969. (The best guide to modern techniques, with neat potted histories of each method.)

PRESSAT, Roland *Population*, C. A. Watts, 1970, Pelican, 1973

SANGER, Margaret *My Fight for Birth Control*, 1932; Farrer Strauss N.Y., 1931
Autobiography, Victor Gollancz, 1939; Norton & Co., N.Y., 1938

SUTHERLAND, Halliday *Control of Life*, Burns Oates, 1951

MISCELLANEOUS

BIRD, Isabella L. *Unbeaten Tracks in Japan*, 1880, reissued by Charles E. Tuttle, 1973

CALDER-MARSHALL, Arthur *The Sage of Sex; A Life of Havelock Ellis*, Rupert Hart-Davis, 1959; Putnam N.Y., 1960

CARPENTER, Edward *Love's Coming of Age*, Swan Sonnenschein, 1902; Doran N.Y., 1911

CHAMBERLAIN, Basil H. *Japanese Things*, 1905, reissued by Charles E. Tuttle, 1971

INGE, Dean W. R. *Outspoken Essays*, Longmans, Green, 1919
Vale, Longmans, Green, 1934

MORPURGO, J. E. *Barnes Wallis*, Longmans, 1972; St Martin's Press N.Y., 1972

ROE, Sir A. V. *The World of Wings and Things*, Hurst & Blackett, 1939; Ryerson Press N.Y., 1939

RUSSELL, Bertrand *Autobiography*, Allen and Unwin, 1975

SULLIVAN, A. M. *The Last Serjeant*, Macdonald, 1952

SUTHERLAND, Halliday *A Time to Keep*, 1934; William Morrow N.Y.
The Arches of the Years, Geoffrey Bles, 1935

TAYLOR, A. J. P. *English History, 1914–1945*, O.U.P. 1965

WATSON, Francis *Dawson of Penn*, Chatto & Windus, 1950

INDEX

Marie Stopes's writings are indexed under the "Stopes, Marie" entry

Abbott, Mary, 224
Abertillery Free Church, 262
Aldred, Guy and Rose, 210–11
Alexandra, Queen, 168
American Birth Control League, 201n
Ancoats Working Men's Brotherhood, 59
Anderson, Sir Maurice Abbot, 211
Anglican Church, and birth control, 156–61, 197, 305
Aquinas, St Thomas, 162
Ashton, Margaret, 142
Aspinall, Rev. E. C., 158
Attlee, Clement, 291–2, 296
Augustine, St, 162
Avory, Mr Justice, 264
Avro, 138–9, 273
Aylmer, John, Bishop of London, 214
Aziz, K. A., 259

Baldwin, Stanley, 258
Bandulska, Miss, 193
Barr, Sir James, 187, 211, 215–16
Barrie, Sir James, 151n
Bassett, Henry, as tepid suitor, 80, 86–7, 91, 97n
Bayliss, Sir William, 211
Bayly, Dr Beddow, 287
"Beale, Courtenay", 204
Beaverbrook, Lord, 192, 206, 207, 289
Becker, Lydia, 18n
Bedford, William Russell, 12th Duke of, 211n
Belloc, Hilaire, 167
Bennett, Arnold, 116, 150, 187
Besant, Annie, 16, 198, 234, 238
Bicknell, John, 253
Bird, Isabella, 69
Birmingham & Midland Institute, 146
Birth Control (Sutherland), 196, 207; libel case over, 213–41
Birth Control News, 200, 207, 258, 265, 269, 270n, 282
Black, Dr Timothy, 309n
Black Record (Vansittart), 44n
Blacker, Dr C. P., 128, 288, 308–9, 315n
Blackie, Walter, 120, 135
Blythe, Ronald, 306, 316
Boden, Mrs Doris, 157
Bodkin, Sir Archibald, 210
Booth, Florence, 186
Bottomley, Horatio, 264
Bourne, Cardinal Francis, 207–8, 239, 240
Box, Muriel, 234n

Brady & Waller (solicitors), 208, 214, 237, 239
Bradlaugh, Charles, and birth control, 176, 196, 199, 214, 217, 222, 234, 238
Brennan, Mr (Stockport consultant), 167
Briant, Keith, 298; his biography of Marie, 19n, 120, 190, 280, 284, 323; first meeting with Marie, 280; Marie's love for, 281, 286–8, 297, 317, 318
Briant, Mrs (mother of Keith), 286, 303
British Association for the Advancement of Science, 16, 17, 20, 119
British Board of Film Censors, 243n, 244
Brown, Monsignor Canon, 162
Brown, Dr E. B., 152, 153
Bryant, Dr Sophie, 30, 31
Buchan, Dr John, 190
Buckie's Bears (H. Stopes-Roe), 254n
Burge, Hubert, Bishop of Southwark, 156
Burgess, Ethel, 141–2, 143, 178n, 299
Burton, Robert, 175
Burton Daily Mail, 245n
Butt, Dame Clara, 187
Buxton, 154
Byrne, Ethel, 185

Cambridge, 38, 40, 303
Carey, Rev. C. S., 157
Carmichael, J. F., 15
Carpenter, Edward, 90–91, 101, 187, 308; and *Married Love*, 120, 133
Carpenter, William, 266
Casti Conubii (papal encyclical, 1930), 271
Catholic Church, and birth control, 162–4, 197–9, 205–6, 207–8, 239–41, 250–1, 260–3, 271
Catholic Times, 205, 207, 325
Catholic Truth Society, 205, 262
CBC (Society for Constructive Birth Control and Racial Progress), 199–200, 204, 207, 210, 211, 227n, 247, 267–8, 270, 281
Chappel, Dr Harold, 227–8
Charles, Ernest, Sutherland's counsel in libel case, 214, 217, 220, 226–7, 228, 229–30
Church Times, 240
Churchill, Winston, 31, 289
Churchill, Mrs Winston, 262
Cinema Commission of Inquiry, 125, 245
Clarke, Austin, 316
Clift, Sidney John, 172–3
Coates, J. F., 5
Comstock Law, 115, 201
Constructive Birth Control and Racial Progress, Society for – *see* CBC

Control of Parenthood, The (ed. Marchant), 183–4
Coward, Noël, 202–3, 269, 295
Cox, Harold, 211n
Cuddeford, Barry, 253–4

Daily Chronicle, 94, 113
Daily Express, 195, 206n, 248, 324
Daily Graphic, 211, 224
Daily Herald, 210
Daily Mail, 173
Daily Mirror, 173, 189, 260n, 299
Daily News, 237
Daily Sketch, 248
Daniels, Nurse E. S., 210
Darwin, Charles, 29, 62, 112, 176, 308
Dawson of Penn, Lord, 197–8
De la Mare, Walter, 298, 314
Dear Brutus (Barrie), 151n
Decline in the Birth Rate, The (Webb), 169n
Denman, Lady, 268n
Dennett, Mary, 201n
Desmond, Shaw, 306
Douglas, Lord Alfred, 125, 282–4, 285, 295–6
Douglas, Lady Olive, 282, 295
Drew, A. C., 147
Duncan, Isadora, 42
Dunlop, Dr Binnie, 127, 139, 148, 204

Edinburgh, 15, 20, 26–8, 257
Edinger, George, 238n
Eliot, T. S., 315
Elizabeth II (as Princess), 254n, 312
Ellis, Elizabeth, 265
Ellis, Havelock, 102, 128, 132n, 187, 204, 308
Eskmeals, 118, 122, 145
Eugenics Review, 150
Eugenics Society, 156, 176–7, 326
Everard & Co., 137, 138
Eze Plage, 324

Fabian Society, 118, 181
Fairfield, Dr Letitia, 272n
Family Doctor, 314
Family Limitation (Aldred), 210
Family Limitation (Sanger), 116n
Family Planning Association, 268, 305, 309, 315n
Fearon, Ernest, 59
Fifield, A. C., 127, 141, 147, 148, 171, 200
Fisher, Dr Evelyne, 155, 285n
Fisher, Geoffrey, Archbishop of Canterbury, 324
Ford, Henry, 208
Forster, E. M., 310
Fox, Dr Adam, Archdeacon of Westminster, 325
Fraser, Sir Hugh, 214
Free Church of Scotland, 21
Friends, Society of, 29–30, 214
Fujii, Kenjiro, 182; botanical studies, 47–8, 56, 63, 70–71, 76, 87; Marie's increasing interest in, 48–50, 51; correspondence with Marie, 52, 54–5, 57–9, 60–61, 63–4, 95; frustrating relationship, 54–5, 57–62; first kiss and "betrothal", 58–9; apparent coldness, 63–4, 81; meets Marie in Japan, 65; break-up of relationship, 70–74, 76–7, 78, 80
Fujii, Shin'nichi, 73

Galton, Sir Francis, 112–13, 176, 308
Gandhi, Mahatma, 259n
Garner, Edith, 81, 82–5, 141
Gates, Dr Reginald Ruggles, 116, 117; marriage to Marie, 88, 91–2; impotence and marital difficulties, 93–100, 103, 104; portrayed in *Vectia*, 95–8; threatens Maude, 100, 103, 104; Marie leaves, 105–6; nullity petition against, 107
General Strike (1926), 258
Givons Grove, 177–8, 208, 224, 247, 251, 273
Glasgow, 115, 205
Goebel, Professor K., 45, 46, 55
Goodman, Alfred, 236, 240
Graves, Robert, 294n
Greenhithe, 32, 33
Greenwood, Walter, 274n
Guy, J. H., 270
Gwynne, H. A., 263–5

Haggard, Sir Rider, 183
Haire, Dr Norman, 198–9, 233, 261, 271
Halifax, Lord, 289
Hall, Commander F., 276n
Hall, Radclyffe, 187n
Hampstead, 41, 57, 165; Denning Road, 28–9, 32, 39; Well Walk, 82, 91, 92, 94, 97, 99, 103, 106, 116
Harding, President Warren, 201
Hardy, Thomas, 95, 276
Hastings, Sir Patrick, Marie's counsel in Sutherland libel case, 211, 214, 215, 221, 225–6, 228, 230–2, 306n
Hawthorne, Dr Jane, 193, 194, 229–30, 246
Hayes, P. J., Roman Catholic Archbishop of New York, 162, 205n
Heap, Alice Gertrude, 146
Hebbes, Nurse Maud, 246
Hedin, Sven, 75
Hemingway, Mrs M. E., 157
Hereditary Genius (Galton), 112
Hewart, Lord Chief Justice, and Stopes v. Sutherland case, 211, 213, 214, 222, 223, 227, 228, 231, 234–6, 238, 243
Hewitt, Charles Gordon: Marie's letters to, 78, 81, 82, 83, 85; devious friendship, 81–6, 88, 91, 97n, 141; and Marie's marriage to Gates 92, 95
Hewlett, Maurice, 87, 276; and *Married Love*, 113, 120
Hill, Professor Leonard, 183
Hindhead, 110, 273, 274
Hitler, Adolf, 128, 165n, 180, 197, 288
Hodges, Frank, 191
Hokkaido, 67–8, 69
Holland, T. H., 124
Holloway, Marie's birth control clinic in, 188–90, 196, 213, 215, 224, 246–7, 257

Howick, Lord, 106
Humphrey, Alvara, 35, 44, 50
Huntington, Charles, 161, 164, 187n, 200, 237, 240, 243
Huxley, Aldous, 168

If (Kipling), 269
"In the New Statesman Office" (Clarke), 316
Inge, W. R., Dean of St Paul's, and birth control, 126–7, 156, 162, 193
Irish Censorship Act (1928), 262
Irish Times, 262

Jack o' Lantern (Tute), 294
Jacobs, Dr Aletta, 177
Jeans, Lady, 275
John, Augustus, 315
John, Dorelia, 315
John Bull, 210, 224
Jones, Dr George, 165–6, 226–7
Joseph, Sir Keith, 326

Karezza (Stockham), 101
Kelly, Sir Gerald, 316
Kennedy, David, 116n
Kidd, Dr Mary, 190
King, Cecil, 313
Kipling, Rudyard, 269, 308
Knecht, Professor, 118
Kuwada, Professor Yoshinari, 74

Lambeth Conference: (1920) 158, 160–1, 197, 214, 305; (1930) 272; (1958) 305
Lancet, The, 190n
Lane, Sir William Arbuthnot, 211, 229
Lawrence, D. H., 90, 131
League of National Life, 207, 260n
Leathard, Audrey, 315n
Leatherhead, 123, 126, 141, 143, 144, 177, 194
Leverhulme, Lord, 274
Literary Guide, 199
Lloyd George, David, 169, 170, 191–2, 206–7
London Mercury, 270
Longhaughton, 106
Love on the Dole (Greenwood), 274n
Love's Coming-of-Age (Carpenter), 90–91
Lublinsky, Professor Paul, 258
Lyle-Samuel, Alexander, 170
Lyttelton, Rev. E., 157
Lytton, Lady Constance, 187, 224

MacAlister, Sir John, 135
McDonald, Sir Claude, 75–6
Macdonald, Helen, 189
MacDonald, J. Ramsay, 267
MacDonald, Malcolm, 289
McIlroy, Professor Anne Louise, 195–6, 211, 214, 230–2
McMurchy, Dr Helen, 92; romantic attachment to Marie, 78–80
McNabb, Father Vincent, 205
Malinowski, Professor B., 259
Malthus, Rev. Thomas, 175

Malthusian League, 127, 176–7; birth control clinic, 198–9, 233
Man and Woman (Ellis), 102
Manchester University, 51–7, 59, 61, 62, 72, 80, 83, 87
Manchester Literary and Philosophical Society, 59, 81
Manhattan, Avro, 310, 323, 324, 325; Marie's love for, 317–21
Marchant, Sir James, 183, 298
Marchant, Rev. James, 126
Marie Stopes Memorial Lectures, 305–6, 307
Mary, Queen, 168
Mathew, Theobald, 214
Maude, Aylmer, 147, 264; his biography of Marie, 43, 120, 259n, 261–2; shares household with Marie and Gates, 94–5, 97, 99, 103; platonic affair with Marie, 95–105, 114, 123–4, 318; portrayed in *Vectia*, 97–9; correspondence with Marie, 99–100, 103–4, 105, 107, 110, 114–15, 122, 124, 141, 143–4, 178; holidays with her, 114, 115; at her wedding to Roe, 127, 143, 144; distress at blow to relationship, 143–4, 145; in Russia, 144–5; on Marie's married happiness, 178; and her birth control campaign, 190, 193, 200; objects to her literary meddling, 269
Mayne, Mrs E. B., 174
medical profession, and birth control, 164–8, 190–1, 261, 314
Medical-Legal Society, 195, 214
Mein Kampf (Hitler), 197
Mensinga, Dr, 176
"Menstrual Curve of Sexual Impulse in Women, The" (Ellis), 132n
Metcalfe, Herbert, 214
Millard, Dr C. Killick, 160n, 161, 165, 193, 194, 211
Mills, George, 225
Mitchell, P. Chalmers, 121
Mitchell, Juliet, 307
Mitchison, Naomi, 128
Montreal, 79, 82
Moore, Henry, 292
Moring, Alexander, Ltd, 314
Morning Post, 192, 263–4, 282
Morpurgo, J. E., 276
Mothers' Clinic for Constructive Birth Control, 186, 188–90, 196, 213, 215, 224, 246–7, 257, 260, 290, 292, 312, 326
Munich, 35, 40–50, 51, 59–60, 164n
Murphy, Harold, 214
Murray, Professor Gilbert, 117
Mussolini, Benito, 272
My Fight for Birth Control (Sanger), 116

National Birth Control Councils, 268
National Birth Rate Commission, 150, 154, 162, 173, 183
National Council of Public Morals, 125, 126
New Phytologist, 54, 63
New Statesman, 264, 306, 308, 313, 316, 326–7
New Witness, 150
New York, 117n, 200–202, 205n

Newman, W. R., 245n
News of the World, 150, 262n
Norbury Park, 274–5, 278, 282, 283–5, 288, 290, 292, 295, 299, 301, 314, 320, 323, 325
North London Collegiate School, 28, 30, 37
Northumberland, Alan Percy, eighth Duke of, 263
Nuffield, Lord, 312

O'Connor, Dr Bernard, 195
O'Connor, T. P., 125, 244–6
Ogura, Professor Yudzuro, 74
Oliver, Professor F. W., 32, 33, 35, 45, 54, 71, 94
Open Country (Hewlett), 87
Openshaw Working Men's Brotherhood, 61
Oxford, 238

Paul, St, 156, 160
Philip, Prince, 312
Phillips, Jenny, 63n, 74n
Philosophy of the Sexes, The, or Every Woman's Book (Waters), 176
Pilgrim, Guy, unsuccessful suitor, 39–40, 47, 64
Pius IX, Pope, 271
Place, Francis, 176
Plain English, 192–3, 224
Portland Bill, 247–8, 249, 293, 312, 325
Pound, Ezra, 262
Powys, Llewellyn, 293
Poynter, J. W., 205, 315
Practitioner, 261
Press, Royal Commission on (1948), 313, 317
Proper Studies (Huxley), 168
Pugh, Raoul, 297
Putnam's, 161, 200
Pyke, Margaret, 5, 268

Queen's Hall meeting (1921), 192–5

Rabagliati, H. V., 214
Rainbow, The (Lawrence), 131
Raper, W. Baldwin, 199n
Rational Dress Society, 18, 24
Raygould, Clarence, 118
Read, Herbert, 295–6
Resvoll, Thekla, 45
Reynolds, C. A., 126
Rhondda Valley, 179, 182
Roberts, G. H., 192
Robie, Dr W. F., 204
Robinson, Dr W. J., 193n, 200
Roe, Sir Alliott Verdon, 137–9, 273
Roe, Humphrey Verdon, 116n, 177, 193, 207, 208, 224, 248, 271, 297; finances *Married Love*, 127, 140, 147; marriage to Marie, 127, 143–4; career in aviation, 137–9; first meeting with Marie, 139; correspondence, 142–3, 145–6, 147, 151, 155, 200–201, 202, 203, 252, 256, 275, 277–9, 288, 302; early married happiness, 145–6, 178; disappointment over first child, 150–4; limerick by, 155; co-partner in birth control work, 185, 188, 194,

195, 208, 247, 268; lack of physical ardour, 203, 272–3, 277–8, 318; growing estrangement, 249–50, 256–7, 260, 272–3, 275, 277–9; financial troubles, 272–3, 274, 277, 298; gives Marie sexual *carte blanche*, 277–8, 292; crumbling of marriage, 278–9, 281; death, 298–9; and son's marriage, 301, 302; ghostly visitation to Marie, 320
Rose, William, 294, 297
Ross, Betty, 275
Rouncefield, Brian, 324
Route, Ettie, 170
Routh, Dr Amand, 152, 153, 166, 174
Royal Free Hospital, 232n
Royal Society of Literature, 325
Russell, Bertrand, 195, 210, 211
Russell, Dora, 211
Russell, John Francis Stanley, second Earl, 195

Sachs, Sadie, 185
St George's High School, Edinburgh, 26–8
St John, Father Stanislaus, 163, 164
St Louis, 91
St Mary's Hospital, Manchester, 140
Sakurai, Professor Joji, 118
Saleeby, Dr C. W., 174
Samuelson, David, 243n
Sanger, Margaret, 120, 122; birth control campaign, 115–17, 185–6, 201n, 205n, 210, 305; rivalry with Marie, 185, 200, 201
Scharlieb, Dr Mary, 174, 183–4, 211
Schreiner, Olive, 131, 308
Scientific and Industrial Research, Department of, 178
Scott, D. W., 35
Scott, Admiral Sir Percy, 192, 193, 194
Scott-Foster, Richard, 252
Scrutton, Lord Justice, 289–9, 264
Sexual Ethics (Sorel), 101
Sexual Question, The (Sorel), 101
Sharp, Evelyn, 237
Shaw, George Bernard, 16, 181, 245n, 266, 277, 293, 307, 319; criticism of *The Race*, 118–19; praise for *Married Love*, 147; and birth control, 195, 199; on Sutherland libel verdict, 237, 240–1; on Marie's "incorrigible pugnacity", 269–70
Shearman, Mr Justice, 89
Shears, Nurse, 265n
Sinoto, Dr Yosito, 74
Skilled Employment and Apprenticeship Association, 183n
Smuts, Field-Marshal Jan C., 321–2
Some Errors in Women's Dress (C. Stopes), 18
Sorel, August, 101
Spectator, 261
Spencer, Philip, 325n
Sporting Times, 242–3
Sportophyte, The, 87–8
Star, The, 161, 188, 261
Starling, Ernest, 101
Stevenson, Frances, 121, 169n, 192, 206, 207
Stockham, Alice B., 101
Stocks, Baroness, 173, 279–80

Stopes, Charlotte (mother), 30, 32, 36, 57, 62, 82, 90, 212; background and education, 15–16; literary work, 16, 28; polemics on New Women, dress and smoking, 16, 18–19, 24, 54; marriage, 16–17; sexual ignorance and frigidity, 19–20, 21, 22; religion, 21, 23, 29; coolness towards daughters, 22, 24, 25–6, 29, 33–4; complaining widowhood, 41, 45, 52–3; Marie's Munich letters to, 43, 47, 48–9; growing tension between Marie and, 53–4, 69–70; increasing demands, 69–70, 74; Marie's letters from Japan, 69–70, 74; and Marie's marriages, 92, 144

Stopes, Henry (father), 36, 41, 56; marriage, 16–17; interest in archaeology, 17, 22, 27, 29, 32; supports Charlotte's enthusiasms, 17–19; sexual imbalance of marriage, 19–21, 25; financial difficulties, 22, 28–9, 31; warm relationship with Marie, 24–6, 29, 33, 34, 151n; last birthday letter to her, 32–3; death, 33

Stopes, Marie: ancestry and birth, 15–21; childhood unhappiness, 22–4; early sense of sin, 23; sense of "burden", 23–4; warm relationship with father, 24–6, 29, 33, 34, 151n; early lack of academic success, 26–8, 30; longing to excel, 28, 30; rejects formalized religion, 29–30, 260n; voracious reading, 29–30; late intellectual development, 30–34; at University College, London, 31–4, 35–6, 43; takes up palaeo-botany, 32–4, 35; dedication to science, 32, 35, 56; double honours degree, 34; awarded Gilchrist Scholarship, 34; appearance, 36, 224, 242, 257, 275, 280, 316; passionate attachments to women, 37–9, 40, 78–80; rejected male suitors, 39–40, 44–5, 47, 80, 86–7; in Munich, 40–51; doctorate for work on cycad ovules, 45–6; relationship with Fujii, 47–50, 52, 54–64, 70–76; junior lecturer and demonstrator in botany at Manchester, 51–6; London Doctorate, 56; coal research, 56, 87; publishes correspondence with Fujii, 57–9; research in Japan, 62–3, 66–76; break-up of relationship with Fujii, 70–76, 82; devious friendship with Hewitt, 81–6; resigns Manchester lectureship, 87; growing professional reputation, 87–8; pseudonyms, 88, 258, 282; sexual ignorance, 89–90, 121; reading of Carpenter and Ellis, 90–91, 101–2; marriage to Gates, 91–3, retains name of Stopes, 93; lecturer in palaeobotany at University College, 94, 104, 117, 178; marital difficulties, 93–100; platonic relationship with Maude, 95–105, 114–15, 123–4, 143–5, 318; leaves Gates, 105–6; nullity petition, 107; mixed ambitions, 109; origins of campaign for sexual education, 109–11, 113–14; development of eugenic ideas, 112–13; financial problems, 117–18; renewed coal research, 118, 121, 122, 146–7; unsuccessful playwriting, 118–19; difficulties over Married Love, 120–3, 126–7; personal dissatisfaction, 123–4;

determination to have child, 124–5, 150–1; publishes Married Love, 127, 139, 140, 141; stresses "mystical oneness" in physical relationship, 129, 133; intellectual confusion, 131–2, 134; marriage to H. V. Roe, 139–44; early married happiness, 145–6, 178; advocacy of contraception, 148–50; still-born child, 151–4; a national figure, 155–74, 179; her prophetic message to the bishops, 160–1, 214, 220–1; questionnaires on clergy's and doctors' contraceptive methods, 158–60, 166–7; campaign against Catholic Church, 164, 197–9, 205–8, 260–3, 313–14, 324; tries to make birth control an election issue, 169–70; class bias, 173–4, 181, 183n, 191; reactionary eugenic and racial views, 180–3, 194; opens birth control clinic, 186–90; plan to subdue striking miners, 191–2; publicity campaigns, 192–5, 200–202, 265–6, 273; recommends use of rubber check pessary, 196, 199, 204, 215, 221, 227–32, 268; founds CBC, 199; American visit, 200–203; egotism, 203–4; libel action, 207–8. 211, 213–36; unsympathetic to other workers, 210; sister's death, 212; and artificial insemination, 217; and "gold pin" controversy, 232–3; loses libel case, 236–8; appeal won, then overruled, 238–40; increasing fame and publicity, 242–3, 246–7; first film, 243–6; dramatic productions, 247, 258, 319; birth of son Harry, 248–9; possessiveness over him, 249, 250, 252, 254–5, 297, 299–304; estrangement from Roe, 249–50, 256–7, 260, 272–3, 275, 277–9; presented at Court, 250; lecture tours, 257; impact abroad, 258–9; paranoia, 260–3, 267–71; lawsuits, 263–5, 266–7; meddling with other authors' work, 269–70, 294; financial worries, 273, 274; given sexual carte blanche by Roe, 277–8, 279; death of marriage, 278–9, 288, 298–9; conviction of indestructibility, 280, 311–12, 316; love for Briant, 281, 286–8, 297, 317, 318; entertains literary lions, 282–5; poetry, 285–7, 292–3, 314; offers to join War Cabinet, 289; other wartime proposals, 289–92; disillusion with modern life, 296–7, 298; death of Roe, 298; opposition to Harry's marriage, 300–4; sense of failure, 305–6, 310, 315; her real achievement, 306–9; continued campaigning, 312–14; has portrait painted, 315–16; love for Avro Manhattan, 317–21; illness, 321, 322–4, 325; belief in re-incarnation, 321–2; death, 325

Stopes, Marie: WRITINGS
Ancient Plants, 87, 120
Bathe, The, an Ecstacy (poem), 25, 256, 314
Black Breeding, 44n
"Brother, The" (poem), 29
Constitution of Coal, The (with Wheeler), 121n, 146
Contraception, Theory, History and Practice, 209n, 246, 256
Don't Tell Timothy (play), 258

Stopes, Marie: WRITINGS – cont.
  Enduring Passion, 256, 272n
  "Flora of the Inferior Oolite of Brora, The",
    63
  "Four Visible Ingredients in Banded
    Bituminous Coal, The", 147n
  "Frank Letter to My Son, A", 299–300
  Germany Miscalculates (film scenario), 118
  "Instead of Tears" (poem), 294
  Journal from Japan, A, 66–7, 68, 69, 73, 75,
    76–7
  Letter to Working Mothers, A, 174
  Love Letters of a Japanese, 57–9, 71
  Love Songs for Young Lovers, 280, 285–6, 293
  Love's Creation (novel), 258, 282
  Maisie's Marriage (film), 243–6
  Man, Other Poems and a Preface, 107–8
  Marriage in My Time, 131, 137
  Married Love, 109, 158, 183n, 194, 215, 243,
    256, 259, 276, 307, 312; writing of, 115,
    116, 122; difficulties of publication, 120–1,
    126–7; publication, 127, 141; financing of,
    139, 140, 147; reaction to, 128–36, 147,
    151, 157, 168, 172, 173; intellectual con-
    fusion, 132, 134; originality of expression,
    132–3; success of, 135–6, 147–8, 155, 243n,
    308; declared obscene in America, 193;
    referred to in libel case, 215–16, 217–19,
    221–2, 226, 228, 235
  "Mrs Jones Does Her Worst", 173
  "Mother, The" (poem), 304
  Mother England, 179
  "Mother-in-Law, The" (poem), 286
  New Gospel, A, 160–1, 163–4, 166, 220, 221,
    305
  Open Letter to the Bishop of St Albans, 291
  Oriri (poem), 287
  Our Ostriches (play), 247
  "Poet's Offspring, A" (poem), 286
  Race, The (play), 111–14, 118–19
  Radiant Motherhood, 173, 178, 180–1, 248,
    252n
  Road to Fairyland, A (stories), 258
  Roman Catholic Methods of Birth Control,
    273
  Sex and the Young, 38
  "Stream, The" (poem), 285
  "To the Old" (poem), 311
  "To Roosevelt and Churchill on their
    Atlantic Charter" (poem), 296
  "Transmutation" (poem), 105
  "True Love" (poem), 287
  Truth About Venereal Disease, The, 256
  Vectia (play), 95–9
  Venus and Methuselah (play), 319
  We Burn (poems), 314, 317
  "Wine That Turned to Vinegar" (poem),
    108
  Wise Parenthood, 148–51, 166, 171, 187,
    235, 243n
Stopes, Winifred (sister), 20, 21, 23, 32, 38,
  56, 57, 63, 82; schooldays, 26, 28; Marie's
  letters to, 41, 43–4, 45, 46, 67, 74, 90–92,
  164n; ill-health and inadequacy, 45, 74, 117,

212; Marie's help for, 45, 53, 62, 117, 212;
  in Munich, 60; death, 212, 242
Stopes-Roe, Dr Harry (son), 145n, 279, 281,
  282n; birth, 242, 248, 257; Marie's besotted
  possessiveness over, 249, 250, 252, 254–5,
  297, 299–304; adopted "brothers", 251–4,
  302; Rousseauesque education, 254, 274;
  early writing, 254n; odd dress, 276; fight for
  independence, 299, 302; marriage, 300–304;
  children, 302n, 304; breach with Marie,
  303–4; partial reconciliation, 317 and n;
  and her death, 325
Stopes-Roe, Mrs Harry (Mary Wallis), 276,
  325; Marie's opposition to, 300–304, 325
Stopes-Roe, Jonathan (grandson), 304, 325
Strachey, J. St Loe, 211n
Streatfeild, Colonel Henry, 168
Studies in the Psychology of Sex (Ellis), 102
Suffragettes, 54, 70, 94, 99
Sullivan, Serjeant, 266; and Stopes v. Suther-
  land case, 214, 215–16, 218–20, 221–3
Sumida River, The (Raybould), 118
Sunday Chronicle, 183, 187
Sunday Dispatch, 150
Sunday Express, 198
Sunday Times, 212, 315
Surgical Manufacturing Company, 233
Sutherland, Dr Halliday G., 195, 264n; attack
  on Marie's birth control campaign, 196, 197,
  207, 208; libel case, 207–8, 211, 213–36, 261;
  verdicts for, 236–40, 242, 243, 250; later
  unsuccessful libel case against Marie, 266,
  274
Sutro, Alfred, 95–6, 258
Swanscombe, 22, 28, 30, 32, 41

Tablet, The, 250, 251
Tanaka, Keiko, 63n, 74
Taylor, A. J. P., 183n
Taylor, Professor Laurie, 305
Teddington, 152
Terry, Ellen, 112
Thurtle, Ernest, 215n
Times, The, 104–5, 155, 192, 198, 215, 242, 248,
  311, 324
Tokyo, 66–7, 68–76, 78
Tute, Warren, 294–5
"Twilight Sleep", 152

Universe, The, 239, 250–1, 264n
University College, London, 31–4, 35, 36,
  39, 43, 94, 104, 117, 178, 186
Unwin, Sir Stanley, 126
Upper Norwood, 18, 26

Vancouver, 78
Vansittart, Lord, 44n
Villars, 102
Voluntary Parenthood League, 201
Vortex, The (Coward), 202, 269

Wakefield, Russell, Bishop of Birmingham,
  125–6, 127, 144, 163, 173; Marie's possible
  letter to, 134–5

Waller, Sir John, 98n
Wallis, Barnes, 276–7, 300, 301–2
Wallis, Mary – see Stopes-Roe, Mrs Harry
Wallis, Molly, 276
Walpole, Hugh, 282, 283–4
Walter, John, 248n
Walworth, Malthusian League clinic in, 198–9, 233
Waters, Dr, 176
Watson, D. M. S., 56, 87
Waugh, Evelyn, 238
Webb, Beatrice, 181
Webb, Sidney, 169n, 181
Wedded Love or Married Misery (Willis), 184
Weiss, Professor F. E., 51, 65, 71–2
Well of Loneliness, The (Hall), 187n
Wells, H. G., 113, 116, 211n, 282, 284, 317
West, Rebecca, 269
Westminster Catholic Federation, 205, 206
Westminster Gazette, 177, 224, 237, 247
Wheeler, Dr R. V., 121, 146, 243, 249
Wilde, Oscar, 18, 213, 282, 295
Wilkinson, Ellen, 215n
Wilkinson, Robin, 252–3, 254
Williams, Robert, 169–70

Willis, Mary, 246–7
Willis, W. N., 184
Willoughby de Broke, Lord and Lady, 174
Wilson, President Woodrow, 116–17
Windsor, Duke of, 168n, 312–13
Wise Wedlock (Beale), 204
Woman Rebel, 115
Woman's Herald, 18
Woman's World, 18
Women's Social and Political Union, 99
Wood, Sir Kingsley, 289n
Woodward, Henry, 93
Woolton, Lord, 290
Wrench, Mollie, 152
Wright, Dr Helena, 151, 259–60, 268, 270
Wuffles (chow), 266–7
Wyss, Clotilde van, Marie's adolescent passion for, 31, 37–9, 40, 47

Yokohama, 64, 65, 76

Zangwill, Edith, 193
Zetetical Society, 16
Zulueta, Father F. M. de, 163–4